Boeing 707 KC-135

and their civil and military derivatives

From the 'Dash 80' to the E-8 J-STARS

Dominique BREFFORT

Colour plates by André JOUINEAU

Translated from the French
by Sally & Lawrence Brown

HISTOIRE & COLLECTIONS

You can fly Boeing jetliners to 135 cities in 70 countries, over the routes of these famous airlines. All continents, all sections of the globe are included. Today's swift Boeing jetliner services make it possible to visit even cities on the far side of the world during the span of a normal vacation!

world—by Boeing jet

Boeing jets are the most proved, most popular jetliners in the world. They are preferred by more airlines and more passengers than *any* other jet. They also hold more speed records (over 240!). Next trip, enjoy the speed and comfort of travel by Boeing 707 or 720!

BOEING Jetliners

LONG-RANGE 707 • MEDIUM-RANGE 720 • SHORT-RANGE 727

Contents

A common ancestor

In March 1952, William M. Allen, the president of the Boeing Aeroplane Co. in September 1945, wrote a memorandum in which he asked his main managers if it was possible for the company to put a civilian transport jet in the skies within two years. This was to be done without jeopardising the current production of military aircraft. He no doubt did not realise that he had marked a turning point for his company.

Founded in 1917, the Boeing company began the long career that we know it for, manufacturing different types of aircraft amongst which were fighter biplanes then monoplanes (F2B, F3B, F4B, P-26), hulled hydroplanes (Model 314 'Clipper'), but also airliners, with the Boeing 247 figuring in the front rank. However, when the Second World War came along, the company, based in the Washington state town of Renton on the west coast of the United States near Seattle, grew considerably. More than 12 700 B-17 Flying Fortresses and 2 750 B-29 Superfortresses would leave its factories as well as those of companies who were working under licence such as Douglas, Lockheed-Vega and Martin.

However, as was the case for many American aviation companies, the end of the war would put the future of Boeing in serious danger. Due to wartime constraints, they had been forced to concentrate on multi engine bombers whilst neglecting other types of aircraft. The official contracts ended at the same time as the war and the company was forced, at the end of 1945, to lay off more than 80% of its 38 000 strong workforce at that time.

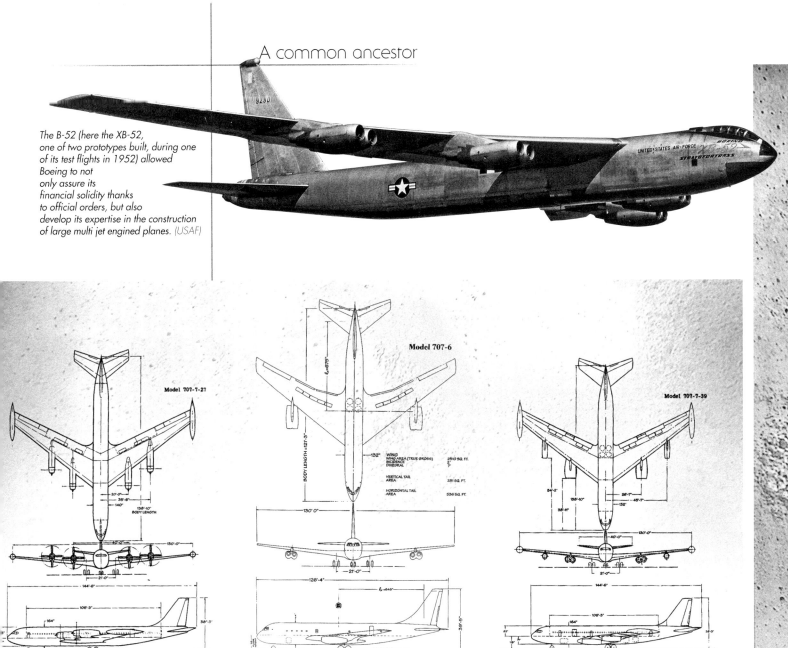

The B-52 (here the XB-52, one of two prototypes built, during one of its test flights in 1952) allowed Boeing to not only assure its financial solidity thanks to official orders, but also develop its expertise in the construction of large multi jet engined planes. (USAF)

Model 707-7-27

Model 707-6

Model 707-7-39

Above. Various studies were carried out by the Boeing engineers before arriving at the final configuration of the Dash 80, all of which did not get past the drawing board. Amongst these projects was the 707-7-27 powered by four turboprops placed on the wings. The 707-6 whose four engines were grouped by pairs in pods, a solution inherited from the B-47 and B-52 but judged inappropriate for a civilian aircraft, or even the six engined 707-7-39. (Boeing)

Boeing saved by a bomber

Below.
As with its predecessor the B-47, the B-52 was a monoplane with high wings whose reactors were placed in pods under the wings with the main undercarriage retracting into the fuselage. Only three B-52A were made, which differentiated from the two prototypes (XB-52 and YB-52) by its cockpit now side by side, the tandem undercarriage and the new engines. (USAF)

Although the situation was serious, it was not a hopeless one for Boeing which naturally had to considerably reduce its output, but whose future had been guaranteed by a project that had been initiated right in the middle of the war. It was in 1943 that the USAAF asked different aviation companies to come up with a plane capable of flying at 800 km/h (500 mph) over a distance of 5 600 km (3,480 miles). Despite these demands that were almost in the domain of science fiction at that time, Boeing submitted in March 1944 its Model 424, a sort of B-29 equip-

ped with pods under the wings, each one containing two jet engines. With this first project being turned down, the company came back with the Model 432 in the following December, this time with the four engines integrated into the fuselage.

This time, the authorities accepted the design and signed a development contract with the aviation company in March 1945. The latter, having benefited from the input of German research after the end of hostilities in Europe, notably in the domain of the swept wing, came up with a new project under the name of the Model 448. This new aircraft was powered

by six fuselage-mounted jet engines and had swept back wings. Using this basic design, more than fifty configurations were studied, the resulting dominating idea was to place the engines under the wings fixed to struts under each wing, the first with two engines and the second with just one. Named the Model 450, this design project was submitted to the USAAF that demanded a few minor modifications, leading a new designation - Model 452 - of which two prototypes were ordered (XB-47 and YB-47). Work began on these in June 1946 and resulted in more than 5 000 hours of wind tunnel tests, a number to be put into perspective with the 50 hours that the B-17 had needed a few years earlier.

The XB-47 having undertaken its maiden flight on 17 December 1947 and the first test flights proving promising, the USAAF ordered ten pre-series B-47A aircraft in September 1948; the aircraft scheduled for delivery from the middle of 1950.

At this time, the United States were involved in the Korean War; the B-47 soon became an important element of national defence and orders came at a steady pace and to such an extent that the Stratojet, as the plane was called, quickly replaced the B-29, 1,600 examples of different versions finally seeing service within no fewer than twenty-eight squadrons. Now the spearhead of the Strategic Air Command, created in March 1946, as well as a key element of the United States policy of dissuasion in the first years of the Cold War, the B-47 remained in this important position for ten years. To this day it remains the most highly produced jet engined bomber of all time with 2,042 leaving the assembly lines. The Stratojet can also be considered as the common ancestor of the B-52, 707 and KC-135 as its rather audacious design, for its time, forced Boeing to resolve a certain number of problems and find solutions that were later taken into consideration in the design of new aircraft.

The dominant position of Boeing as the almost exclusive supplier of strategic bombers to the USAAF quickly found itself strengthened by the appearance of what can be considered as its direct heir, the B-52, for which the watchword seems to have been: bigger, stronger!

This gigantic plane, whose career is far from over as we write these lines, first appeared in January 1946, when the USAAF began to look for a successor to the B-36 which, at

the time, had not yet flown. Boeing, thanks to its position and its expertise in the field of heavy bombers, soon put itself forward and submitted, in April of the same year, its Model 462 which was in fact just a larger B-29 equipped with six turboprops. The latter, Wright T-35s, proved to be very difficult to get right and the whole project was considerably held up.

However, the USAAF finally ordered two prototypes in July 1948 (respectively designated XB-52 and YB-52), with 20° swept wings and powered by four T-35 engines. Even before these planes were put into construction, Boeing proposed replacing them with a more modern version powered by turbojets that could be delivered in 1951.

The USAAF having accepted this proposition, the Seattle company began production of the Model 464-49, a bomber with a vague resemblance to the B-47 but with a 35° swept wing and, above all, eight Pratt and Whitney J57 engines installed in twos in pods suspended on struts. The American authorities were almost immediately won over by the project to the point that, in February 1951, a first order of thirteen examples of the series was made, even though the first prototype had not yet left the ground. The maiden flight, undertaken by a second prototype, the YB-52, contrary to expectations, took place on 15 April 1952 with the XB-52 following suit on 2 October the same year. Two years later, on 5 August 1954 to be precise, the first production aircraft (B-52A) took off. The construction of the massive bomber, named the Stratofortress in homage to its glorious predecessors became a priority in this same year with the discovery of the Soviet Myasichev Mya-4 'Bison' jet engined strategic bomber.

Boeing is forced to look at the civilian market once more

At the end of the forties, the future of Boeing seemed to be largely guaranteed due to the military orders that mostly stemmed from the Cold War, and its expertise in the field of heavy multi-engined aircraft, notably jets, meant that the aviation company could not now be

Opposite.

The Dash 80 was also used as a demonstration aircraft for the future KC-135. It is seen here during its seventh flight on 22 July 1954, simulating in flight refuelling (no probe has been fitted) with a B-52 whilst flying over the first example of a Stratotanker surrounded by a large crowd on the Renton factory runway. (Boeing)

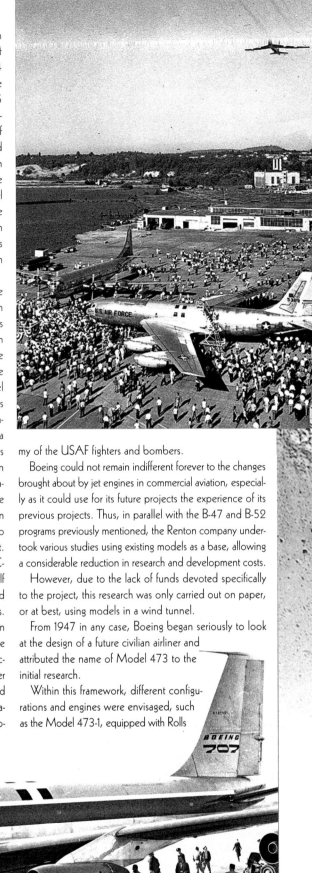

1. Sixty-five examples of the Boeing 247, designed in 1933, were built. Most of them were put into service by Boeing Air Transport and a few by Lufthansa. Capable of carrying ten passengers, this twin-engined, entirely metallic aircraft with its automatic pilot and retracting undercarriage, is considered as being the first modern civilian transporter. It was quickly overtaken by the Douglas DC-2 and remained in service during the duration of the Second World War with several used by the military under the name of C-73.
2. Designed by the British company De Havilland, to whom we owe several of the great aeronautical success stories such as the Tiger Moth or the Mosquito, the DH 106 Comet I was the first jet airliner. The maiden flight of this four-engined plane (the engines were placed in the wing roots) took place on 17 July 1949 and entered into service in January 1952. Despite its profoundly groundbreaking character and its undeniable technological success, the Comet was a commercial disaster as a design fault was at the origin of a series of disasters that began in 1953. After two long years of investigations that revealed a structural defect, the design of a plane with improved performance, the Comet 4, was able to be launched; however in the intervening years, the two American giants, Douglas and Boeing had developed their own airliners, the 707 and the DC-8 respectively.
3. The Model 307 or Sratoliner was based on the B-17 from which it took the wings and tail plane. It had a pressurised cabin and ten examples were made, beginning its commercial career with TWA in 1940, the only company along with Pan Am to use this type.

Below.

The Boeing 367-80 seen on the Renton factory runway, surrounded by many people and bearing, at the front of the fuselage, the emblems of airline companies (Qantas, Air France, Lufthansa, TWA, etc.) The cargo hold door, typical of this one-off prototype, was the only point of access for both the cabin and cockpit. (J. Delmas collection).

called into question. However, Boeing had been behind in the civilian market which had been covered since the end of the Second World War by Douglas (with its DC-3, DC-4 and soon DC-6) or Lockheed (Model 10 to 14 and of course the L-049 Constellation) amongst others. Indeed, in 1945 Boeing had only produced 150 multi-engined modern commercial aircraft, that is to say made entirely of metal and out of this number more than half were the model 247 [1] that dated from the beginning of the thirties. However, in the domain of civilian air travel, things were rapidly evolving. The De Havilland Comet [2] had inaugurated the era of civilian air travel in 1949. Of course we know of the troubles that this plane saw; problems that considerably penalised its career, even when its serious teething problems were resolved, but it was in a way at the origin of the revolution that the introduction of jet engines represented in civilian travel.

It should not be forgotten that up to the beginning of the fifties, this mode of propulsion was still the object of much reticence on the part of the main constructors, especially as the piston engine was at its height and that the future path seemed rather to pass by an intermediate solution such as the turbopropulser. After the war, Boeing placed itself once more in the civilian market with a long-range airliner, the Model 377 Stratocruiser. The successor of the Stratoliner [3], it was based on the B-29 and took advantage of the technical advances of the latter, whilst its main exterior characteristic was a pressurised bilobal fuselage. Boeing made 56 of these planes between 1947 and 1950 which more or less saved its civilian branch, especially as it was bought by several foreign companies, a first for Boeing. The commercial exploitation of the Stratocruiser began over the Pacific in 1949, between San Francisco and Honolulu (Hawaii) when Pan Am brought into service the first of the twenty-five aircraft that it had bought. But it was above all the military version of this plane, the C-97, that met the greatest success, allowing Boeing to pull itself out of the doldrums brought about by the end of the Second World War and the cessation of most of the official contracts. Indeed, the Model 367 or C-97, the design of which began even before the end of the Second World War and whose prototype flew on 9 November 1944, saw a total production of 888 aircraft between 1947 and 1958. Nearly a quarter of these (219 to be exact) were tankers (KC-97) that played a crucial role within the SAC from 1950, after having replaced the old B-50s and considerably lengthening the autono-

my of the USAF fighters and bombers.

Boeing could not remain indifferent forever to the changes brought about by jet engines in commercial aviation, especially as it could use for its future projects the experience of its previous projects. Thus, in parallel with the B-47 and B-52 programs previously mentioned, the Renton company undertook various studies using existing models as a base, allowing a considerable reduction in research and development costs.

However, due to the lack of funds devoted specifically to the project, this research was only carried out on paper, or at best, using models in a wind tunnel.

From 1947 in any case, Boeing began seriously to look at the design of a future civilian airliner and attributed the name of Model 473 to the initial research.

Within this framework, different configurations and engines were envisaged, such as the Model 473-1, equipped with Rolls

Royce Nene engines installed in pods held by struts, or the twin-engined 473-11. None of these, however, were attractive to airlines because of their short range that made two stopovers necessary if travelling coast to coast across the United States. It would not be until 1949 that the situation progressed a little. Indeed, at this time, Boeing had acquired a certain experience thanks to the B-47 and B-52, whilst the arrival of better engines now allowed for a greater take off weight for the future plane had consequently more range due to an increased quantity of fuel carried. From mid 1949 the 473-25 and 473-60 were presented, with an outline close to that of the B-52, that is to say with jet engines instal-

using turbojets, these being the British Bristol Olympus (367-68) or the American Pratt & Whitney J57 (367-71). Having tried, in 1951, to sell to the USAF the idea of a jet transport/tanker plane capable of efficiently completing its fleet of B-47s, Boeing saw itself turned down by the official authorities who cited a lack of budget for such an acquisition. Due to a lack of openings in this branch, Boeing saw itself forced, therefore, to carry on with its research in the field of commercial aviation.

A new start

The aviation company therefore decided to go back to the drawing board and in September 1951, began the first research into an aircraft upon which most of the previously envisaged solutions were definitively abandoned. Indeed, from the outset, it was decided to deal with the problem of the installation of the main undercarriage by using aerofoils placed low down with a central section to house the landing gear.

Below.
This view of the Dash 80 landing allows us to see how the underneath of the plane was decorated. A bare metal fuselage with the rear painted yellow and the wings dark red upon which is painted the name of the aviation company and the registration.
(D. Breffort Collection)

led in pairs in pods and bicycle undercarriage. Another configuration envisaged the following year was the 473-47 destined for the American home market, a twin engined aircraft with a shape similar to that of the future 737 but with 18° swept back wings and a Stratocruiser cockpit. One of the main problems faced by Boeing engineers at this time was the installation of the main undercarriage which was made difficult by the fact that the swept back wing was, on the envisaged models, placed high up in the fuselage as with the B-47 and B-52. In these conditions, the undercarriage which was most of the time of the bicycle type, as on these bombers, should have retracted into the cabin, separating it into two. Other solutions were of course looked at, such as the installation of the landing gear in under wing pods, but these different configurations increasingly came up against the desire of airlines that much preferred planes with median straight wings, or wings set low on the fuselage. Whilst a team of engineers looked at the possibilities brought about by the Model 473, a second team worked on an offshoot of the Model 367/377 that had lead to the C-97, KC-97 and Stratocruiser. This time it was not only about designing a new airliner, but also increased performance in order to gain new military contracts. In 1948 the replacement of classic piston engines by turboprops was thus envisaged (Model 367-15 with Allison T-38 engines), the goal being to increase the speed of flying tankers that would refuel increasingly faster jet aircraft. The end of 1950 saw the appearance of the Model 367-60, a C-97 equipped with turboprops and a gull wing in order to ensure sufficient ground clearance for the propellers, whilst the following year, Boeing envisaged

Although 35° swept wings were finally chosen, notably because they allowed for a reduction in wingspan whilst retaining an identical wing surface, the undercarriage was now situated both very close to the centre of gravity to aid retrac-

Below.
The three men who carried out the first flights with the Boeing 367-80. From left to right, Richard 'Dix' Loesch, Alvin 'Tex' Johnston (pilots) and L. A. 'Bert' Binegar (flight engineer). (Boeing)

4. This particular designation showed the radically different character of this new aircraft, the design of which wanted to be radically different from its previous planes and distanced itself from previous studies. The 400, 500 and 600 numbers had already been attributed to other productions, notably to missiles, and the 700 series was logically chosen. Finally, the last number - 7 - was chosen as it was a reminder of the company's previous successes, the 247, 377, but also B-17! Next, this combination of numbers was (and still is) used to designate production aircraft such as the 747, 777 or the recent 787, but also one-off projects that never amounted to anything such as the supersonic SST 2707 ('the 707 of the year 2000!') or the 7J7 which was to be designed in a partnership with Japan.
5. We can question the pertinence and above all the efficiency of such disinformation, notably with Boeing's direct competitors such as Douglas who would not have been duped, like the great rivals of the time, the Soviets, by this manipulation. In any case, the 'Dash 80' took off for the first time in July 1954; it had been an open secret for some time and the aircraft had the same registration N70700!

Below.
The Boeing 367-80 on the Renton runway, along with several civilian and military propeller planes. The white cross on a black background was added to the upper fuselage during the test flight period to make the plane more easily visible in flight.
(J. Delmas collection).

tion on take off, and far back enough to avoid the tail making contact with the ground if there was much weight in this area. An initial study, named Model 707-1 [4], was submitted mid November 1951 and consisted of an aircraft powered by four J57 turbojets mounted by pairs in pods, like the B-47, and whose 3.10 metre fuselage could carry 72 first class passengers. The project was rapidly modified, notably with an increase in the wing surface and the diameter of the fuselage, leading to the Model 707-6 from the spring of the following year. This four engined aircraft, 38.50 metres (126 ft) long and with a 39.60 metre (130 ft) wingspan, whose engines (still the J57) were also mounted in pairs as with its predecessor, would carry 76 passengers sitting in rows of four and looked to be clearly superior to the De Havilland Comet that was on the point of entering into service.

An audacious gamble

In April 1952, William Allen, the Boeing boss, asked his main branch managers in writing, if it was wise to undertake a study for a future jet tanker and transport aircraft. The replies that arrived even before the end of the month were positive and the general atmosphere seemed to be fairly euphoric due to the maiden flight of the B-52 a few days previously. Allen wrote a report that he submitted to the company board in which he recommended that the company should go ahead. Thus, on 22 April 1952, the Boeing boardroom voted a budget of 15 million dollars, an amount that quickly increased to 16 million and taken from the company's own funds (this represented double the profits made by the company the

previous year), destined to finance the research and development of a future aircraft based on the studies undertaken on the 707-6 and logically named the 707-7. This was unofficially unveiled to the public under the designation Model 367-80 (rapidly simplified to 'Dash-Eighty') so that it would be believed that the aircraft was in fact just an extrapolation of the KC-97 equipped with turbojets [5].

On 8 May 1952, William Allen gave the go ahead for the construction of a prototype destined to prove the feasibility of both a jet airliner and an identical military jet plane that could be used for transport with the MATS (Military Airlift Transport Command) and as a tanker for the Strategic Air Command.

In fact, contrary to what has long been said, the risk taken by Boeing at the time was not as high as that, as the financial situation of the company was much improved, mostly due to the large orders for KC-97 tankers B-47 bombers and soon the B-52.

Also, the company could count on the future official orders for a military version (transport and above all a tanker) with the USAF covering some of the costs of necessary research for its program.

It was in September 1952 that the project was officially presented, that is just a few days after Douglas announced that it too was working on a similar aircraft, the future DC-8. This announcement, mainly aimed at airline companies, had been voluntarily held back up to this date so that the competition would not gain too much of a head start. In the interval, various configurations were envisaged for the 707-7, these mainly being for the disposition and placement of

Opposite.
In December 1957, the 367-80 received a JT4A-3 engine in the number two position and a JT3C-4 in number three under the wings. The latter was replaced by a JT3C-6 the following April. The fifth engine, a rear mounted JT3C-4, appeared in April 1961, replaced in January 1962 by a JT8D-1 before being deleted in July 1962. Used intensely at this time, the aircraft has lost its sheen and shows many signs of fatigue and wear. (Boeing).

the engines; these could be not only turbojets (707-7-39 with six engines of which a pair was mounted under each wing, but also turboprops (707-7-27), mounted on the wings.

Finally, in order to increase the plane's range, it was envisaged for a while to add extra fuel tanks at the wingtips, a little like Lockheed had done with the Super Constellation, these tanks being shaped like those of the F-104 Starfighter.

The construction of a prototype effectively began in October 1952, led by Edward C. Wells, who worked at Boeing on all the large aircraft, from the B-17 to the 747, and helped in the field of aerodynamics by George Schairer, an engineer of German origin and one of the supporters of the swept wing. A mock up of the cabin, equipped with a sound system that was supposed to give the impression of flight, was made in great secrecy in a hangar at New York and a few carefully chosen personalities were authorised to see it. At the same time, a mostly wooden made replica of the plane was made at the Renton factory and was destined to solve different technical problems such as the placement of cables and hoses or the functioning of the motivators and control surfaces. The engine chosen was the Pratt & Whitney JT3, the civilian version of the J57 that equipped, amongst others, the B-52. This was a way of reassuring civilians, not yet convinced by the reliability of this type of propulsion whilst also having some of the research finances covered in the meantime by the military. These four turbojets, following the recommendations of the ATA, were now installed separately (to avoid any collateral damage in the event of a problem with one of them) on struts under the wings and separated in such a way as to evenly distribute the stress on the wings.

The beginning of a legend

The 'roll-out', the official presentation of the prototype, took place on 15 May 1954, that is two weeks before the date originally planned. Painted in bright yellow and reddish brown colours, the

Dash 80 had a particularly appropriate registration - N70700 - and was named 'Jet Stratoliner' and 'Jet Stratotanker', by Mrs William E. Boeing herself, as this single aircraft was destined essentially to serve as a demonstration aircraft both for the future civilian Model 707 and the military KC-135.

At this time, no single order had been made for the aircraft whose appearance, apart from its bright colours, was more that of a military transport plane with its particularly small number of windows (ten on the right and six on the left). On the other hand, the risk taken by Boeing was carefully calculated as the Seattle company knew that, as the USAF had just ordered the B-52, that it would soon need a suitable tanker, that is a jet propulsed one.

Finally, it was clear that the large passenger jet represented the future and that this should be explored by the Seattle company if it was to avoid being left behind once more, not only by Douglas and its DC-8, but also by other foreign competitors such as the British, Soviets (Tupolev) and even the French (Sud-Est with its Caravelle).

The insurance policy taken out for this prototype was the most expensive ever asked for a plane. It notably stipulated that one pilot would take the controls, this being Alvin M. Johnston, nicknamed 'Tex' [6]. It has to be said that this was a particularly good choice as, after having begun his career on the Bell P-39 and having flown the prototype of the first jet designed in the United States, the XP-59, he had practically saved the B-47 program after joining Boeing in 1949.

Having flown the YB-52 for the first time on 15 April 1952, Tex Johnston was practically the only man in the world at this time with knowledge of heavy multi jet engines. The maiden flight was postponed for a few days due to an incident

6. This nickname was due to his habit of always wearing cowboy boots!

Opposite.
It was in April 1961 that the Dash 80 received the JT3C-6 engine at the left rear of the fuselage as part of the trials program for the future triple jet 727. The nozzle was specially equipped with an angled extension so that the flow would be led over the left stabilizer. (J. Delmas collection)

on 21 May 1954. After a failure in the left undercarriage leg, the wingtip and number one reactor were slightly damaged and some time was needed to deal with the problem and make sure that the stresses brought about when braking hard would finally be of no consequence to the structure of the landing gear. Finally, on 15 July 1954, the 38th birthday of the Boeing company, at 14.14 hrs, the 367-80 took off for the very first time. The plane having no emergency exit system, the crew was voluntarily reduced to only two men, Alvin Johnston at the controls and Richard L. ' Dix ' Loesch at his right. Watched from the ground by several thousand Boeing employees and the inhabitants of the region of Seattle, the Dash 80, escorted by a F-86 Sabre chase plane, it remained in the air for more than an hour before landing on the Boeing runway where it was warmly welcomed by William Allen in person, but also by those who had worked on it, notably the engineers Edward Wells and George Schairer.

A long series of tests

The second flight took place two days later and this time lasted two hours and twenty minutes during which the aircraft reached an altitude of 8,320 metres (27,300 ft) and flying at nearly 780 km/h (485 mph). After a first series of eight-day tests which showed the aircraft's excellent flying capacities, it was obviously well suited to both a civilian role and that of a tanker for the B-52 should the configuration interest the military. The Dash 80 returned to the workshops in order to undergo the modifications necessary to more intensive

future tests that were planned. Having only just started flying again, the plane was slightly damaged when landing on 5 August after a fault with the brakes that forced Tex Johnston to leave the runway to slow the plane down. The forward undercarriage was damaged in this emergency manoeuvre and the Dash 80 was immobilised for repairs until the following 20 September. Several test periods were then undertaken without any significant incident until mid June 1955. The plane then went back to the factory to have an in flight refuelling probe added similar to that on the KC-97 as well as a cabin for its operator placed under the empennage at the rear of the fuselage. This extra equipment was destined to show the validity of the concept to the USAF and did not take anything away from the aircraft's performance. In any case it did not prevent Tex Johnston from doing two rolls with the four-engined aircraft during the Gold Cup Boating Competition, an annual nautical fete at Lake Washington. One can imagine the anger of the Boeing boss when he saw his precious plane carrying out such manoeuvres without incident! An anger that increased when the test pilot said to him that he had already rehearsed such a manoeuvre when at altitude. However, William Allen did not take any measures against his cowboy of a pilot, but he never forgave him for this 'exploit' that remains almost unique in the annals of aviation history.

After having simulated several rendezvous with a B-52 on 15 September 1955, the Dash 80, still equipped with its refuelling system, then undertook various lengthy flights destined to prove its endurance. One notable flight was a return trip from Seattle via Denver and Los Angeles that lasted a little under six hours (5 h 48), this was in fact its longest flight since it had firs taken to the skies. A month later, on 16 October, the plane undertook its first coast-to-coast flight from Seattle to Andrews (Maryland) in 4 h 27. The return leg, due to exceptional favourable winds took an almost identical time.

At the end of 1955, the Dash 80 had carried out more than two hundred test flights but its career did not end here as more tests followed at a fair pace in the months and years to come. The plane was used as a platform for trials of all sorts of equipment destined not only for the future versions of the 707/KC-135 (installation of a weather radar in the nose, which meant redesigning the latter, engine noise reducers, leading edge flaps, brakes, sound proofing the cabin, reverse thrusters etc.), but also other Boeing projects.

It was after having being used to test out various models of turbo reactors, sometimes simultaneously mounted under the wings, that a fifth propulser was added to the left side of the fuselage in April 1961 as part of the elaboration program of the Boeing 727. After having been used to a promotional end in order to attract future customers, civilian as well as military, the Dash 80 was lent to NASA at the end of 1962 and used mostly for research into the boundary limit; air flow over wing surfaces and principally the function of blown flaps. It was also used, this time directly by Boeing, in 1964 when it took part in a competition for the heavy transport CX-HLS (Cargo Experimental- Heavy Logistics Support) that should have been won by the Lockheed C-5 Galaxy. To this end, the plane was equipped with an 'all terrain' undercarriage that allowed it to land on hastily made runways. After two series of tests carried out respectively by NASA (simulation of the low speed characteristics for the future supersonic SST) and Boeing (system for automatic landing) which ended on 22 January 1970, the Dash 80 was finally given to the National Air & Space Museum of the Smithsonian Institution. It flew to Dulles International Airport (Washington DC) on 26 May 1972. The museum did not have at this time the infrastructure necessary for the permanent exhibition of an aircraft of this size. The following day it sent to the army storage facility (Military Aircraft Storage & Disposition Center) at Davis-Monthan in the Arizona desert where it remained for more than eighteen years. Repatriated to its hometown of Renton in May 1990, it was initially made airworthy in order to take part in the 75th anniversary of Boeing in July 1991, then definitively sent by air in August 2003 to the new building of the Smithsonian's National Air and Space Museum, the Steven F. Udvar-Hazy Center built near Dulles airport where it now makes the most of a well earned rest.

rejected it - quite the contrary. The general atmosphere was even rather favourable as in 1953, general Curtis E. LeMay, the chief at the time of the Strategic Air Command, had envisaged the purchase of a fleet of two hundred tankers programmed for the following fiscal year. However, despite this individual desire, there was much incertitude within the USAF as to the type of plane needed for the future tanker. Several projects, including two submitted by Douglas based on the DC-8 and the other equipped with the (XC-132) turboprop were put forward. An official invitation for proposal was launched in May 1954 and saw six aviation companies take part [7]. With the authorities hesitating as we have seen, Boeing, on 22 July of the same year got a head start that would turn out to be decisive by organising a series of simulated in-flight refuelling between a Dash 80 and a B-52. So whilst they were talking of the use of a new tanker, Boeing's tanker was flying! The result of this was not long in coming and on 30 July, the ARDC (Air Research & Defence Command), whilst waiting for the results of the invitation for proposal, recommended the purchase of between 70 and 100 (interim tankers) based on the 367-138B and rapidly renamed by Boeing the Model 717, a designation that would be used for all the aircraft specifically designed for the military market. What was still only a simple declaration of intention was finalised a few days later, thanks once more to the unfailing support of general LeMay, an enthusiastic supporter of the Dash 80 [8]. On 5 August 1954, the USAF announced that it was to purchase 29 aircraft, with a further order a few days later, 27 August, for 88 more aircraft. So Boeing came out as the official winner of an invitation for proposal the results of which were kept under wraps.

It was only in February 1955 that the USAF made public its decision... declaring Lockheed as the winner with its Model L-193! The Burbanks company, which had had solid political support, notably in California where it was based,

7. Boeing, Convair, Douglas, Lockheed, Martin and Fairchild.
8. Curtis LeMay, literally wrapped up on his first flight with the Dash 80 said, for example, to the Boeing bosses ' meanwhile, build me some of these... '.

The military is the first to fire!

As we have seen, the Dash 80 was destined, due to its unique character, to interest not only civilian customers but also the military, the latter soon showing its interest. Remember that even though the USAF had not envisaged the financing ab initio of the Boeing project it had not

received an order based on one prototype whilst 169 new KC-135 were being ordered from Boeing! In a way, the official winner of the competition was authorised to build one aircraft whilst its 'unlucky' rival had, at the same time, to build a veritable fleet of tankers. This crazy situation did not last as Lockheed finally never made numerous examples of its tanker because the USAF did not want to have two distinct fleets of aircraft destined to carry out the same mission. Amongst other things, this meant specific training for crews, the impossibility of interchanging the two aircraft and an even more complicated management of spare parts as everything would have to be multiplied by two. Although Boeing finally won, in reality if not on paper, its audacious gamble, it owed much to the influence of the SAC which had been used to Boeing aircraft for many years (B-29, B-47, KC-97 and now the B-52) and had never had cause to complain: to cut it short, with a jet tanker designed at Renton, they were in familiar territory!

The civilians at last

Although the future of the Dash 80 and its descendants was assured thanks to the large orders made by the USAF, taking the great financial weight off Boeing and its president's shoulders at the same time, the civil market remained to be conquered, the companies still doubting the efficiency and utility of a large jet passenger plane. They were hardly encouraged by the tragedy that blighted the beginning of the De Havilland Comet's career. A non-negligible parameter is that a jet airliner of this type at the beginning of the fifties cost almost four times more than a propeller plane like the Douglas DC-7 or the Lockheed Super Constellation and Starliner, the 'stars' of the day. The Boeing salesmen were tasked with selling the plane all over the world and many pilots were invited to Renton to fly the 'Dash Eighty'. Despite these efforts, buyers were not exactly banging on the door; no company was ready to be the first to take the leap and risk considera-

ble amounts of money in acquiring a fleet of commercial jets.

Finally, more than a year after the plane's maiden flight on 13 October 1955, Pan Am became the first company to take the leap, heralding the long saga of the 707. Indeed it was on this day that the company director, Juan Trippe, ordered twenty production aircraft designated 707-120. In fact he wanted to be the first to have jet aircraft and, a little like the USAF previously, took no chances at the time by ordering twenty-five Douglas DC-8. This model only existed on paper [9] so the new Boeings allowed him to fill the gap and show, whatever the cost, his position as leader. This first order got the ball rolling as one month later, it was American Airlines' turn to order thirty 707 aircraft. This company was rapidly followed by ten others. Things had been slow to take off at the beginning but now it was a logjam; the main airline companies (Continental, Braniff, Air France, Sabena, etc.) were literally queuing up to buy the new plane after having radically changed their point of view in terms of commercial exploitation. Pan Am put its first aircraft into service over the Atlantic on 26 October 1958, more than four years after the maiden flight of the Dash 80, 184 Boeing 707 aircraft, its direct descendant had already been ordered.

9. The Douglas DC-8 did not finally fly until May 1958, whilst the 707 was already in service with Pan Am.

Opposite.
The first 707-120, without any registration number, during its official presentation on 28 October 1957 at Renton. Having carried out its maiden flight on 20 December of the same year, it first served as a training aircraft to familiarise crews and to define new routes before being delivered to its owner, Pan Am, on 30 November 1958.
(J. Delmas collection)

THE BOEING 120

We have just seen that the military, and mainly the USAF, quickly realised the interest represented by the new Boeing four engined jet. The same could not exactly be said for civilian companies.

In reality, two parameters played against Boeing in this domain. Firstly a certain reticence, which is understandable, on the part of civilians after the series of dramatic accidents concerning the De Havilland Comet I[1] where six planes (out of seventeen) were lost in one and a half years, these companies judging that it was urgent to... wait. However, the particular attitude of the Seattle company was no stranger either to this phenomenon. Indeed, seeing that the civil market was difficult to conquer whilst, at the same time, being certain that the

Opposite.
This 707-131 (c/n 7663/ N736TW) was used from 1959 to 1971 by TWA before being sold to Israel Aircraft Industries. Note the inscription 'StarStream 707 ' on the rear of the fuselage, a lot of companies using a typical name to their new jet aircraft for promotional use.
(J. Guillem collection)

military tanker orders would be a lot easier to obtain, Boeing firstly concentrated on the development of its KC-135 that had received orders as soon as the prototype had flown. There would always be time, later, to obtain civilian orders. In fact it was the competition that forced Boeing to cease this apparent immobility. On 7 June 1955, Douglas, taking advantage of its dominant position in the field of commercial aircraft, mainly thanks to its DC-7, officially confirmed that it was undertaking the design of a future civil jet with a better performance than the Dash 80, the future DC-8 [2].

Below. Used by Pan Am as 'Jet Clipper Resolute' (N758PA) from May 1961 to December 1970, this 707-121 (c/n 18084) was sold to MCA Leasing in October 1978. Re-registered, it was leased to the charter company Southeast from January to February 1979 with its new name 'Boriqueen'. (J. Guillem collection)

Below.
Sold to Cranbourne Corp. in
December 1971, this former TWA
707-131 (c/n 17668) was offered for
sell to Air Manila International,
painted in this Philippine company
livery, but the transaction never took
place. (J. Guillem collection)

For this, Douglas respected the main wishes of the companies that wanted an aircraft with a wider fuselage, capable of crossing the Atlantic without a stop over, something that the Boeing project did not offer. Next it was Convair's turn to join in the adventure with its Model 22 that was initially named the Skylark 600 then quickly the 880, a smaller aircraft but one that was more rapid, a higher speed being the key to future success according to the constructor.

Presented in 1956, the Convair 880 drew its inspiration from both the previous military aircraft made by the company and the Boeing and Douglas projects notably with jet engines (derived from the General Electric J79 installed on the Phantom II, engines that offered good performance and safety but were particularly noisy and fuel guzzling) mounted on struts and with a pronounced swept wing. However, its essential characteristic was its maximum speed of 600 mph (965 km/h, or 880 feet per second, hence its name). The number of passengers carried was sacrificed in order to achieve this speed. The Convair 880 and its longer range version, the 880M, were only marginally successful, as in the meantime, Boeing had come up with its 720 series. Therefore, only 65 of these planes were made at Fort Worth (Texas) between 1959 and 1962, with the aircraft

entering into commercial service on 15 May 1960. The company tried to reverse the trend in 1961 with the Model 990, a longer plane equipped with turbofan engine and modified wings, but this turned out to be a complete flop as only 37 were sold, sealing the fate of the company that never managed to recover from its financial losses.

A question of diameter

With its competitors now at its heels, mostly Douglas, Boeing was forced, even before the launch of its first production aircraft, to take another look at its project in order to present not only an aircraft superior to all others, but above all, a plane capable of immediately answering the main needs of the airlines. We have previously seen that different variants, as much with the wings (a more and more pronounced sweep, wings positioned on the fuselage) as with the disposition of the engines, had successively been studied on paper. It was finally decided that the future aircraft, as well as its military counterpart, had a slightly larger fuselage and wings than on the 'Dash 80'. However, it was above all the diameter of the fuselage, and consequently the future disposition of the passengers

1. The first production De Havilland Comet 1 took off on January 1951 and was immediately a huge success. This was the first certified commercial jet, it flew 50% faster than the best piston-engined planes of the day (DC-6, Constellation) and was quickly ordered in series, notably by British airlines. Unluckily a series of tragedies after entering into regular service, the first one being the BOAC aircraft that crashed off the island of Elba on 10 January 1954, killing all the passengers. Another accident happened in the April of the same year and the whole fleet was grounded. The reasons for these accidents (one due to a weakness in one of the windows) were discovered at the end of a long series of tests and simulations. The resistance of the pressurised areas were also tested in water-filled tanks. The Comet only went back into service in 1958, in a modified version (Mark 4 with a lengthened fuselage and equipped with extra fuel tanks in the wings) that became the first civil transport jet aircraft to be used for trans Atlantic flights a few weeks

before Pan Am and its Boeing 707 aircraft. However, at this period, the time spent dealing with these teething problems had led to the commercial airlines losing interest in this model, especially given that they were now being offered new aircraft that performed better and were apparently safer.

2. The DC-8 prototype carried out its maiden flight on 30 May 1958, several weeks before the Pan Am Boeing 707 entered into commercial service, and received its official certificate at the end of the following August. The first version entered into service (10 series) on 18 September 1959, it was powered by Pratt & Whitney JT3C engines and destined for domestic United States flights. The first two customers were United and Delta Airlines. The delay in the program allowed Boeing to gain superiority, the Santa Monica firm's plane, despite its undeniable qualities and successive versions was never able to catch up.

in the cabin that was the object of long debate and research. The first studies (Model 707-1) envisaged using a 3,10 m (122 inches) diameter fuselage which was much less than that offered by the propeller aircraft of the day. In these conditions the cabin could only hold 72 passengers. This number was rapidly revised, and the Model 707-2, therefore, received a 3,35 m (132 inches) diameter. Although this dimension, that was finally chosen for the Dash 80, was identical to that of the upper deck of the Boeing 377 and allowed for passengers to be seated in rows of four, it still remained inferior to that of most of the commercial airliners of the day, starting with the Lockheed Super Constellation and Starliner. As we have seen, the model of the cabin was made when the decision to make the plane was taken and quickly showed the ideal dimension to be 3,66 m (144 inches) as it allowed passengers in rows of four in first class, with five in tourist class and 6 in economy [3]). However, here too, Boeing still remained below its competitors proposals, attracted by the future DC-8 and its 3,73 m (147 inches diameter fuselage. Seriously threatened, notably when United Airlines

twenty planes on 13 October 1955.

This contract was slightly modified as the airplane demanded aircraft equipped with the latest model fuselage that was 3,76 m (148 in) wide. A few months later, a second revision was undertaken at the end of which it was decided that only six aircraft, the first six of this version, would be bought, the others being the second generation 707-320 models with JT4A engines. In order to differentiate the different buyers, Boeing quickly elaborated a particular system of designation. From now on, in the number identifying the version, the two last numbers would be attributed to an airline in the chronological order of orders placed.

The Pan Am planes, the first company to buy, were designated 707-121, whilst those of United Airlines (second buyer) became 707-122, and those of American 707-123 and so on. [5] As the years passed and the buyers became more numerous, an alphanumeric system was introduced as the two number system was not enough.

The ' roll out ' of the first production aircraft (c/n 17586, destined for Pan Am) took place on 28 October 1957 at Renton, and the plane undertook its maiden flight two months later on 20 December 1957. The official certificate was given in September the following year and the beginning of the commercial exploitation by Pan Am, was able to take place a few days later on 26 October 1958. Beforehand, the airline, whose first plane was named by the First Lady [6], Mamie Eisenhower, had used the first 707-121 planes to perfect the training of its crews, notably by carrying out freight flights between New York and San Juan in Porto Rico, as well as some promotional demonstrations destined for the press, between, amongst others, the United States and Great Britain. [7]

announced its decision to choose the Douglas plane, Boeing decided to play its last card by making use of the rivalry between the main American airlines. The latter wanted now to have a fleet of jet planes for their domestic and international routes. It was American Airlines that allowed the Renton aviation company to regain the initiative. Wanting to be the first airline to offer jet aircraft transcontinental links, it declared that it was ready to buy several examples of the Boeing 707 on the condition that its fuselage would be increased to 3,76 m (148 inches). This increase, which came late and was costly, and that allowed for an ideal cabin configuration whatever the number of passengers carried, was accepted by Boeing that just beat its two main rivals the Douglas DC-8 (one inch, or 2,54 cm more) and the De Havilland Comet 4 (0,38 m/15 inches more) [4].

The first orders, the first successes

It was finally Pan Am that was the first to order the new plane, officially designated the 707-120, signing a contract for

Above.
The second Boeing 707 to be made (c/n 17587) was delivered to Pan Am only nine months after its first flight on 21 March 1958. It is seen here during a certification flight, with a particularly appropriate registration number at the rear of the fuselage (N707PA).
(V. Gréciet collection)

Above, right.
The 707 assembly line at the Boeing factory at Renton with, in the foreground, c/n 17696 destined for the Australian Quantas company.
(Qantas)

Opposite.
The very first production Boeing 707 during construction at the Renton factory. This aircraft (c/n 17586), was named 'Jet Clipper Constitution and did not have originally planned for symbolic registration of -N707PA -, this being finally attributed to the second production aircraft.
(J. Delmas collection)

Below.
The Australian company, Quantas, was the first to buy the short version of the Boeing 707-120, the -138. The aircraft entered into service on the Sydney-San Francisco route in July 1959. These two close-ups of VH-EBG, delivered in the September of the same year and named within the fleet, 'City of Hobart' , show the ferry pod, a profiled container hung under the left wing containing a spare engine. (Qantas)

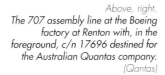

When the first transatlantic flights began at the end of October 1958, the flights between New York-Idlewild and Paris-Le Bourget sometimes comprised a stop over, notably in the west east direction, depending on weather conditions. Very quickly, other capital cities were linked, starting with Rome on 9 November, then London on the 16th of the same month.

Pan Am used its 707-121 planes over the Atlantic for only a brief period as it replaced them starting from August 1959 with the 707-321 when these were put into service, keeping the old JT3C engined models for shorter trips such as the Caribbean or South America. In total, 63 of these planes of the very first version [8], longer than the 367-80 (ten extra feet, or three metres) and with a wider fuselage (by six inches, 15 cm) were made. Powered by four Pratt & Whitney JT3C-6 engines (the civil version of the J57, a reactor installed, amongst others, on the F-100, F-101 and F-102 as well as the B-52), it was 43,78 metres (144 ft 6 in) long and had a wingspan of 39,65 metres (130' 10"). The 707-120 could cross the United States from coast to coast whilst at least one

cation was made to this version during production with the addition of two Krueger type flaps to the wings' leading edge between the two exterior engine pods. This system, which functioned at the same time as the usual high lift flap, was destined to slow down the stalling process at low speed.

After Pan Am, which ended up with largest fleet of 707s of all models (126 planes bought new and others second hand), the airlines quickly pressed their 707 aircraft into service. National Airlines, that had gone with the DC-8 but had not yet received any of these aircraft when the traditional Christmas holiday rush began, rented a few planes from Pan Am for the 1958 end of year tourist destinations. American Airlines now joined in at

stop over was required for crossing the Atlantic. The cabin could seat, depending on the chosen configuration by the buyers, 124 passengers in first class and 179 in tourist class, with access via two doors situated on the left side of the fuselage, one in front of the wing's leading edge and the other behind the trailing edge. The hold doors were situated under the floor of the cabin situated on either side of the plane, on the right, this particular configuration later becoming common on all of Boeing's commercial aircraft. At the beginning, the 707-120 was equipped with a small size vertical stabiliser with a non-assisted rudder. These elements were later modified (raised vertical stabiliser, hydraulically assisted rudder) on planes made from the end of 1959 or added to older aircraft.

In some cases, a rear ventral fin was added which was destined to improve the aircraft's stability in the case of asymmetry in engine function, protecting at the same time the rear of the fuselage in the case of too steep a take off. Another modifi-

the beginning of 1959 by using its new four-engined planes for the coast to coast New York-Los Angeles run starting from 25 January, thus beating by two months TWA that had, at the beginning, chosen to go with the smaller and faster Convair 880, but above all, beating United whose DC-8 aircraft only began this run in September 1959. It was also to American that the unfortunate privilege fell of losing a 707, when one of its planes (c/n 17641) crashed during a training flight between Calverton (Maryland) and New York on 15 August 1959. This company was above all the first to use the 707 for domestic flights in the United States with the 'Flagship Oklahoma' linking the first time Los Angeles to New York-Idlewild on 25 January 1959. Due to the limited autonomy of the 707-120, diversions were inevitable in the case of bad weather conditions, notably when there were high winds at altitude. However, as the original design of the plane was good, there were not many teething problems and the incidents limited to a few problems

3 Contrary to what is done today, the planes of the 1950s and 1960s did not have mixed cabins and only carried one type of passenger.

4. This diameter was later a reference for other Boeing success stories, notably the 727, 737 and 757.

5. This system was later kept, at least as long as the airlines lasted, but this time without reference to the order of the orders. This is why American Airlines now has the 767-223.

6. The first Pan Am 707-121 was named 'Clipper America', the word, 'Clipper' (or 'Jet Clipper') had been chosen as a reminder of the 1930s' Sikorsky seaplanes. Most of this airline's Boeings were named in this way.

The plane used by the Beatles during their North American tour in 1964 was especially named 'Clipper Beatles'! Four 707-121 aircraft bore the name 'Clipper America' in order that at least one of them would be the first to fly.

7. The first transatlantic flight of the new four-engined Boeing was between New York and London with a VIP passenger, Juan Trippe, the Boeing boss. It was not the first jet engined transatlantic flight in fact, the BOAC Comet 4 had been making this run since 4 October 1954.

8. Pan Am = 6 (-121), American Airlines = 25 (-123), Continental = 5 (-124), TWA = 15 (-131), Qantas = 7 (-138), Cubana for Western = 2 (-139) to which should be added three 707-153/(V) C-137 for the USAF.

The 707-120

with the hydraulic system, air conditioning and the engine water injectors. The main undercarriage had in some cases shown signs of weakness and its design was rapidly modified during production whilst the original fuselage tail cone made from magnesium that was subjected to extreme fatigue from the noise of the engines, was replaced by one made from aluminium with an interior layer of glass fibre.

The test flights began on 20 March 1959 and the first plane (registered VH-EBA) was delivered to the Australian airline the following 16 July, beginning its regular service at the end of the same month.

The 707-138 began to be used on the Sydney-London run in September 1959 and returned to Boeing two years later in order to be re-equipped with improved performance turbofans. This 'short' variant was also the first to carry a 'ferry pod', a profiled pod held by a strut between the fuselage and the number 2 engine and destined to carry a spare reactor to airports outside the usual maintenance sites.

A special version, the 707-220

This version was especially made for use from airports situated at high altitude and in a hotter than usual atmosphere. It had the Pratt & Whitney JT4A-3 engines, identical turbojets to that of its direct rival the DC-8-20, and only five were finally made, all ordered by Braniif on 5 December 1955 with the designation 707-227. The airline had chosen these special models for its Central and South America destinations, regions where there were several of the highest airports in the world (4 070 m/13,350 ft for La Paz in Bolivia, 2 812 m/9,225 ft for Quito in Ecuador, etc.) and where the ambient temperatures were higher than average. Apart from its different engines, almost identical to those of the 707-320, and despite the preliminary studies that had envisaged using a shortened fuselage and even install extra fuel tanks on the wing tips, the 707-220 was finally identical to the 707-120.

The first production example carried out its maiden flight on 11 May 1959, the official certificate was given on the following 5 November, and this despite the loss of a plane that happened following the phenomenon of 'Dutch Roll' during a test flight on 19 October that caused the deaths of four crew members. The pilot had not been able to stabilise the aircraft after having lost three of its engines during involuntary manoeuvres. Brannif brought into service the surviving four aircraft at the end of December 1959, initially on United States domestic flights, then, from April 1960 on its New York-Buenos Aires run with successive stop overs at Panama and Lima.

These planes were rendered obsolete by the arrival models equipped with turbofans used in the Latin American network until the beginning of 1971. They were then firstly put into storage then finally destroyed in May 1984.

Braniff's El Dorado Super Jet...
the Different and Superior BOEING 707-227

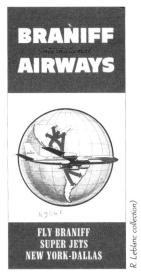

The Australian 707-138

The first variant of the 707-12 was especially made for the Australian airline Quantas and showed Boeing's willingness to satisfy the demands of its customers, a costly policy initially but one that would pay off later as it tended to reinforce loyalty. Seven were made and designated as the 707-138; it was an aircraft with a slightly shortened fuselage (by 10 feet/3,03 m, making a total length that went from 43,78 m/144' 6" to 40,75 m/134' 6") at the level of the wings' trailing edges. Although this slight reduction made the plane better adapted for certain runways, both shorter and bumpier, like that of Nadi on the Fiji Islands, it limited, on the other hand, the maximum number of passengers it could carry.

The aircraft was equipped with extra fuel tanks placed at the centre of the fuselage and it could carry almost 15,000 more litres (3,960 US gall) of fuel than the standard model, giving it enough autonomy and reducing the structural mass at the same time. Quantas particular needed planes that had good endurance, capable of crossing the sea over long distances, notably between the stop overs on its San Francisco-Sydney run or certain flights over 4,000 kms (2,500 miles).

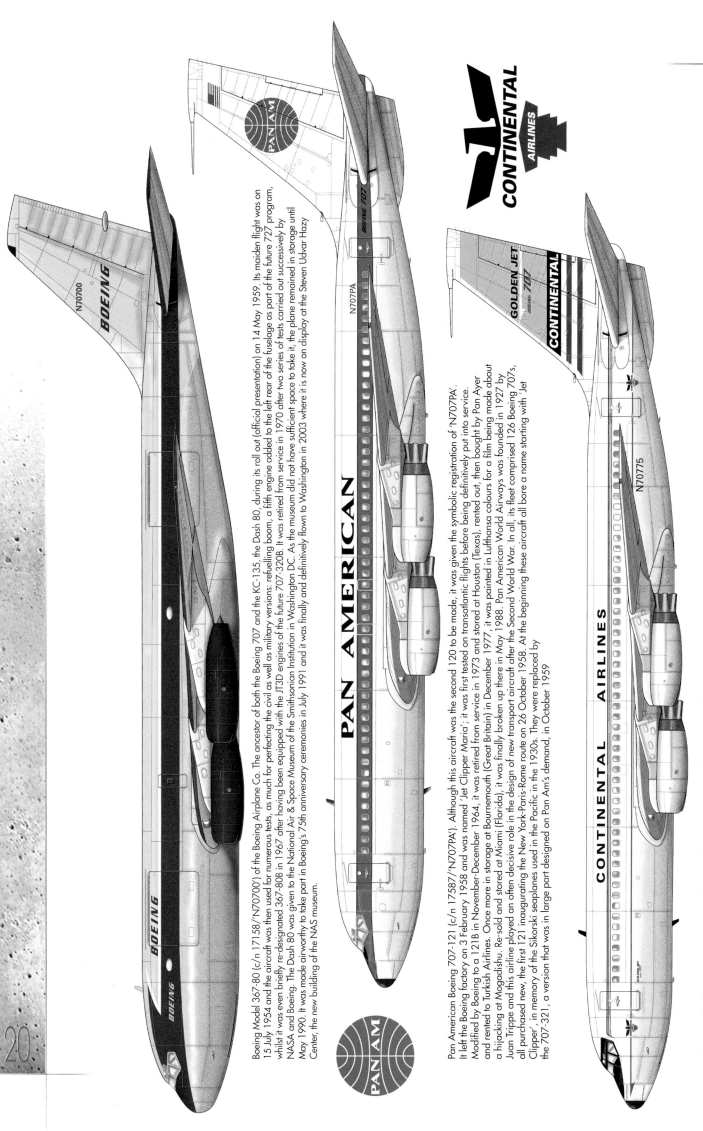

Boeing Model 367-80 (c/n 17158/'N70700') of the Boeing Airplane Co. The ancestor of both the Boeing 707 and the KC-135, the Dash 80, during its roll out (official presentation) on 14 May 1959. Its maiden flight was on 15 July 1954 and the aircraft was then used for numerous tests, as much for perfecting the civil as well as military versions: refuelling boom, a fifth engine added to the left rear of the fuselage as part of the future 727 program, whilst it was even briefly re-designated 367-80B in 1967 after having been equipped with the JT3D engines of the future 707-320B. It was retired from service in 1970 after two series of tests carried out successively by NASA and Boeing. The Dash 80 was given to the National Air & Space Museum of the Smithsonian Institution in Washington DC. As the museum did not have sufficient space to take it, the plane remained in storage until May 1990. It was made airworthy to take part in Boeing's 75th anniversary ceremonies in July 1991 and it was finally and definitively flown to Washington in 2003 where it is now on display at the Steven Udvar Hazy Center, the new building of the NAS museum.

Pan American Boeing 707-121 (c/n 17587/'N707PA'). Although this aircraft was the second 120 to be made, it was given the symbolic registration of 'N707PA'. It left the Boeing factory on 3 February 1958 and was named 'Jet Clipper Maria'; it was first tested on transatlantic flights before being definitively put into service. Modified by Boeing to a 121B in November-December 1964, it was retired from service in 1973 and stored at Houston (Texas), rented out, then bought by Pan Ayer and rented to Turkish Airlines. Once more in storage at Bournemouth (Great Britain) in December 1977, it was painted in Lufthansa colours for a film being made about a hijacking at Mogadishu. Re-sold and stored at Miami (Florida), it was finally broken up there in May 1988. Pan American World Airways was founded in 1927 by Juan Trippe and this airline played an often decisive role in the design of new transport aircraft after the Second World War. In all, its fleet comprised 126 Boeing 707s, all purchased new, the first 121 inaugurating the New York-Paris-Rome route on 26 October 1958. At the beginning these aircraft all bore a name starting with 'Jet Clipper', in memory of the Sikorski seaplanes used in the Pacific in the 1930s. They were replaced by the 707-321, a version that was in large part designed on Pan Am's demand, in October 1959

Continental Airlines Boeing 707-124 (c/n 17611 /'N70775'). Delivered to Continental on 16 July 1959, this plane exploded in mid air near Unionville (Missouri) on the Chicago-Kansas City route. This accident, which killed the forty-five people on board the plane, is considered to be the first case of sabotage concerning a civil plane. The FBI inquest determined that the explosion, which broke the fuselage at the tail plane, was caused by a bomb placed at the rear, in the toilets, by an individual who wanted to get the money for his wife from a recently subscribed life insurance. The history of Continental Airlines, who took this name in 1937, goes back in fact to 1934 when its planes began flying on the El Paso-Albuquerque route. The first Boeing 124 was ordered in December 1955 for the Chicago-Los Angeles route. The third American domestic airline (after AA and Braniff), its aircraft flew more than other airlines (up to eleven hours a day !) ; this version was replaced, from April 1962.

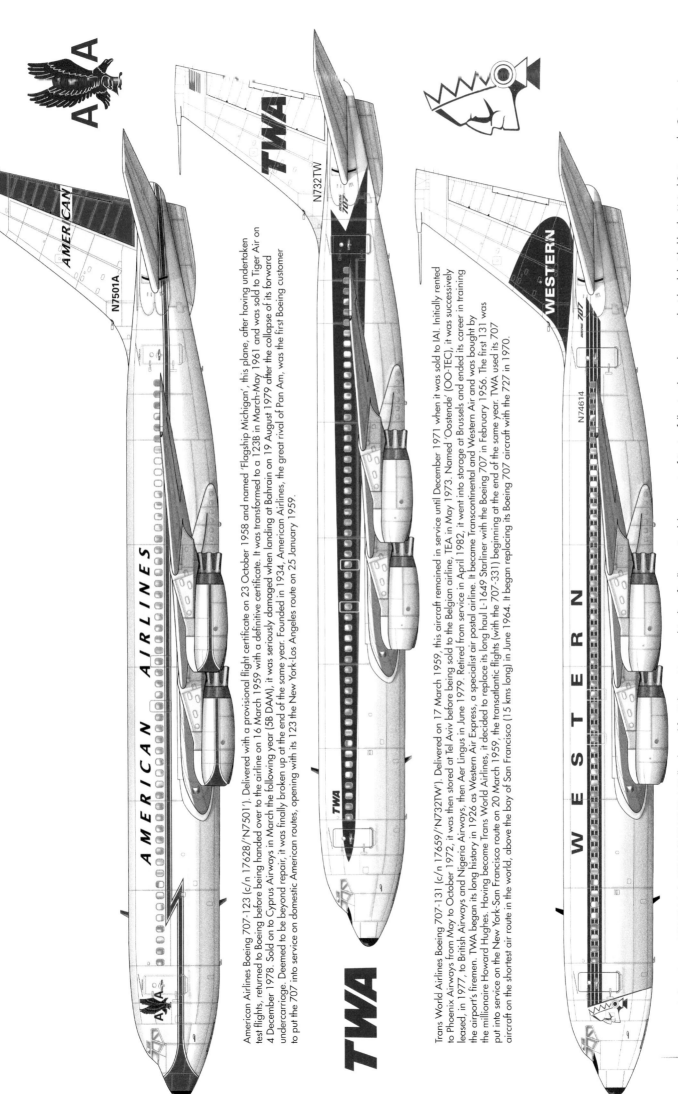

American Airlines Boeing 707-123 (c/n 17628/'N7501'). Delivered with a provisional flight certificate on 23 October 1958 and named 'Flagship Michigan', this plane, after having undertaken test flights, returned to Boeing before being handed over to the airline on 16 March 1959 with a definitive certificate. It was transformed to a 123B in March-May 1961 and was sold to Tiger Air on 4 December 1978. Sold on to Cyprus Airways in March the following year (5B DAM), it was seriously damaged when landing at Bahrain on 19 August 1979 after the collapse of its forward undercarriage. Deemed to be beyond repair, it was finally broken up at the end of the same year. Founded in 1934, American Airlines, the great rival of Pan Am, was the first Boeing customer to put the 707 into service on domestic American routes, opening with its 123 the New York-Los Angeles route on 25 January 1959.

Trans World Airlines Boeing 707-131 (c/n 17659/'N732TW'). Delivered on 17 March 1959, this aircraft remained in service until December 1971 when it was sold to IAI. Initially rented to Phoenix Airways from May to October 1972, it was then stored at Tel Aviv before being sold to the Belgian airline, TEA in May 1973. Named 'Oostende' (OO-TEC), it was successively leased, in 1977, to British Airways and Nigeria Airways, then Aer Lingus in June 1979. Retired from service in April 1982, it went into storage at Brussels and ended its career in training the airport's firemen. TWA began its long history in 1926 as Western Air Express, a specialist air postal airline. It became Transcontinental and Western Air and was bought by the millionaire Howard Hughes. Having become Trans World Airlines, it decided to replace its long haul L-1649 Starliner with the Boeing 707 in February 1956. The first 131 was put into service on the New York-San Francisco route on 20 March 1959, the transatlantic flights (with the 707-331) beginning at the end of the same year. TWA used its 707 aircraft on the shortest air route in the world, above the bay of San Francisco (15 kms long) in June 1964. It began replacing its Boeing 707 aircraft with the 727 in 1970.

Western Airlines Boeing 707-139 (c/n 17904/'N74614'). Initially planned for Cubana Airways, this plane finally remained the property of Boeing following the embargo on the island decided by the United States on the Castro regime. It was leased to Western Airlines on 4 May 1960 to 22 September 1962. It was sold to Sally Leasing Corp the following December and rented to Pan Am ('N779PA' 'Jet Clipper Southern Cross'). On 7 April 1964, the aircraft, arriving from San Juan (Porto Rico), left the runway when landing at New York-JFK and its fuselage broke in two ; however, there were no victims. Beyond repair, it was broken up there shortly after. Western Airlines boasts of being the oldest United States airline. Under this name, it goes back in any case to 1941, and began putting into service its first leased Boeing 707-139 aircraft in June 1960, replacing them with the 720 two years later. Western was finally taken over by Delta Airlines in September 1986.

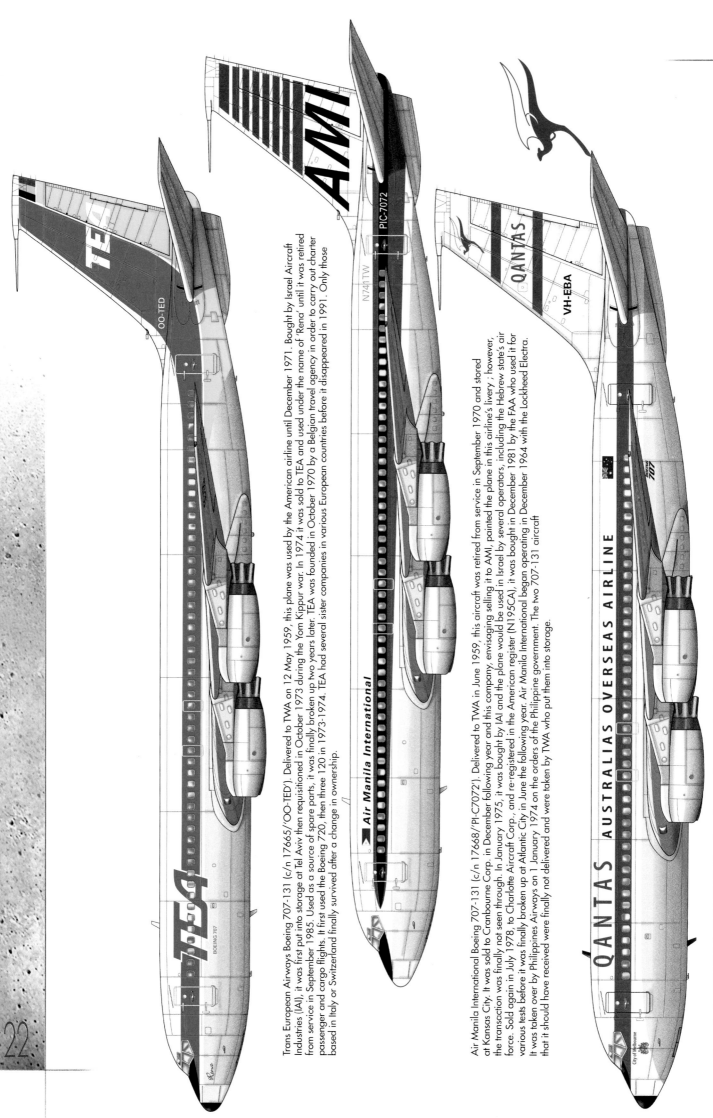

Trans European Airways Boeing 707-131 (c/n 17665/'OO-TED'). Delivered to TWA on 12 May 1959, this plane was used by the American airline until December 1971. Bought by Israel Aircraft Industries (IAI), it was first put into storage at Tel Aviv then requisitioned in October 1973 during the Yom Kippur war. In 1974 it was sold to TEA and used under the name of 'Rena' until it was retired from service in September 1985. Used as a source of spare parts, it was finally broken up two years later. TEA was founded in October 1970 by a Belgian travel agency in order to carry out charter passenger and cargo flights. It first used the Boeing 720, then three 120 in 1973-1974. TEA had several sister companies in various European countries before it disappeared in 1991. Only those based in Italy or Switzerland finally survived after a change in ownership.

▶ Air Manila International

Air Manila International Boeing 707-131 (c/n 17668/'PI-C7072'). Delivered to TWA in June 1959, this aircraft was retired from service in September 1970 and stored at Kansas City. It was sold to Cranbourne Corp. in December following year and this company, envisaging selling it to AMI, painted the plane in this airline's livery ; however, the transaction was finally not seen through. In January 1975, it was bought by IAI and the plane would be used in Israel by several operators, including the Hebrew state's air force. Sold again in July 1978, to Charlotte Aircraft Corp., and re-registered in the American register (N195CA), it was bought in December 1981 by the FAA who used it for various tests before it was finally broken up at Atlantic City in June the following year. Air Manila International began operating in December 1964 with the Lockheed Electra. It was taken over by Philippines Airways on 1 January 1974 on the orders of the Philippine government. The two 707-131 aircraft that it should have received were finally not delivered and were taken by TWA who put them into storage.

QANTAS AUSTRALIAS OVERSEAS AIRLINE

Qantas Boeing 707-138 (c/n 17696/'VH-EBA'). Delivered on 16 July 1959 and named 'City of Melbourne', this aircraft was transformed to a 138B in August-September 1961. It was sold to Pacific Western in November 1967 and ended its career with the Royal Saudi Air Force as prince Bandar's private plane. Qantas ordered this particular Boeing 707-120 variant from Boeing for flights to particular destinations, notably the island of Nadji in the Fiji Islands, which was both a tourist destination and a stopover on the Australia-United States route. Seven 707-138 were made and were characterised by a three metre (10 ft) shorter fuselage, a lower fuselage ventral fin and a cabin that could hold 154 passengers. The original engines, an improved version of the JT3C, were rapidly changed for turbofans (138B).

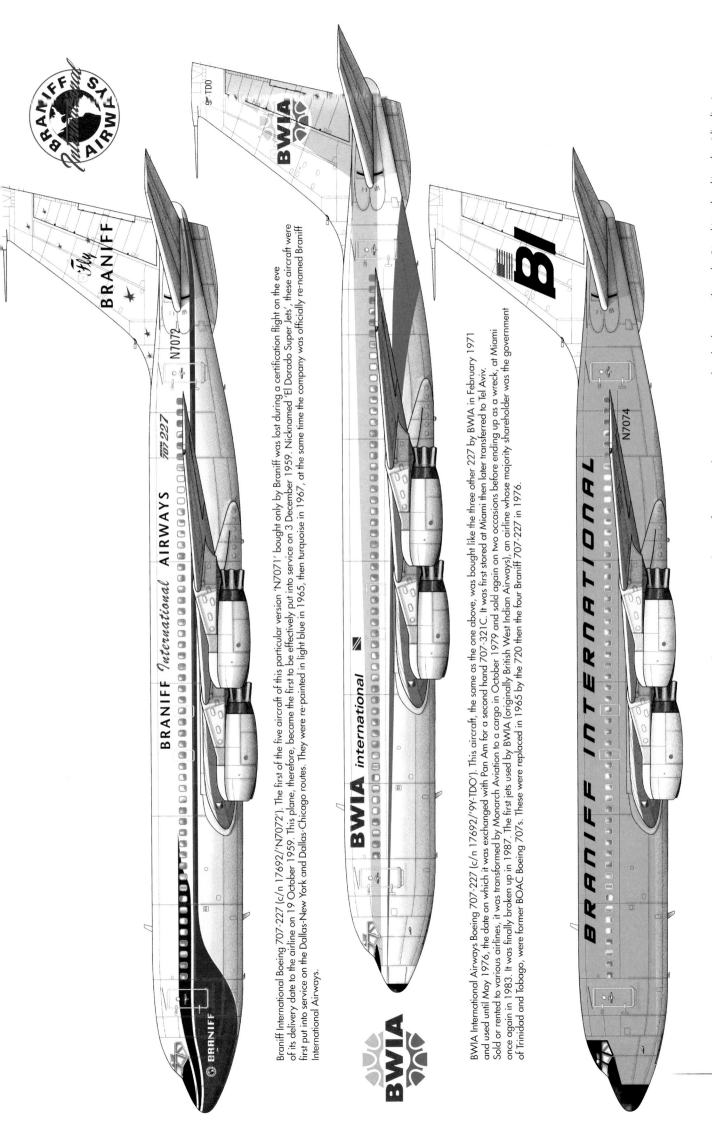

Braniff International Boeing 707-227 (c/n 17692/'N7072'). The first of the five aircraft of this particular version 'N7071' bought only by Braniff was lost during a certification flight on the eve of its delivery date to the airline on 19 October 1959. This plane, therefore, became the first to be effectively put into service on 3 December 1959. Nicknamed 'El Dorado Super Jets', these aircraft were first put into service on the Dallas-New York and Dallas-Chicago routes. They were re-painted in light blue in 1965, then turquoise in 1967, at the same time the company was officially re-named Braniff International Airways.

BWIA International Airways Boeing 707-227 (c/n 17692/'9Y-TDO'). This aircraft, the same as the one above, was bought like the three other 227 by BWIA in February 1971 and used until May 1976, the date on which it was exchanged with Pan Am for a second hand 707-321C. It was first stored at Miami then later transferred to Tel Aviv. Sold or rented to various airlines, it was transformed by Monarch Aviation to a cargo in October 1979 and sold again on two occasions before ending up as a wreck, at Miami once again in 1983. It was finally broken up in 1987. The first jets used by BWIA (originally British West Indian Airways), an airline whose majority shareholder was the government of Trinidad and Tobago, were former BOAC Boeing 707s. These were replaced in 1965 by the 720 then the four Braniff 707-227 in 1976.

Braniff International Airways Boeing 707-227 (c/n 17694/'Braniff N7074'). Delivered to Braniff on 21 January 1960, this aircraft was painted turquoise in 1965 when the designer Alexander Girard introduced into the airline liverie of different colours (seven in all) for each aircraft in its fleet. Bought by BWIA in May 1971, it was named 'Bird of Paradise' and exchanged at the end of its use for a Pan Am 707-321C. Stored at Miami, it was, like its counterparts, sold on many occasions to various airlines or companies that rented it or sub let it until May 1981, the date on which it was scrapped at Moses Lake (Washington state) when owned by Sonico Inc.

23

Above.
The 707-328 'Château de Chambord' (c/n 17614/ F-BHSB) was delivered to Air France in December 1959. It is seen here in Air France colours during a test flight before being delivered in the region of Seattle.
(J. Delmas collection)

THE BOEING 707-320

The 707-120 had still not entered into service when Boeing undertook the study of a derivative and improved version, a plane capable of crossing the Atlantic without a stopover and in any weather. This resulted in the 707-320 'Intercontinental' whose fate was more enviable than that of its predecessor.

Although the latest generation piston engine airliners such as the Lockheed Starliner or Douglas DC-7 were capable of crossing the Atlantic without a stopover, the first version of the 707 had to, on the other hand, make a stop over at Gander (Newfoundland) in order to cross the ocean from west to east and at Keflavik, Iceland for the return. To give its four-engined plane real intercontinental capacities, Boeing decided to give it more muscle and above all, more endurance.

New engines and wings

To this end, the aircraft's fuselage was lengthened by a little more than two metres (6' 7"), the wingspan increased and the original engines replaced by the JT4A-3 engine that could produce 7,166 kg (15,800 lb) of thrust. Although more fuel could be carried (96,360 litres/25,455 US gall), increasing the autonomy by more than 2,500 kms (1,550 miles), giving it a range of 7,500 kms (4,660 miles) without a stopover and a full payload, the aircraft was, on the other hand, heavier than the 707-120 (between 18 and 20% depending on the configuration).

Faced with a heavier take off weight, Boeing was forced with improving the engines, the wing surface and the lift systems. The first problem was solved by mounting new reactors, which were, by the way, the same as those used by the great rival of the day, the Douglas DC-8. These jet engines did not have the water injection system that was as polluting as it was diffi-

PAN AMERICAN
WELCOMES YOU TO

PARIS

Helpful
Information
For
Arriving
Passengers

(R. Leblanc collection)

Below.
Operated by Pan Am who named it 'Westward Ho' from January 1960 to August 1972, this 707-331 (c/n 17604/N726PA) was sold to Lease Air Corp on 15 August 1972 and immediately leased to Aeronauts International travel club. When the latter ceased operations, in August 1975, this plane was repossessed by Pan Am. (J. Guillem collection)

The turn in the road will take you to other quiet
peaceful villages like Buckland-in-the-Moor.

Only your dreams get you there faster...

Fly the fastest Jets to England - 6½ hours on Pan Am!

ional travelers can now fly Jet
* direct to Europe from 11 of
's major gateway cities.
the East Coast, you can fly Jets
Europe from New York, Bos-
iladelphia* and Washington/
e*. From the Midwest, you can
direct from Chicago and Detroit.

And from the West Coast, Pan Am Jets
will fly you *direct* from Los Angeles,
San Francisco, Portland and Seattle over
the Polar route.
Serene in the hands of the world's
most experienced airline, you travel at
speeds up to 600 miles an hour aboard
the newest, biggest, fastest, most power-

ful fleet of over-ocean jetliners in the
world—the Jet Clipper fleet.
To date, more than 300,000 passen-
gers have flown the Atlantic on Pan Am
Jet Clippers. For first-class *President
Special* or low-cost Economy service,
call your Travel Agent or any of Pan
Am's 66 offices in the U.S. and Canada.
*Trade-Mark, Reg. U.S. Pat. Off., 1958 Juve

WORLDS MOST [logo] EXPERIENCED AIRLINE

---

1. In detail 20 examples (-321) to la Pan Am,
21 to Air France (-328), seven to Sabena
(-329), 12 to TWA (-331) plus six others finally delivered to Pan Am and finally 3 to SAA
(-344).

cult to implement and whose performance was 17
to 35% superior. The wings were also greatly
modified as the surface and wingspan were increased, going respectively from 43,15 m/142' 5" (in
place of 39,65 m/130' 10") and 268,80 m²
(2,892 sq ft), whilst the original 35° sweep
remained.

To achieve this increase, Boeing did not change
the general shape but only modified the junction
between the wing and the fuselage by adding an
element known as a glove. The wingtips were also
changed, whilst the engines that now protruded
more, were further away from the cabin (the gap
going from 8,28 m/27' 2" to 10,06 m/33') greatly reducing the noise levels inside the latter. Finally new ailerons were used both on the wings
leading and trailing edges, this reduced the landing
approach speed by 10% despite the increase in
overall mass.

The fuselage maintained an identical diameter
but, due to its increased length, the cabin could
now take 104 first class passengers (instead of 96)
and 165 to 180 in economy class with gaps
between seats varying between 1 metre (3' 3")
and 85 cms (2' 10"). The plane was certified for
a maximum capacity of 189 people.

Finally, several elements were also modified, notably with
the reinforced undercarriage, or the horizontal tail plane that
was larger and whose span was increased from 12,09 m (39'
8") to 13,92 m (45' 8"). A certain number of covering panels
were also reinforced.

The first production models, as with the first production

707-120, were equipped with the short vertical stabiliser and
the manually-operated rudder. These elements were quickly
replaced by a heightened tail plane and a hydraulically-assis-
ted rudder and were often added later to old planes. As for
the engines, depending on customers, these were Pratt &
Whitney JT4A-3, or JT4A-5.

The first example of this new plane undertook its maiden
flight on 11 January 1959, that is nine months after that of the
first 707-120, and was delivered in the following August, its
official certification having been given a few days earlier. Once
again, it was Pan Am that was the first to receive and put into
service this model. Its order went back to the end of December 1955 when, as we have seen, it had decided to only buy
six of the 707-120 initially planned and to go with this version
for the rest of its order. The company officially began to use
its 707-321 planes on 26 August 1959. The first New York
to London flight took place on the following 10 October,
the new plane, replacing on this destination the 707-121.
Also in October, the Pan Am ' Clipper Fleet Wing ' accomplished the first round the world flight by a 707, leaving from
San Francisco with successive stop overs at Manille, Karachi,
Rome with the return via the Pole and Anchorage, making
55 flying hours with sixteen stop overs.

All over the world!

In the end, the 707-320 would sell better than its predecessor a total of 69 planes[1], that is as many as all of the variants
of DC-8; the interested customers soon placed their orders,
most of the time even before the maiden flight of the model.
Air France, the first non-American company to acquire the
four-engined Boeing, ordered its ten 707-328 in Novem-

2. The airport of Idlewild was renamed John Fitzgerald Kennedy International Airport in December 1963, in memory of the United States president who had been assassinated a few weeks previously.

ber 1955 but did not immediately officially announce this so as not to disturb the transactions in view of buying the Caravelle that were going on at the same time. The first French 707 landed at Orly on 6 November 1959, the crews having undergone training in the United States in the previous weeks. Its commercial life began the following 31 January on the Paris-Orly/New York-Idlewild [2] line and the first accident with a plane of the national French company happened on 27 July

1961 when the 'Château de Versailles' (constructor n° 17 613) crashed at Hamburg airport after an aborted take off, injuring ten passengers and crew.

Sabena was the second European company to buy this intercontinental version and received the first of its seven 707-329 that it had ordered on 4 December 1959, that is only a few days after the French. On the other hand, it began its flights across the Atlantic on 23 January 1960, beating Air France

caractéristiques du **BOEING 707 INTERCONTINENTAL** **LE PLUS SPACIEUX DES AVIONS NOUVEAUX**

ENVERGURE : 43,41 M
LONGUEUR : 46,60 M
HAUTEUR : 11,85 M
SURFACE ALAIRE : 268,70 M2
LARGEUR DE LA CABINE (intérieur) : 3,53 M
HAUTEUR DE LA CABINE (intérieur) : 2,18 M
VOLUME DES SOUTES A BAGAGES ET FRET : 48,139 M3
TYPE DES MOTEURS :
4 TURBO-RÉACTEURS PRATT ET WHITNEY JT 4 A3
PUISSANCE AU DÉCOLLAGE :
18.000 KG DE POUSSÉE STATIQUE
CAPACITÉ DE CARBURANT : 89.000 L
POIDS MAXIMUM AU DÉCOLLAGE : 141.060 KG
LONGUEUR DE PISTE :
au décollage : 2.700 m
à l'atterrissage : 2.080 m
CHARGE MARCHANDE : 17.600 KG SUR 5.800 KM
RAYON D'ACTION : 7.400 KM AVEC 9.600 KG
VITESSE : 1.000 KM/H
NOMBRE DE PLACES :
DE 115 À 189 SELON LES AMÉNAGEMENTS

Longue comme la moitié d'un terrain de football, la coque géante de l'Intercontinental est divisée en plusieurs cabines dont l'insonorisation et la climatisation parfaites assurent aux passagers une atmosphère agréable et reposante pendant tout le voyage.

LEGENDE

1 *coupole du radar mét*
2 *entrée classe économi*
3 *cabine 1re classe*
    (8 FAUTEUILS TRES LARGES PAR RANG
4 *bar-promenoir*
5 *cabine classe économi*
    (6 FAUTEUILS DE FRONT)
6 *office arrière*
7 *toilettes arrière*
8 *entrée 1re classe*

26

Above and right opposite.
The Air France 707-328 'Château de Versailles' (c/n 17613/F-BHSA) was damaged on 27 July 1961 at Hamburg after a failed take off. Nobody was injured, but the aircraft was deemed to be beyond repair. It did not yet have 4,000 flying hours.
(R. Leblanc collection)

to this emblematic destination by a week, and at the same time becoming the first non-American airline to operate on this line.

Sabena's 707-329 aircraft were soon put to the test in the summer of 1960 with the evacuation of Belgian nationals from the Congo. The transatlantic flights were suspended during this period and the planes transported 7,000 civilians at the height of this crisis between 9 and 22 August. At this time, one of the aircraft carried out a veritable record flight, carrying 300 passengers instead of the usual one hundred

Opposite.
'How to recognise the new 707 Astrojet'. Extract from an American Airlines advertising leaflet. (R. Leblanc collection)

One of the Air France 707-328 taking off from one of the Renton factory runways (no doubt F-BHSA 'Château de Versailles', c/n 17613). At the edge of the runway is a USAF KC-135A, an aircraft that was quite different from its civilian cousin despite appearances.
(R. Leblanc collection)

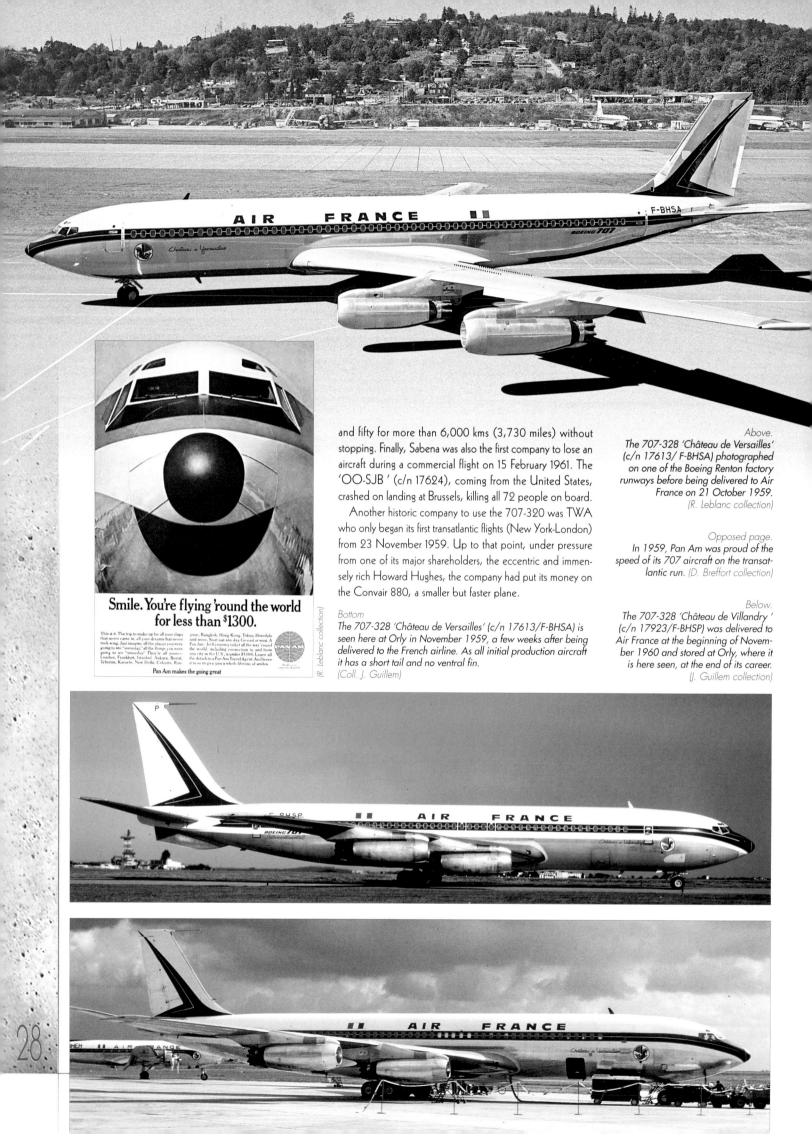

AIR FRANCE

F-BHSA

Boeing 707

Château de Versailles

and fifty for more than 6,000 kms (3,730 miles) without stopping. Finally, Sabena was also the first company to lose an aircraft during a commercial flight on 15 February 1961. The 'OO-SJB ' (c/n 17624), coming from the United States, crashed on landing at Brussels, killing all 72 people on board.

Another historic company to use the 707-320 was TWA who only began its first transatlantic flights (New York-London) from 23 November 1959. Up to that point, under pressure from one of its major shareholders, the eccentric and immensely rich Howard Hughes, the company had put its money on the Convair 880, a smaller but faster plane.

Bottom
The 707-328 'Château de Versailles' (c/n 17613/F-BHSA) is seen here at Orly in November 1959, a few weeks after being delivered to the French airline. As all initial production aircraft it has a short tail and no ventral fin.
(Coll. J. Guillem)

Above.
The 707-328 'Château de Versailles' (c/n 17613/ F-BHSA) photographed on one of the Boeing Renton factory runways before being delivered to Air France on 21 October 1959.
(R. Leblanc collection)

Opposed page.
In 1959, Pan Am was proud of the speed of its 707 aircraft on the transatlantic run. (D. Breffort collection)

Below.
The 707-328 'Château de Villandry ' (c/n 17923/F-BHSP) was delivered to Air France at the beginning of November 1960 and stored at Orly, where it is here seen, at the end of its career.
(J. Guillem collection)

F-BHSP **AIR FRANCE** Boeing 707 Intercontinental *Château de Villandry*

AIR FRANCE

Through the magic of Pan Am's Jet Clippers, this is *your* year to visit Europe.

6 hours 55 minutes to Europe

With the end of summer begins Europe's most beautiful season. The summer crowds are gone; a more colorful time begins at a more leisurely pace. This can be your year to visit the Continent, and *this Fall* is the perfect time.

Today, Europe is well within the limits of 2 weeks' vacation time and the average vacation budget. Abroad, prices are generally reduced for Fall. And with Pan Am Jet Clipper* economy-class service, New York to London is only $272 one way, $492⁶⁰ round trip. Pan Am Jets are fastest to Europe and offer the only service to Paris and Rome as well.

In addition to economy class, Pan Am's deluxe *President Special* service is available on every flight. For reservations, call your Travel Agent or any of Pan Am's 61 offices in the United States and Canada.   *Trade-Mark, Reg. U.S. Pat. Off.

World's Most Experienced Airline

Pan Am Jet Clippers...world's fastest airliners...the only economy-class Jet service... the only Jets to all three: London, Paris and Rome.

SEULEMENT HUIT HEURES POUR RELIER LA FRANCE AUX U.S.A. lorsque vous voyagez à bord d'un Boeing 707 Intercontinental... l'avion de transport à réaction le plus spacieux du monde et qui a fait ses preuves

BOEING 707 Intercontinental

5

Air France advertising leaflet. (R. Leblanc collection)

Brunch in Europe...dinner in Los Angeles

You can make this flight *today*, aboard Boeing 707s!

You can leave Europe in a 707 jetliner at 11 AM, have a 3½-hour visit in New York, and land at Los Angeles that same evening in time for dinner. Like the 131,000 passengers who have already flown in this superb Boeing jet, you'll find the flight exhilarating—yet serene and wonderfully comfortable. There's no vibration, no travel fatigue. You arrive rested and refreshed. Make your next trip in the Boeing 707, the most flight-tested airliner ever to enter commercial service.

BOEING 707 and 720

(Ph. Bruno collection)

Caravelle

BOEING 707 INTERCONTINENTAL LES DEUX MEILLEURS "JETS"

SUR LE PLUS GRAND RÉSEAU DU MONDE

AIR FRANCE

30

Opposite.
The unusual livery of the Air France 707-328 (c/n 17920/ F-BHSK, 'Château de Vizille'), photographed at Nairobi (Kenya) in May 1964, is explained by the fact that at this time it was rented out to the Air Madagascar company that had only partially repainted it. Back again within the Air France fleet, it was retired from service in January 1977, stored briefly at Orly and destroyed a few months later.
(J. Delmas collection)

Opposite.
'Jet Clipper Mercury ', this 707-321 (c/n 17602/ N724PA) delivered to Pan Am in December 1959 was leased to Yugoslavian national airline JAT from June to October 1971. Repainted in this operator colour scheme, it retained its original registration number.
(J. Guillem collection).

Below.
In March 1962, Air Afrique rented out the 'Château de Pau ' (707-328 c/n 17619/ F-BHSG) to Air France and, therefore, modified the livery of this aircraft initially used for carrying passengers then freight. Air France took this plane back, photographed here in 1962 at Abidjan and it was sold to Royal Air Maroc in September 1977. (J. Delmas collection)

Bottom.
Operated during ten years by Pam Am who named it 'J. Cl. Defiance', this 707-331 (c/n 17683) was leased to Air Vietnam in March 1973. Renamed ' Companion of Peace ' and reregistered after being purchased by this South Vietnamese airline in December, it was flown to Hong Kong and stored after the collapse of the South Vietnamese government in April 1975. It was finally repossessed by Pan Am a few months later, because of unpaid bills…
(J. Guillem collection).

Delivered to Sabena in June 1960, this 707-329 (c/n 17627/ OO-SJE) was destroyed by fire after an accident on landing at Tenerife airport on 15 February 1978.
(J. Guillem collection).

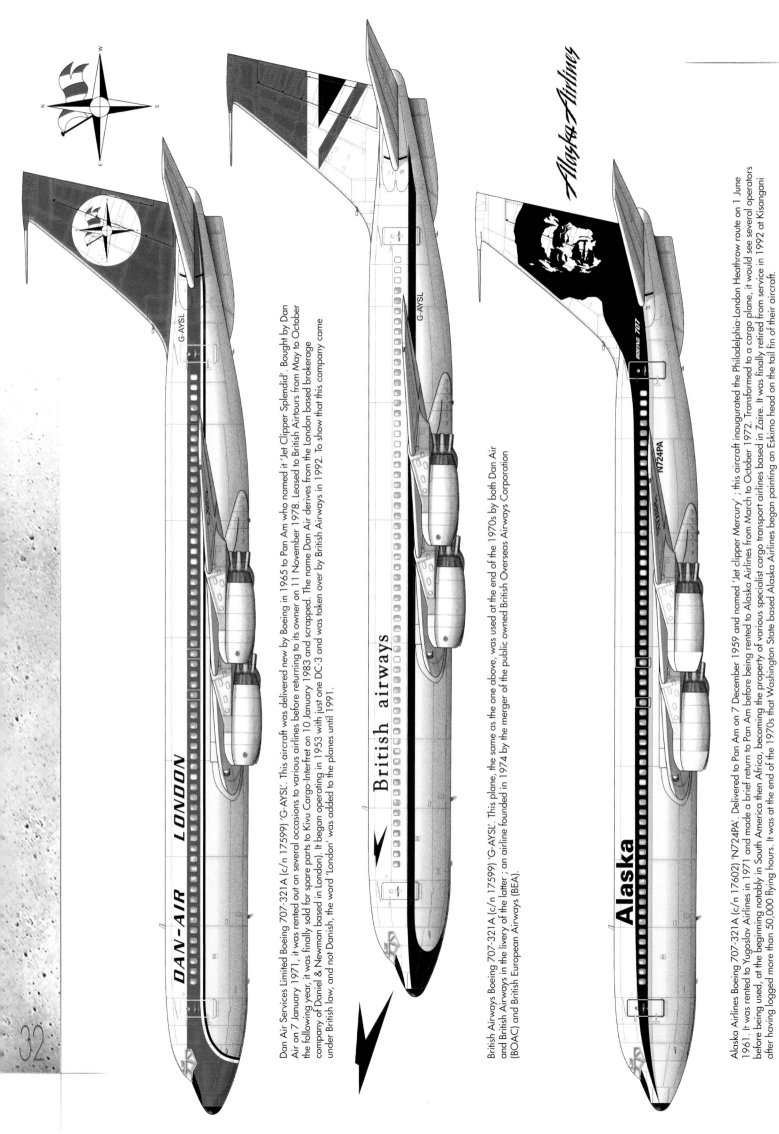

DAN-AIR LONDON

G-AYSL

Dan Air Services Limited Boeing 707-321A (c/n 17599) 'G-AYSL'. This aircraft was delivered new by Boeing in 1965 to Pan Am who named it 'Jet Clipper Splendid'. Bought by Dan Air on 7 January 1971, it was rented out on several occasions to various airlines before returning to its owner on 11 November 1978. Leased to British Airtours from May to October the following year, it was finally sold for spare parts to Kivu Cargo-Interfret on 10 January 1983 and scrapped. The name Dan Air derives from the London based brokerage company of Daniel & Newman based in London). It began operating in 1953 with just one DC-3 and was taken over by British Airways in 1992. To show that this company came under British law, and not Danish, the word 'London' was added to the planes until 1991.

British airways

G-AYSL

British Airways Boeing 707-321A (c/n 17599) 'G-AYSL'. This plane, the same as the one above, was used at the end of the 1970s by both Dan Air and British Airways in the livery of the latter ; an airline founded in 1974 by the merger of the public owned British Overseas Airways Corporation (BOAC) and British European Airways (BEA).

Alaska Airlines

BOEING 707

N724PA

Alaska

Alaska Airlines Boeing 707-321A (c/n 17602) 'N724PA'. Delivered to Pan Am on 7 December 1959 and named 'Jet clipper Mercury' ; this aircraft inaugurated the Philadelphia-London Heathrow route on 1 June 1961. It was rented to Yugoslav Airlines in 1971 and made a brief return to Pan Am before being rented to Alaska Airlines from March to October 1972. Transformed to a cargo plane, it would see several operators before being used, at the beginning notably in South America then Africa, becoming the property of various specialist cargo transport airlines based in Zaire. It was finally retired from service in 1992 at Kisangani after having logged more than 50,000 flying hours. It was at the end of the 1970s that Washington State based Alaska Airlines began painting an Eskimo head on the tail fin of their aircraft.

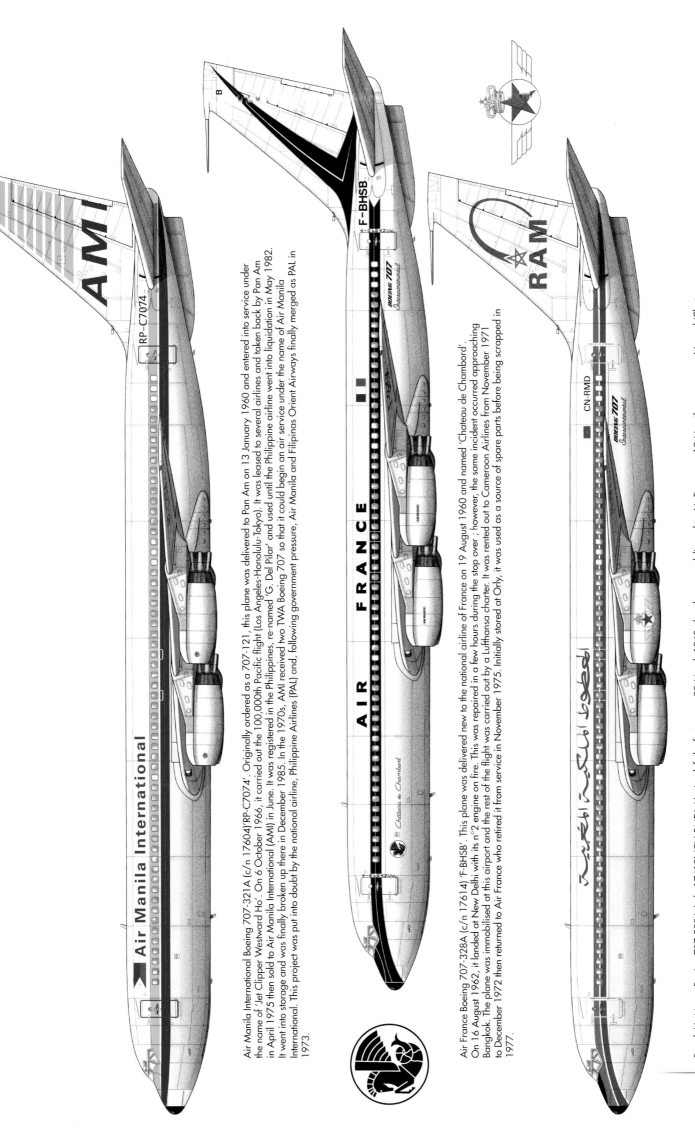

Air Manila International

Air Manila International Boeing 707-321A (c/n 17604) 'RP-C7074'. Originally ordered as a 707-121, this plane was delivered to Pan Am on 13 January 1960 and entered into service under the name of 'Jet Clipper Westward Ho'. On 6 October 1966, it carried out the 100,000th Pacific flight (Los Angeles-Honolulu-Tokyo). It was leased to several airlines and taken back by Pan Am in April 1975 then sold to Air Manila International (AMI) in June. It was registered in the Philippines, re-named 'G. Del Pilar' and used until the Philippine airline went into liquidation in May 1982. It went into storage and was finally broken up there in December 1985. In the 1970s, AMI received two TWA Boeing 707 so that it could begin an air service under the name of Air Manila International. This project was put into doubt by the national airline, Philippine Airlines (PAL) and, following government pressure, Air Manila and Filipinas Orient Airways finally merged as PAL in 1973.

Air France Boeing 707-328A (c/n 17614) 'F-BHSB'. This plane was delivered new to the national airline of France on 19 August 1960 and named 'Chateau de Chambord'. On 16 August 1962, it landed at New Delhi with its n°2 engine on fire. This was repaired in a few hours during the stop over ; however, the same incident occurred approaching Bangkok. The plane was immobilised at this airport and the rest of the flight was carried out by a Lufthansa charter. It was rented out to Cameroon Airlines from November 1971 to December 1972 then returned to Air France who retired it from service in November 1975. Initially stored at Orly, it was used as a source of spare parts before being scrapped in 1977.

Royal Air Maroc Boeing 707-328A (c/n 17619) 'CN-RMD'. Having left the factory on 28 March 1960, the plane was delivered to Air France on 12 May the same year. Named 'Chateau de Pau', it was retired from service by the French airline on 1 September 1977. It was bought by Royal Air Maroc on 29 September 1977 and sold to Israel in November 1978, going to the Heyl Ha' Avir (Israeli air force) in April 1980. It was used as a cargo and transport plane with the registration 4X-JYN'. In 1991, it was bought by Israel Aircraft Industry and finally scrapped in November 1993.

33

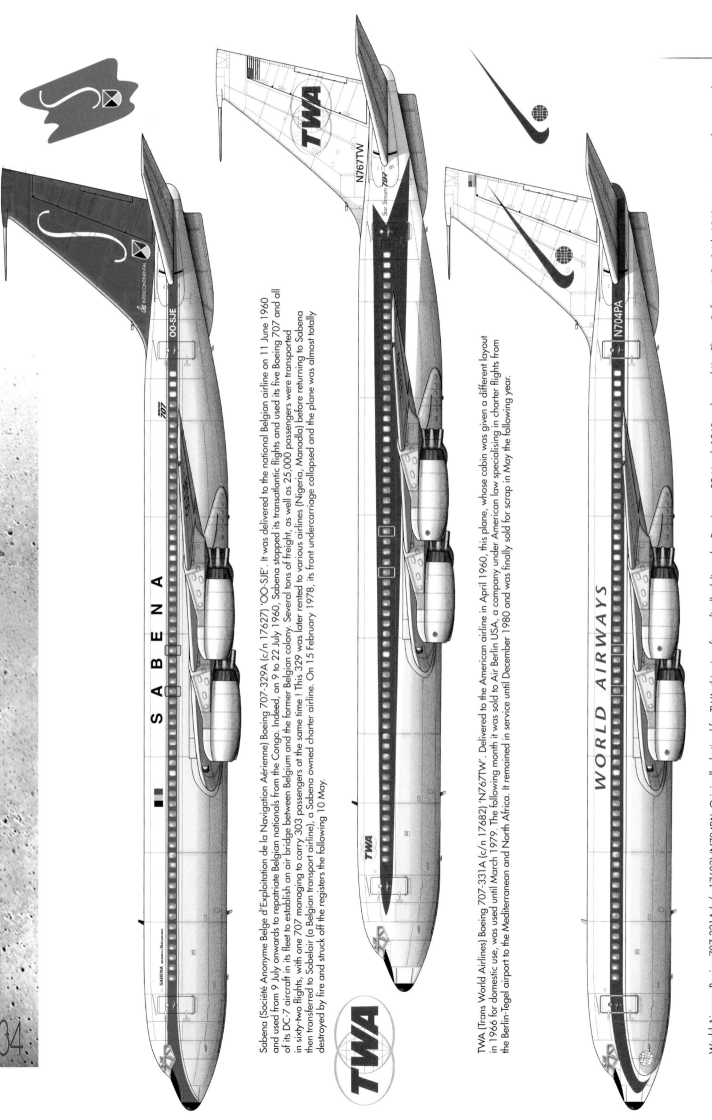

34

SABENA

OO-SJE

Sabena (Société Anonyme Belge d'Exploitation de la Navigation Aérienne) Boeing 707-329A (c/n 17627) 'OO-SJE'. It was delivered to the national Belgian airline on 11 June 1960 and used from 9 July onwards to repatriate Belgian nationals from the Congo. Indeed, on 9 to 22 July 1960, Sabena stopped its transatlantic flights and used its five Boeing 707 and all of its DC-7 aircraft in its fleet to establish an air bridge between Belgium and the former Belgian colony. Several tons of freight, as well as 25,000 passengers were transported in sixty-two flights, with one 707 managing to carry 303 passengers at the same time ! This 329 was later rented to various airlines (Nigeria, Manadla) before returning to Sabena then transferred to Sobelair (a Belgian transport airline), a Sabena owned charter airline. On 15 February 1978, its front undercarriage collapsed and the plane was almost totally destroyed by fire and struck off the registers the following 10 May.

N767TW

TWA (Trans World Airlines) Boeing 707-331A (c/n 17682) 'N767TW'. Delivered to the American airline in April 1960, this plane, whose cabin was given a different layout in 1966 for domestic use, was used until March 1979. The following month it was sold to Air Berlin USA, a company under American law specialising in charter flights from the Berlin-Tegel airport to the Mediterranean and North Africa. It remained in service until December 1980 and was finally sold for scrap in May the following year.

WORLD AIRWAYS

N704PA

World Airways Boeing 707-321A (c/n 17683) 'N704PA'. Originally destined for TWA, this aircraft was finally delivered to Pan Am on 23 March 1960 and named 'Jet Clipper Defiance'. On 2 July 1962, it was temporarily re-named 'Jet Clipper America' for the 100,000th Atlantic flight. It was rented to World Airways in 1972 then to Air Vietnam under the name of 'Companion of Peace' the following year, it remained immobilised at Hong Kong after the fall of South Vietnam. Re-registered in the United States in December 1975, it was finally broken up at Carson City in June 1977. World Airways was created in 1948 and frequently worked under contract for the United States government, notably during the Vietnam War where it transported men and materiel from its home airport of Oakland (California).

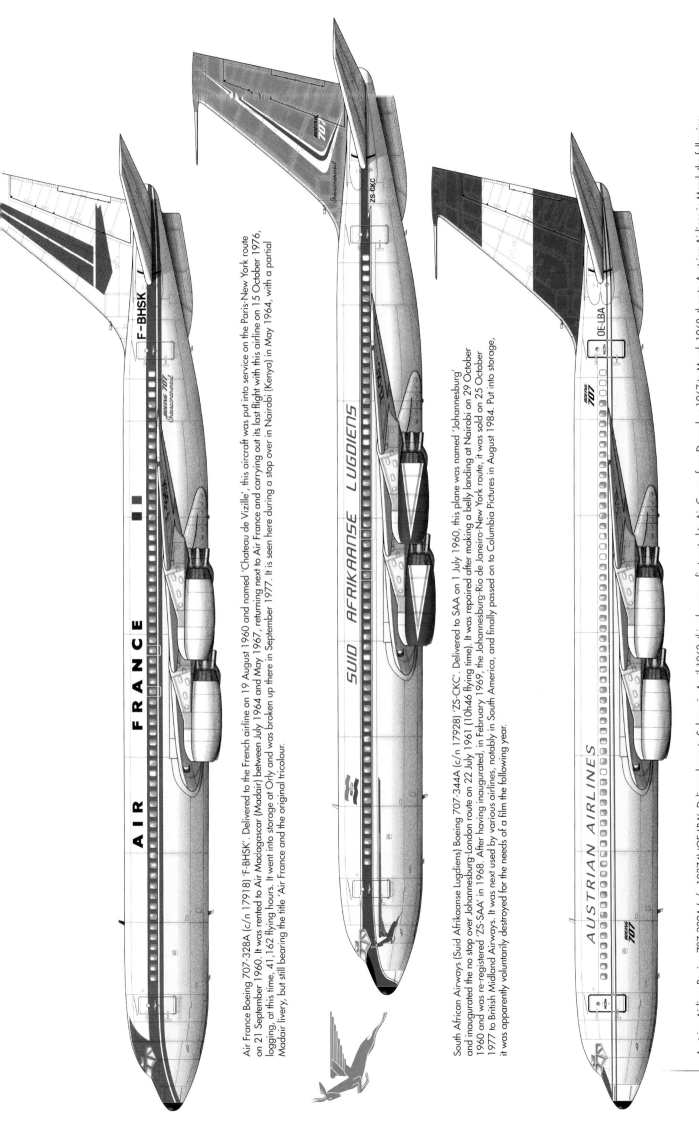

AIR FRANCE

F-BHSK

Air France Boeing 707-328A (c/n 17918) 'F-BHSK'. Delivered to the French airline on 19 August 1960 and named 'Château de Vizille', this aircraft was put into service on the Paris-New York route on 21 September 1960. It was rented to Air Madagascar (Madair) between July 1964 and May 1967, returning next to Air France and carrying out its last flight with this airline on 15 October 1976, logging, at this time, 41,162 flying hours. It went into storage at Orly and was broken up there in September 1977. It is seen here during a stop over in Nairobi (Kenya) in May 1964, with a partial Madair livery, but still bearing the title 'Air France and the original tricolour.

SUID AFRIKAANSE LUGDIENS

ZS-CKC

South African Airways (Suid Afrikaanse Lugdiens) Boeing 707-344A (c/n 17928) 'ZS-CKC'. Delivered to SAA on 1 July 1960, this plane was named 'Johannesburg' and inaugurated the no stop over Johannesburg-London route on 22 July 1961 (10h46 flying time). It was repaired after making a belly landing at Nairobi on 29 October 1960 and was re-registered 'ZS-SAA' in 1968. After having inaugurated, in February 1969, the Johannesburg-Rio de Janeiro-New York route, it was sold on 25 October 1977 to British Midland Airways. It was next used by various airlines, notably in South America, and finally passed on to Columbia Pictures in August 1984. Put into storage, it was apparently voluntarily destroyed for the needs of a film the following year.

AUSTRIAN AIRLINES

OE-LBA

Austrian Airlines Boeing 707-329A (c/n 18374) 'OE-LBA'. Delivered new to Sabena in April 1962, this plane was first rented to Air Congo from December 1967 to March 1968, then to Austrian Airlines in March the following year, before returning to Sabena in March 1968. It was rented once more to Air Algérie who used it to fly pilgrims to Mecca in December 1974. It returned to Sabena before being lent to Mandala Nusantara Airlines. In January 1977, it was bought by the Israeli air force where it was converted to an electronic reconnaissance (ELINT) aircraft, being used notably in 1982 to jam Syrian communications during the attack launched against missile launch bases in South Lebanon.

The BOEING 707-420

Above.
This 707-465 (c/n 18372) was delivered to Cunard Eagle in February 1962 and registered in Bermuda (VR-BBW) until September, when it was taken back by BOAC-Cunard (G-ARWD) who kept it until October 1966. (J. Guillem collection)

The growing success of the 707 quickly encouraged jet engine manufacturers to contact the Renton company and offer their services. However, it was only Britain's Rolls Royce that managed to fulfil this desire, ending up by developing a new version, the 707-420.

Globally, this version was no more than 707-320 'Intercontinental' with four Rolls Royce Conway 508 engines capable of producing 7,937 kg (17,500 lb) of thrust, in place of the original Pratt & Whitney JT4A engines. These new engines were in fact different from their American

Below.
Delivered to BOAC in April 1960, this 707-436 (c/n 17705/G-APFD) was successively transferred to BEA in February 1973 and to British Airtours in April 1974, before being leased to Air Mauritius between October 1977 and April 1979. Retaining its original registration number, it was repainted in the Mauritian airline colour scheme and named 'City of Port Louis'. (J. Guillem collection)

counterparts as they were of the 'by-pass turbofan' type, that is to say equipped with a fan installed in front of the axial flow compressor, which meant an increased thrust but, at the same time, a reduction in fuel used.

Now a direct competitor to the identically engined Douglas DC-8-40, the 707-420, as it was designated, was specially designed for airlines of Commonwealth countries that were in this way, not subject to custom duties normally imposed on engines made outside of this economic sphere. Also, the British airline BOAC was still waiting for the De Havilland Comet 4, the program of which was constantly delayed. BOAC had also, in 1955, suffered from the abandon of the Vickers VC-7 program, and showed itself to be particularly attracted by this British engine equipped version. The latter was seen as a sort of compensation for all these prevarications, and was in large part at the origin of its production.

Above.
The Douglas DC-8 was always the direct rival of the Boeing 707 and was a great success when it first flew. There were fewer made than its rival but it performance was often very close or even slightly superior. The DC-8-40 version, like this Capitol Airlines plane, was the first commercial jet equipped with turbofans, these being the Rolls-Royce Conway identical to those on the Boeing 707-420. This version was only slightly successful, firstly because of a lack of enthusiasm on the part of American airlines for buying a foreign engine, but most of all because of the appearance of the Pratt & Whitney JT3D in 1961. (D. Breffort collection).

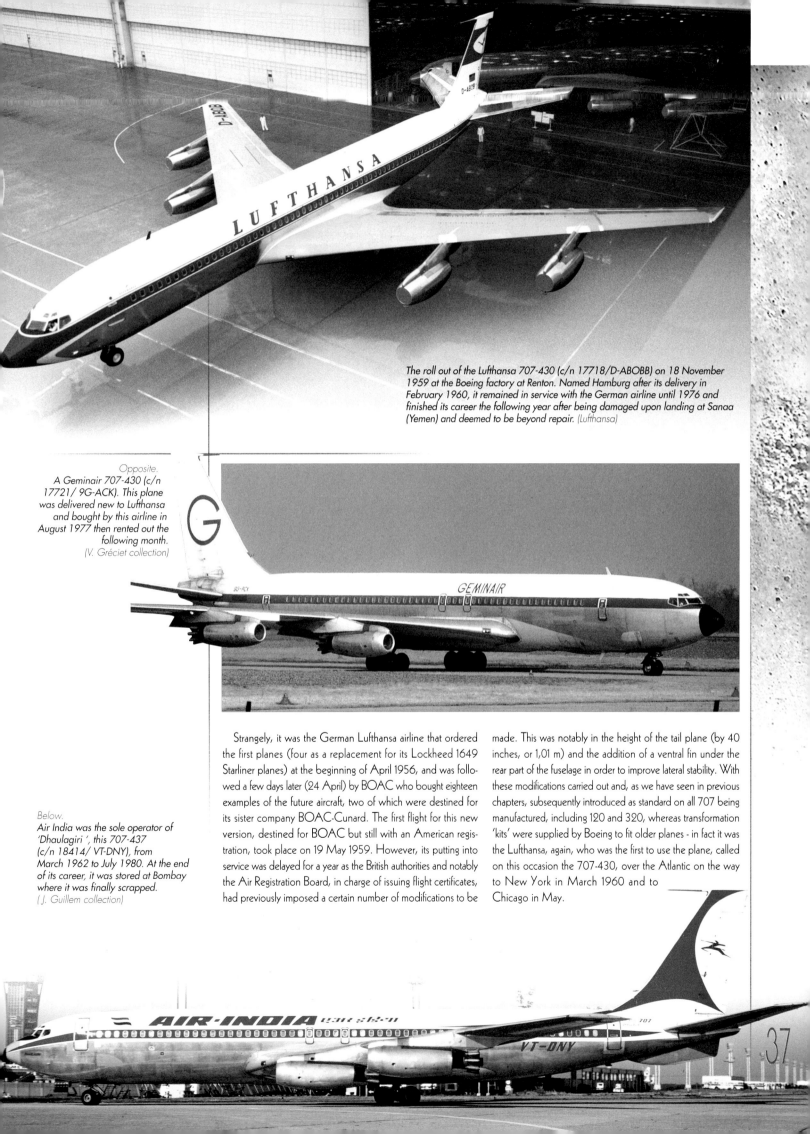

The roll out of the Lufthansa 707-430 (c/n 17718/D-ABOBB) on 18 November 1959 at the Boeing factory at Renton. Named Hamburg after its delivery in February 1960, it remained in service with the German airline until 1976 and finished its career the following year after being damaged upon landing at Sanaa (Yemen) and deemed to be beyond repair. *(Lufthansa)*

Opposite.
A Geminair 707-430 (c/n 17721/ 9G-ACK). This plane was delivered new to Lufthansa and bought by this airline in August 1977 then rented out the following month.
(V. Gréciet collection)

Below.
Air India was the sole operator of 'Dhaulagiri ', this 707-437 (c/n 18414/ VT-DNY), from March 1962 to July 1980. At the end of its career, it was stored at Bombay where it was finally scrapped.
(J. Guillem collection)

Strangely, it was the German Lufthansa airline that ordered the first planes (four as a replacement for its Lockheed 1649 Starliner planes) at the beginning of April 1956, and was followed a few days later (24 April) by BOAC who bought eighteen examples of the future aircraft, two of which were destined for its sister company BOAC-Cunard. The first flight for this new version, destined for BOAC but still with an American registration, took place on 19 May 1959. However, its putting into service was delayed for a year as the British authorities and notably the Air Registration Board, in charge of issuing flight certificates, had previously imposed a certain number of modifications to be made. This was notably in the height of the tail plane (by 40 inches, or 1,01 m) and the addition of a ventral fin under the rear part of the fuselage in order to improve lateral stability. With these modifications carried out and, as we have seen in previous chapters, subsequently introduced as standard on all 707 being manufactured, including 120 and 320, whereas transformation 'kits' were supplied by Boeing to fit older planes - in fact it was the Lufthansa, again, who was the first to use the plane, called on this occasion the 707-430, over the Atlantic on the way to New York in March 1960 and to Chicago in May.

As for the BOAC aircraft, they were mostly delivered by air and without any seats in the cabin, these being fitted in Great Britain. The regular transatlantic service began on 27 May 1960.

This version, the first to be fitted with turbofan engines, ended up as a failure due to its engines that were not as good as the American JT3D but that above all guzzled more fuel. Only 37 of these planes were built [1] and BOAC was even strongly criticised for having chosen the 707 instead of the VC-10 produced locally. BOAC ended up by having a mixed fleet with Vickers, judged superior by the crews and passengers, and the 707-436, the latter progressively sold back to Boeing or ceded to BEA from 1974, a company that would merge with BOAC a little later on within the future British Airways, and used until 1983 when they were replaced by Boeing Jumbo Jets. Another handicap encountered by the aircraft was its passenger capacity (a maximum of 189 passengers) that was the same as a standard 707-320, a characteristic of which the change in engines had no influence, reducing the attractiveness of this version. All the first hand buyers of this Rolls Royce Conway engined 707 were non-American airlines, a first for this aircraft, Air India ordering three in September 1956. The first of these planes was delivered by

JET TO YOUR HOLIDAY IN NORTH AMERICA

LONDON, MANCHESTER, GLASGOW OR SHANNON TO U.S.A. & CANADA

Serving New York Boston Washington
Baltimore Los Angeles San Francisco Honolulu
Chicago Detroit Montreal Toronto

R. Leblanc collection

Top
Israeli airline El Al operated this 707-458 (c/n 18357/ 4X-ATC) from February 1962 to January 1980. It is here seen at Paris-Orly in August 1978. (J. Guillem collection)

Above.
Delivered new to BOAC in May 1960, this 707-436 (c/n 17707/ G-APFF) was used by British Airways from April 1974, following the reorganization of British airlines operators. Transferred to British Airtours in May 1974, it was briefly leased by British Airways in October 1977.
(J. Guillem collection)

Below.
Air Wing International Boeing 707-436 (N888NW). This aircraft (c/n 17705) began its career in 1960 with BOAC who transferred it to British Airtour in February 1973. Later sold to an American company, it was bought by Air Wing in August 1981 to be used by International Mailing & Printing. It was never used and was sold once more and finally broken up at Fort Lauderdale (Florida) in August 1986.
(D. Breffort collection)

A Lufthansa 707-430 lands at dusk. The noise reducers at the rear of the Rolls Royce Conway engines are clearly visible. (Lufthansa)

Opposite.
This Boeing 707-458 (c/n 18357) was bought by El Al in 1962 who sold it on to Zaire Aero Service in February 1980. Recovered by the Israeli airline after maintenance fees were left unpaid, it was bought by Wolf Aviation in November 1983. Damaged at Isiro (Zaire) in July 1984 and deemed to be beyond repair, the aircraft was destroyed a short time after at Kinshasa airport.
(D. Breffort collection)

1. Five for Lufthansa (707-430), eighteen for BOAC/Cunard (-436), six for Air India (-437), three for Varig (-441), three for El Al (-458) to which should be added two for Eagle Cunard (-465) one of which was finally delivered to BOAC.

air and also set a record on 21 February 1960 by flying directly from the sub continent to the west coast of the United States with a stopover in London. Two months later, the Indian airline began its regular flights, initially in the direction of the British capital (19 April), then to New York (14 May) and to Tokyo the in January following year. Air India, that dropped its last Lockheed Super Constellation aircraft in June 1962, had a mixed fleet made up of Boeing aircraft and the De Havilland Comet rented from BOAC. One of its aircraft was lost in January 1966 when it crashed into a mountain in the Swiss Alps. In an ironic twist of fate, it was almost exactly the same place and in the same weather conditions that one its Super Constellations was lost fifteen years earlier.

Below.
British Airtours Boeing 707-436 (c/n 17716/G-APFO). This plane began its career in November 1960 with BOAC before being used by this airline that resulted from the merging, in April 1974, of BEA, BOAC and other British airlines.
(D. Breffort collection)

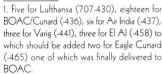

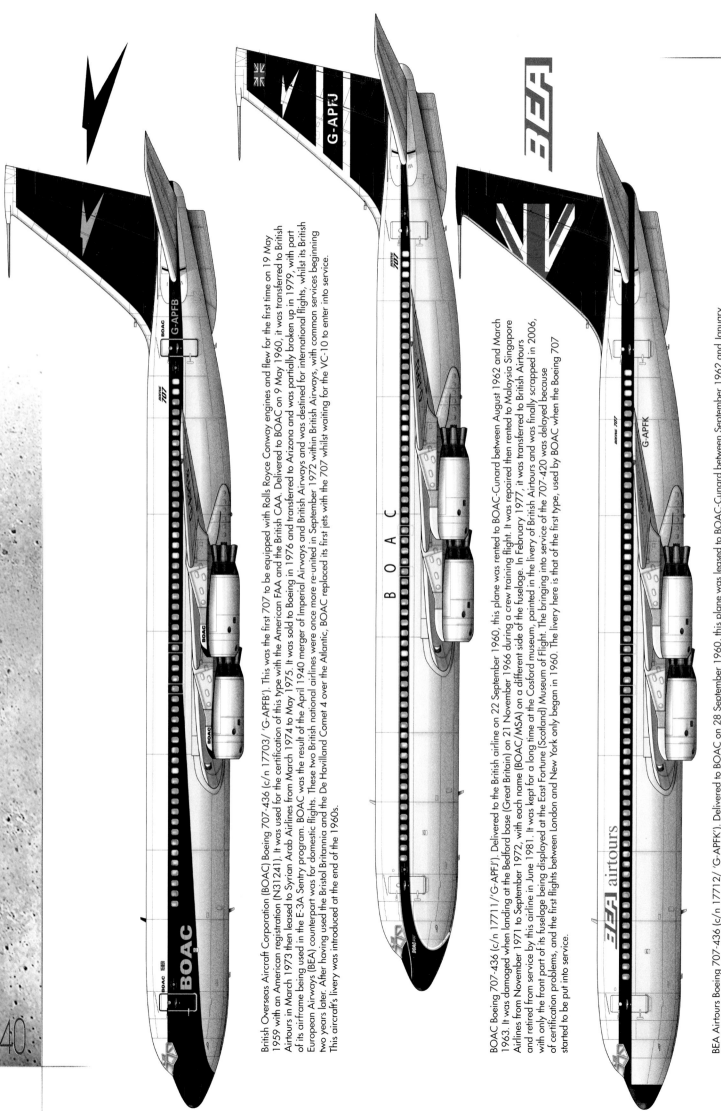

British Overseas Aircraft Corporation (BOAC) Boeing 707-436 (c/n 17703/ 'G-APFB'). This was the first 707 to be equipped with Rolls Royce Conway engines and flew for the first time on 19 May 1959 with an American registration (N31241). It was used for the certification of this type with the American FAA and the British CAA. Delivered to BOAC on 9 May 1960, it was transferred to British Airtours in March 1973 then leased to Syrian Arab Airlines from March 1974 to May 1975. It was sold to Boeing in 1976 and transferred to Arizona and was partially broken up in 1979, with part of its airframe being used in the E-3A Sentry program. BOAC was the result of the April 1940 merger of Imperial Airways and British Airways and was destined for international flights, whilst its British European Airways (BEA) counterpart was for domestic flights. These two British national airlines were once more re-united in September 1972 within British Airways, with common services beginning two years later. After having used the Bristol Britannia and the De Havilland Comet 4 over the Atlantic, BOAC replaced its first jets with the 707 whilst waiting for the VC-10 to enter into service. This aircraft's livery was introduced at the end of the 1960s.

BOAC Boeing 707-436 (c/n 17711/ 'G-APFJ'). Delivered to the British airline on 22 September 1960, this plane was rented to BOAC-Cunard between August 1962 and March 1963. It was damaged when landing at the Bedford base (Great Britain) on 21 November 1966 during a crew training flight. It was repaired then rented to Malaysia Singapore Airlines from November 1971 to September 1972, with each name (BOAC/MSA) on a different side of the fuselage. In February 1977, it was transferred to British Airtours and retired from service by this airline in June 1981. It was kept for a long time at the Cosford museum, painted in the livery of British Airtours and was finally scrapped in 2006, with only the front part of its fuselage being displayed at the East Fortune (Scotland) Museum of Flight. The bringing into service of the 707-420 was delayed because of certification problems, and the first flights between London and New York only began in 1960. The livery here is that of the first type, used by BOAC when the Boeing 707 started to be put into service.

BEA Airtours Boeing 707-436 (c/n 17712/ 'G-APFK'). Delivered to BOAC on 28 September 1960, this plane was leased to BOAC-Cunard between September 1962 and January 1967, and then transferred to BEA Airtours in December 1971. This airline was re-named British Airtours in April 1974 and the plane was next briefly rented to Iran Air in March the following year. Its career ended tragically on 17 March 1977 at Glasgow-Prestwick when, put off balance during an engine breakdown simulation, it crashed and caught fire after its left wing touched the runway. There were, however, no deaths.

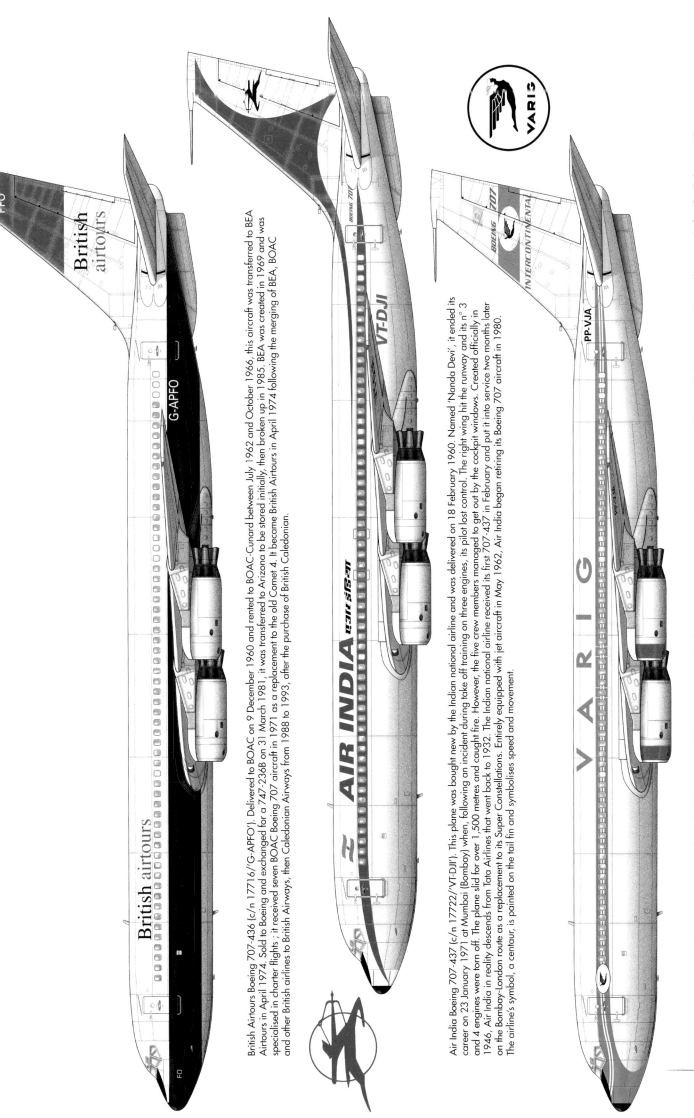

British airtours

British airtours

G-APFO

British Airtours Boeing 707-436 (c/n 17716/'G-APFO'). Delivered to BOAC on 9 December 1960 and rented to BOAC-Cunard between July 1962 and October 1966, this aircraft was transferred to BEA Airtours in April 1974. Sold to Boeing and exchanged for a 747-236B on 31 March 1981, it was transferred to Arizona to be stored initially, then broken up in 1985. BEA was created in 1969 and was specialised in charter flights ; it received seven BOAC Boeing 707 aircraft in 1971 as a replacement to the old Comet 4. It became British Airtours in April 1974 following the merging of BEA, BOAC and other British airlines to British Airways, then Caledonian Airways from 1988 to 1993, after the purchase of British Caledonian.

BOEING 707

VT-DJI

AIR INDIA एयर इंडिया 707-20

Air India Boeing 707-437 (c/n 17722/'VT-DJI'). This plane was bought new by the Indian national airline and was delivered on 18 February 1960. Named 'Nanda Devi', it ended its career on 23 January 1971 at Mumbai (Bombay) when, following an incident during take off training on three engines, its pilot lost control. The right wing hit the runway and its n° 3 and 4 engines were torn off. The plane slid for over 1,500 metres and caught fire. However, the five crew members managed to get out by the cockpit windows. Created officially in 1946, Air India in reality descends from Tata Airlines that went back to 1932. The Indian national airline received its first 707-437 in February and put it into service two months later on the Bombay-London route as a replacement to its Super Constellations. Entirely equipped with jet aircraft in May 1962, Air India began retiring its Boeing 707 aircraft in 1980. The airline's symbol, a centaur, is painted on the tail fin and symbolises speed and movement.

BOEING 707 INTERCONTINENTAL

PP-VJA

VARIG

VARIG Boeing 707-441 (c/n 17905/'PP-VJA'). Delivered to the Brazilian airline in June 1960, this plane remained in service until September 1979, the date on which it was stored at Rio de Janeiro before finally being sold to RDC Marine and transferred to Houston. It was finally sold for spare parts by Business Cash Flow (BCF) Aviation (Congo) in July 1989 and was broken up the following year. The Empresa de Viacção Aérea Rio-Grandense (VARIG) was created in 1927 with the help of Germany. This company, the currently the largest in Brazil and Latin America, constantly grew by buying several airlines such as Panair do Brazil in 1965. After having first used its SE Caravelle aircraf on the Rio de Janeiro-New York route, VARIG started replacing them with the 707-441 in 1960, then with the Boeing 727.

41

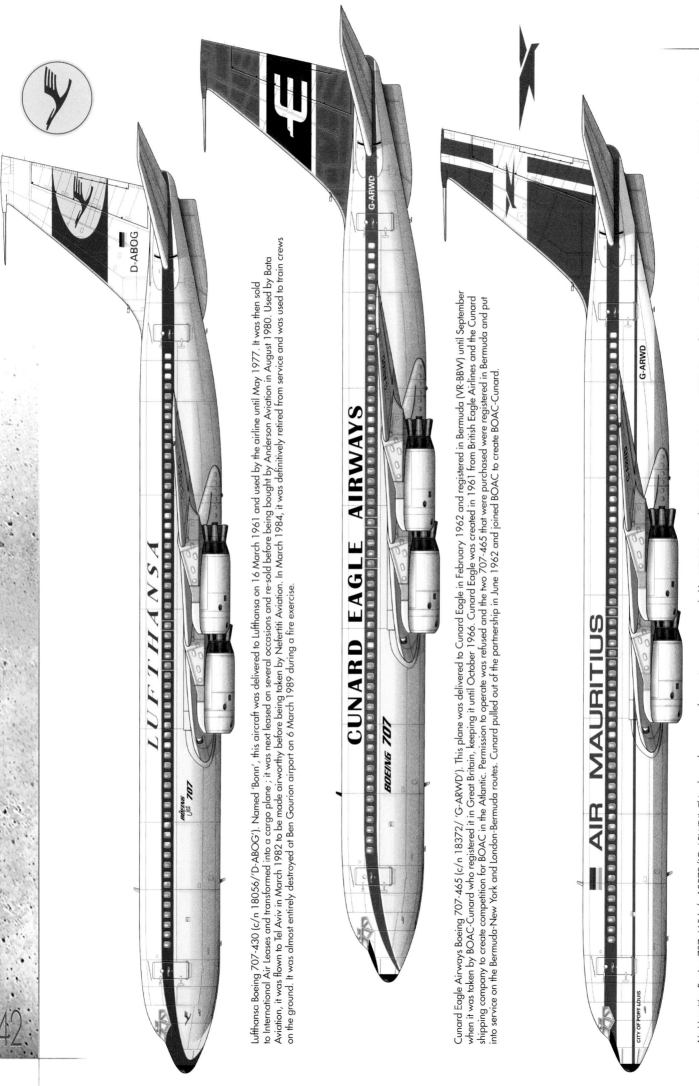

LUFTHANSA

D-ABOG

BOEING 707

CUNARD EAGLE AIRWAYS

G-ARWD

AIR MAURITIUS

G-ARWD

CITY OF PORT LOUIS

Lufthansa Boeing 707-430 (c/n 18056/'D-ABOG'). Named 'Bonn', this aircraft was delivered to Lufthansa on 16 March 1961 and used by the airline until May 1977. It was then sold to International Air Leases and transformed into a cargo plane ; it was next leased on several occasions and re-sold before being bought by Anderson Aviation in August 1980. Used by Bata Aviation, it was flown to Tel Aviv in March 1982 to be made airworthy before being taken by Nefertiti Aviation. In March 1984, it was definitively retired from service and was used to train crews on the ground. It was almost entirely destroyed at Ben Gourion airport on 6 March 1989 during a fire exercise.

Cunard Eagle Airways Boeing 707-465 (c/n 18372/ 'G-ARWD'). This plane was delivered to Cunard Eagle in February 1962 and registered in Bermuda (VR-BBW) until September when it was taken by BOAC-Cunard who registered it in Great Britain, keeping it until October 1966. Cunard Eagle was created in 1961 from British Eagle Airlines and the Cunard shipping company to create competition for BOAC in the Atlantic. Permission to operate was refused and the two 707-465 that were purchased were registered in Bermuda and put into service on the Bermuda-New York and London-Bermuda routes. Cunard pulled out of the partnership in June 1962 and joined BOAC to create BOAC-Cunard.

Air Mauritius Boeing 707-465 (c/n 18372/'G-ARWD'). This plane, the same as the previous one, was ceded by BOAC-Cunard to BEA Airtours in January 1973. It was first rented to DETA in January and February 1975, then leased by Air Mauritius from April 1979 to April 1981 after having been named 'City of Port Louis'. In May 1981, it was sold to Boeing and taken to Arizona where it was broken up shortly after. Air Mauritius, the national airline of this Indian Ocean island, was created in June 1967 thanks to the participation of British Airways, Air France and Air India. At the beginning it was limited to flights between Mauritius and the neighbouring island of La Reunion. It began opening its first regular international routes in 1977 with two Boeing 707-400 rented by BA, planes used until the purchase of two 707-344B in March 1981. The Air Mauritius emblem is the Phaeton Rubicola, a bird commonly called Paille-en-Queue (white-tailed tropicbird) and typical to this region.

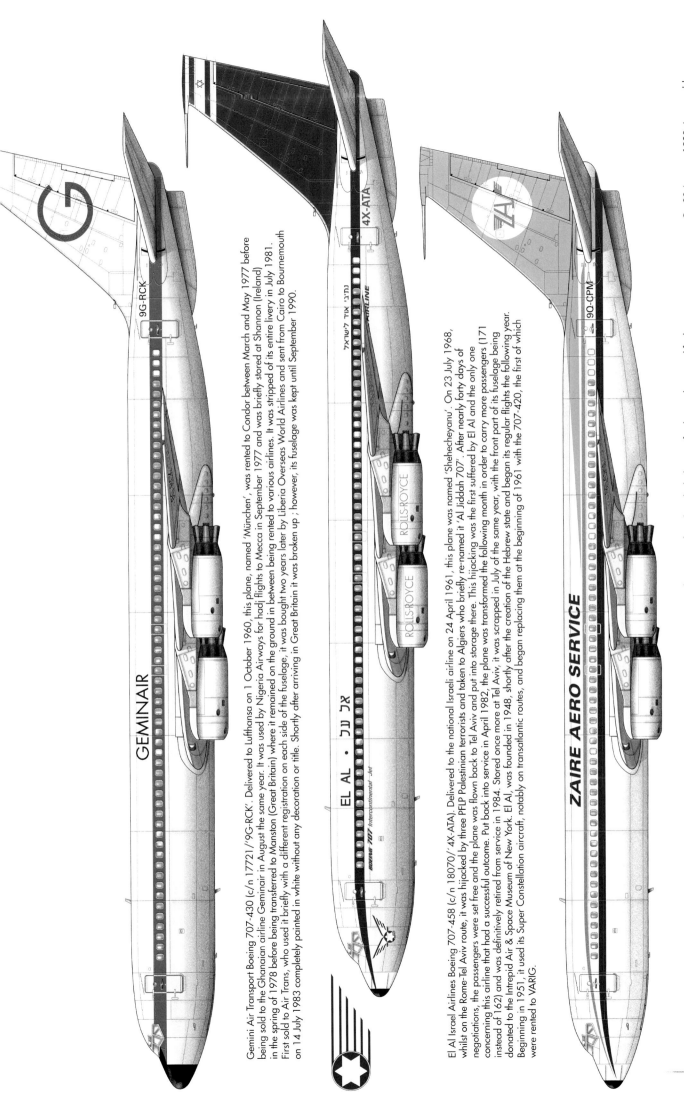

GEMINAIR

9G-RCK

Gemini Air Transport Boeing 707-430 (c/n 17721/'9G-RCK'. Delivered to Lufthansa on 1 October 1960, this plane, named 'München', was rented to Condor between March and May 1977 before being sold to the Ghanaian airline Geminair in August the same year. It was used by Nigeria Airways for hadj flights to Mecca in September 1977 and was briefly stored at Shannon (Ireland) in the spring of 1978 before being transferred to Manston (Great Britain) where it remained on the ground in between being rented to various airlines. It was stripped of its entire livery in July 1981. First sold to Air Trans, who used it briefly with a different registration on each side of the fuselage, it was bought two years later by Liberia Overseas World Airlines and sent from Cairo to Bournemouth on 14 July 1983 completely painted in white without any decoration or title. Shortly after arriving in Great Britain it was broken up ; however, its fuselage was kept until September 1990.

4X-ATA

EL AL · אל על

EL AL Israel Airlines Boeing 707-458 (c/n 18070/'4X-ATA). Delivered to the national Israeli airline on 24 April 1961, this plane was named 'Shehecheyanu'. On 23 July 1968, whilst on the Rome-Tel Aviv route, it was hijacked by three PFLP Palestinian terrorists and taken to Algiers who briefly re-named it 'Al Jiddah 707'. After nearly forty days of negotiations, the passengers were set free and the plane was flown back to Tel Aviv and put into storage there. This hijacking was the first suffered by El Al and the only one concerning this airline that had a successful outcome. Put back into service in April 1982, the plane was transformed the following month in order to carry more passengers (171 instead of 162) and was definitively retired from service in 1984. Stored once more at Tel Aviv, it was scrapped in July of the same year, with the front part of its fuselage being donated to the Intrepid Air & Space Museum of New York. El Al, was founded in 1948, shortly after the creation of the Hebrew state and began its regular flights the following year. Beginning in 1951, it used its Super Constellation aircraft, notably on transatlantic routes, and began replacing them at the beginning of 1961 with the 707-420, the first of which were rented to VARIG.

ZAIRE AERO SERVICE

9Q-CPM

Zaire Aero Service Boeing 707-458 (c/n 18357/'9Q-CPM'). Delivered to El Al on 15 February 1962, this aircraft was transferred to El Al Charter after having been modified to carry more passengers. On 29 January 1980, it was sold to Zaire Aero Service, and was delivered during a regular El Al flight from Tel Aviv to Kinshasa (Zaire). Back in Israel for maintenance, it was taken back by El Al in July 1981 as the maintenance bills had not been paid. Stored at Tel Aviv, it was sold to Wolf Aviation in November 1983 and re-registered (9Q-CWR). Its career ended in July 1984, following an accident landing at Isiro-Matari (Zaire) with no casualties in July ; it went to Kinshasa to be repaired and finally scrapped in July 1986 after its repair was abandoned. ZAS, founded in 1976, was specialised in cargo and passenger charter flights. Indeed, to this end, it leased two Boeing 320C and passenger charter flights. Indeed, to this end, it leased two Boeing 320C and bought one 707-458 which remained in service until it disappeared in 1985.

THE BOEING 720

After the undeniable international success of the 707-320, Boeing turned to the domestic United States market with a smaller version specially designed for these destinations.

The design of the Model 720, the short version of the four-engined Boeing, was the result of the combination of several elements. On one hand the desire of the plane manufacturer to offer its customers, notably North American airlines specialised in short and medium haul flights, a lighter and faster aircraft than the standard 707 that could use shorter runways than those of the main international airports, but also the desire not to let the competition get ahead, especially by Convair who announced in April 1956 that it was working on its Model 22 Skylark, the future 880.

Seeing the threat beforehand, Boeing had begun two months earlier to look at a new plane, initially called the 707-020 in 1957 [1] during the promotion of the plane, then finally the 720.

At the outset, a radically different design, and a taste of the future 737, with only two jet engines had been studied. It finally ended up, in order to satisfy the demands of airlines, closely resembling the 707-120, but both lighter and shorter.

The fuselage was indeed shortened by ten inches (2,54 m), and was now 39,65 m (130' 10") in length, whilst the fuel load was set at 53 800 litres (14,212 US gall), reducing range (a little more than 8,400 km/5,220 miles) but reducing consi-

Above.
The first Boeing 720 (c/n 17907) carried out its roll out on 30 October 1959 but was not delivered to its first owner, United Airlines, until a year later. (J. Delmas collection)

1. This designation was rapidly abandoned so that it would not be confused with versions reserved for the military (C-135, KC-135, etc.) that were already using it. It was finally re-used for the MD 695 when MacDonnell Douglas merged with Boeing.

Below.
Used by Boeing to get the type's certificate, the first 720 (c/n 17907) underwent a long series of tests before delivery. On this occasion, a test pattern was painted on the fuselage.
(J. Delmas collection)

Above.
This 720-022 (c/n 18075) was initially part of the United Airlines fleet from 1962 until 1972 before being used by Air Viking from May 1974 to the end of 1975 when the Icelandic airline went into receivership.
(J.C. Bertrand collection)

derably the aircraft's take off weight. This reduction in weight was also reinforced by the use of a different type of aluminium from that previously used in the manufacture of the plane. The plane was also a little faster than the standard 707-120 and could take two types of different jet engine, the Pratt & Whitney JT3C-12 or C-7 with or without water injection. The first had a slightly higher thrust at take off (9%). As for

Above.
Delivered to United in October 1960, the first Boeing 720 was firstly named 'Mainliner Walter T. Varney', then 'Captain F. M. Crismore' and used by the American airline until the end of 1972. It was scrapped in July 1982 after a lot of corrosion was found due to its being stored outside for a long time.
(J. Delmas collection)

Above.
Air Rhodesia, renamed Air Zimbabwe in April 1980 after the country gained its independence, used three old United 720-025 until 1982. (V. Gréciet collection)

BOEING *720* WORLD'S NEWEST JETLINER

It's new, sleek, fast... designed specially to serve cities not now on the jet-travel map, as well as major centers. The pure-jet 720 cruises at more than 600 miles an hour and operates easily from shorter run-ways. It is the newest jet by Boeing, world's most experienced builder of jetliners. United Air Lines will be the first to put 720s in service. Watch for the introduction of the exciting 720, newest of the jets.

Philippe Bruno collection

the cabin, shortened by 2,50 metres (8 ft), in the same way as the fuselage and whose interior had been thus been changed, it could take 141 passengers in tourist class and 88 in first class. The wings were also modified with an addition, at the level of the area situated between the fuselage and inside engine pods, of an extension, as with the 707-320. This increased the wing surface without modifying the wingspan whilst the chord was slightly increased at the level of the leading edge. The aircraft's stability, notably at low speed, already improved by the reduction in weight, was increased by the appearance on the exterior of the wings, of two Krueger flaps at the level of the leading edge that deployed at the same time as the high-lift flap.

Below.
Operated during ten years by United Airlines, from February 1961 to the end of 1972, this 720-022 (c/n 18049/ N421MA) was purchased in March 1977 by MCA who leased it to Guatemalan carrier Aviateca between April and September of that year. (J. Guillem collection)

It was United Airlines, the airline that was a priority for Boeing as it had ordered the Douglas DC-8-10 and -20, that ordered the first eleven examples of this new version designated the 720-022 on 17 November 1957. It was followed by American Airlines, that had also opted for the DC-8 for its long haul flights, but who wanted a simpler plane for other destinations, that was the first to show interest in this version. They ordered 25 planes on 31 July 1958, putting them into service in July 1960. The first flight of a plane of this type

buying twenty SE Caravelle planes in February 1959. They kept their Boeing aircraft for more than ten years as they only replaced them with other Boeing aircraft, the three engine 727, in 1972. The two first examples of the 720 were equipped with a short tail plane and the non-assisted rudder of the 707-120 and -320 of the beginning of the series. These planes were, like their counterparts, later fitted with standard elements. In all, 65 Boeing 720 planes were made[2], a modest sales figure but one which should be seen in parallel with the relati-

2. Twenty nine for United Airlines (720-022) who thus had the biggest fleet of any single airline, ten for American Airlines (-023, later fitted with new engines and redesignated -023B), fifteen for Eastern (-025), five for Braniff (-027), one for Federal Aviation Agency (that would be used by NASA for crash-tests in 1984), three for Aer Lingus (-048) and finally two for Pacific Northern Airlines (-062).

(constructor number 17907, a -022 destined for United) took place on 23 November 1959 and its commercial use was logically initiated by United Airlines on 5 July the following year on the Chicago-Denver-Los Angeles route, the certificate having been given the previous month.

United had completed its fleet of medium-haul aircraft by

vely low research and production costs that the design of this model had engendered, the plane proving to be profitable for the Renton based company. However, the global profitability of the 707 was not assured at the end of the 1950s as, at this time, although Boeing's order books comprised a little more than 180 examples of five different types, they had

Below.
Different musical group but same plane (see p. 48), 'Caesars Chariot' *was used by the Bee Gees during their USA tour in 1979. On this occasion, it received this elegant livery displaying the title (Spirits having flown) of the thirteenth album of this group released the same year. (Coll. J. Guillem)*

The boeing 720

Below.
Operated by Eastern Airlines from January 1982 to June 1970,
this Boeing 720-025 (c/n 18240/ N8711E) was sold to Aero American in September 1972 and leased to Club America from October 1972 to April 1973.
(J. Guillem collection).

N8711E

NG FLOWN

THE TOUR, 79

N7224U

only cornered a little more than a third of the commercial jet market. This deficit had been caused by the costs incurred by the necessary research for the manufacture of new models in order to cover the ever-increasing competition. The Boeing 707, and above all its direct and newly engined off shoot, the 720B, produced until 1967, was progressively replaced its designated successor, the three engine 727 that appeared in 1964. The fleet of second hand 720 aircraft was used by charter airlines. In 1966, ageing problems appeared with the wing covering, this forced Boeing to undertake modifications to solve this problem; this work was carried out at Wichita.

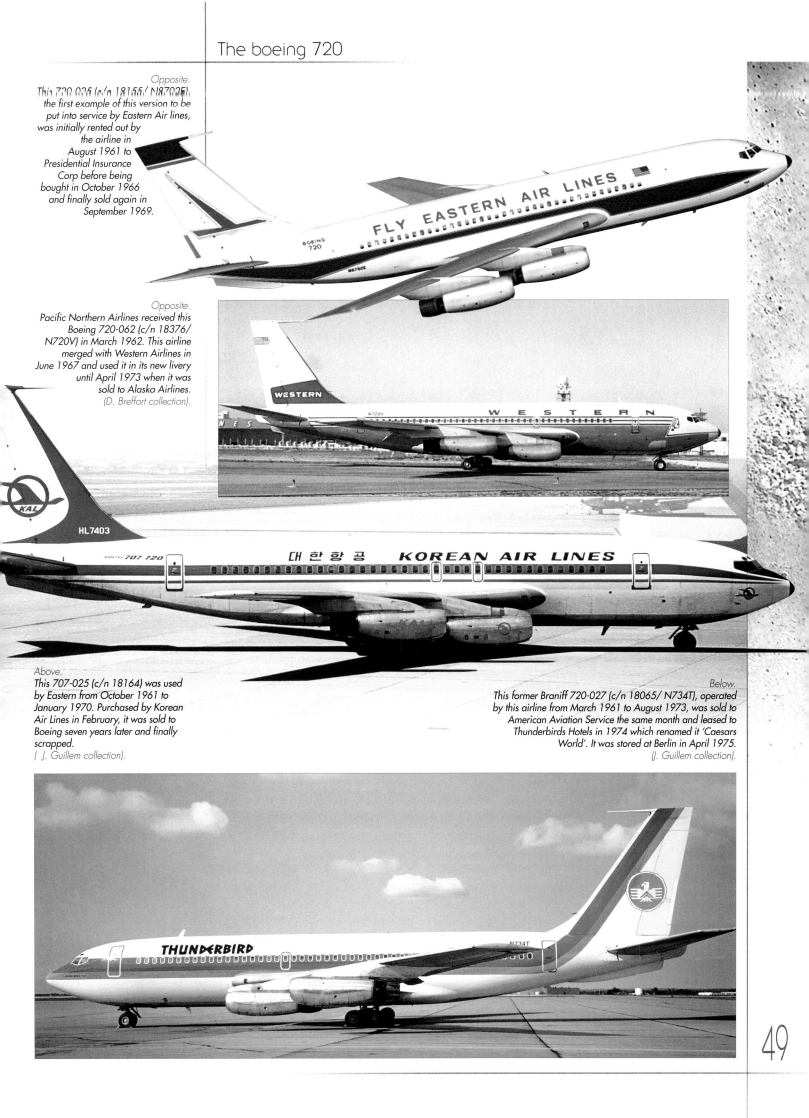

The boeing 720

Opposite.
This 720-025 (c/n 18155/ N8703E), the first example of this version to be put into service by Eastern Air lines, was initially rented out by the airline in August 1961 to Presidential Insurance Corp before being bought in October 1966 and finally sold again in September 1969.

Opposite.
*Pacific Northern Airlines received this Boeing 720-062 (c/n 18376/ N720V) in March 1962. This airline merged with Western Airlines in June 1967 and used it in its new livery until April 1973 when it was sold to Alaska Airlines.
(D. Breffort collection).*

Above.
This 707-025 (c/n 18164) was used by Eastern from October 1961 to January 1970. Purchased by Korean Air Lines in February, it was sold to Boeing seven years later and finally scrapped.
(J. Guillem collection).

Below.
This former Braniff 720-027 (c/n 18065/ N734T), operated by this airline from March 1961 to August 1973, was sold to American Aviation Service the same month and leased to Thunderbirds Hotels in 1974 which renamed it 'Caesars World'. It was stored at Berlin in April 1975.
(J. Guillem collection).

49

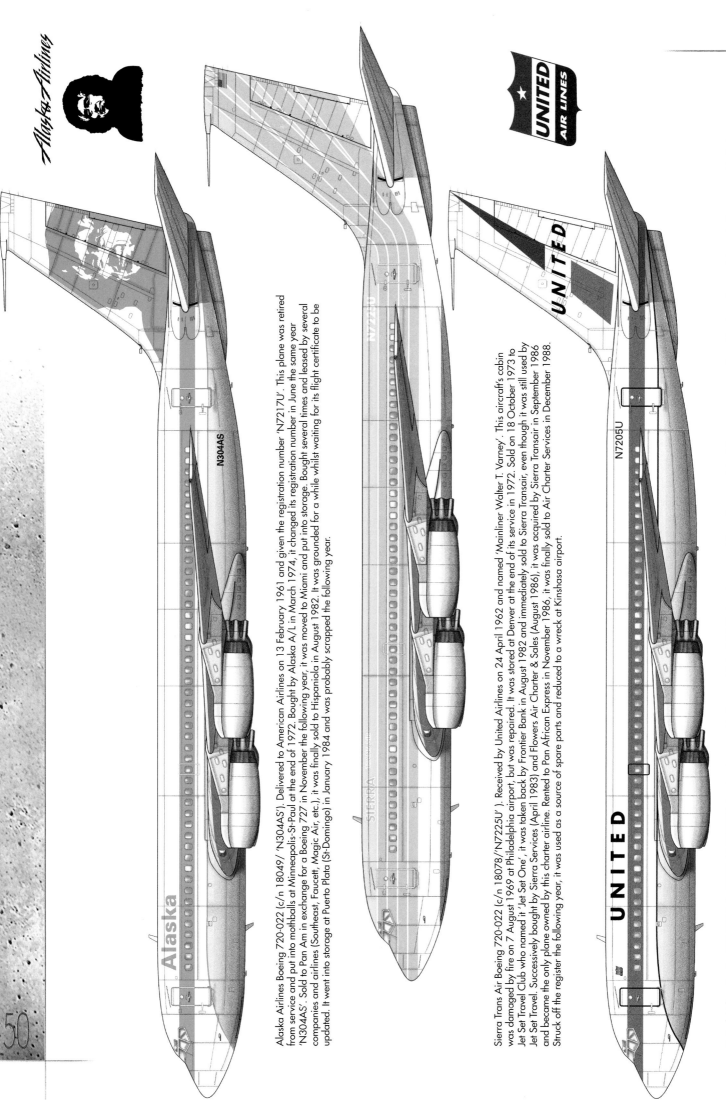

Alaska

Alaska Airlines Boeing 720-022 (c/n 18049/ 'N304AS'). Delivered to American Airlines on 13 February 1961 and given the registration number 'N7217U'. This plane was retired from service and put into mothballs at Minneapolis-St-Paul at the end of 1972. Bought by Alaska A/L in March 1974, it changed its registration number in June the same year 'N304AS'. Sold to Pan Am in exchange for a Boeing 727 in November the following year, it was moved to Miami and put into storage. Bought several times and leased by several companies and airlines (Southeast, Faucett, Magic Air, etc.), it was finally sold to Hispaniola in August 1982. It was grounded for a while whilst waiting for its flight certificate to be updated. It went into storage at Puerto Plata (St-Domingo) in January 1984 and was probably scrapped the following year.

SIERRA

Sierra Trans Air Boeing 720-022 (c/n 18078/ 'N7225U'). Received by United Airlines on 24 April 1962 and named 'Mainliner Walter T. Varney'. This aircraft's cabin was damaged by fire on 7 August 1969 at Philadelphia airport, but was repaired. It was stored at Denver at the end of its service in 1972. Sold on 18 October 1973 to Jet Set Travel Club who named it 'Jet Set One', it was taken back by Frontier Bank in August 1982 and immediately sold to Sierra Transair, even though it was still used by Jet Set Travel. Successively bought by Sierra Services (April 1983) and Flowers Air Charter & Sales (August 1986), it was acquired by Sierra Transair in September 1986 and became the only plane owned by this charter airline. Rented to Pan African Express in November 1986, it was finally sold to Air Charter Services in December 1988. Struck off the register the following year, it was used as a source of spare parts and reduced to a wreck at Kinshasa airport.

UNITED

United Airlines Boeing 720-022 (c/n 17911/ 'N7205U'). Leaving the assembly lines on 13 April 1960, this plane was delivered to United the following 20 May and used by the airline until the end of 1972. Mothballed at Denver, it was sold for spare parts in March 1976 to Aviation Sales Co and finally destroyed at the end of the same year. United Airlines was the first airline to use the Boeing 720 and began by using it on the Chicago-Denver-Los Angeles route at the beginning of July 1960. United remained the biggest domestic airline up to the end of the 1970s and started to progressively replace its 720s

N304AS

N7225U

N7205U

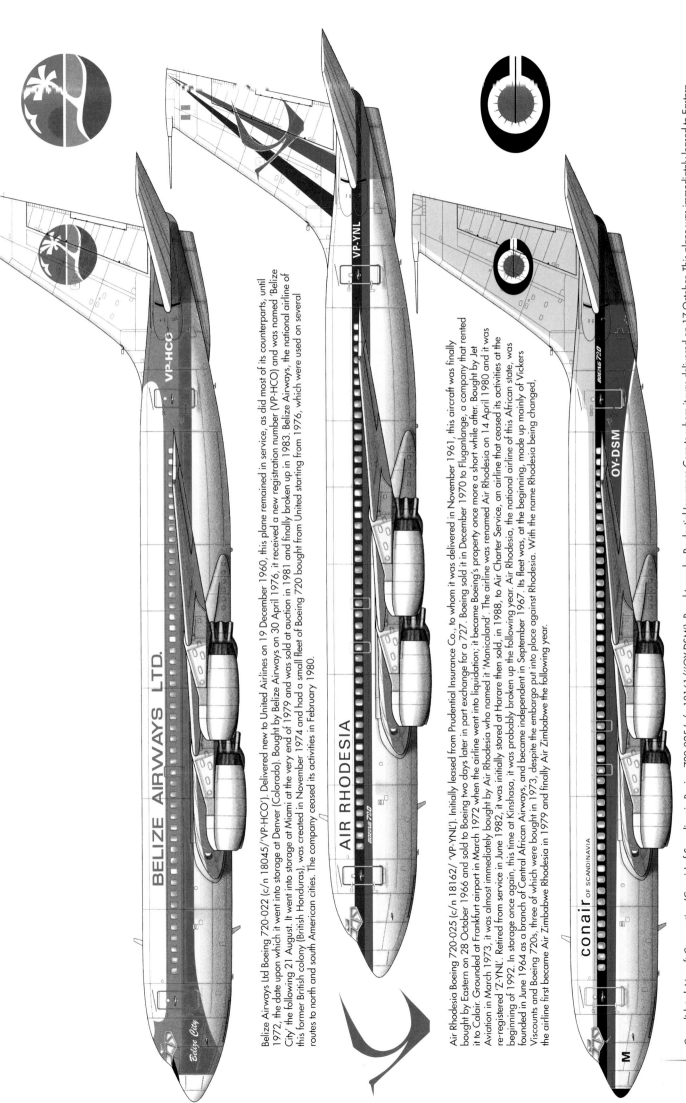

BELIZE AIRWAYS LTD.

Belize Airways Ltd Boeing 720-022 (c/n 18045/'VP-HCO'). Delivered new to United Airlines on 19 December 1960, this plane remained in service, as did most of its counterparts, until 1972, the date upon which it went into storage at Denver (Colorado). Bought by Belize Airways on 30 April 1976, it received a new registration number (VP-HCO) and was named 'Belize City' the following 21 August. It went into storage at Miami at the very end of 1979 and was sold at auction in 1981 and finally broken up in 1983. Belize Airways, the national airline of this former British colony (British Honduras), was created in November 1974 and had a small fleet of Boeing 720 bought from United starting from 1976, which were used on several routes to north and south American cities. The company ceased its activities in February 1980.

AIR RHODESIA

Air Rhodesia Boeing 720-025 (c/n 18162/ 'VP-YNL'). Initially leased from Prudential Insurance Co., to whom it was delivered in November 1961, this aircraft was finally bought by Eastern on 28 October 1966 and sold to Boeing two days later in part exchange for a 727. Boeing sold it in December 1970 to Fluganlange, a company that rented it to Calair. Grounded at Frankfurt airport in March 1972 when the airline went into liquidation; it became Boeing's property once more after. Bought by Jet Aviation in March 1973, it was almost immediately bought by Air Rhodesia who named it 'Manicaland'. The airline was renamed Air Rhodesia on 14 April 1980 and it was re-registered 'Z-YNL'. Retired from service in June 1982, it was initially stored at Harare then sold, in 1988, to Air Charter Service, an airline that ceased its activities at the beginning of 1992. In storage once again, this time at Kinshasa, it was probably broken up the following year. Air Rhodesia, the national airline of this African state, was founded in June 1964 as a branch of Central African Airways, and became independent in September 1967. Its fleet was, at the beginning, made up mainly of Vickers Viscounts and Boeing 720s, three of which were bought in 1973, despite the embargo put into place against Rhodesia. With the name Rhodesia being changed, the airline first became Air Zimbabwe Rhodesia in 1979 and finally Air Zimbabwe the following year.

conair OF SCANDINAVIA

Consolidated Aircraft Corporation (Conair) of Scandinavia Boeing 720-025 (c/n 18161/'OY-DSM'). Bought new by Prudential Insurance Corp to whom it was delivered on 17 October. This plane was immediately leased to Eastern Airlines who bought it in October 1966. Exchanged by Boeing for a 727 on 20 November 1969, it went into storage before being sold to Conair on 30 April 1971, the plane was once more stored, this time at Copenhagen, where it was accidentally destroyed by fire in July 1984 whilst being broken up. Conair was founded by the eccentric Danish millionaire, Simon Ove Spies who bought the charter airline, Flying Enterprise, when it went into bankruptcy. Specialised in charter flights to southern Europe and North Africa, it initially used five old Eastern Boeing 720s in 1971. These were replaced by the 720B ten years later.

51

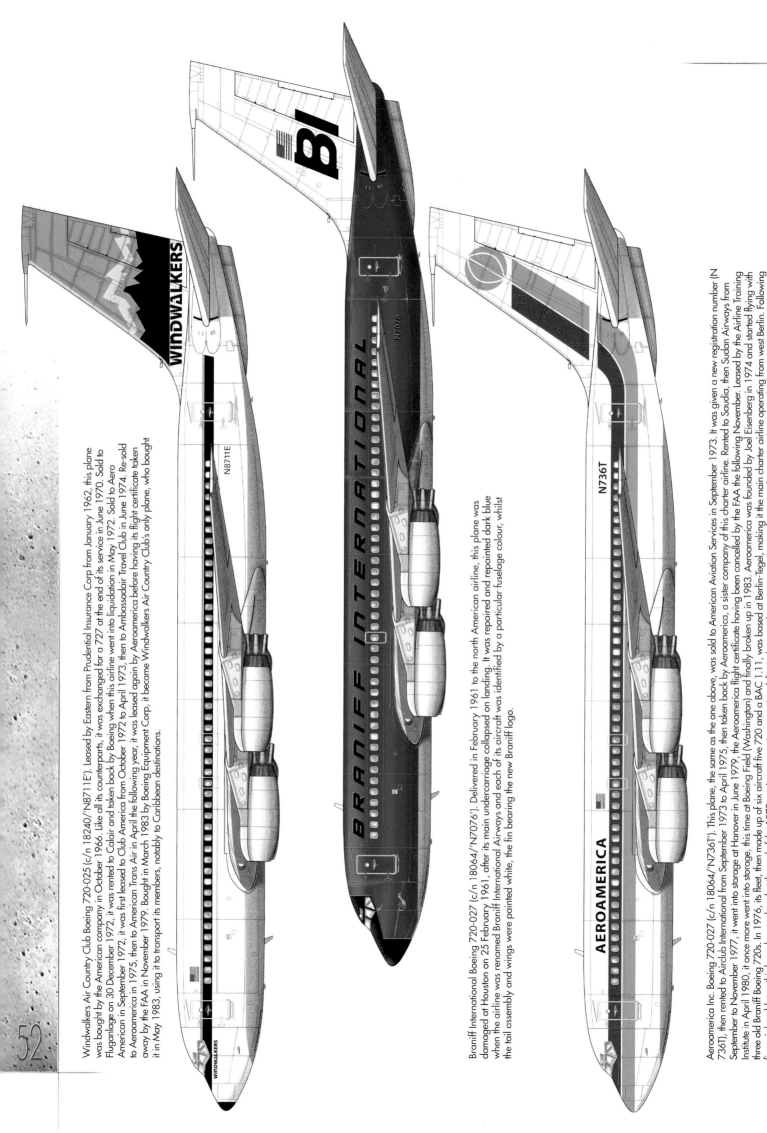

Windwalkers Air Country Club Boeing 720-025 (c/n 18240/'N8711E'). Leased by Eastern from Prudential Insurance Corp from January 1962, this plane was bought by the American company in October 1966. Like all its counterparts, it was exchanged for a 727 at the end of its service in June 1970. Sold to Fluganlage on 30 December 1972, it was rented to Calair and taken back by Boeing when this airline went into liquidation in May 1972. Sold to Aero American in September 1972, it was first leased to Club America from October 1972 to April 1973, then to Ambassadair Travel Club in June 1974. Re-sold to Aeroamerica in 1975, then to American Trans Air in April the following year, it was leased again by Aeroamerica before having its flight certificate taken away by the FAA in November 1979. Bought in March 1983 by Boeing Equipment Corp, it became Windwalkers Air Country Club's only plane, who bought it in May 1983, using it to transport its members, notably to Caribbean destinations.

Braniff International Boeing 720-027 (c/n 18064/'N7076'). Delivered in February 1961 to the north American airline, this plane was damaged at Houston on 25 February 1961, after its main undercarriage collapsed on landing. It was repaired and repainted dark blue when the airline was renamed Braniff International Airways and each of its aircraft was identified by a particular fuselage colour, whilst the tail assembly and wings were painted white, the fin bearing the new Braniff logo.

Aeroamerica Inc. Boeing 720-027 (c/n 18064/'N736T'). This plane, the same as the one above, was sold to American Aviation Services in September 1973. It was given a new registration number (N 736T), then rented to Airclub International from September 1973 to April 1975, then taken back by Aeroamerica, a sister company of this charter airline. Rented to Saudia, then Sudan Airways from September to November 1977, it went into storage at Hanover in June 1979, the Aeroamerica flight certificate having been cancelled by the FAA the following November. Leased by the Airline Training Institute in April 1980, it once more went into storage, this time at Boeing Field (Washington) and finally broken up in 1983. Aeroamerica was founded by Joel Eisenberg in 1974 and started flying with three old Braniff Boeing 720s. In 1976, its fleet, then made up of six aircraft five 720 and a BAC 1.11, was based at Berlin-Tegel, making it the main charter airline operating from west Berlin. Following financial problems, this branch was closed at the end of the 1979 tourist season. Aeroamerica definitively ceased its activities in 1981, after its certificate was taken away for financial and safety reasons.

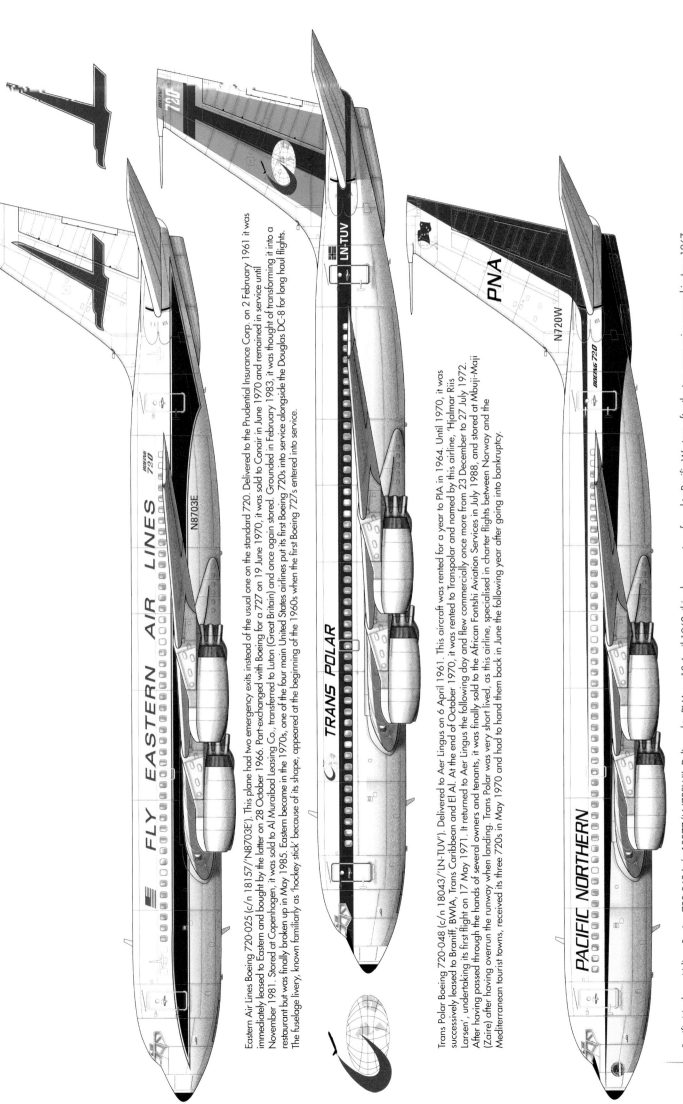

Eastern Air Lines Boeing 720-025 (c/n 18157//N8703E'). This plane had two emergency exits instead of the usual one on the standard 720. Delivered to the Prudential Insurance Corp. on 2 February 1961 it was immediately leased to Eastern and bought by the latter on 28 October 1966. Part-exchanged with Boeing for a 727 on 19 June 1970, it was sold to Conair in June 1970 and remained in service until November 1981. Stored at Copenhagen, it was sold to Al Muraibad Leasing Co., transferred to Luton (Great Britain) and once again stored. Grounded in February 1983, it was thought of transforming it into a restaurant but was finally broken up in May 1985. Eastern became in the 1970s, one of the four main United States airlines put its first Boeing 720s into service alongside the Douglas DC-8 for long haul flights. The fuselage livery, known familiarly as 'hockey stick' because of its shape, appeared at the beginning of the 1960s when the first Boeing 727s entered into service.

Trans Polar Boeing 720-048 (c/n 18043//'LN-TUV'). Delivered to Aer Lingus on 6 April 1961. This aircraft was rented for a year to PIA in 1964. Until 1970, it was successively leased to Braniff, BWIA, Trans Caribbean and El Al. At the end of October 1970, it was rented to Transpolar and named by this airline, 'Hjalmar Riis Larsen,' undertaking its first flight on 17 May 1971. It returned to Aer Lingus the following day and flew commercially once more from 23 December to 27 July 1972. After having passed through the hands of several owners and tenants, it was finally sold to the African Fontshi Aviation Services in July 1988, and stored at Mbuji-Maji (Zaire) after having overrun the runway when landing. Trans Polar was very short lived, as this airline, specialised in charter flights between Norway and the Mediterranean tourist towns, received its three 720s in May 1970 and had to hand them back in June the following year after going into bankruptcy.

Pacific Northern Airlines Boeing 720-062 (c/n 18377// N720W'). Delivered to PNA on 18 April 1962, this plane was transferred to Pacific Western after the two companies merged in June 1967. Bought in April 1973 by Alaska Airlines, it changed its registration number (N302AS) then went to Pan Am where it was exchanged for a Boeing 727 in December 1975. Taken to Miami, it was stored there, and then sold to F. B. Ayer & Associates who rented it to Aeroamerica in April 1976. Stored at Berlin-Tempelhof the same year, it was broken up in 1978 after having been used for training purposes by the airport's fire service. Pacific Northern was created in 1932 under the name of Woodley Airways, and began with regional flights in southwest Alaska. It became Pacific Northern in 1945 and began regular flights between Anchorage and Seattle, in competition with Northern Airlines. In October 1967, PNA was taken over by Western Airlines.

CARGO AND UPGRADED VERSIONS

With the appearance of new, improved performance jet engines, most of the 707 versions had a second youth starting at the beginning of the 1960s. Production lines even restarted with this, whilst some older aircraft were refitted at the factory to conform to the new standards.

All these new versions, which incorporated, apart from their new engines with turbofans, some of the improvements appearing during production, were identified by a B suffix, added to their initial designation. This was the case for newly made aircraft or others that had returned to the factory for modifications.

Opposite.
Photographed in flight before being delivered, this 707-138B (c/n 18067) still bears its American registration. It was delivered in July 1961 to the Australian Quantas company who used it until the end of 1968 under the name of 'City of Darwin'.
(J. Delmas collection)

Opposite.
Delivered to Qantas in July 1959, this 707-138 (c/n 17696/VH-EBA) was named 'City of Melbourne'. Modified into a -138B by Boeing in September 1961, it was sold to Pacific Western in November 1967 and ended its career as the private plane of the Saudi Arabian Prince Bandar within this country's air force. (Qantas)

Below.
This Boeing 707-123 (c/n 17636/ N7509A), delivered to American Airlines in April 1959, kept some of its original livery when it was leased by Air Berlin from May to November 1980. (D. Breffort collection).

1. In detail 31 for American Airlines (707-123B), 41 for TWA (-131B) and 6 for Qantas (-138B).

The 707-120B

Very logically, it was the first version to be made, the 707-120, that was affected; the prototype of the new aircraft, in fact rather a variant, undertook its maiden flight on 22 June 1960. The official certificate was, on the other hand, given much later on 1 March the following year. Apart from the new Pratt & Whitney JT3D-3 engines with double flow turbofans, this version had the wing extension that appeared on the 720, as well as extra Krueger flaps on the leading edge and an enlarged horizontal tail plane. Compared with its predecessor, the 707-120B had a reduced take off run, this being without the need for water injection, a system that was as polluting (noise and smoke) as it was complicated. Its rate of climb was improved, and its range increased thanks to its improved performance engines (8,164 kg/18,000 lb of thrust) and consumed less fuel, whilst its maximum speed (Mach 0.91), that is 1,006 km/h (625 mph) or cruising speed (992 km/h - 616 mph - at 7 575 m - 24,850 ft - altitude) was higher. Seventy-eight new 707-120B aircraft were made [1], at the beginning under the impulse of Boeing itself and American

55

The new rules concerning the reduction of noise emitted by civilian jet aircraft, created at the very beginning of the 1980s, were at the origin of the elaboration of various systems named hushkits, destined to reduce the noise caused by these engines. Initially, at the beginning of the 1973, Boeing itself had carried out tests on noise reducers on a 707-331B rented from TWA. These tests were not continued, essentially because there was not much interest shown on the part of the owners of these four-engine planes.

More exacting standards concerning noise reduction by the ICAO (International Civil Aviation Organisation), and the FAR (Flight Airworthiness Regulations) appeared. Chapter 2, stage 2. These literally forbade from flying in Europe, the United States and many other parts of the globe, noisy aircraft; the Boeing 707 still in service and designed at a time when noise pollution was not taken into consideration was directly threatened. In order to allow these aircraft, owned by airlines that were often financially incapable of acquiring new aircraft, to continue flying, various companies specialising in aeronautics designed systems to reduce noise levels to a level in line with the new official standards. In the end, only two companies, Comtran and QNC (Quiet Nacelle Corporation) to a far lesser extent (this concerned five 707-320B and C) produced the hushkits that could be installed on the original Pratt & Whitney JT3D engines. The first aircraft thus equipped were delivered starting in May 1985. These systems comprised of the addition of sound proofing materials in a redesigned engine pod, equipped with an air vent and long fan gas discharge vents. Also, the conversion proposed by Comtran did not only concern the engines; the cabin was also modified (the use of fireproofed material in order to come into line with new regulations), as well as the avionics. Despite its cost (two million dollars), this transformation remained nonetheless interesting as it was less than the cost of a new aircraft. The modification of a 707-330 being without contest the most economically interesting because of its range and its carrying capacity that was larger than that of older versions. Thus, in 1991, more than one hundred and fifty 707-320B and C were fitted with hushkits with only six 707-320B and two 720B. Later, other aircraft were transformed by re-using noise reduction systems taken from old planes. New, even more draconian standards (stage 3) were written up in 1994 and came into effect in Europe on 1 January 2000 and 1 April for the United States. From now on, no aircraft that did not respect these standards were authorised to fly in these countries and could not even figure on the national register. Planes older than 25 years had to be retired from service, unless they obtained a derogation that was valid for a maximum of three years. To satisfy these new standards, that concerned not only the 707 aircraft still in service, but also the DC-8 that used the same engines, various companies (Comtran, Burbank Aeronautical II) designed and tested their own systems, notably to be able to be part of the call for tenders sent out for the conversion of the OC-135B « Open Skies ». These transformations, which now concerned a very reduced number of civil aircraft still in service but, on the other hand, a lot more military aircraft (E-3 Sentry, J-STARS, KC-135E) that used the same engines were more and more challenged by a simple re-engining (by the CFM 56 or its military variant); this was more expensive but much more straightforward.

Top.
A 707-138B of the Montana Austria Flugbetrieb (c/n 18068/OE-IRA). The Austrian airline bought this plane from Qantas in 1977 and used it until May 1981 when it went into receivership. (V. Gréciet collection)

Above.
A Boeing 707-323B-H (c/n 20179/S7-LAS) of Ligne Aérienne Seychelles seen at Mombasa (Kenya) in 1987. This plane began its career in September 1969 with American Airlines. Sold in December 1986 to Middle East Leasing, it was rented out to LAS from December 1986 to November 1987. (D. Breffort collection)

Airlines who ordered the first plane in November 1959. Other airlines soon showed an interest in the improved performance. Many old planes were thus modernised by Boeing [2], and notably those of the original fleets of Quantas and Pan Am, as well as the three VC-137 VIP transports bought by the USAF. This converting of old aircraft could take two different forms according to their owners' wishes. This was a straightforward change of engines, or the modification as well of the wings. It was American Airlines that had the biggest fleet of this version (fifty-four aircraft, of which more than half were bought new), and they were the first

to put it into regular service in the spring of 1961. The last 707-120B, an aircraft destined for Pan Am, left the assembly lines right at the beginning of 1969.

The 720B

Although the 707-120B was effectively the first of the four-engine plane's modernised variants to enter into service; this modernisation was in fact thought up by Boeing for its 720, essentially in order to counter the threat posed by the very promising Convair 990, mostly thanks to its General Electrics CJ-805 engines. Pratt & Whitney having also, and with its own money, designed a turbofan called the JT3D, Boeing made the most of the opportunity to offer its customers a new range of planes with this engine. This allowed them, for a reduced cost, to cover the market and avoid being left behind by its direct competitors.

The situation in the middle of 1958, was fairly delicate for Boeing as American Airlines, its second customer for the four-engine plane, had, as we have seen, modified much of its original order for the 707-120 for the 720 that corresponded better to its needs. At the same time, Convair was trying to attract the airline by promoting the fact that its next model 990 was faster. Boeing was worried that American Airlines would end up by going for this

---

2. In total 39 aircraft: six for Pan Am (-121B including a -139B for Western originally destined for Cubana), twenty three for American Airlines (-123B), seven for Qantas (-138B) and three for the USAF (707-153B/VC-137B).

Opposite.
A 707-123B of Transavia Holland (c/n 17646/PH-TVA). First delivered to American Airlines in August 1959 who named it 'Flagship Kentucky', this plane was bought by this Dutch airline on 17 March 1972 who renamed it 'Province Zeeland'. (V. Gréciet collection)

aircraft equipped with double flow turbofan engines (707-190B and 720B), thus shattering the hopes of the Texas-based company that ended up by making only thirty Convair 990. These long and difficult discussions ended up being worthwhile for Boeing as it allowed it to make a lot more of its turbofan-equipped 707 than all of the other versions of the four-engine plane (644 new planes of the three main versions, to which should be added more than a hundred others destined for the military market, as well as refitted planes), and position itself as the undeniable main civilian jet constructor.

The first 720B carried out its maiden flight on 6 October 1960, that is a little under four months after that of the 707-120B that was also equipped with new engines, the certificate being awarded in March the following year, a few days before it entered into service, whilst the last plane left the production lines in September 1967. In all, ninety-nine Boeing 720B were made [3], to which should be added ten planes that were refitted for American Airlines.

The 707-320B

Initially overtaken, at the beginning of the 1960s by Douglas and its turbofan equipped DC-8-50, Boeing quickly saw the interest in equipping this type of engine on its intercontinental version of its 707. This meant a reduction in fuel

Above.
The 'Château de Vincennes'(707-328B c/n 18456/F-BHSV), on one of the parking areas of Boeing's Renton factory on the banks of Lake Washington. It has the livery of its first owner, Air France, who used it from December 1962 to April 1983.
(J. Delmas collection)

Opposite.
After its withdrawal from service by American Airlines in November 1974, this 701-123B (c/n 17647) was purchased by Quebecair who operated it until January 1979. Today, the front section of its fuselage is preserved in the Sinsheim Museum of Techniques, in Germany.
(J. Guillem collection).

plane, which is what happened in October 1958 when it ordered 25 aircraft. Boeing, however, did not settle for this and, after long and tough negotiations, managed to get American Airlines to go back on its decision the following year. The airline accepted to renegotiate its previous contracts for

used, and, therefore, an increase in range, whilst obtaining an increased thrust at take off, amongst others, that could increase the global mass of the plane.

As had been the case with the 707-120B, this version did not content itself with being equipped with new genera-

Boeing 707-320C delivered new

DESIGNATION	AIRLINE	QUANTITY	DESIGNATION	AIRLINE	QUANTITY	DESIGNATION	AIRLINE	QUANTITY
-309C	China Airlines	2	-347C	Western	5	-384C	Olympic Airways	4
-311C	Wardair	1	-348C	Aer Lingus	4	-385C	American Airlines	1
-321C	Continental Airlines	2	-349C	Flying Tiger	4	-386C	Iran Air	4
	Pan American	34	-351C	Northwest Orient	26	-387C	Aerolineas Argentinas	2
-323C	American Airlines	36	-355C	Air France	1	-396C	Wardair	1
-324C	Continental Airlines	11		Executive Jet	2	-399C	British Caledonian	2
-327C	Braniff	9	-358C	El Al	2	-3B4C	MEA	4
-328C	Air France	8	-360C	Ethiopian Airlines	1	-3B5C	Korean Airlines	1
-329C	Sabena	7	-365C	British Eagle	1	-3D3C	Alia Royal Jordanian	2
-330C	Lufthansa	6		Caledonian	1	-3F9C	Nigeria Airways	3
-331C	TWA	15	-366C	Egypt Air	9	-3H7C	Air Cameroun	1
-336C	BOAC	7	-368C	Saudi Arabian Airlines	7	-3J6C	CAAC	6
-337C	Air India	2	-369C	Kuwaiti Airways	5	-3J8C	Sudan Air	2
-338C	Qantas	21	-370C	Iraqi Airways	3	-3K1C	Tarom	4
-340C	Pakistan International	7	-372C	Airlift	2	-3L5C	Libyan Arab Airlines	1
-341C	Varig	3	-373C	TWA	2	-3L6C	Aviation Services & Support	1
-344C	South African Airways	5		World Airways	9			
-345C	Varig	5	-379C	Varig	1	**TOTAL**		**305**

Above.
Delivered to Pan Am in February 1968, this 707-321BA-H, (c/n 19693/N491PA) remained in service with the American airline until 1979. It is seen here at Abidjan airport in the Ivory Coast, equipped with a ferry pod containing a spare engine and in Air Afrique livery, a partner airline on some African routes. (J. Delmas collection)

Opposite.
Withdrawn from service by Qantas in March 1968, this 707-138B (c/n 17702) was leased by British Eagle in March 1968. Christened 'Phoenix', it was only used for a short period, the airline going bankrupt in November that same year…
(J. Guillem collection)

Opposite.
After a long career with Pan Am, this 707-321BA-H (c/n 18837) was sold in October 1980 to the Le Point association which became Point Air in April the following year. Rented to Minerve in August 1981, it went into storage at Orly when this company ceased its activities in February 1987.
(J. Delmas collection)

Opposite.
This Braniff International Boeing 707-138B (c/n 18740/N108BN), the last of this version to be made, began its career with Qantas in September 1964 and was used until it was sold on to Regency Income Corp in 1969. It was then rented by Braniff until 1973. As a matter of interest, this aircraft is still in service and owned now by the actor John Travolta, repainted in Qantas livery and specially registered 'N707JT'. (J. Guillem collection).

Below.
After a short career with Qantas, all the 707-138B were operated by minor airlines. This aircraft (c/n 18067) was purchased by BWIA in September 1969 and used by this airline from Trinidad and Tobago until 1977.
(J. Guillem collection)

tion JT3D engines, each producing a ton of extra thrust, but was also modified structurally. The wingspan was increased by forty inches (1,01 m) and the wing surface was also increased thanks to the use of different exterior wing panels of which the wing tips were rounded.

The wing's leading edge, between the fuselage and the inside engine pods were slightly moved forward which increased the lift, notably at low speeds, whilst the trailing edge flaps

were redesigned. Thanks to this apparently small increase (five extra inches, or 0.13 m), the aircraft saw its range increase by 15%, to a maximum of 8,830 km (5,487 miles). All the 707-320B aircraft were of course equipped with the heightened tail plane that was characteristic of the planes at middle and the end of production, whilst their cabin could hold, according to the configurations, between 189 and 219 passengers.

It was Pan Am that was the first customer of the new aircraft,

3. Twelve aircraft for American Airlines (720-023B), three for Pan Am, originally destined for American (-023B), eight for Continental (-024B), eight for Lufthansa (-030B), four for Pakistan International Airlines (-040B), twenty seven for Western (-047B), seventeen for Northwest Orient (-051B), two for El Al (-058B), three for Avianca (-059B), three for Ethiopian Airlines (-060B) and two for Saudia (-068B).

the first of which flew on 31 January 1962 and was put into service the following June. Because of its great endurance, the 707-320B was in priority used on longer flights over 7,000 km (4,350 miles), such as Los Angeles-London or San Francisco-Tokyo. Northwest Orient Airlines, that had begun to use the DC-8 on domestic United States flights, quickly declared itself to be a little dissatisfied with the Douglas four-engine plane and, after having initially ordered from Boeing a few of its 720, accepted the offer of the latter to quite simply replace its DC-8 fleet with the 707-351B. Northwest, having accepted, and no longer buying any more Douglas aircraft sounded the beginning of the end for Douglas who had not really taken into consideration the criticisms of its customers. They were finally bought by Boeing at the end of the 20th century.

At the end of production, a few aircraft were equipped with the improved wings that were used on the cargo version, measuring 1.05 m (3' 5") more than on a standard 707-320B

(44,16 m - 145' 9"- instead of 43,15 m - 142' 5" -, that is a wing surface that went from 269 m² - 2,892 sq ft -to 280 m² - 2,942 sq ft). This variant, named the 707-320B « Advanced » or more simply the 707-320BA, now had a range of 9,900 km (6,150 miles). It was also equipped with two extra Krueger flaps on the wings' leading edge, modified flaps on the trailing edge and engine hoods with additional enlarged air vents so that more air could be pulled in on take off. The last 707-320B, a version which was the first to use the alphanumeric system to designate its customers, was delivered in 1971. A fair number of these aircraft, at the end of their careers, were transformed into cargo planes or offered to the military market.

The 707-320C

Pan Am, a little after the improved intercontinental version came into service, asked Boeing to make it a variant destined to carry freight. This took the form of production 707-320B (double flow jet engines and a modified wing surface) that was equipped with a cargo door that was a little

similar to that on the Dash 80. Rectangular in shape (3,38 m by 2,31 m/11' by 7' 7"), it was placed on the left side of the fuselage, between the cockpit and the wing's leading edge. In order to take freight in the cabin that had been transformed into a hold, the floor of the latter was reinforced and equipped with tie-down points whilst the undercarriage was also strengthened to deal with the extra weight, the maximum load now being 39 metric tonnes (43 tons). The great majority of the 320C to be made were of the 'convertible'or 'combi'type, that is to say, they could, according to the needs of the user, carry either freight or passengers (maximum capacity varying from 195 to 219, or a combination of both). The cabin windows were still in place, as well as the passenger access doors. It was only in October 1962 that the first all cargo aircraft appeared, initially ordered by American Airlines and with covered up windows, whilst the internal equipment (seats, galleys, etc.), as well as the air conditioning system, had become useless and were removed. The extra weight compared to a 'convertible'was not negligible (5,800 kg/12,875 lb) and allowed the increase of the payload in proportion. The maiden flight of a convertible 707, a -321C bought by Pan Am, the first airline to have

ordered this type in April 1962, took place on 19 February 1963; it was put into service on 17 June the same year, as much over the Atlantic as the Pacific. Pan Am, by this strategic choice, gained a large part of the freight transport market the following year thanks to its fleet that ended up comprising more than thirty of these aircraft. Boeing's old adversary, Douglas, also offered its own cargo version of its four engine plane, the DC-8-54CF [4] which flew a few weeks before the 707 in January 1963, but which could not rival the 707 and finally only achieved half the sales of Boeing.

During the Vietnam war, the cargo 707s were much used to carry freight between the United States and south east Asia. Some airlines, such as Pan Am, signed contracts with the

Opposite.
Property of Monarch who purchased it in November 1971, this 720-051B (c/n 18381), here captured during landing, was leased to Cyprus Airways from March 1977 to January 1978. (J. Guillem collection).

Above.
Purchased by Monarch from Northwest in September 1971, this 720-051B (c/n 18381/G-AZFB) was leased to Iraqi Airways between August and November 1974. (J. Guillem collection)

Above, right.
When it belonged to MEA, this former American Airlines 720-023B (c/n 18026) was the only plane of this type leased to Libyan Arab Airlines, from July 1976 to May 1977. It was destroyed during a shelling in Beyrouth, on 16 June 1982. (J. Guillem collection)

Opposite.
Ports of Call Travel Club, who became Skyworld Airlines in September 1985, operated this 707-323B-H (c/n 20176/N712PC) until July 1989, when it ceased operations. The aircraft was then stored at Denver, Colorado. (J. Guillem collection)

4. The 54CF series was the first of the DC-8 to have a cargo door (3,56 m x 2,16 m) in order to be used, like the -320C in an all cargo version, all passenger or mixed.
Douglas delivered its first DC-8-54CF to TCA (future Air Canada) in January 1963. Later, Douglas also offered a version that could carry a heavier load, the 55CF as well as the 54AF, a cargo only aircraft without a cabin arrangement and windows that was only bought by United (15 aircraft). A cargo only aircraft without cabin facilities and portholes of which only United bought fifteen.

army. The Flying Tiger Line, the oldest north American freight company, also ordered both the DC-8 and the 707-320C to replace its propeller powered CL-44D and Lockheed L-1049C aircraft. It received its first Boeing in September 1965. The Flying Tiger Line only used these planes for four years, its fleet being made up of planes rented from Aer Lingus, El Al or Caledonian, before replacing them with the 747 and the DC-8-63F. Flying Tiger was, however, the first company to fly around the pole on 14 November 1965, one of its planes carrying out a return trip from Honolulu via Christchurch (New Zealand) and the Antarctic, a distance of 43,200 km (26,844 miles) undertaken in 62 hours 30 minutes. In total, three hundred and five 707-320C were made, many airlines finally preferred it to the passenger transport version, notably from the time the « Jumbo-jet » appeared. The last 707-3F9C was bought by Nigeria Airways, and was delivered new to this airline in January 1978. A certain number of aircraft still with an important potential, were

bought by the USAF of US Navy and transformed respectively into the C-18 and E-6 Mercury.

Apart from these versions, it should be pointed out that Northwest Orient Airlines received from May 1963 onwards, five 707-351B specially named SCD (for Side Cargo Door), the cabin of which was divided in two lengthwise and equipped with a cargo door, but without a reinforced floor and the system of attaching freight that was characteristic of the versions traditionally destined for carrying freight. These planes, that could carry an extra load of 4.5 tonnes, were put into service above the Pacific from July 1963. In November of the same year, Northwest bought real convertibles (707-351C) that it used until September 1978.

The only 707-700

At the end of the 1970s, Boeing, using its own money, made a demonstrator destined to attract future customers that would be interested in either having their fleet of old 707 aircraft fitted with new engines, or buying a new plane of which production would be restarted. With this objective, a 707-320C (constr. n° 21956) taken brand new from the produc-

Above.
Delivered to American Airlines as a non-convertible
cargo in July 1965, this 707-323C-H
(c/n 18938/N7559A) was destroyed by a shelling at
Beyrouth on 16 June 1982. At this time he belonged to
the Lebanese company TMA for five years.
(J. Guillem collection)

Opposite.
Loading freight onto a TWA 707-331C.
The monoblock door opened towards the top using
actuators and did not have any windows. Freight was
placed on pallets and slid into the plane using rollers
placed on the floor. The cabin windows were
protected, inside, by mobile when this was turned into
a hold. (J. Delmas collection).

Opposite.
Delivered to MSA (Malaysia Singapore Airlines) in July 1968, this 707-312B-H (c/n 19738) was first registered '9M-AOT', then '9V-BFB' in June 1972, a few weeks before being transferred to Singapore Airlines when MSA ceased operations.
(J. Guillem collection)

Opposite.
Destined for Pan Am but finally delivered to Continental in August 1964, this 707-321H (c/n 18825) was leased by DAS Air Cargo (5X-DAR) in February 1986. It was destroyed by a fire on 25 November 1992 after crashing on landing at a military barracks in Kano (Nigeria) during a sand storm.
(J.-C. Bertrand collection)

Opposite.
American Airlines sub-leased this 707-323C-H (c/n 20089) from BCal from June 1972 to December 1973. Named 'City of Renfrew', this plane was damaged by a fire in its cabin on 10 August 1972. It was put back in service after being repaired.
(J. Guillem collection)

Opposite.
This 707-373C-H (c/n 19179/ N372WA) was delivered in May 1966 to World Airways who sold it to Portuguese airline TAP in July 1974. (J. Guillem collection)

Below.
After being leased from two different owners from 1974, this 720-023B (c/n 18033) was purchased by Ecuatoriana in April 1977. Named 'Imbabura', it belly-landed at Tel-Aviv on 10 May that year. Repaired and re-registered (HC-BDP), it staid in service until December 1984.
(J. Guillem collection)

tion lines, was equipped with four CFM56 engines and began its test flights at the end of November 1979 after having been specially decorated. This project was rapidly abandoned, the civilian market showing hardly any interest for this offer which concerned a plane, which at that time, had been overtaken by new planes, notably made by Boeing (737 and, above all, the 747). The manufacture of a new plane could not have been achieved without costly structural modifications (lengthening of the fuselage, different wings, larger and reinforced undercarriage), whilst only fitting new engines turned out to be of little interest financially.

Although, the 707-700, as the plane was named, did not finally have any descendants, it was, however extremely useful to Boeing as the experience gained during its trials was much used for the elaboration of certain versions of the 737 (notably from the 300 series as it was equipped with CFM 56 engines), and also served to define the procedures for replacing the engines of part of the KC-135 fleet. After this series of tests, the prototype was finally re-equipped with JT3D engines, sold to the Moroccan government in March 1982 and later transformed as a flying tanker for the Moroccan air force.

Above.
'Imbabura', a 720-023B (c/n 18037) leased by Ecuatoriana from January 1975 to April 1984, in its 'ethnic' livery with a military code on the tail. It has here been photographed at Quito airport, with the Andes on the background. (J. Guillem collection)

Above, left.
This 707-348C-H (c/n 19410) was briefly leased from the Canadian airline Transair by Aer Lingus, between December 1973 and April 1974 for charters to the United States and the Caribbean. Re-registered (CF-TAI), it was also renamed 'Fort Garry'. (J. Guillem collection)

Above, right.
Owned by Aer Lingus for fifteen years, this 707-348C-H (c/n 19001/5A-DIY) was sold to United Arab Airlines in June 1981; this carrier was renamed Jamahiriya Air Transport in June 1983 and finally Jamahiriya Arab Airlines in June 1986. (J. Guillem collection)

Opposite.
The sole Nile Safari Aviation 707-338C (c/n 19622/ST-ALL) photographed during landing, at the end of the eighties, shortly before this airline ceased operations with aircraft of this size. Originally delivered to Qantas in January 1968, this aircraft enjoys a long career as it is still in service, after having become the first production E-8C in 1992! (D. Breffort collection).

Opposite.
*After having begun its career with Pan Am in November 1967 under the name 'Jet Clipper Sovereign of the Seas', this non-convertible cargo 707-321C-H (c/n 19370/F-BYCN), was used by Air France between October 1975 and November 1982, the date upon which it was definitively withdrawn from service.
It is seen here in 1979, in its new livery introduced shortly before by the French airline throughout its fleet.
(J. Delmas collection).*

*After having sold this 707-338C-H (c/n 19622)
to Itel in October 1977, Qantas leased it until
22 December of that year, pending the delivery
of a Boeing 747. On that occasion, the aircraft
received this particularly appropriate livery
('Have a Qantastic Christmas').
(J. Guillem collection)*

Above.
The Air France 'Château de Langeais' (707-328C-H - c/n 19916/F-BLCK) was delivered to the French national airline in December 1968 and used until November 1982. Damaged after an emergency landing at Ostende on 26 November 1997 whilst under the ownership of Memphis Air (Egypt), it was repaired and went back into service in August 1998.
(R. Leblanc collection).

Top.
Delivered to Sudan Airways in June 1974, this 707-3J8C-H (c/n 20897) was still in service with this airline in January 2006.
(J. Guillem collection)

Above.
Hoping to give a second youth to the 707, Boeing transformed this 707-320C (c/n 21956) directly on the assembly lines by giving it new CFM56 engines. Specially decorated, this prototype, named 'Bob Silvey', began its test flights at the end of November 1979 but did not have any descendants, at least in the civil domain.
(J. Guillem collection)

Above.
Acquired in April 1974 and re-sold in June 1987 by the Yugoslavian airline JAT, this 707-351C (c/n 19411/YU-AGJ) was delivered new to Northwest in December 1966.
(V. Gréciet collection)

Below.
Landing at Hong Kong-Kaï Tak of Cathay Pacific Airways 707-351C 'VR-HHB'. This former Northwest aircraft (c/n 18747) was operated by this Hong Kong airline between July 1975 and April 1980, the date upon which the 707s' fleet was replaced by Boeing 747s. (J. Guillem collection)

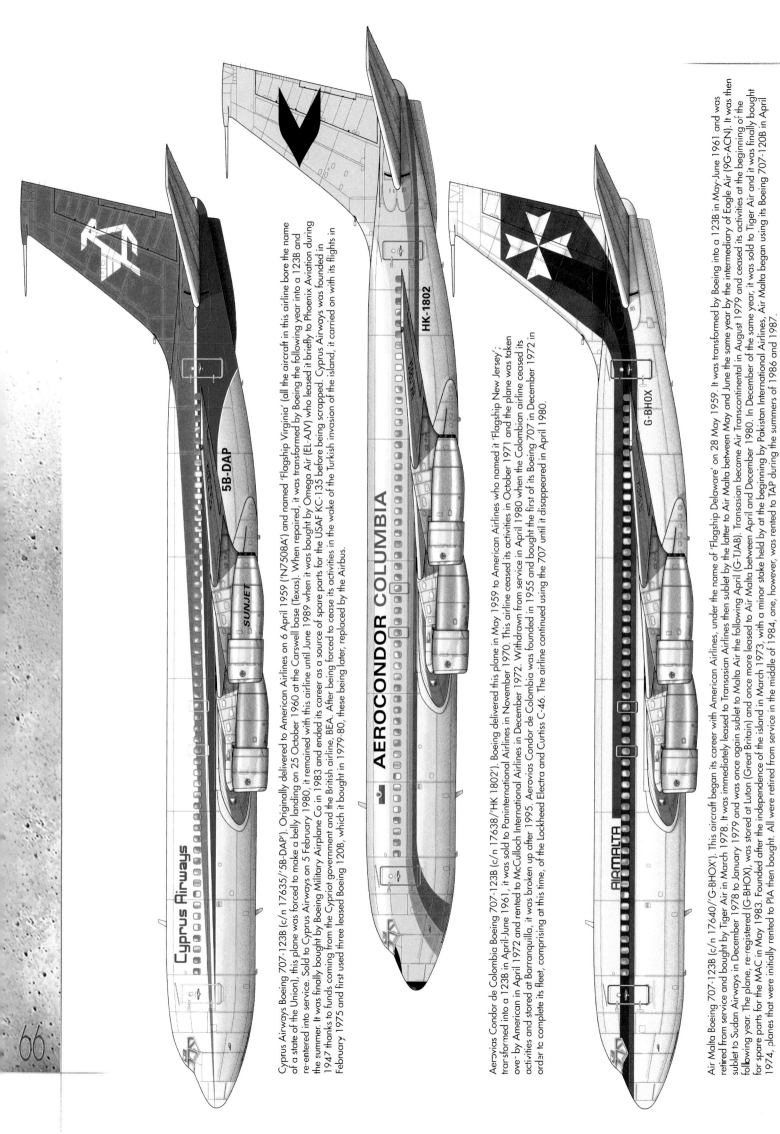

Cyprus Airways

5B-DAP

SUNJET

Cyprus Airways Boeing 707-123B (c/n 17635/'5B-DAP'). Originally delivered to American Airlines on 6 April 1959 ('N7508A') and named 'Flagship Virginia' (all the aircraft in this airline bore the name of a state of the Union), this plane was forced to make a belly landing on 25 October 1960 at the Carswell base (Texas). When repaired, it was transformed by Boeing the following year into a 123B and re-entered into service. Sold to Cyprus Airways on 5 February 1980, it remained with this airline until June 1989 when it was bought by Omega Air (EL-AJV) who leased it briefly to Phoenix Aviation during the summer. It was finally bought by Boeing Military Airplane Co in 1983 and ended its career as a source of spare parts for the USAF KC-135 before being scrapped. Cyprus Airways was founded in 1947 thanks to funds coming from the Cypriot government and the British airline, BEA. After being forced to cease its activities in the wake of the Turkish invasion of the island, it carried on with its flights in February 1975 and first used three leased Boeing 120B, which it bought in 1979-80, these being later, replaced by the Airbus.

AEROCONDOR COLUMBIA

HK-1802

Aerovias Condor de Colombia Boeing 707-123B (c/n 17638/'HK 1802'). Boeing delivered this plane in May 1959 to American Airlines who named it 'Flagship New Jersey'; transformed into a 123B in April-June 1961, it was sold to Paninternational Airlines in November 1970. This airline ceased its activities in October 1971 and the plane was taken over by American in April 1972 and rented to McCulloch International Airlines in December 1972. Withdrawn from service in April 1980 when the Colombian airline ceased its activities and stored at Barranquilla, it was broken up after 1995. Aerovias Condor de Colombia was founded in 1955 and bought the first of its Boeing 707 in December 1972 in order to complete its fleet, comprising at this time, of the Lockheed Electra and Curtiss C-46. The airline continued using the 707 until it disappeared in April 1980.

AIRMALTA

G-BHOX

Air Malta Boeing 707-123B (c/n 17640/'G-BHOX'). This aircraft began its career with American Airlines, under the name of 'Flagship Delaware' on 28 May 1959. It was transformed by Boeing into a 123B in May-June 1961. It was retired from service and bought by Tiger Air in March 1978. It was immediately leased to Transasian Airlines then sublet by the latter to Air Malta between May and June the same year by the intermediary of Eagle Air (9G-ACN). It was then sublet to Sudan Airways in December 1978 to January 1979 and was once again sublet to Malta Air the following April (G-TJAB). Transasian became Air Transcontinental in August 1979 and ceased its activities at the beginning of the following year. The plane, re-registered (G-BHOX), was stored at Luton (Great Britain) and once more leased to Air Malta between April and December 1980. In December of the same year, it was sold to Tiger Air and it was finally bought for spare parts for the MAC in May 1983. Founded after the independence of the island in March 1973, with a minor stake held by at the beginning by Pakistan International Airlines, Air Malta began using its Boeing 707-120B in April 1974, planes that were initially rented from PIA then bought. All were retired from service in the middle of 1984, one, however, was rented to TAP during the summers of 1986 and 1987.

66.

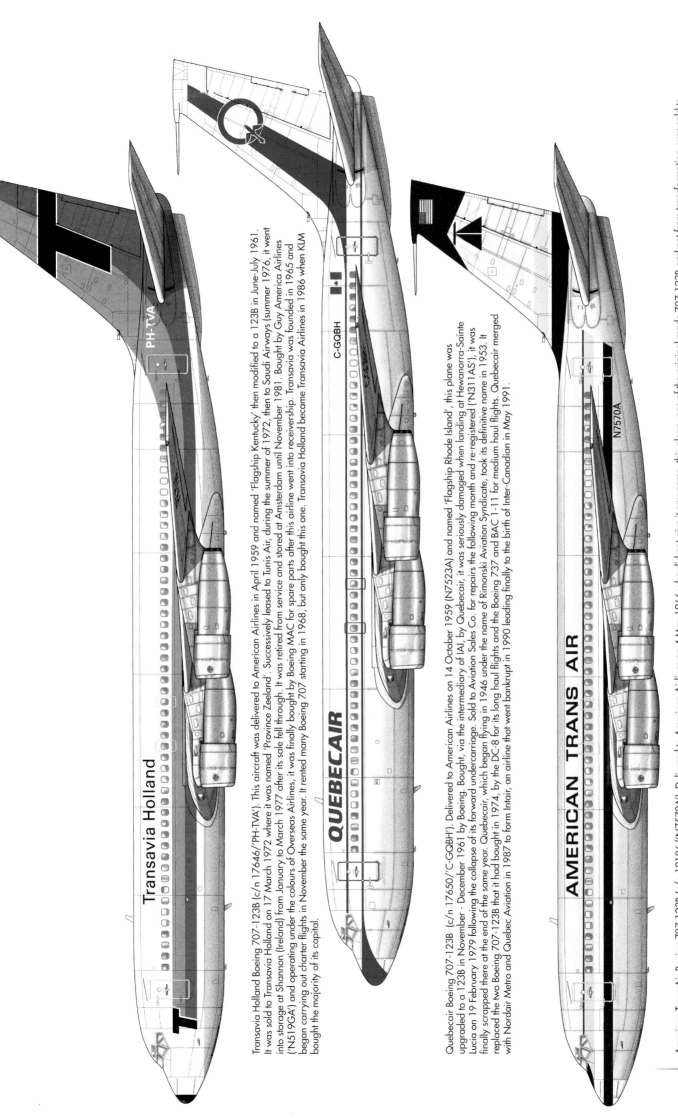

Transavia Holland

Transavia Holland Boeing 707-123B (c/n 17646/'PH-TVA'). This aircraft was delivered to American Airlines in April 1959 and named 'Flagship Kentucky' then modified to a 123B in June-July 1961. It was sold to Transavia Holland on 17 March 1972 where it was named 'Province Zeeland'. Successively leased to Tunis Air, during the summer of 1972, then to Saudi Airways (summer 1976, it went into storage at Amsterdam until November 1981. Bought by Guy America Airlines ('N519GA') and operating under the colours of Overseas Airlines, it was finally bought by Boeing MAC for spare parts after this airline went into receivership. Transavia was founded in 1965 and began carrying out charter flights in November the same year. Transavia Holland became Transavia Airlines in 1986 when KLM bought the majority of its capital.

QUEBECAIR

Quebecair Boeing 707-123B (c/n 17650/'C-GQBH'). Delivered to American Airlines on 14 October 1959 (N7523A) and named 'Flagship Rhode Island', this plane was upgraded to a 123B in November - December 1961 by Boeing. Bought, via the intermediary of IAI, by Quebecair, it was seriously damaged when landing at Hewanorra-Sainte Lucia on 19 February 1979 following the collapse of its forward undercarriage. Sold to Aviation Sales Co. for repairs the following month and re-registered ('N311AS'), it was finally scrapped there at the end of the same year. Quebecair, which began flying in 1946 under the name of Rimonski Aviation Syndicate, took its definitive name in 1953. It replaced the two Boeing 707-123B that it had bought in 1974, by the DC-8 for its long haul flights and the Boeing 737 and BAC 1-11 for medium haul flights. Quebecair merged with Nordair Metro and Quebec Aviation in 1987 to form Intair, an airline that went bankrupt in 1990 leading finally to the birth of Inter-Canadian in May 1991.

AMERICAN TRANS AIR

American Trans Air Boeing 707-123B (c/n 19186/'N7570A'). Delivered to American Airlines on 4 May 1966 who did not give it any name, this plane, one of the original made 707-123B and not from transformation, was sold to American Trans Air on 1 May 1981 who kept it until the end of 1984 before letting it go to Boeing Equipment Holding Corp. who rented it temporarily to American Trans Air whilst this airline was waiting for delivery of new more modern aircraft. It was finally sold to Boeing MAC on 20 August 1985, where it was used for spare parts for the modernisation of the KC-135 and was broken up shortly after. ATA was founded in August 1973, originally to use three Boeing 720 for the Ambassadair Travel Club, an association based at Indianapolis organising flights all over the world for its members. Next, American Trans Air, carrying out regular or charter flights, nationally or internationally, finally sold all of its aircraft to Boeing in exchange for the 727 or Lockheed Tristar.

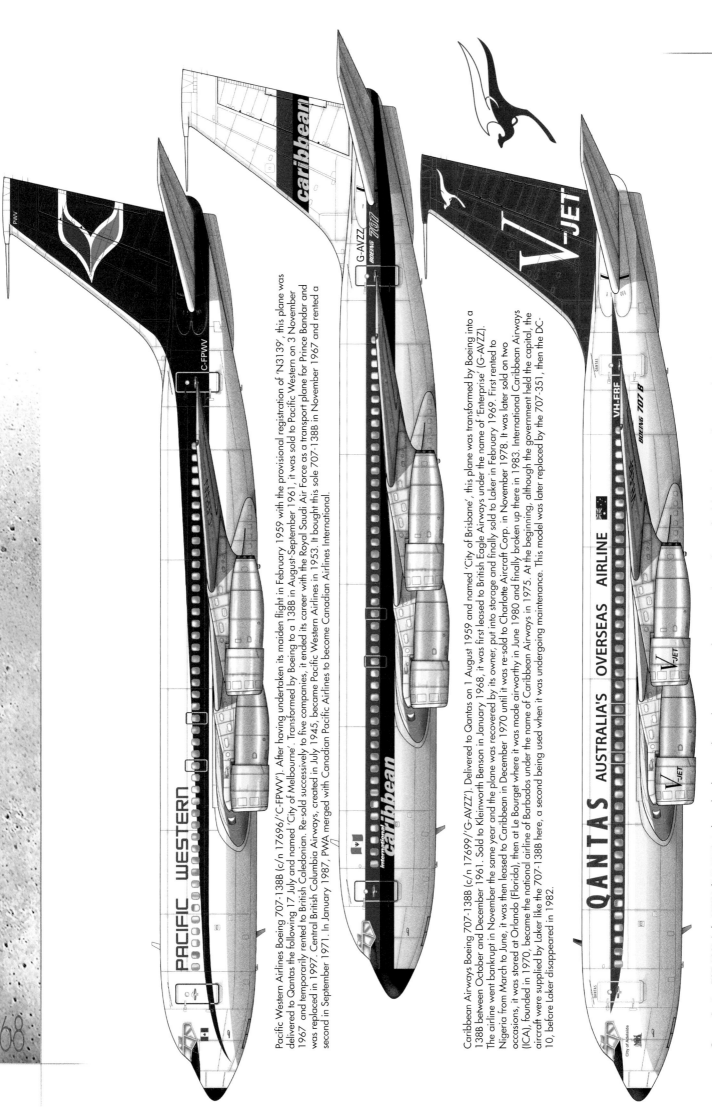

Pacific Western Airlines Boeing 707-138B (c/n 17696/'C-FPWV'). After having undertaken its maiden flight in February 1959 with the provisional registration of 'N3139', this plane was delivered to Qantas the following 17 July and named 'City of Melbourne'. Transformed by Boeing to a 138B and named 'City of Melbourne'. Transformed by Boeing on 3 November 1967 and temporarily rented to British Caledonian. Re-sold successively to five companies, it ended its career with the Royal Saudi Air Force as a transport plane for Prince Bandar and was replaced in 1997. Central British Columbia Airways, created in July 1945, became Pacific Western Airlines in 1953. It bought this sole 707-138B in November 1967 and rented a second in September 1971. In January 1987, PWA merged with Canadian Pacific Airlines to become Canadian Airlines International.

Caribbean Airways Boeing 707-138B (c/n 17699/'G-AVZZ'). Delivered to Qantas on 1 August 1959 and named 'City of Brisbane', this plane was transformed by Boeing into a 138B between October and December 1961. Sold to Kleinworth Benson in January 1968, it was first leased to British Eagle Airways under the name of 'Enterprise' (G-AVZZ). The airline went bankrupt in November the same year and the plane was recovered by its owner, put into storage and finally sold to Laker in February 1969. First rented to Nigeria from March to June, it was then leased to Caribbean in December 1970 until it was re-sold to Charlotte Aircraft Corp. in November 1978. It was later sold on two occasions, it was stored at Orlando (Florida), then at Le Bourget where it was made airworthy in June 1980 and finally broken up there in 1983. International Caribbean Airways (ICA), founded in 1970, became the national airline of Barbados under the name of Caribbean Airways in 1975. At the beginning, although the government held the capital, the aircraft were supplied by Laker like the 707-138B here, a second being used when it was undergoing maintenance. This model was later replaced by the 707-351, then the DC-10, before Laker disappeared in 1982.

Qantas Boeing 707-138B (c/n 17701/'VH-EBF'). Delivered to the Australian airline on 4 September 1959 and named 'City of Adelaide', this aircraft was transformed to a 138B in November - December 1961 and used until 1968. Bought by F. B. Ayer & Associates (re-named Pan Ayer in May 1976), it was leased to Standard Airways (N792SA) until August 1969 when the airline went bankrupt, and stored at New York. In 1971, it went to Hamburg to be used by the German airline Air Commerz (D-ADAQ), then rented for a few months to Air Alaska. Successively stored, leased or purchased by different companies from september 1972 to august 1979, it then returned to the United States and went into storage at Burbank, being finally broken up at the end of 1986. Queensland And Northern Territory Aerial Services, created in 1920 and nationalised in 1947, became Qantas in August 1967.

68

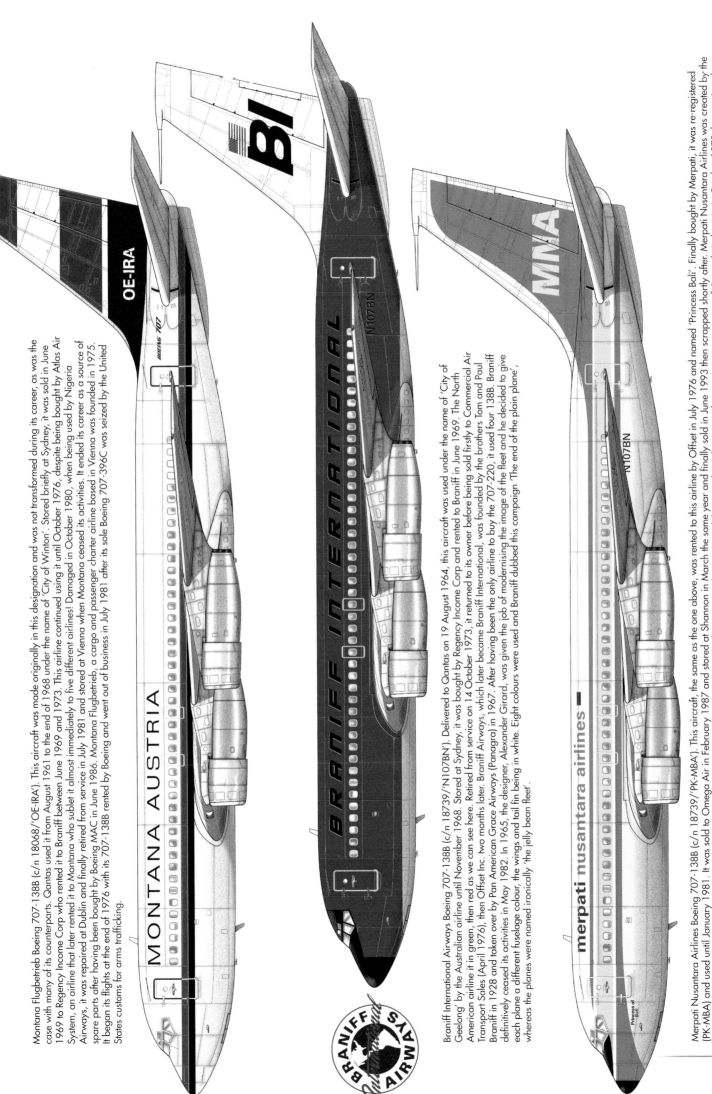

Montana Flugbetrieb Boeing 707-138B (c/n 18068/'OE-IRA'). This aircraft was made originally in this designation and was not transformed during its career, as was the case with many of its counterparts. Qantas used it from August 1961 to the end of 1968 under the name of 'City of Winton'. Stored briefly at Sydney, it was sold in June 1969 to Regency Income Corp who rented it to Braniff between June 1969 and 1973. This airline continued using it until October 1976, despite being bought by Atlas Air System, an airline that later rented it to Montana who sublet it almost immediately to five different airlines! Damaged in October 1980, when being used by Nigeria Airways, it was repaired at Dublin and finally retired from service in July 1981 and stored at Vienna when Montana ceased its activities. It ended its career as a source of spare parts after having been bought by Boeing MAC in June 1986. Montana Flugbetrieb, a cargo and passenger charter airline based in Vienna was founded in 1975. It began its flights at the end of 1976 with its 707-138B rented by Boeing and went out of business in July 1981 after its sole Boeing 707-396C was seized by the United States customs for arms trafficking.

MONTANA AUSTRIA

Braniff International Airways Boeing 707-138B (c/n 18739/'N107BN'). Delivered to Qantas on 19 August 1964, this aircraft was used under the name of 'City of Geelong' by the Australian airline until November 1968. Stored at Sydney, it was bought by Regency Income Corp and rented to Braniff in June 1969. The North American airline it in green, then red as we can see here. Retired from service on 14 October 1973, it returned to its owner before being sold firstly to Commercial Air Transport Sales (April 1976), then Offset Inc. two months later. Braniff Airways, which later became Braniff International, was founded by the brothers Tom and Paul Braniff in 1928 and taken over by Pan American Grace Airways (Panagra) in 1967. After having been the only airline to buy the 707-220, it used four 138B. Braniff definitively ceased its activities in May 1982. In 1965, the designer, Alexander Girard, was given the job of modernising the image of the fleet and he decided to give each plane a different fuselage colour, the wings and tail fin being in white. Eight colours were used and Braniff dubbed this campaign 'The end of the plain plane', whereas the planes were named ironically 'the jelly bean fleet'.

Merpati Nusantara Airlines Boeing 707-138B (c/n 18739/'PK-MBA'). This aircraft, the same as the one above, was rented to this airline by Offset in July 1976 and named 'Princess Bali'. Finally bought by Merpati, it was re-registered (PK-MBA) and used until January 1981. It was sold to Omega Air in February 1987 and stored at Shannon in March the same year and finally sold in June 1993 then scrapped shortly after. Merpati Nusantara Airlines was created by the Indonesian government in 1962. It rented several Boeing 707 to transport pilgrims to Mecca, the first in November 1971 and the second in July 1976. It became a sister company of Garauda Indonesia in October 1978, but continued to operate under its own name and livery as its management remained independent.

merpati nusantara airlines

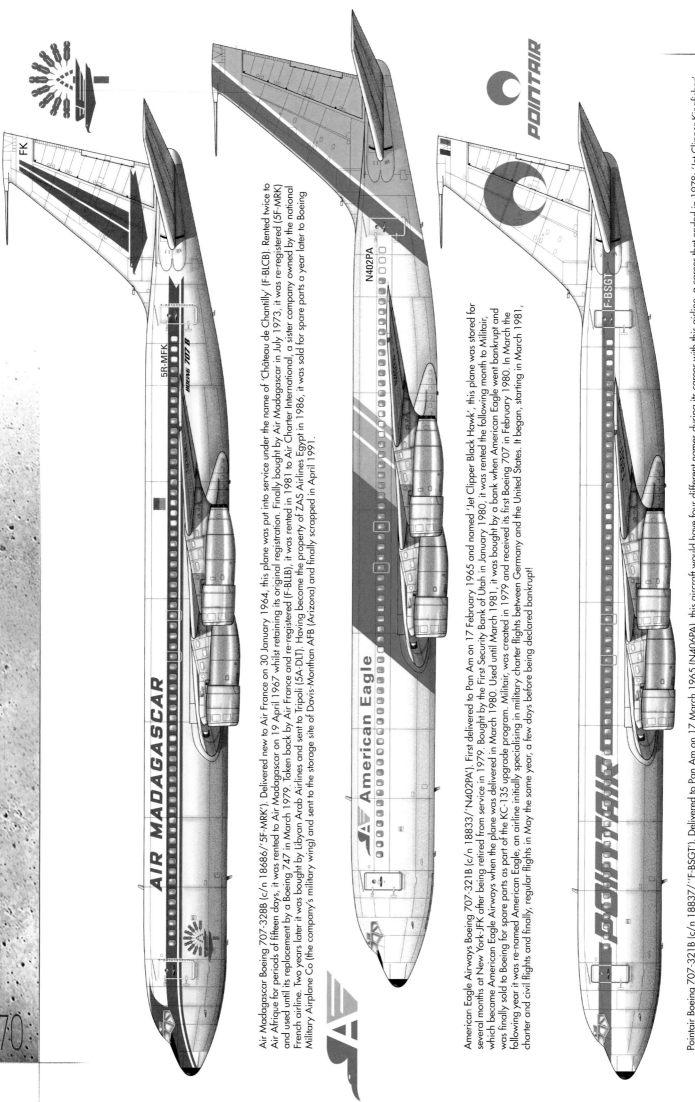

AIR MADAGASCAR

5R-MFK

BOEING 707 B

Air Madagascar Boeing 707-328B (c/n 18686/'5F-MRK'). Delivered new to Air France on 30 January 1964, this plane was put into service under the name of 'Château de Chantilly' (F-BLCB). Rented twice to Air Afrique for periods of fifteen days, it was rented to Air Madagascar on 19 April 1967 whilst retaining its original registration. Finally bought by Air Madagascar in July 1973, it was re-registered (5F-MRK) and used until its replacement by a Boeing 747 in March 1979. Taken back by Air France and re-registered (F-BLLB), it was rented in 1981 to Air Charter International, a sister company owned by the national French airline. Two years later it was bought by Libyan Arab Airlines and sent to Tripoli (5A-DLT). Having become the property of ZAS Airlines Egypt in 1986, it was sold for spare parts a year later to Boeing Military Airplane Co (the company's military wing) and sent to the storage site of Davis-Monthan AFB (Arizona) and finally scrapped in April 1991.

American Eagle

N402PA

American Eagle Airways Boeing 707-321B (c/n 18833/'N402PA'). First delivered to Pan Am on 17 February 1965 and named 'Jet Clipper Black Hawk', this plane was stored for several months at New York-JFK after being retired from service in 1979. Bought by the First Security Bank of Utah in January 1980, it was rented the following month to Militair, which became American Eagle Airways when the plane was delivered in March 1980. Used until March 1981, it was bought by a bank when American Eagle went bankrupt and was finally sold to Boeing for spare parts as part of the KC-135 upgrade program. Militair, was created in 1979 and received its first Boeing 707 in February 1980. In March the following year it was re-named American Eagle, an airline initially specialising in military charter flights between Germany and the United States. It began, starting in March 1981, charter and civil flights and finally, regular flights in May the same year, a few days before being declared bankrupt!

POINTAIR

F-BSGT

Pointair Boeing 707-321B (c/n 18837/''F-BSGT'). Delivered to Pan Am on 17 March 1965 (N406PA), this aircraft would have four different names during its career with this airline, a career that ended in 1978: 'Jet Clipper Kingfisher', 'JCI Early Bird' during the Telstar satellite tests, 'JCI 'Sverige (March-April 1977) and once more 'Jet Clipper Kingfisher'. Bought by the French airline SATT on 28 June 1978, it was rented to Aerotour in April 1980 then bought on 23 October the same year by the Le Point association and became Point Air in April 1981, it was rented to Minerve in August 1981. Retried from service and stored at Orly in June 1984, it was bought by an Equator company and rented to Naganagini, a Burkina Faso airline (XT-ABZ) from February 1987 to October 1990 when it was finally bought for spare parts for the upgrade of the KC-135. Founded by the Le Point tour operator at the end of 1980, this airline, which became Point Air in April the following year, used two Boeing 707-321B and a 336C (rented in March 1984 and registered in Burkina Faso), until March 1987. They were replaced by the Douglas DC-8 until December of this same year, when it was taken over by Minerve.

70

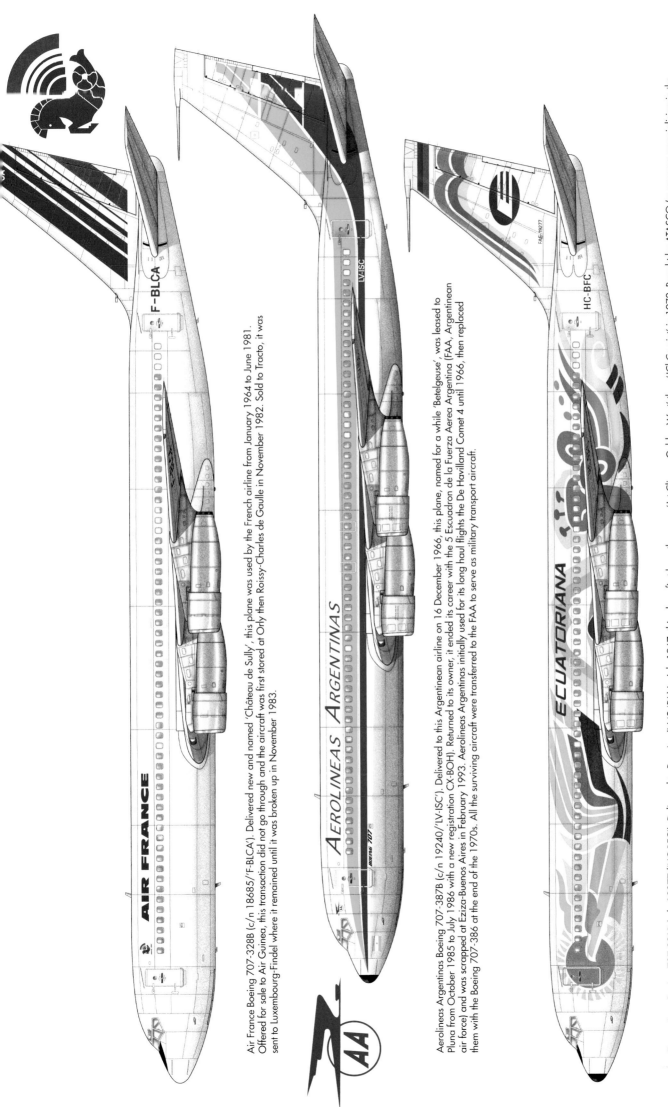

F-BLCA

AIR FRANCE

Air France Boeing 707-328B (c/n 18685/'F-BLCA'). Delivered new and named 'Château de Sully', this plane was used by the French airline from January 1964 to June 1981. Offered for sale to Air Guinea, this transaction did not go through and the aircraft was first stored at Orly then Roissy-Charles de Gaulle in November 1982. Sold to Tracto, it was sent to Luxembourg-Findel where it remained until it was broken up in November 1983.

LV-ISC

AEROLINEAS ARGENTINAS

BOEING 707

Aerolineas Argentinas Boeing 707-387B (c/n 19240/'LV-ISC'). Delivered to this Argentinean airline on 16 December 1966, this plane, named for a while 'Betelgeuse', was leased to Pluna from October 1985 to July 1986 with a new registration CX-BOH). Returned to its owner, it ended its career with the 5 Escuadron de la Fuerza Aerea Argentina (FAA, Argentinean air force) and was scrapped at Eziza-Buenos Aires in February 1993. Aerolineas Argentinas initially used for its long haul flights the De Havilland Comet 4 until 1966, then replaced them with the Boeing 707-386 at the end of the 1970s. All the surviving aircraft were transferred to the FAA to serve as military transport aircraft.

HC-BFC

FAE-19277

ECUATORIANA

Ecuatoriana Boeing 707-321B (c/n 19277/'HC-BFC'). Delivered to Pan Am (N424PA) in July 1967, this plane first bore the name 'Jet Clipper Golden West' then 'JCI Comjet' in 1972. Bought by ATASCO (a company specialising in the sale and maintenance of planes) in March 1978, it was rented the following month to Ecuatoriana and bore, as well as its registration (HC-BFC), a military serial derived from the constructor number (FAE 19277). Named successively, 'Mandbi' then 'Chimborazo', it was used until the Ecuador government suspended the airline's activities in March 1994. The Compania Ecuatoriana de Aviacion was founded in 1974 and began by renting a first Boeing 707-321B in September 1976, which was followed by four others as well as a Douglas DC-10. This 'psychedelic' livery, one of the most spectacular borne by a Boeing 707 was in fact inspired by traditional American Indian art and was only used by this aircraft at the beginning of the 1980s.

71

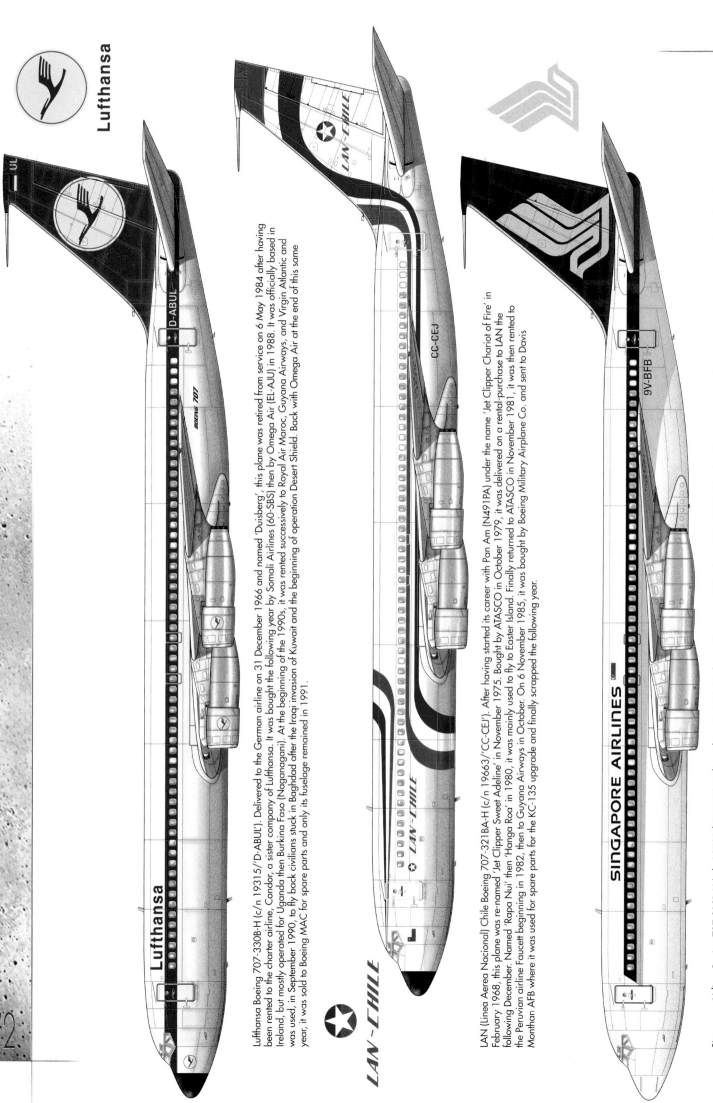

Lufthansa

LAN-CHILE

SINGAPORE AIRLINES

Lufthansa Boeing 707-330B-H (c/n 19315/'D-ABUI'). Delivered to the German airline on 31 December 1966 and named 'Duisberg', this plane was retired from service on 6 May 1984 after having been rented to the charter airline, Condor, a sister company of Lufthansa. It was bought the following year by Omega Air (EL-AJU) in 1988. It was officially based in Ireland, but mostly operated for Uganda then Burkina Faso (Naganagani). At the beginning of the 1990s, it was rented successively to Royal Air Maroc, Guyana Airways, and Virgin Atlantic and was used, in September 1990, to fly back civilians stuck in Baghdad after the Iraqi invasion of Kuwait and the beginning of operation Desert Shield. Back with Omega Air at the end of this same year, it was sold to Boeing MAC for spare parts and only its fuselage remained in 1991.

LAN (Linea Aerea Nacional) Chile Boeing 707-321BA-H (c/n 19663/'CC-CEJ'). After having started its career with Pan Am (N491PA) under the name 'Jet Clipper Chariot of Fire' in February 1968, this plane was re-named 'Jet Clipper Sweet Adeline' in November 1975. Bought by ATASCO in October 1979, it was delivered on a rental-purchase to LAN the following December. Named 'Rapa Nui' then 'Hanga Roa' in 1980, it was mainly used to fly to Easter Island. Finally returned to ATASCO in November 1981, it was then rented to the Peruvian airline Faucett beginning in 1982, then to Guyana Airways in October. On 6 November 1985, it was bought by Boeing Military Airplane Co. and sent to Davis Monthan AFB where it was used for spare parts for the KC-135 upgrade and finally scrapped the following year.

Singapore Airlines Boeing 707-312B-H (c/n 19738/'9V-BFB'). Delivered new to MSA (Malaysia Singapore Airlines) on 3 July 1968, this aircraft was re-registered '9V-BFB' on 30 June 1972 and transferred in October of the same year to Singapore Airlines after the Singapore government disbanded MSA. The new airline completed its 707 fleet with three extra cargo aircraft in 1976-1977, he passenger flights being carried out at this time by the Boeing 747 and the DC-10.

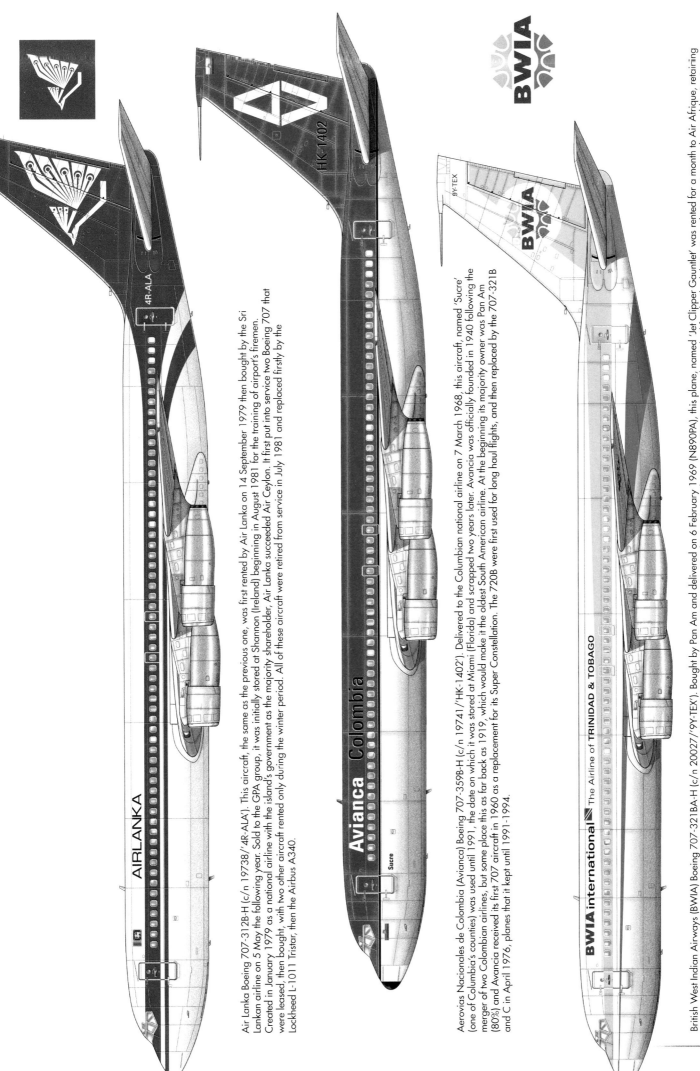

AIRLANKA

4R-ALA

Air Lanka Boeing 707-312B-H (c/n 19738//4R-ALA). This aircraft, the same as the previous one, was first rented by Air Lanka on 14 September 1979 then bought by the Sri Lankan airline on 5 May the following year. Sold to the GPA group, it was initially stored at Shannon (Ireland) beginning in August 1981 for the training of airport's firemen. Created in January 1979 as a national airline with the island's government as the majority shareholder, Air Lanka succeeded Air Ceylon. It first put into service two Boeing 707 that were leased, then bought, with two other aircraft rented only during the winter period. All of these aircraft were retired from service in July 1981 and replaced firstly by the Lockheed L-1011 Tristar, then the Airbus A340.

HK-1402

Avianca Colombia

Sucre

Aerovias Nacionales de Colombia (Avianca) Boeing 707-359B-H (c/n 19741/'HK-1402'). Delivered to the Columbian national airline on 7 March 1968, this aircraft, named 'Sucre' (one of Columbia's counties) was used until 1991, the date on which it was stored at Miami (Florida) and scrapped two years later. Avianca was officially founded in 1940 following the merger of two Colombian airlines, but some place this as far back as 1919, which would make it the oldest South American airline. At the beginning its majority owner was Pan Am (80%) and Avancia received its first 707 aircraft in 1960 as a replacement for its Super Constellation. The 720B were first used for long haul flights, and then replaced by the 707-321B and C in April 1976, planes that it kept until 1991-1994.

9Y-TEX

BWIA international ✈ The Airline of **TRINIDAD & TOBAGO**

British West Indian Airways (BWIA) Boeing 707-321BA-H (c/n 20027//9Y-TEX'). Bought by Pan Am and delivered on 6 February 1969 (N890PA), this plane, named 'Jet Clipper Gauntlet' was rented for a month to Air Afrique, retaining its original livery with only the renting airline's name on the fuselage. Sold to BWIA on 16 January 1976, it remained in service until January 1983. It was used a test bed for the 'hush kit' noise reducing systems and was sold to Boeing MAC on 18 October 1985 for spare parts and was finally destroyed in 1991. BWIA was initially 90% owned by the government of Trinidad and Tobago had its capital completely nationalised in 1976. It first used the BOAC supplied Boeing 707 before buying several, keeping them until 1983.

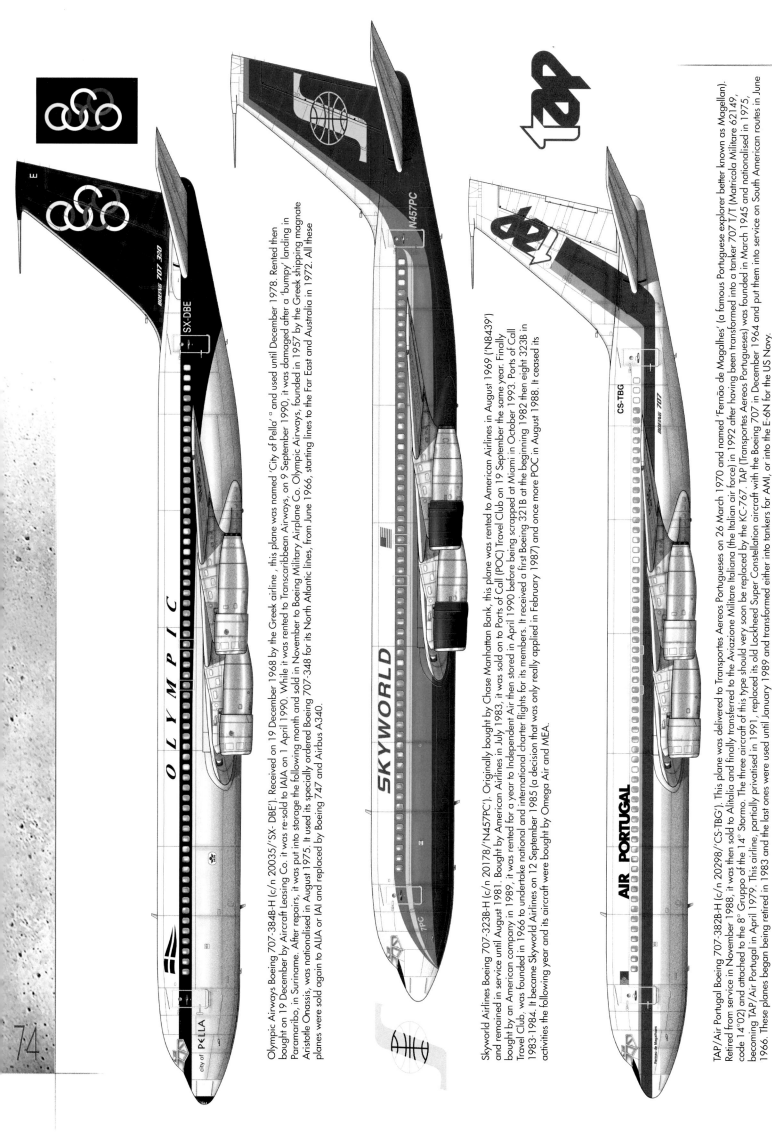

OLYMPIC

BOEING 707 320

SX-DBE

city of PELLA

SKYWORLD

N457PC

7PC

AIR PORTUGAL

BOEING 707

CS-TBG

Fernão de Magalhães

Olympic Airways Boeing 707-384B-H (c/n 20035/'SX- DBE'). Received on 19 December 1968 by the Greek airline, this plane was named 'City of Pella' " and used until December 1978. Rented then bought on 19 December by Aircraft Leasing Co. it was re-sold to IAIA on 1 April 1990. While it was rented to Transcaribbean Airways, on 9 September 1990, it was damaged after a 'bumpy' landing in Paramaribo, in Suriname. After repairs, it was put into storage the following month and sold in November to Boeing Military Airplane Co. Olympic Airways, founded in 1957 by the Greek shipping magnate Aristotle Onassis, was nationalised in August 1975. It used its specially ordered Boeing 707-348 for its North Atlantic lines, from June 1966, starting lines to the Far East and Australia in 1972. All these planes were sold again to ALIA or IAI and replaced by Boeing 747 and Airbus A340.

Skyworld Airlines Boeing 707-323B-H (c/n 20178/'N457PC'). Originally bought by Chase Manhattan Bank, this plane was rented to American Airlines in August 1969 ('N8439') and remained in service until August 1981. Bought by American Airlines in July 1983, it was sold on to Ports of Call (POC) Travel Club on 19 September the same year. Finally bought by an American company in 1989, it was rented for a year to Independent Air then stored in April 1990 before being scrapped at Miami in October 1993. Ports of Call Travel Club, was founded in 1966 to undertake national and international charter flights for its members. It received a first Boeing 321B at the beginning 1982 then eight 323B in 1983-1984. It became Skyworld Airlines on 12 September 1985 (a decision that was only really applied in February 1987) and once more POC in August 1988. It ceased its activities the following year and its aircraft were bought by Omega Air and MEA.

TAP/Air Portugal Boeing 707-382B-H (c/n 20298/'CS-TBG'). This plane was delivered to Transportes Aereos Portugueses on 26 March 1970 and named 'Fernão de Magalhes' (a famous Portuguese explorer better known as Magellan). Retired from service in November 1988, it was then sold to Alitalia and finally transferred to the Aviazione Militare Italiana (the Italian air force) in 1992 after having been transformed into a tanker 707 T/T (Matricola Militare 62149, code 14°02) and attached to the 8° Gruppo of the 14° Stormo. The three aircraft of this type should very soon be replaced by the KC-767. TAP (Transportes Aereos Portugueses) was founded in March 1945 and nationalised in 1975, becoming TAP/Air Portugal in April 1979. This airline, partially privatised in 1991, replaced its old Lockheed Super Constellation aircraft with the Boeing 707 in December 1964 and put them into service on South American routes in June 1966. These planes began being retired in 1983 and the last ones were used until January 1989 and transformed either into tankers for AMI, or into the E-6N for the US Navy.

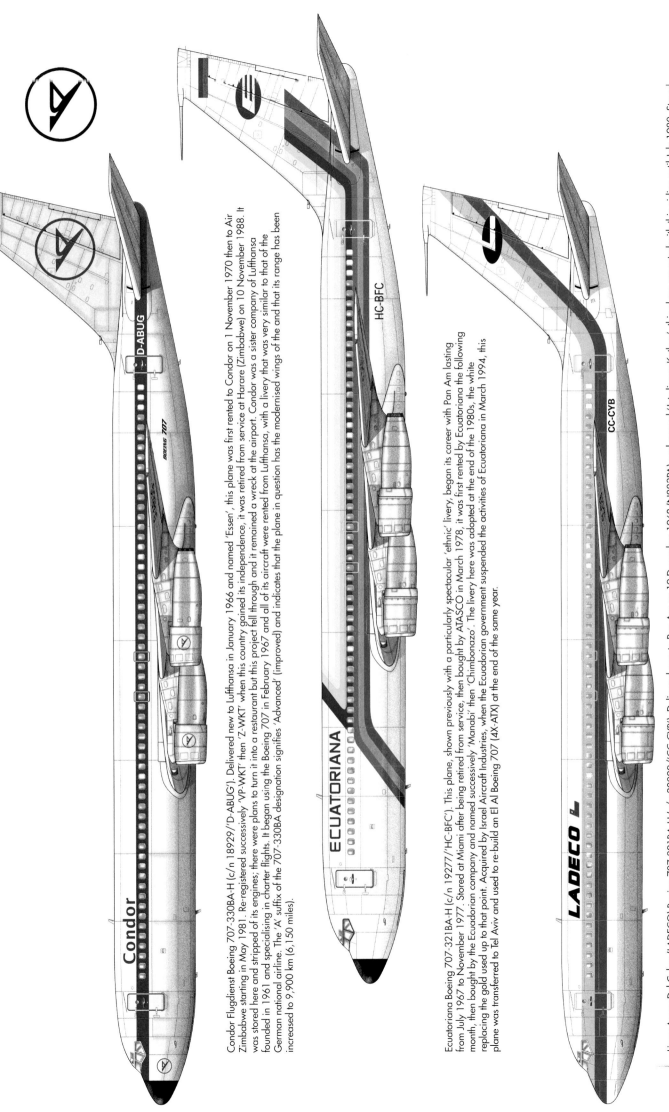

Condor

D-ABUG

BOEING 707

Condor Flugdienst Boeing 707-330BA-H (c/n 18929/'D-ABUG'). Delivered new to Lufthansa in January 1966 and named 'Essen', this plane was first rented to Condor on 1 November 1970 then to Air Zimbabwe starting in May 1981. Re-registered successively 'VP-WKT' then 'Z-WKT' when this country gained its independence, it was retired from service at Harare (Zimbabwe) on 10 November 1988. It was stored here and stripped of its engines; there were plans to turn it into a restaurant but this project fell through and it remained a wreck at the airport. Condor was a sister company of Lufthansa founded in 1961 and specialising in charter flights. It began using the Boeing 707 in February 1967 and all of its aircraft were rented from Lufthansa, with a livery that was very similar to that of the German national airline. The 'A' suffix of the 707-330BA designation signifies 'Advanced' (improved) and indicates that the plane in question has the modernised wings of the and that its range has been increased to 9,900 km (6,150 miles).

ECUATORIANA

HC-BFC

Ecuatoriana Boeing 707-321BA-H (c/n 19277/'HC-BFC'). This plane, shown previously with a particularly spectacular 'ethnic' livery, began its career with Pan Am lasting from July 1967 to November 1977. Stored at Miami after being retired from service, then bought by ATASCO in March 1978, it was first rented by Ecuatoriana the following month, then bought by the Ecuadorian company and named successively 'Manabi' then 'Chimbonazo'. The livery here was adopted at the end of the 1980s, the white replacing the gold used up to that point. Acquired by Israel Aircraft Industries, when the Ecuadorian government suspended the activities of Ecuatoriana in March 1994, this plane was transferred to Tel Aviv and used to re-build an El Al Boeing 707 (4X-ATX) at the end of the same year.

LADECO L

CC-CYB

Linea Aerea Del Cobre (LADECO) Boeing 707-321BA-H (c/n 20022/'CC-CYB'). Delivered new to Pan Am on 19 December 1968 (N883PA) and named 'Jet clipper Kathay', this plane operated with this airline until July 1980. Stored successively at Miami (Florida), Marana (Arizona), Stansted (Great Britain) and once more at Marana, it was sold to Global International Airlines in May 1983. Taken back by Pan Am in September of the same year, it was sold to Falcon Aircraft Conversions in August the following year for use with the New World Travel Club. Equipped with 'hush kits' in January 1985 whilst flying under the colours Kinshasa Airways, it was rented to LADECO at the end of March 1989 until December 1994. Next rented to JARO International, it was used from September to November 1996 by the singer Michael Jackson for a world tour, bearing at this time the logo of Kingdom Entertainment. Registered in Zaire (9Q-CWQ), it was still visible at Damascus airport (Syria) in 2007. LADECO was founded in September 1958 and first used a 707-327C in December 1988, then this 321B the following year. This Chilean airline, a large part of which was owned at the beginning by Iberia, was absorbed by LAN in 2001.

75

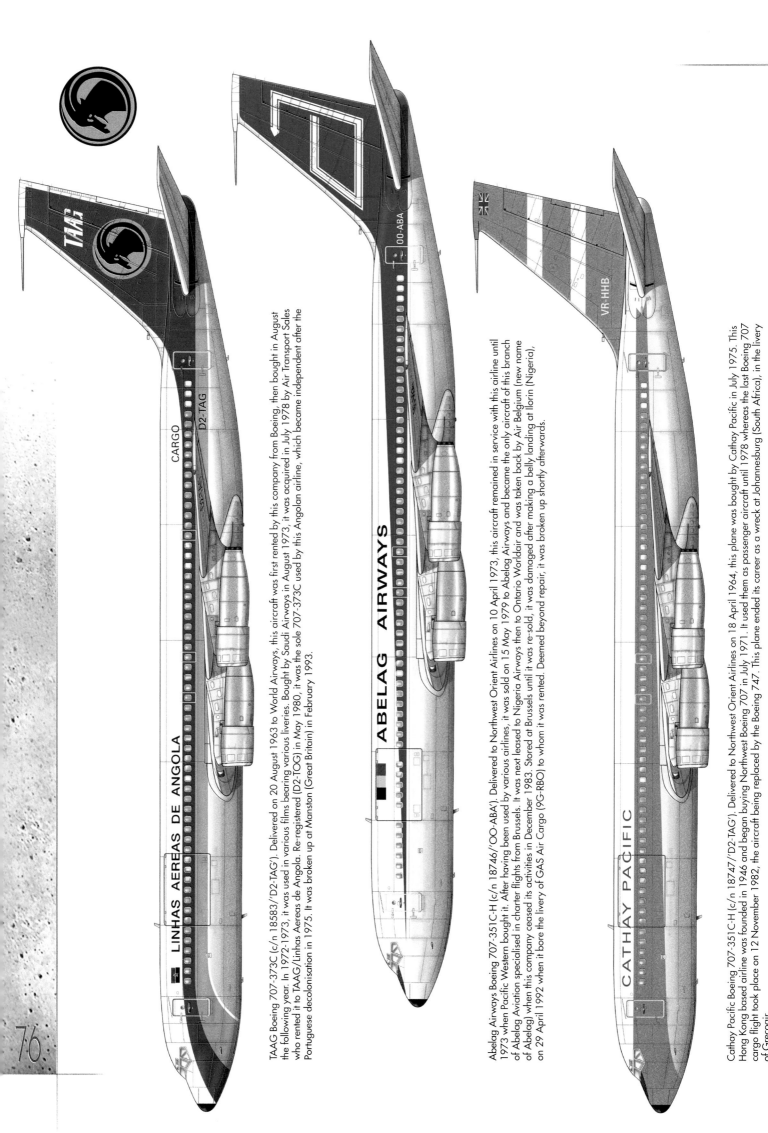

LINHAS AEREAS DE ANGOLA

CARGO

D2-TAG

TAAG Boeing 707-373C (c/n 18583/'D2-TAG'). Delivered on 20 August 1963 to World Airways, this aircraft was first rented by this company from Boeing, then bought in August the following year. In 1972-1973, it was used in various films bearing various liveries. Bought by Saudi Airways in August 1973, it was acquired in July 1978 by Air Transport Sales who rented it to TAAG/Linhas Aereas de Angola. Re-registered (D2-TOG) in May 1980, it was the sole 707-373C used by this Angolan airline, which became independent after the Portuguese decolonisation in 1975. It was broken up at Manston (Great Britain) in February 1993.

ABELAG AIRWAYS

OO-ABA

Abelag Airways Boeing 707-351C-H (c/n 18746/'OO-ABA'). Delivered to Northwest Orient Airlines on 10 April 1973, this aircraft remained in service with this airline until 1973 when Pacific Western bought it. After having been used by various airlines, it was sold on 15 May 1979 to Abelag Airways and became the only aircraft of this branch of Abelag Aviation specialised in charter flights from Brussels. It was next leased to Nigeria Airways then to Ontario Worldair and was taken back by Air Belgium (new name of Abelag) when this company ceased its activities in December 1983. Stored at Brussels until it was re-sold, it was damaged after making a belly landing at Ilorin (Nigeria), on 29 April 1992 when it bore the livery of GAS Air Cargo (9G-RBO) to whom it was rented. Deemed beyond repair, it was broken up shortly afterwards.

CATHAY PACIFIC

VR-HHB

Cathay Pacific Boeing 707-351C-H (c/n 18747/'D2-TAG'). Delivered to Northwest Orient Airlines on 18 April 1964, this plane was bought by Cathay Pacific in July 1975. This Hong Kong based airline was founded in 1946 and began buying Northwest Boeing 707 in July 1971. It used them as passenger aircraft until 1978 whereas the last Boeing 707 cargo flight took place on 12 November 1982, the aircraft being replaced by the Boeing 747. This plane ended its career as a wreck at Johannesburg (South Africa), in the livery of Grecoair.

76

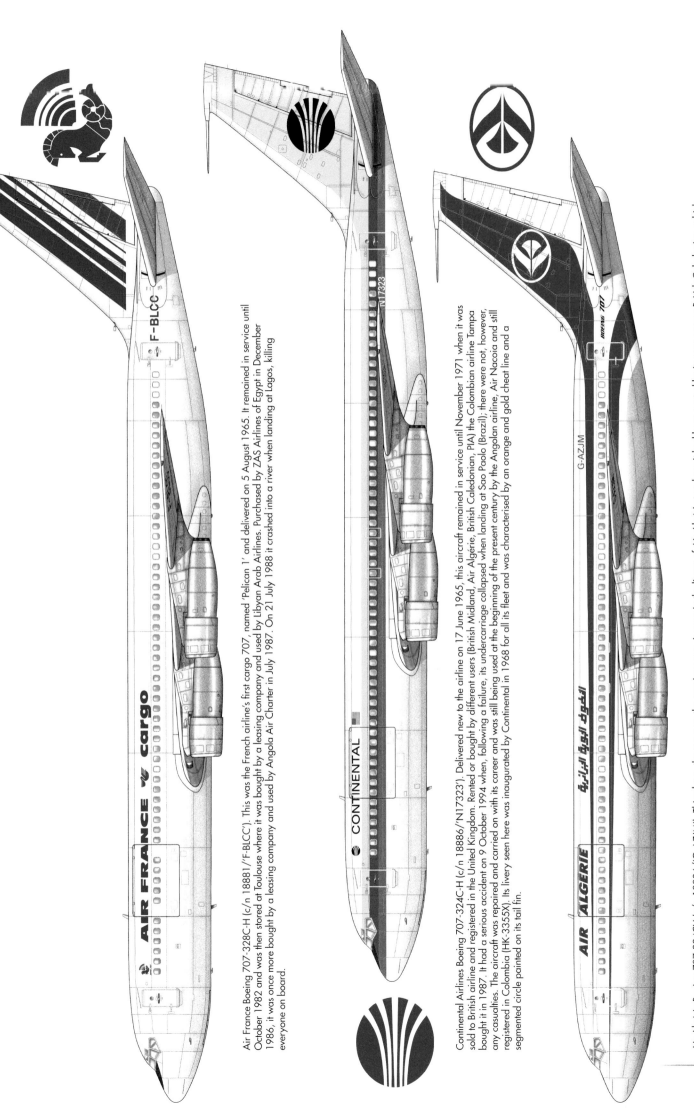

AIR FRANCE cargo

F-BLCC

Air France Boeing 707-328C-H (c/n 18881/'F-BLCC'). This was the French airline's first cargo 707, named 'Pelican 1' and delivered on 5 August 1965. It remained in service until October 1982 and was then stored at Toulouse where it was bought by a leasing company and used by Libyan Arab Airlines. Purchased by ZAS Airlines of Egypt in December 1986, it was once more bought by a leasing company and used by Angola Air Charter in July 1987. On 21 July 1988 it crashed into a river when landing at Lagos, killing everyone on board.

CONTINENTAL

N17323

Continental Airlines Boeing 707-324C-H (c/n 18886/'N17323'). Delivered new to the airline on 17 June 1965, this aircraft remained in service until November 1971 when it was sold to British airline and registered in the United Kingdom. Rented or bought by different users (British Midland, Air Algérie, British Caledonian, PIA) the Colombian airline Tampa bought it in 1987. It had a serious accident on 9 October 1994 when, following a failure, its undercarriage collapsed when landing at Sao Paolo (Brazil); there were not, however, any casualties. The aircraft was repaired and carried on with its career and was still being used at the beginning of the present century by the Angolan airline, Air Nacoia and still registered in Colombia (HK-3355X). Its livery seen here was inaugurated by Continental in 1968 for all its fleet and was characterised by an orange and gold cheat line and a segmented circle painted on its tail fin.

AIR ALGERIE الخطوط الجوية الجزائرية

BOEING 707

G-AZJM

AIR ALGERIE

Air Algérie Boeing 707-324CH (c/n 18886/'G-AZJM'). This plane, the same as the previous one, is seen in the livery of Air Algérie to whom it had been rented by its new owner, British Caledonian, which explains its British registration. It was once more leased to the Algerian airline from 8 July 1978 to 15 January 1980, still bearing the same registration. This was the only 707-324C used by Air Algérie, the first of these four-engined aircraft being one that was rented to PIA in 1972 after the airline was nationalised. All of the Boeing 707 was initially rented to transport pilgrims to Mecca, then for cargo flights to Europe, North and East Africa and the Middle East.

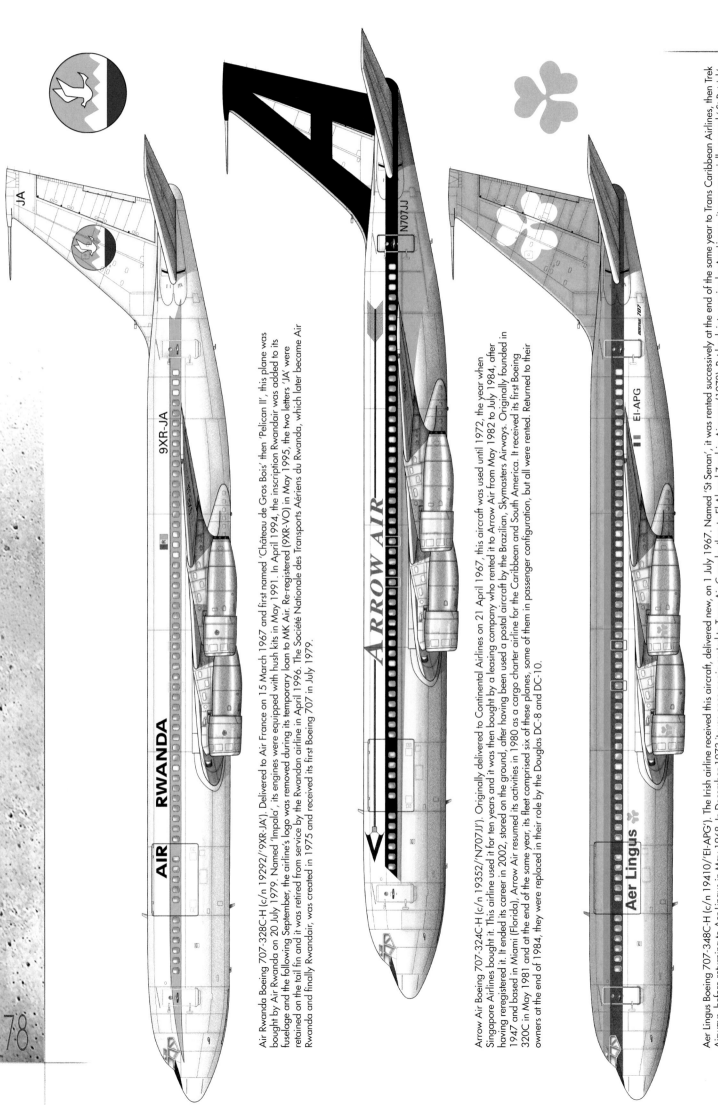

Air Rwanda Boeing 707-328C-H (c/n 19292/'9XR-JA'). Delivered to Air France on 15 March 1967 and first named 'Château de Gros Bois' then 'Pelican II', this plane was bought by Air Rwanda on 20 July 1979. Named 'Impala', its engines were equipped with hush kits in May 1991. In April 1994, the inscription Rwandair was added to its fuselage and the following September, the airline's logo was removed during its temporary loan to MK Air. Re-registered (9XR-VO) in May 1995, the two letters 'JA' were retained on the tail fin and it was retired from service by the Rwandan airline in April 1996. The Société Nationale des Transports Aériens du Rwanda, which later became Air Rwanda and finally Rwandair, was created in 1975 and received its first Boeing 707 in July 1979.

Arrow Air Boeing 707-324C-H (c/n 19352/'N707JJ'). Originally delivered to Continental Airlines on 21 April 1967, this aircraft was used until 1972, the year when Singapore Airlines bought it. This airline used it for ten years and it was then bought by a leasing company who rented it to Arrow Air from May 1982 to July 1984, after having reregistered it. It ended its career in 2002, stored on the ground, when it had been used a postal aircraft by the Brazilian, Skymasters Airways. Originally founded in 1947 and based in Miami (Florida), Arrow Air resumed its activities in 1980 as a cargo charter airline for the Caribbean and South America. It received its first Boeing 320C in May 1981 and at the end of the same year, its fleet comprised six of these planes, some of them in passenger configuration, but all were rented. Returned to their owners at the end of 1984, they were replaced in their role by the Douglas DC-8 and DC-10.

Aer Lingus Boeing 707-348C-H (c/n 19410/'EI-APG'). The Irish airline received this aircraft, delivered new, on 1 July 1967. Named 'St Senan', it was rented successively at the end of the same year to Trans Caribbean Airlines, then Trek Airways, before returning to Aer Lingus in May 1968. In December 1973 it was once again rented to Trans Air Canada, then to El Al and Zambia Airways (1978). Put back into service by Aer Lingus, it was especially named ' St Patrick' for Pope John-Paul II's visit to Ireland on 29 September to 1 October 1979. In June 1981, its sale to United African Airlines fell through and it was stored at Dublin. After two other attempts to sell it failed, it was rented for three months to Libyan Arab Airlines March 1981 and returned to Dublin in May. Bought by Sudan Airways ('ST-AIM') on 1 September 1982, it crashed into the Nile a few kilometres from Khartoum (Sudan) on the 10th of the same month whilst on route for Saudi Arabia. The aircraft was completely destroyed but the eleven-man crew managed to escape.

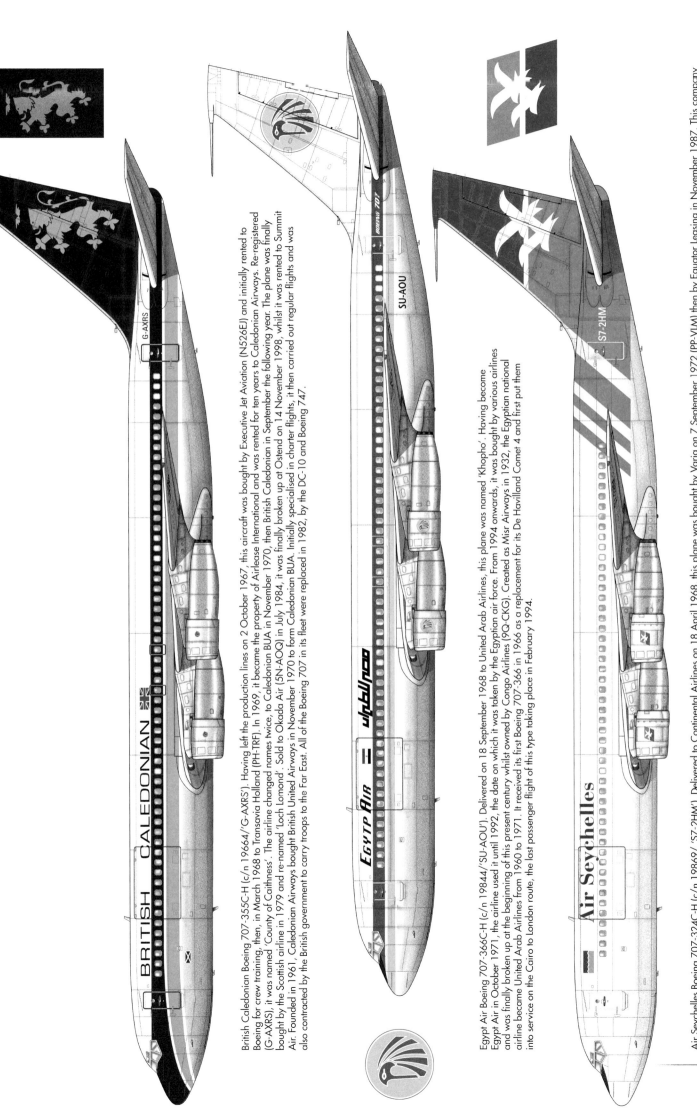

BRITISH CALEDONIAN

G-AXRS

British Caledonian Boeing 707-355C-H (c/n 19664/'G-AXRS'). Having left the production lines on 2 October 1967, this aircraft was bought by Executive Jet Aviation (N526EJ) and initially rented to Boeing for crew training, then, in March 1968 to Transavia Holland (PH-TRF). In 1969, it became the property of Airlease International and was rented for ten years to Caledonian Airways. Re-registered (G-AXRS), it was named 'County of Caithness'. The airline changed names twice, to Caledonian BUA in November 1970, then British Caledonian in September the following year. The plane was finally bought by the Scottish airline in 1979 and re-named 'Loch Lomond'. Sold to Okada Air (5N-AOQ) in July 1984, it was finally broken up at Ostend on 14 November 1998, whilst it was rented to Summit Air. Founded in 1961, Caledonian Airways bought British United Airways in November 1970 to form Caledonian BUA. Initially specialised in charter flights, it then carried out regular flights and was also contracted by the British government to carry troops to the Far East. All of the Boeing 707 in its fleet were replaced in 1982, by the DC-10 and Boeing 747.

EGYPT AIR

BOEING 707

SU-AOU

Egypt Air Boeing 707-366C-H (c/n 19844/'SU-AOU'). Delivered on 18 September 1968 to United Arab Airlines, this plane was named 'Khopho'. Having become Egypt Air in October 1971, the airline used it until 1992, the date on which it was taken by the Egyptian air force. From 1994 onwards, it was bought by various airlines and was finally broken up at the beginning of this present century whilst owned by Congo Airlines (9Q-CKG). Created as Misr Airways in 1932, the Egyptian national airline became United Arab Airlines from 1960 to 1971. It received its first Boeing 707-366 in 1966 as a replacement for its De Havilland Comet 4 and first put them into service on the Cairo to London route, the last passenger flight of this type taking place in February 1994.

Air Seychelles

S7-2HM

Air Seychelles Boeing 707-324C-H (c/n 19869/ 'S7-2HM'). Delivered to Continental Airlines on 18 April 1968, this plane was bought by Varig on 7 September 1972 (PP-VLM) then by Equator Leasing in November 1987. This company equipped it with hushkits and leased it to Air Seychelles (S7-2HM) from January 1988 to October 1989. Transformed into a cargo in 1990, it ended its career stored at Luanda (Angola) in 2002, in the livery of Angola Air Charter (D2-TOK). Founded in 1976, Seychelles Airways became Air Seychelles in 1979 and used only two rented 707-324C, which were replaced in October 1989 by a sole Boeing 767 for its long haul flights.

79

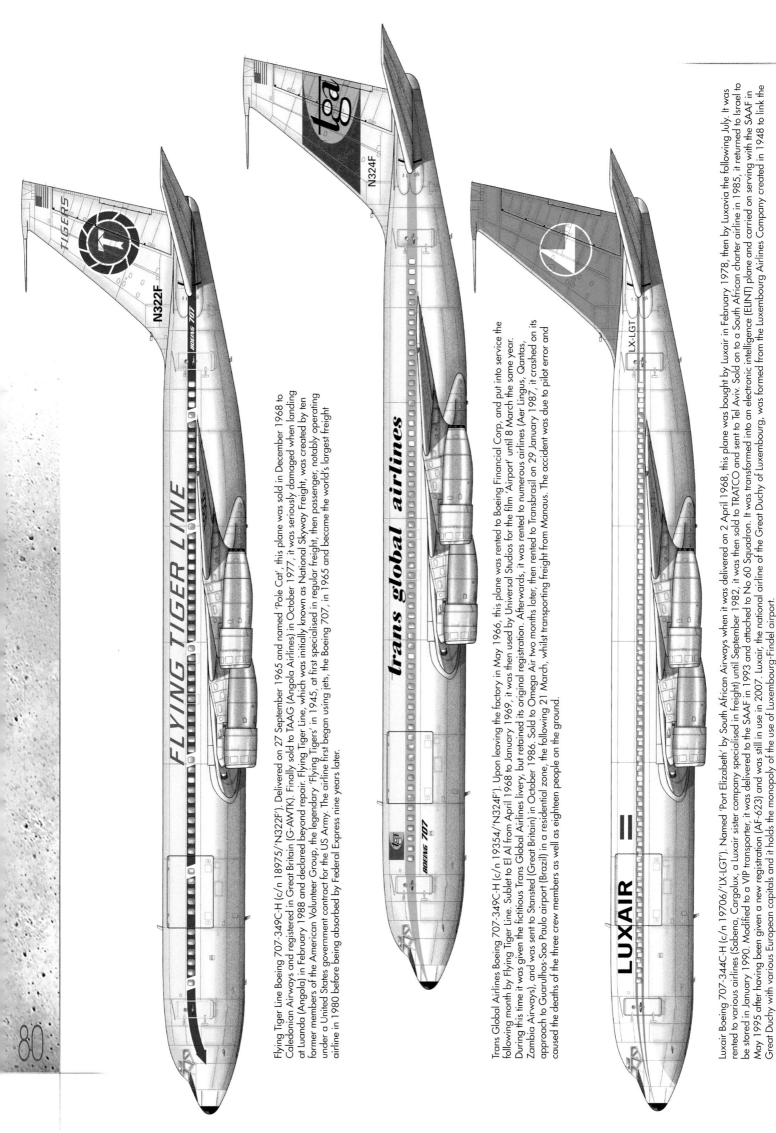

FLYING TIGER LINE

N322F

BOEING 707

TIGERS

Flying Tiger Line Boeing 707-349C-H (c/n 18975/'N322F'). Delivered on 27 September 1965 and named 'Pole Cat', this plane was sold in December 1968 to Caledonian Airways and registered in Great Britain (G-AWTK). Finally sold to TAAG (Angola Airlines) in October 1977, it was seriously damaged when landing at Luanda (Angola) in February 1988 and declared beyond repair. Flying Tiger Line, which was initially known as National Skyway Freight, was created by ten former members of the American Volunteer Group, the legendary 'Flying Tigers' in 1945, at first specialised in regular freight, then passenger, notably operating under a United States government contract for the US Army. The airline first began using jets, the Boeing 707, in 1965 and became the world's largest freight airline in 1980 before being absorbed by Federal Express nine years later.

trans global airlines

N324F

tga

BOEING 707

Trans Global Airlines Boeing 707-349C-H (c/n 19354/'N324F'). Upon leaving the factory in May 1966, this plane was rented to Boeing Financial Corp, and put into service the following month by Flying Tiger Line. Sublet to El Al from April 1968 to January 1969, it was then used by Universal Studios for the film 'Airport' until 8 March the same year. During this time it was given the fictitious Trans Global Airlines livery, but retained its original registration. Afterwards, it was rented to numerous airlines (Aer Lingus, Qantas, Zambia Airways), and was sent to Stansted (Great Britain) in October 1986. Sold to Omega Air two months later, then rented to Transbrasil on 29 January 1987, it crashed on its approach to Guarulhos-Sao Paulo airport (Brazil) in a residential zone, the following 21 March, whilst transporting freight from Manaus. The accident was due to pilot error and caused the deaths of the three crew members as well as eighteen people on the ground.

LUXAIR

LX-LGT

Luxair Boeing 707-344C-H (c/n 19706/'LX-LGT'). Named 'Port Elizabeth' by South African Airways when it was delivered on 2 April 1968, this plane was bought by Luxair in February 1978, then by Luxavia the following July. It was rented to various airlines (Sabena, Cargolux, a Luxair sister company specialised in freight) until September 1982, it was then sold to TRATCO and sent to Tel Aviv. Sold on to a South African charter airline in 1985, it returned to Israel to be stored in January 1990. Modified to a VIP transporter, it was delivered to the SAAF in 1993 and attached to No 60 Squadron. It was transformed into an electronic intelligence (ELINT) plane and carried on serving with the SAAF in May 1995 after having been given a new registration (AF-623) and was still in use in 2007. Luxair, the national airline of the Great Duchy of Luxembourg, was formed from the Luxembourg Airlines Company created in 1948 to link the Great Duchy with various European capitals and it holds the monopoly of the use of Luxembourg-Findel airport.

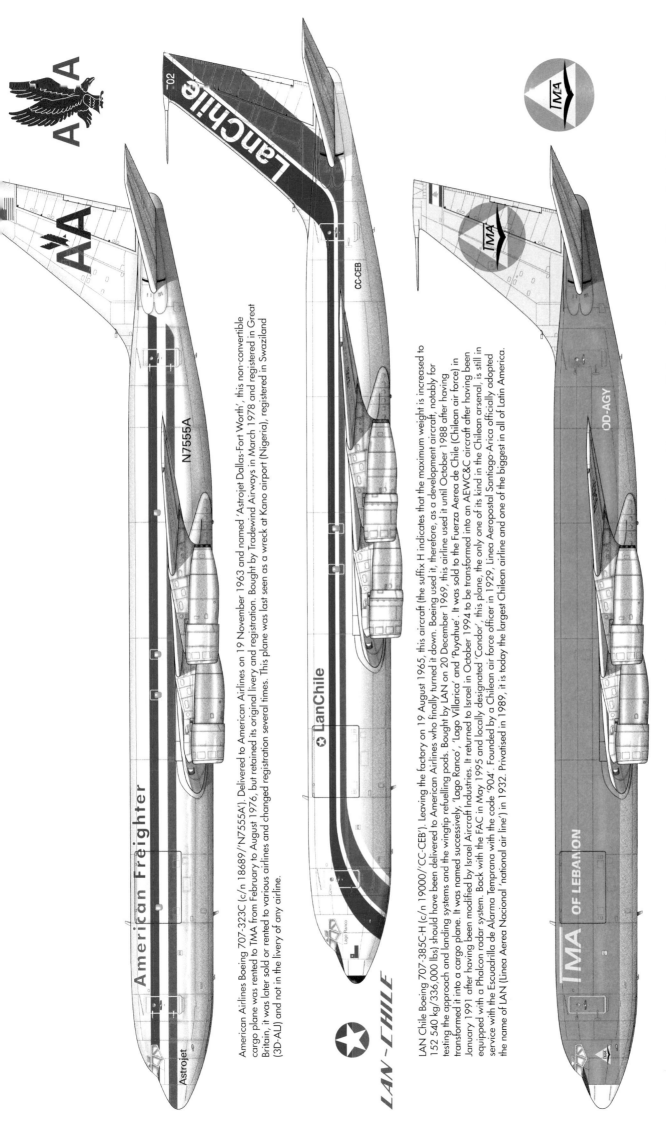

American Freighter

Astrojet

N7555A

American Airlines Boeing 707-323C (c/n 18689//N7555A'). Delivered to American Airlines on 19 November 1963 and named 'Astrojet Dallas-Fort Worth', this non-convertible cargo plane was rented to TMA from February to August 1976, but retained its original livery and registration. Bought by Tradewind Airways in March 1978 and registered in Great Britain, it was later sold or rented to various airlines and changed registration several times. This plane was last seen as a wreck at Kano airport (Nigeria), registered in Swaziland (3D-ALJ) and not in the livery of any airline.

LanChile

CC-CEB

LanChile

Lago Ranco

LAN-CHILE

LAN Chile Boeing 707-385C-H (c/n 19000//CC-CEB'). Leaving the factory on 19 August 1965, this aircraft (the suffix H indicates that the maximum weight is increased to 152 540 kg/336,000 lbs) should have been delivered to American Airlines who finally turned it down. Boeing used it, therefore, as a development aircraft, notably for testing the approach and landing systems and the wingtip refuelling pods. Bought by LAN on 20 December 1969, this airline used it until October 1988 after having transformed it into a cargo plane. It was named successively, 'Lago Ranco', 'Lago Villarica' and 'Puyahue'. It was sold to the Fuerza Aerea de Chile (Chilean air force) in January 1991 after having been modified by Israel Aircraft Industries. It returned to Israel in October 1994 to be transformed into an AEWC&C aircraft after having been equipped with a Phalcon radar system. Back with the FAC in May 1995 and locally designated 'Condor', this plane, the only one of its kind in the Chilean arsenal, is still in service with the Escuadrilla de Alarma Temprana with the code '904'. Founded by a Chilean air force officer in 1929, Linea Aeropostal Santiago-Arica officially adopted the name of LAN (Linea Aerea Nacional 'national air line') in 1932. Privatised in 1989, it is today the largest Chilean airline and one of the biggest in all of Latin America.

TMA OF LEBANON

OD-AGY

Trans Mediterranean Airways (TMA) Boeing 707-321C-H (c/n 19105//OD-AGY'). This aircraft began its career on 22 May 1966, when it was delivered to Braniff who painted it entirely yellow; all of its 707 fleet had a different colour. In 1971, it was rented to TMA who used it until 1980 after having transformed it into a non-convertible cargo. Rented to Golf Air in January 1981, it came back to TMA a month later and remained in service until March 1992 when Kuwait Airways leased it. Back once more with TMA during the summer of 1996, it was rented again by Kuwait at the end of 1996. Stored at Beirut, in remained there in the hope of an potential buyer; its current fate is not known with certitude. The Lebanon airline TMA was founded in 1953 and was specialised in freight transport, originally for the Arab-American petrol company Aramco. It began using jet aircraft in 1966 by buying a first Boeing 707-331C. After having been a very prosperous airline and one of the biggest specialising in airfreight, TMA experienced great difficulties during the Lebanese Civil War (1976-90), which left it on the verge of disappearing.

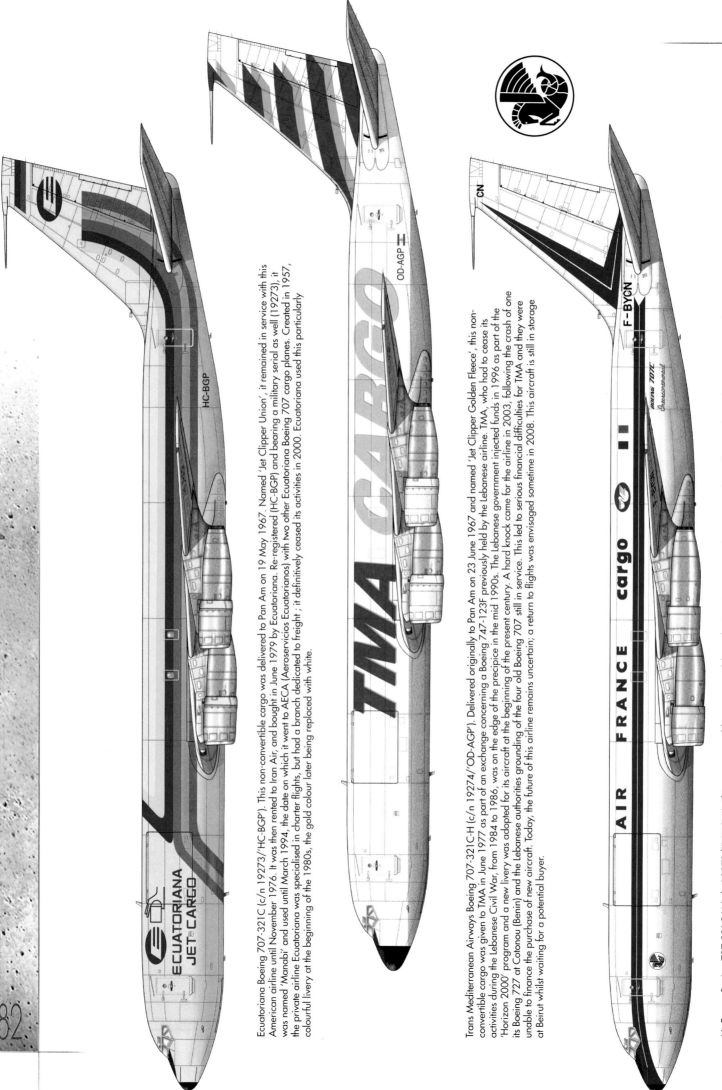

Ecuatoriana Boeing 707-321C (c/n 19273//HC-BGP). This non-convertible cargo was delivered to Pan Am on 19 May 1967. Named 'Jet Clipper Union', it remained in service with this American airline until November 1976. It was then rented to Iran Air, and bought in June 1979 by Ecuatoriana. Re-registered (HC-BGP) and bearing a military serial as well (19273), it was named 'Manabi' and used until March 1994, the date on which it went to AECA (Aeroservicios Ecuatorianos) with two other Ecuatoriana Boeing 707 cargo planes. Created in 1957, the private airline Ecuatoriana was specialised in charter flights, but had a branch dedicated to freight ; it definitively ceased its activities in 2000. Ecuatoriana used this particularly colourful livery at the beginning of the 1980s, the gold colour later being replaced with white.

Trans Mediterranean Airways Boeing 707-321C-H (c/n 19274//OD-AGP). Delivered originally to Pan Am on 23 June 1967 and named 'Jet Clipper Golden Fleece', this non-convertible cargo was given to TMA in June 1977 as part of an exchange concerning a Boeing 747-123F previously held by the Lebanese airline. TMA, who had to cease its activities during the Lebanese Civil War, from 1984 to 1986, was on the edge of the precipice in the mid 1990s. The Lebanese government injected funds in 1996 as part of the 'Horizon 2000' program and a new livery was adopted for its aircraft at the beginning of the present century. A hard knock came for the airline in 2003, following the crash of one its Boeing 727 at Cotonou (Benin) and the Lebanese authorities grounding of the four old Boeing 707 still in service. This led to serious financial difficulties for TMA and they were unable to finance the purchase of new aircraft. Today, the future of this airline remains uncertain; a return to flights was envisaged sometime in 2008. This aircraft is still in storage at Beirut whilst waiting for a potential buyer.

Air France Boeing 707-321C-H (c/n 19370//F-BYCN). This non-convertible cargo was delivered to Pan Am in November 1967 and initially named 'Jet Clipper Sovereign of the Seas' then 'Clipper Starlight' in 1977. Bought by Air France on 1 October 1975, it remained the property of the national French airline until November 1981 and was notably used for its Antilles network.

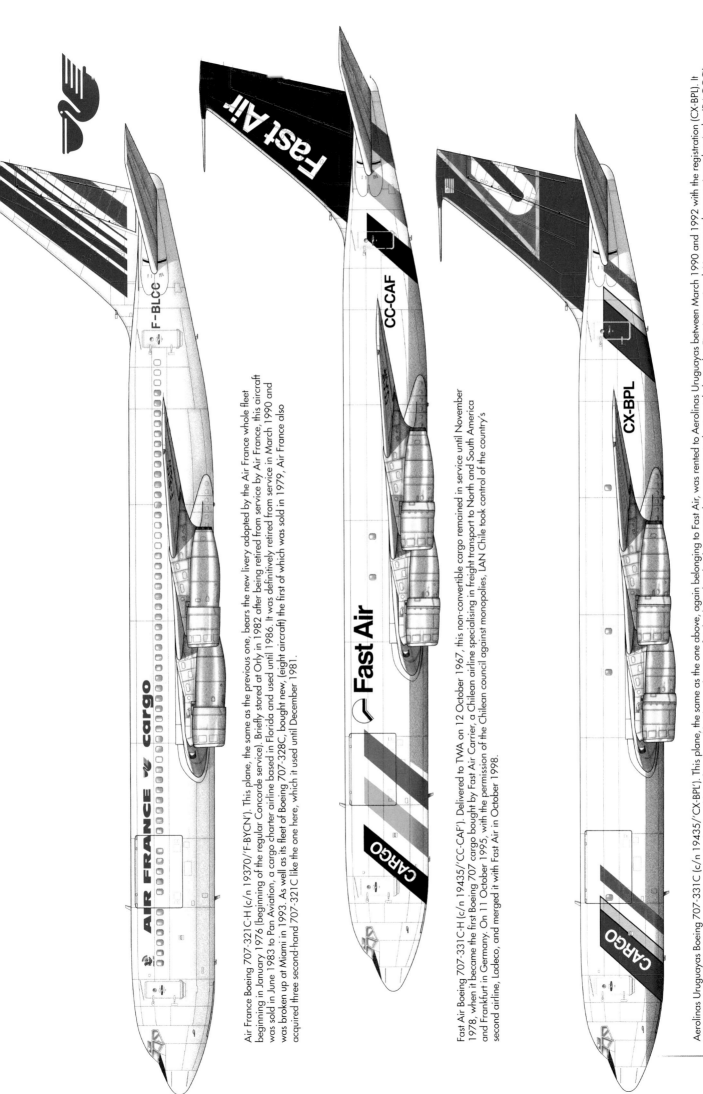

Air France Boeing 707-321C-H (c/n 19370/'F-BYCN'). This plane, the same as the previous one, bears the new livery adopted by the Air France whole fleet beginning in January 1976 (beginning of the regular Concorde service). Briefly stored at Orly in 1982 after being retired from service by Air France, this aircraft was sold in June 1983 to Pan Aviation, a cargo charter airline based in Florida and used until 1986. It was definitively retired from service in March 1990 and was broken up at Miami in 1993. As well as its fleet of Boeing 707-328C, bought new, (eight aircraft) the first of which was sold in 1979, Air France also acquired three second-hand 707-321C like the one here, which it used until December 1981.

Fast Air Boeing 707-331C-H (c/n 19435/'CC-CAF'). Delivered to TWA on 12 October 1967, this non-convertible cargo remained in service until November 1978, when it became the first Boeing 707 cargo bought by Fast Air Carrier, a Chilean airline specialising in freight transport to North and South America and Frankfurt in Germany. On 11 October 1995, with the permission of the Chilean council against monopolies, LAN Chile took control of the country's second airline, Ladeco, and merged it with Fast Air in October 1998.

Aerolinas Uruguayas Boeing 707-331C (c/n 19435/'CX-BPL'). This plane, the same as the one above, again belonging to Fast Air, was rented to Aerolinas Uruguayas between March 1990 and 1992 with the registration (CX-BPL). It ended its career on 16 January 1997, seriously damaged by a fire caused by the overheating of its brakes when landing at Kinshasa airport. At the time it belonged to First International Airways and was registered at Aruba (P4-OOC). Aerolinas Uruguayas, a Uruguayan airline specialising in freight, only had this one 707-331C used for regular flights to South America and the United States. This airline's activities were transferred to Aerovenca in June 1995 and ceased definitively shortly afterwards.

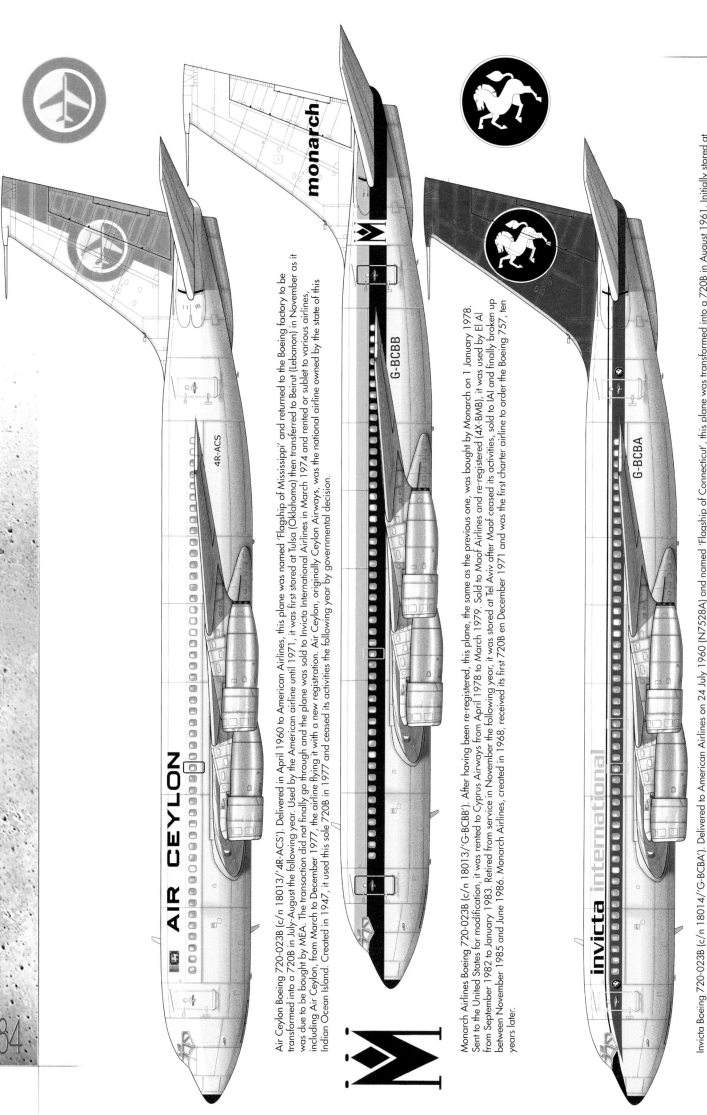

AIR CEYLON

4R-ACS

Air Ceylon Boeing 720-023B (c/n 18013/'4R-ACS'). Delivered in April 1960 to American Airlines, this plane was named 'Flagship of Mississippi' and returned to the Boeing factory to be transformed into a 720B in July-August the following year. Used by the American airline until 1971, it was first stored at Tulsa (Oklahoma) then transferred to Beirut (Lebanon) in November as it was due to be bought by MEA. The transaction did not finally go through and the plane was sold to Invicta International Airlines in March 1974 and rented or sublet to various airlines, including Air Ceylon, from March to December 1977, the airline flying it with a new registration. Air Ceylon, originally Ceylon Airways, was the national airline owned by the state of this Indian Ocean Island. Created in 1947, it used this sole 720B in 1977 and ceased its activities the following year by governmental decision.

monarch

G-BCBB

Monarch Airlines Boeing 720-023B (c/n 18013/'G-BCBB'). After having been re-registered, this plane, the same as the previous one, was bought by Monarch on 1 January 1978. Sent to the United States for modification, it was rented to Cyprus Airways from April 1978 to March 1979. Sold to Maof Airlines and re-registered (4X-BMB), it was used by El Al from September 1982 to January 1983. Retired from service in November the following year, it was stored at Tel Aviv after Maof ceased its activities, sold to IAI and finally broken up between November 1985 and June 1986. Monarch Airlines, created in 1968, received its first 720B en December 1971 and was the first charter airline to order the Boeing 757, ten years later.

invicta international

G-BCBA

Invicta Boeing 720-023B (c/n 18014/'G-BCBA'). Delivered to American Airlines on 24 July 1960 (N7528A) and named 'Flagship of Connecticut', this plane was transformed into a 720B in August 1961. Initially stored at Tulsa, then Beirut, as it was due to be sold to MEA, it was sent to Great Britain after the sale fell through and modified. Sold to Invicta and re-registered (G-BCBA), it was rented successively, sublet and finally stored at Luton and repainted in the Monarch livery, the airline that finally bought it in September 1977. Once more rented several times, it was sold to Maof Airlines in October 1981 and used by El Al the following year. First sold to IAI in November 1985, it was bought for spare parts in January 1986, first Omega Air, then by Boeing MAC. Invicta, a freight and passenger charter airline based in Great Britain, was founded in 1964 and merged with British Midland in 1968 but took back its name the following year. In 1973 it went through financial problems and European Ferries acquired 70 % of its capital. After having received two 720B in 1973, Invicta was sold to Universal Air Transport and disappeared in 1975.

84

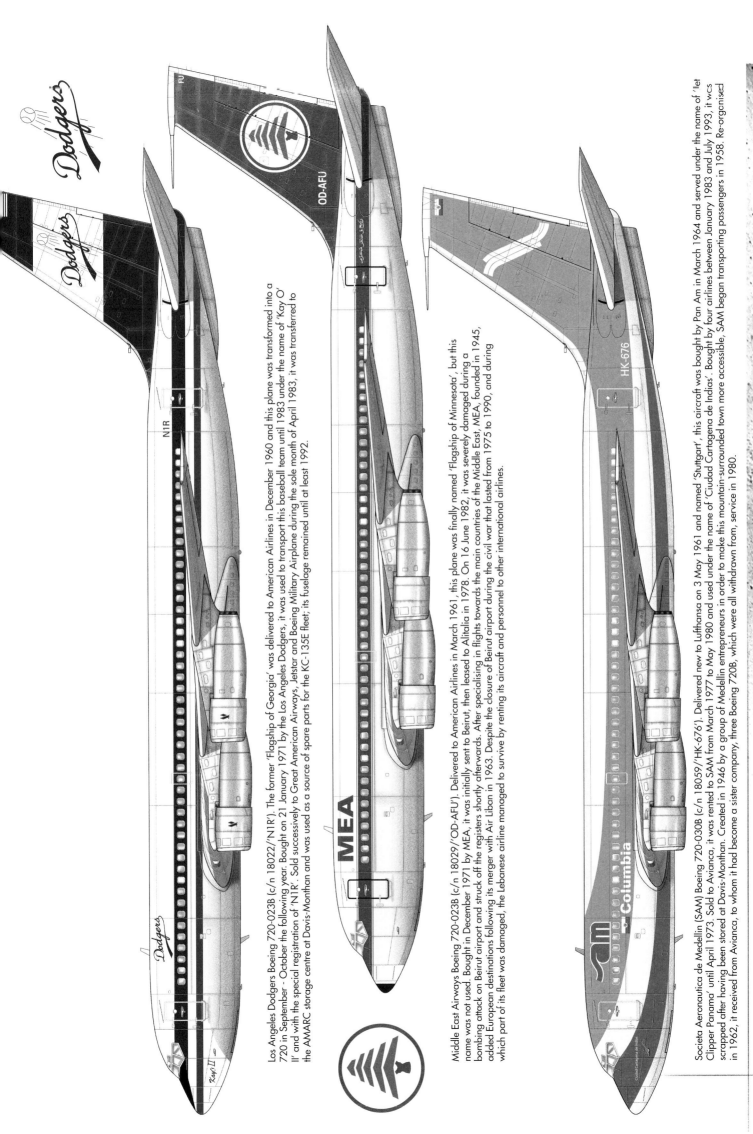

Los Angeles Dodgers Boeing 720-023B (c/n 18022/N1R'). The former 'Flagship of Georgia' was delivered to American Airlines in December 1960 and this plane was transformed into a 720 in September - October the following year. Bought on 21 January 1971 by the Los Angeles Dodgers, it was used to transport this baseball team until 1983 under the name of 'Kay O' II' and with the special registration of 'N1R'. Sold successively to Great American Airways, Jetstar and Boeing Military Airplane during the sole month of April 1983, it was transferred to the AMARC storage centre at Davis-Monthan and was used as a source of spare parts for the KC-135E fleet; its fuselage remained until at least 1992.

Middle East Airways Boeing 720-023B (c/n 18029/'OD-AFU'). Delivered to American Airlines in March 1961, this plane was finally named 'Flagship of Minnesota', but this name was not used. Bought in December 1971 by MEA, it was initially sent to Beirut, then leased to Alitalia in 1978. On 16 June 1982, it was severely damaged during a bombing attack on Beirut airport and struck off the registers shortly afterwards. After specialising in flights towards the main countries of the Middle East, MEA, founded in 1945, added European destinations following its merger with Air Liban in 1963. Despite the closure of Beirut airport during the civil war that lasted from 1975 to 1990, and during which part of its fleet was damaged, the Lebanese airline managed to survive by renting its aircraft and personnel to other international airlines.

Societa Aeronautica de Medellin (SAM) Boeing 720-030B (c/n 18059/'HK-676'). Delivered new to Lufthansa on 3 May 1961 and named 'Stuttgart', this aircraft was bought by Pan Am in March 1964 and served under the name of 'Jet Clipper Panama' until April 1973. Sold to Avianca, it was rented to SAM from March 1977 to May 1980 and used under the name of 'Ciudad Cartagena de Indias'. Bought by four airlines between January 1983 and July 1993, it was scrapped after having been stored at Davis-Monthan. Created in 1946 by a group of Medellin entrepreneurs in order to make this mountain-surrounded town more accessible, SAM began transporting passengers in 1958. Re-organised in 1962, it received from Avianca, to whom it had become a sister company, three Boeing 720B, which were all withdrawn from, service in 1980.

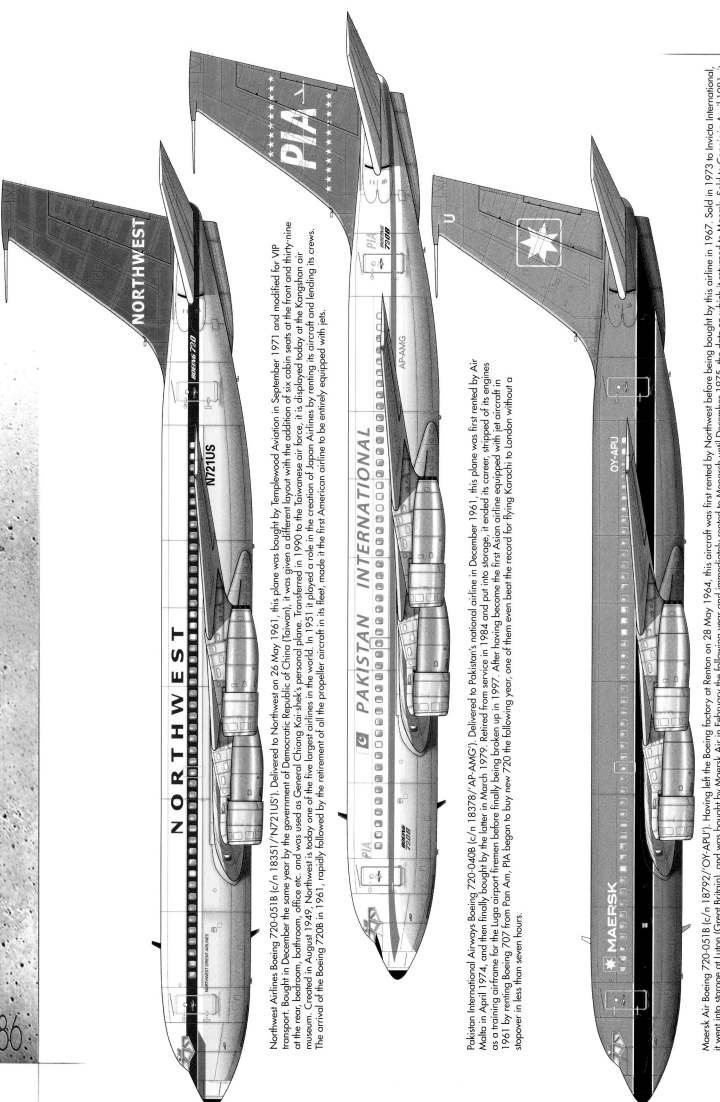

Northwest Airlines Boeing 720-051B (c/n 18351/'N721US'). Delivered to Northwest on 26 May 1961, this plane was bought by Templewood Aviation in September 1971 and modified for VIP transport. Bought in December the same year by the government of Democratic Republic of China (Taiwan), it was given a different layout with the addition of six cabin seats at the front and thirty-nine at the rear, bedroom, bathroom, office etc. and was used as General Chiang Kai-shek's personal plane. Transferred in 1990 to the Taiwanese air force, it is displayed today at the Kangshan air museum. Created in August 1949, Northwest is today one of the five largest airlines in the world. In 1951 it played a role in the creation of Japan Airlines by renting its aircraft and lending its crews. The arrival of the Boeing 720B in 1961, rapidly followed by the retirement of all the propeller aircraft in its fleet, made it the first American airline to be entirely equipped with jets.

Pakistan International Airways Boeing 720-040B (c/n 18378/'AP-AMG'). Delivered to Pakistan's national airline in December 1961, this plane was first rented by Air Malta in April 1974, and then finally bought by the latter in March 1979. Retired from service in 1984 and put into storage, it ended its career, stripped of its engines as a training airframe for the Luga airport firemen before finally being broken up in 1997. After having become the first Asian airline equipped with jet aircraft in 1961 by renting Boeing 707 from Pan Am, PIA began to buy new 720 the following year, one of them even beat the record for flying Karachi to London without a stopover in less than seven hours.

Maersk Air Boeing 720-051B (c/n 18792/'OY-APU'). Having left the Boeing factory at Renton on 28 May 1964, this aircraft was first rented by Northwest before being bought by this airline in 1967. Sold in 1973 to Invicta International, it went into storage at Luton (Great Britain), and was bought by Maersk Air in February the following year and immediately rented to Monarch until December 1975, the date on which it returned to Maersk. Sold to Conair in April 1981, it was damaged when landing at Salzburg (Austria) on 12 February 1987. It was not repaired and was sold for spare parts to Boeing MAC in May 1987. Maersk Air, a low cost Danish airline founded in 1969, was part of the A.P. Moller-Maersk specialised in maritime transport. It bought its first Boeing 707 en 1973, these aircraft being the first to fly in the airline's traditional colours (shades of blue and a white seven-point star on the tail fin). Faced with serious financial problems, Maersk was bought by an Icelandic investment fund in 2005 and absorbed by Sterling European Airlines.

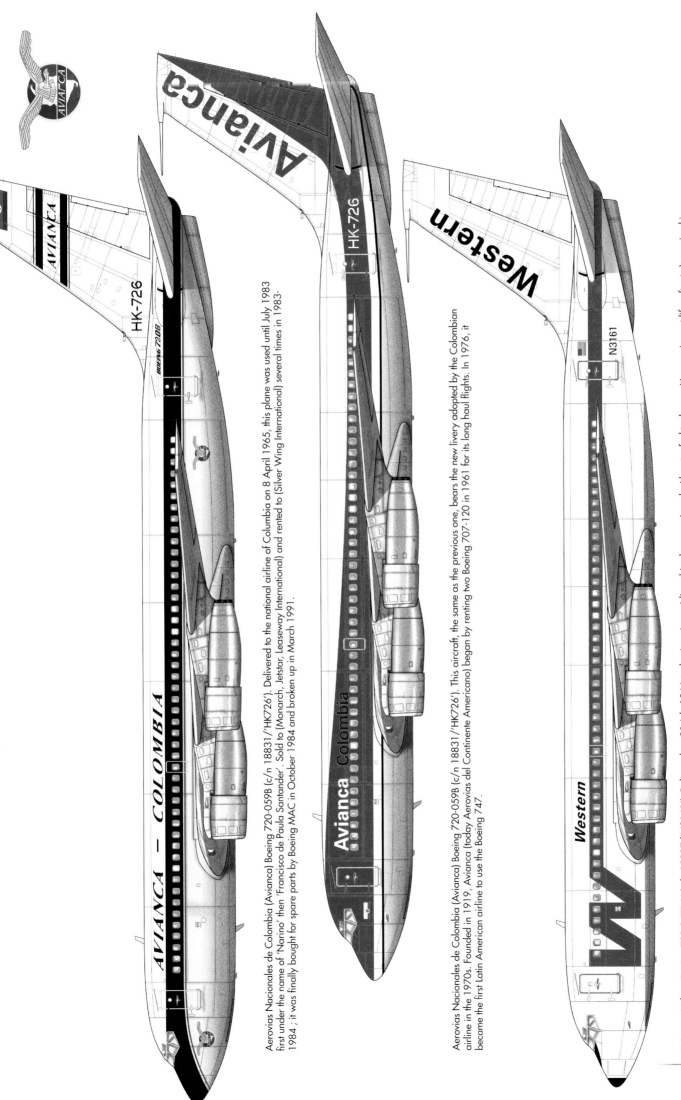

Aerovias Nacionales de Colombia (Avianca) Boeing 720-059B (c/n 18831/'HK726'). Delivered to the national airline of Columbia on 8 April 1965, this plane was used until July 1983 first under the name of 'Narino' then 'Francisco de Paula Santander'. Sold to (Monarch, Jetstar, Leaseway International) and rented to (Silver Wing International) several times in 1983-1984 ; it was finally bought for spare parts by Boeing MAC in October 1984 and broken up in March 1991.

Aerovias Nacionales de Colombia (Avianca) Boeing 720-059B (c/n 18831/'HK726'). This aircraft, the same as the previous one, bears the new livery adopted by the Colombian airline in the 1970s. Founded in 1919, Avianca (today Aerovias del Continente Americano) began by renting two Boeing 707-120 in 1961 for its long haul flights. In 1976, it became the first Latin American airline to use the Boeing 747.

Western Airlines Boeing 720-047B-H (c/n 19207/'N3161'). Delivered on 30 July 1966 to the American airline, this plane, equipped with extra fuel tanks, maritime equipment life rafts etc.) remained in service until September 1979, the date on which it was sold to Wicklund Aviation. Stored at Van Nuys (California), it was bought for spare parts by Boeing MAC in March 1983 and stored at Davis-Monthan and sold a final time to National Aircraft and broken up at Tucson (Arizona) in 1992. Western Airlines, based in California, became after the war one of the United States biggest domestic airlines, its fleet being entirely made up of jets at the end of the 1960s. Its Boeing 720 remained in service longer than planned in order to replace the DC-10 that was grounded for a while. Hit full on by the de-regulation measures, the activities of Western were finally taken over by Delta Airlines in 1987.

The Military Versions of the 707

Initially designed only for the civil market, the Boeing 707 had a second lease of life at the end of its career. This happened at the end of the 20th century, via certain specialised versions, and is likely to continue for some time to come.

Although the 'Dash 80' was the precursor for an important lineage of military aircraft, used almost exclusively by the United States and which a large part of the 820 aircraft made is still in service today, it also led to, but later and in a more roundabout way as it received new engines and underwent transformations, a non negligible amount of military versions (250 aircraft). These planes, destined originally for transport duties, often VIPs, became more and more specialised, culminating with the best known of all, the E-3 Sentry, popularly known as the AWACS and based on the 707-320 'Intercontinental'.

Above.
VC-137B s/n 62-6000 'Air Force One' at the German airfield of Berlin Tempelhof during president Reagan's visit to the Federal Republic of Germany. (USAF)

Opposite.
VC-137C s/n 65-6974 of the 89th MAW photographed in 1992 at Andrews AFB. (USAF)

Below.
VC-137C s/n 58-6971 brought back the former hostages from the American Embassy at Teheran to Andrews in January 1981. Note the different livery of VC-137B 'Air Force One' compared to the darker VC-137C. (USAF)

89th Military Airlift Wing insignia.

EXPERTO CREDE

The VC-137A and B

The first military 707 aircraft were in fact the three VC-137A bought new and delivered to the USAF in 1959. Originally destined, as their designation indicates, for the transportation of VIPs, two of them would soon become famous throughout the world by becoming the new 'Air Force One', the aircraft whose special role was to carry the president of the United States. Based on the 707-120 and designated by Boeing as the 707-153 (this being the number attributed to the USAF), these three aircraft differed from the transport C-135 (see following chapters) by their fuselage which was both wider (0,41 m/1' 4") and longer (42,32 m/138' 10" in all), but especially by their windows, of which there were far more, which explains why a new designation was chosen by the USAF.

The engines were the Pratt & Whitney JT3C-6 equipped with a noise-reducing system that relied on a crown of twenty tubes placed at the rear of the engine. The electrical system was slightly different from a standard civil aircraft and the cabin, which could carry thirty-six to forty passengers, was specially set up for the transportation of VIPs with twenty-two more comfortable VIP seats, a conference table, fold-down beds, communica-

tion posts and so on. The usual crew comprised between seven and seventeen men and women.

The first aircraft (s/n 58-6970), that flew on 7 April 1959, was specially attached to the president of the Union and thus became the first jet to be called Air Force One, along with two propeller aircraft, a Lockheed VC-121 and a Douglas VC-118.

Its internal layout was even more refined than that of its homologues, notably with a separate cabin placed in front of the wing, equipped with reclining seats, several offices and even a conference room equipped with ultra modern communication systems. The VC-137A were delivered from May 1959 to the 1289th Air Transport Squadron of the 1254th Air Transport Wing, a unit specialised in missions Special Air Missions (SAM).

Between February and May 1963, these planes were transformed by the Lockheed factory into VC-137B and equipped with more powerful JT3D-3 turbofan engines (8 164 kg/18,000lbs of thrust each), like many of the civil 707-120 of the time. Thanks to these new engines, the range was increased (1,850 km/1,150 miles more) and these aircraft, in the same livery as their successors, the VC-137C, that had just entered into service, replaced the latter, despite their inferior performance. Declassified into C-137B under president Jimmy Carter at the end of the 1970s, and therefore relieved of some of their luxury fittings, these planes also received a slightly less prestigious livery and were finally replaced in 1998 by four Boeing 757-200.

The V-137C

In order to become the new Air Force One during the official retirement of the propeller planes previously allocated this role, the USAF bought from Boeing, ten years apart, two new aircraft, designated VC-137C and which were based on the 707-320B 'Intercontinental', the denomination of Boeing being 707-353B. Powered by JT3D-3 turbofans, these planes had a range of 11,000 km/6,835 miles (that is 4,000 km/2,485 miles more than the previous VC-137A) at a cruising speed of 880 km/h (545 mph). The first aircraft (serial 62-6000, sometimes called 'SAM 6000', SAM being the abbreviation of Special Air Mission) had similar fittings to its predecessors, with an added presidential suite at the rear and an increased passenger load (50 passengers). On the other hand, particular attention had been paid to the external livery, as it had been done by the famous designer Raymond Loewy, the man behind the Coca-Cola bottle and the Marlboro logo. He was advised by the First Lady herself, Jackie Kennedy. Nothing had been left to chance, not even the base colour of the fuselage cockade, which matched the stripe painted on the fuselage! Ordered in 1961, the plane was delivered to the USAF on 9 October the

following year and used by the presidential couple for its main official visits, notably abroad. It was even the scene of a sad ceremony when vice-president Lyndon B. Johnson was sworn in whilst bringing back the body of John F. Kennedy who had been assassinated a few hours earlier at Dallas, Texas, in November 1963.

Ten years later, in April 1972, a second VC-137C (serial 72-7000) was delivered to the USAF, identical to the previous except for the rear of the fuselage, not equipped with a ventral fin that both improved lateral stability and acted as a shock absorber in the case of too steep a take off.

These two aircraft remained in service with the 89th Military Airlift Wing at Andrews (Maryland), which took over from the 1254th ATW in January 1966 in its role of VIP transportation. Replaced as Air Force One in September 1990 by a Boeing VC-25 (the military designation for a 747) then declassified into a C-137C by the Carter administration, these aircraft were repainted in the classic livery of the SAM and finally retired from service, and put into storage, in 1998 and 2001 respectively.

As well as these two VC-137C, two old 707-320 were supplied to the USAF, who renamed them C-137C. The first was a civil 707-320C that had been seized by the US customs in 1985, whilst the second (a 707-320B) was bought from Buffalo Airways in 1987. Both were also attached to the 89th AW and used for transporting VIPs, notably the vice president of the United States. They were used until 1998, the date on which one was transformed into an E-8C.

The C-18

In order to respect the change in the way of designating military aircraft in the United States, which came into use in 1962, and according to which, the same aircraft had the same name, whatever its service branch (USAF, USN, USMC, etc.), all the military 707 aircraft delivered after this date were given the basic C-18 designation. This was the case particu-

larly for the nine 707-323C sold by American Airlines to the USAF in June 1982 which were initially destined for transport missions and training. Important areas of corrosion were found on one of these aircraft and it was scrapped before even entering into service; a second plane, with the same fault, was used a little later as a source of spare parts. As had been, without doubt, the intention of the USAF from the beginning, four aircraft were transformed in 1985 into EC-18B ARIA and two others into EC-18D, the last (c/n 19380/serial 81-0898), renamed C-18B, was firstly kept at the Grumman factory at Melbourne (Florida) before finally being transformed into a E-8C.

The EC-18

As we have just seen, in 1985 four C-18A were transformed into EC-18B ARIA (Advanced Range Instrumented Aircraft) in order to take over the role of the old EC-135N. For this, they were given a bulbous nose similar to the latter and had a directional radar antenna that was 2,12 m (7') in diameter. Thus modified, these planes were longer (by 5,45 m/18') than the EC-135N, with a higher carrying load and, above all, much better and more modern electronic equipment. Destined

VC-137C s/n 62-6000 began its career as Air Force One in 1962. President Kennedy and his wife used it for all their trips. It had a particular livery and its cabin housed, amongst other things, a presidential suite. (USAF)

Above.
'Air Force Two', VC-137C s/n 68-6970 photographed at Wright Patterson AFB in 1982, was at this time used by vice president George Bush. (USAF)

Below.
VC-137 s/n 65-973 at Eielson AFB, Alaska, in 1991, during an official visit by members of the United States government and general staff to boost the morale of troops during operation 'Desert Storm'. (USAF)

for use as communication relays, they were also as a test centre for various equipment, notably the pursuit of missiles or space vehicles. The EC-18B carried, for example, many cameras and photographic equipment on the left side of the fuselage, the underside of the wing on this side was even painted black to avoid reflections when taking photographs. At first based at Wright Paterson with the 4950th Test Wing, the EC-18B were attached, in 1994, as were all the ARIA programme aircraft, to the 452nd Flight Test Squadron, of the 412th Test Wing at Edwards in California. From June 2000, they were used for training the crews of the E-6 Mercury.

The 412th TW also had, during this time, the only two EC-18D AMMCA (Advanced Cruise Missile Mission Control Aircraft). These planes were specially modified by the E-Systems Company for remote control trials for cruise missiles. In the bulbous nose of these aircraft was a small pursuit radar antenna as well as a AN/APG 63 fighter radar used both for searching and surveillance and a third radar for the weather. Three technicians were in the plane specially for the cruise missile, launched from a B-52, and its eventual destruction, in the case of an incident. Based at Edwards. Once the trials were over, the two planes were once more modified, this time into a E-8C.

Delivered in September 1967 to American Airlines, this 707-348C-H (c/n 19518) was acquired by the USAF in June 1982. Redesignated C-18A with the serial number 81-0893, it was modified into an EC-18B and used by the 452nd FLTS of the 412th TW.
(J. Guillem collection)

The training TC-18

The training of E-3 Sentry crews proved to be very expensive if carried out on operational aircraft, the USAF decided to use, to this end starting in the 1980s, old civil aircraft, without much of the electronic equipment, beginning with the Radome, but, on the other hand, with a cockpit that imitated that of the E-3, as well as an imitation in-flight refuelling probe.

Two old TWA 707-331 were therefore bought by the USAF who named them TC-18E attaching them to the 552nd Airborne Control Wing at Tinker (Oklahoma), the unit of all the USAF's Sentry aircraft. Used until March 1992 with civil serial numbers, the date upon which they were given military serials, they were briefly replaced by a C-18A and a EC-18D whose bulbous nose had been replaced by that of a standard 707. The US Navy wanted, like the USAF, to reduce training costs for the crews of its new E-6 Mercury. It used two civil 707 aircraft (the -331C (H) of the Portuguese airline TAP), renamed TC-18F, which flew until August 1995 with civil serial

numbers before being bought by the Navy and receiving an official BuNo. Attached to the NTSU (Naval Training Support Unit) at Tinker, these two planes, designated In Flight Trainer or IFT were used for flight training not only for future pilots, but also for navigators and mechanics on the future Mercury. These training periods had a duration that varied between four and twelve weeks, the crews having previously undergone a basic training on a flight simulator. Without the operational avionics of the production Mercury, the TC-18F had JT3D engines instead of the CFM 56 and were retired from service respectively in 1999 and 2001.

Finally, still on the topic of the familiarisation missions for crews, we should mention the only GE-8C aircraft, based on

Above.
At the parking area of the Edwards base in 1996, an EC-18D (s/n 81-0893) in the foreground, rubs shoulders with the NKC-135E s/n 55-3135. Despite appearances, the first is a former American Airlines 707-323C, whilst the second began its career as a KC-135 tanker. (USAF)

EC-18D s/n 81-0895 of 452nd Flight Test Squadron at the Edwards base, flying over California. Apart from their function as test beds, these aircraft whose appearance was close to the EC-135N although they were longer, have also been used for training E-6 Mercury crews since 2000. (USAF)

Below.
Former American Airlines 'Astrojet San Francisco', this 707-323C (c/n 19381- s/n 81-0895) became one of the two EC-18D AMMCA specially modified for remote control trials for cruise missiles. In 2002, once these tests were over, it was once more modified, this time into an E-8C.
(J. Guillem collection).

a 707-348C and destined for ground training as indicated by its G for Ground prefix, within the J-STARS programme at the Robins base.

The E-6 Mercury

In order to keep a communications network between the authorities and commanders in the environment of a nuclear war, starting with the NCA (National Command Authority), and the triple nuclear component (submarines, ballistic missiles and bombers) of the United States, the US Navy made a system in the 1960s called TACAMO (Take Charge And Move Out) using extremely modified Lockheed C-130 Hercules. The essential mission of these planes was to receive, verify, and retransmit EAM (Emergency Action Messages) that come from or to the American strategic forces and mainly the missile carrying submarines.

For this, the aircraft had to be able to communicate on virtually every possible radio frequency VLF (Very Low Frequency/) to SHF (Super High Frequency/) and replace the system of land ELF (Extremely Low Frequency) transmissions that are very vulnerable in the event of a nuclear strike.

The main component of this system was the sixteen aircraft mainly based at Tinker (Oklahoma) and the alert bases in California (Travis) and Maryland (Patuxent River) assembled within the Strategic Command Wing 1 (STRATCOMWING 1 or SCW 1) of the US Navy, made up the VQ-3 squadron 'Iron Men', VQ-4 'Shadows' and VQ-7 'Roughnecks' These planes carried out flights in closed circuits (racetracks) above the oceans, according to predefined zones, the missions lasting six to ten hours, with the possibility of extending them with in-flight refuelling. Until 1992, two TACAMO aircraft flew everyday, one above the Atlantic and the other over the Pacific. At the beginning, the trials for this system were undertaken by the Lockheed KC-130 equipped with VLF and wire antenna, then, from 1966, the EC-130Q appeared. This was more specialised and the equipment was continuously improved, they were attached to the VQ-3 and VQ-4.

In order to modernise this fleet, and having been able to use a conclusive experiment on the subject carried out by the NADC (Naval Air Development Center) in Warminster, in Pennsylvania, thanks to having been able to use the NKC-135A lent by the Air Force, the US Navy signed a contract with Boeing in 1984 for sixteen aircraft, designated E-6A and initially named Hermes, then finally Mercury. These planes, based on the 707-320 and powered by four CFM International F108-CF-100 turbofans, the military version of the CFM 56, had the following equipment:

- An in-flight refuelling receptacle that allowed the plane to remain in the air up to 72 hours.

- A system named DAISS (Digital Airborne Intercontinental Switching System) for automatic retransmission of signals to different communication systems.

- Two deployable very low frequency antennas (VLF), one 7,925 m (26,000') long from the fuselage (LTWA/Long Trailing Wire Antenna) and the other 1,220 m/4,000' (STWA/Short Trailing Wire Antenna) from the tail cone, to which is added ten fixed antennas on and under the fuselage as well as at the wingtips and the tailplane.

- A system for satellite communication (MILSTAR, for Military Strategic Tactical and Relay).

- A system for the automatic sending of transmission (on printers or screens) named MCS (Mission Computer System).

- A HPTS (High Power Transmit Unit), a high power amplifier (200 kW) for the trailing antennas that kept contact with the missile carrying submarines (SSBN) when they were submerged.

- Very low frequency transmission and receiving equipment (VLF) AN/U, coupled with a communication centre AN/USC-14.

- And finally a system of managing the flying controls to ensure an optimal coordination between the plane's trajectory and the best radio links, the trailing antennas having to remain as horizontal as possible. Also, all the planes have a reinforcement skin to protect against corrosion and their fuselage is

specially designed to deal with the extra stress caused by the manoeuvres undertaken in their missions (turns within the racetracks) while the antennas are deployed.

The prototype's maiden flight was on 19 February 1987 and the sixteen E-CA began to be delivered to the Navy in August 1989, one of them remained with Boeing where it was transformed into a YE-6B for the USAF. The arrival of new aircraft was subordinate to the dismantling of essential equipment installed on the Lockheed EC-130Q, the two types were used together for a short period. The fleet of Mercury was distributed between the Pacific (eight aircraft with the VQ-3 based at NAS Barbers Point, Hawaii, the first unit to be transformed at the end of 1989) and the east coast of the United States (seven planes delivered between 1990 and 1993 to VQ-4 at Patuxent River, Maryland); each time a plane was kept on alert on the ground for fifteen minutes.

Normally carrying a crew of eleven[1], the E-6A can carry out missions of nearly seventy-two hours with a change over crew by refuelling in flight, its range being over 10,000 km. They are protected against EMP (Electro Magnetic Pulse) caused by a nuclear explosion that is particularly dangerous for electric and electronic systems. The Mercury differs from the USAF E-3 with its pods placed at the wingtips containing satellite equipment (SATCOM) as well as ESM antennas and of course their trailing antennas linked to two winches, one of which is placed in the fuselage, the other in the rear tip. These trailing cables act as wire antennas and create a wavelength capable of penetrating the surface of the sea and reaching submarines wherever they may be immersed in the world. Crew training is carried out, for the flight crew, by the CFCTS (Contract Flight Crew Training System) at the Tinker air base where there are two IFT (Flight Trainer), for the Boeing TC-18F, destined notably for teaching the in-flight refuelling techniques and for the on board specialists of the NTSU (Naval Training Support Unit).

After having undertaken a series of trials, starting in 1992, with one if its Mercury aircraft, the US Navy decided to trans-

Above.
In order to test the concept in full size, a Boeing 707 was disguised as a Mercury and given US Navy markings as well as a two tone livery identical to the USAF EC/RC-135 that was finally rejected. (US DoD)

---

1. Four flying crew (pilot, co-pilot, navigator and) and seven specialists (Airborne Command Officer, Airborne Command Supervisor, two airborne communication specialists, two on board technicians and an operator for the trailing antenna winches).

form part of its E-6B fleet, a version that combined both the functions of the E-6A TACAMO and that of the USAF EC-135C 'Looking Glass'. Apart from the links and the traditional control of submersed submarines, these aircraft are now also able to serve as Airborne Command Posts and, for example, control the firing of land based ballistic missiles; their communications systems, working in VHF and taken from the old EC-135C having been improved with this in mind. This combination of missions was mostly caused by the end of the Cold War and the subsequent need to unify the control systems for the launching of missiles based on land, sea or air. The modernisation of the aircraft took place within the CPM programme (Command Post Modification) and was materialised by the installation of the ALCS (Airborne Launch Control System). This meant an extra bump on the fuselage that protected the communication satellite antenna 'Pacer Link Milstar'. The cabin was given an area for the new specialist crew members, which meant that the rest area usually placed there had to be moved to the rear of the aircraft. Finally, the number of crew was now

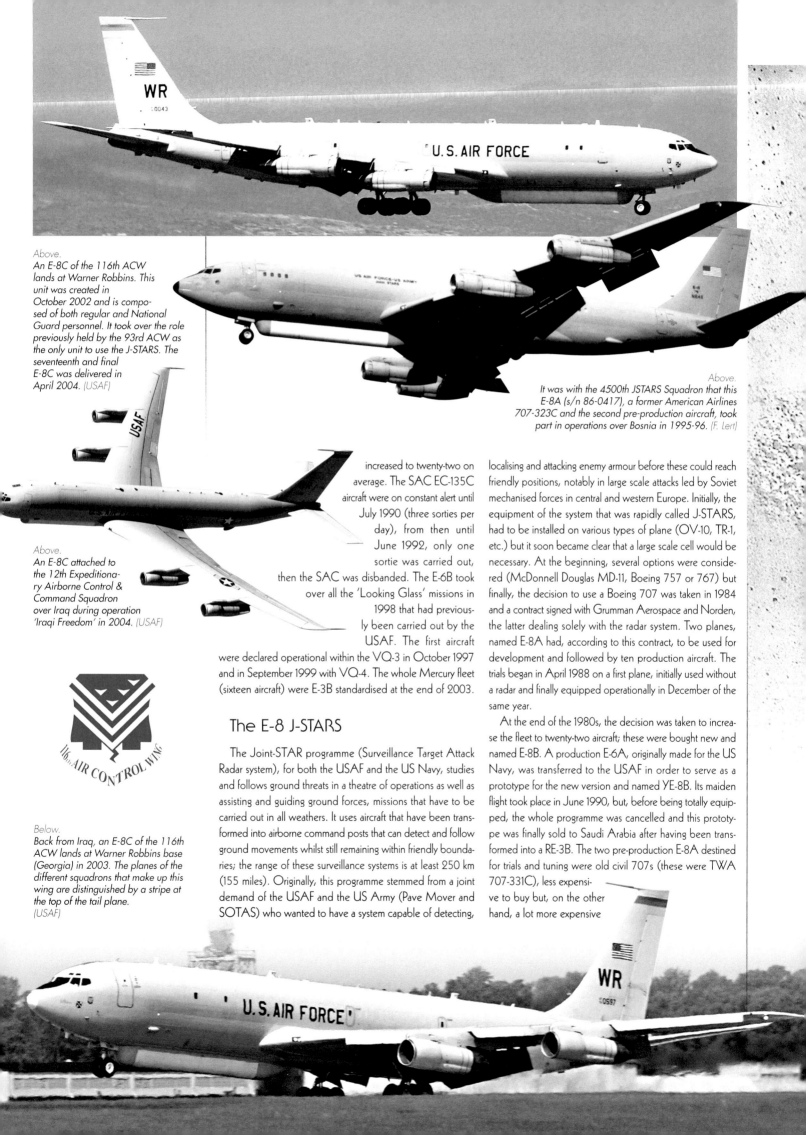

Above.
An E-8C of the 116th ACW lands at Warner Robbins. This unit was created in October 2002 and is composed of both regular and National Guard personnel. It took over the role previously held by the 93rd ACW as the only unit to use the J-STARS. The seventeenth and final E-8C was delivered in April 2004. (USAF)

Above.
It was with the 4500th JSTARS Squadron that this E-8A (s/n 86-0417), a former American Airlines 707-323C and the second pre-production aircraft, took part in operations over Bosnia in 1995-96. (F. Lert)

Above.
An E-8C attached to the 12th Expeditionary Airborne Control & Command Squadron over Iraq during operation 'Iraqi Freedom' in 2004. (USAF)

116ᵗʰ AIR CONTROL WING

Below.
Back from Iraq, an E-8C of the 116th ACW lands at Warner Robbins base (Georgia) in 2003. The planes of the different squadrons that make up this wing are distinguished by a stripe at the top of the tail plane. (USAF)

increased to twenty-two on average. The SAC EC-135C aircraft were on constant alert until July 1990 (three sorties per day), from then until June 1992, only one sortie was carried out, then the SAC was disbanded. The E-6B took over all the 'Looking Glass' missions in 1998 that had previously been carried out by the USAF. The first aircraft were declared operational within the VQ-3 in October 1997 and in September 1999 with VQ-4. The whole Mercury fleet (sixteen aircraft) were E-3B standardised at the end of 2003.

The E-8 J-STARS

The Joint-STAR programme (Surveillance Target Attack Radar system), for both the USAF and the US Navy, studies and follows ground threats in a theatre of operations as well as assisting and guiding ground forces, missions that have to be carried out in all weathers. It uses aircraft that have been transformed into airborne command posts that can detect and follow ground movements whilst still remaining within friendly boundaries; the range of these surveillance systems is at least 250 km (155 miles). Originally, this programme stemmed from a joint demand of the USAF and the US Army (Pave Mover and SOTAS) who wanted to have a system capable of detecting,

localising and attacking enemy armour before these could reach friendly positions, notably in large scale attacks led by Soviet mechanised forces in central and western Europe. Initially, the equipment of the system that was rapidly called J-STARS, had to be installed on various types of plane (OV-10, TR-1, etc.) but it soon became clear that a large scale cell would be necessary. At the beginning, several options were considered (McDonnell Douglas MD-11, Boeing 757 or 767) but finally, the decision to use a Boeing 707 was taken in 1984 and a contract signed with Grumman Aerospace and Norden, the latter dealing solely with the radar system. Two planes, named E-8A had, according to this contract, to be used for development and followed by ten production aircraft. The trials began in April 1988 on a first plane, initially used without a radar and finally equipped operationally in December of the same year.

At the end of the 1980s, the decision was taken to increase the fleet to twenty-two aircraft; these were bought new and named E-8B. A production E-6A, originally made for the US Navy, was transferred to the USAF in order to serve as a prototype for the new version and named YE-8B. Its maiden flight took place in June 1990, but, before being totally equipped, the whole programme was cancelled and this prototype was finally sold to Saudi Arabia after having been transformed into a RE-3B. The two pre-production E-8A destined for trials and tuning were old civil 707s (these were TWA 707-331C), less expensive to buy but, on the other hand, a lot more expensive

to transform. The production costs of future aircraft constantly rose and, the 707 production line having been closed when Japan bought the AWACS modified 767, it was decided, in November 1989, to use old civil aircraft and rename them E-8C. Boeing finally withdrew from the programme and Grumman took over, making a plane destined for permanent trials and designated T3. The initial order for twenty-two aircraft was reduced to E-8C; this amount comprised also the two pre-production E-8A aircraft, the twentieth being destined to remain with Northrop-Grumman as a test bed. In 1997, this number was once more reduced due to budget cutbacks to thirteen aircraft. NATO and the RAF were contacted at this time to see if, as possible customers, they would share the production costs. Whilst still undergoing evaluation, the two pre-production E-8A were used operationally by the 4411th J-STARS Squadron, based at Riyadh during the Gulf War in January 1991. They carried out fifty sorties and nearly 500 flying hours, notably guiding with great precision Apache AH-64 and Cobra AH-1 combat helicopters, towards Iraqi armour. Their efficiency in this role was such that a high-ranking USAF officer said 'with them, mobile targets did not remain so for very long'.

One of them saw service again along with the first production E-8C in the peacekeeping operation 'Joint Endeavour' in Bosnia from December 1995, this time with the 4500th J-STARS (Prov) squadron based in Germany. The first E-8A (s/n 86-0416) was next transformed into a training TE-8A and the second quite simply retired from service.

The first two aircraft having been transformed after a general overhaul of the airframe and an eventual replacement of the parts deemed to be doubtful beginning in April 1992, and the authorisation to transform six other machines having been granted the following year, the maiden flight of the E-8C took place in March 1994. The first production aircraft (P.1) was delivered to the USAF in August 1995 and the new aircraft began to be delivered to the 93rd ACW at Robins (Georgia), especially created for this, starting in June 1996 at the rate of roughly one every six months. The following year, the unit was operational with five aircraft (including the two test planes) and it received the last E-8C (P.17) in March 2005. Based on the 707-320C, the E-8 differs on the outside by its radar and high performance communication system, a canoe shaped radome measuring twelve metres (39') in length and containing a 7.30 m (24') long

An E-8C of the 128th EACCS taking off for a mission over Iraq in April 2004 during operation 'Iraqi Freedom'. The belly area of the airframe is mostly unpainted so that it does not interfere with radar transmissions. (USAF)

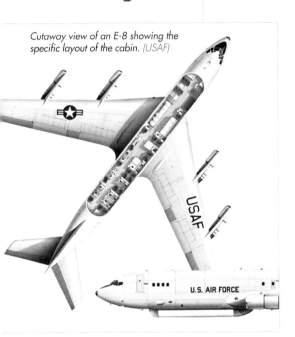

Cutaway view of an E-8 showing the specific layout of the cabin. (USAF)

The E-8 J-STARS

N°	C/N	S/N	Delivery date	Note
FSD-1	19626	86-0416	August 1987	E-8A pre-production. Used for J-STARS training
FSD-2	19574	86-0417	Nov. 1988	E-8A pre-production
YE-8B	24503	88-0322		E-8B prototype. Program cancelled. Scrapped
FSD-3	19621	90-0175	March 1994	E-8C pre-production. Used for J-STARS training
P-1	19622	92-3289	June 1996	E-8C LRIP production
P-2	19295	92-3290	Dec. 1996	E-8C LRIP production
P-3	19294	93-0597	1998	E-8C LRIP production
P-4	19296	93-1097	1998	E-8C LRIP production
P-5	19293	94-0284	1999	E-8C LRIP production
P-6	19442	94-0285	1999	E-8C
P-7	20016	95-0121	2000	E-8C
P-8	20495	95-0122	2000	E-8C
P-9	20319	96-0042	April 2001	E-8C Damaged by hurricane 'Rita' Sept. 2005
P-10	20316	96-0043	August 2001	E-8C Block 20
P-11	19986	97-0100	Nov 2001	E-8C Block 20
P-12	20317	97-0200	2002	E-8C Block 20
P-13	20318	97-0201	2002	E-8C Block 20
P-14	19998	99-006	2002	E-8C Block 20
P-15	20043	00-2000		E-8C Block 20
P-16	19581	02-9111	April 2005	E-8C Block 20 ex C-18 s/n 81-0896

Opposite.
An artist's impression of how the E-8 J-STARS is used in the field, and its importance in the organisation of the battlefield. (USAF)

Below.
This E-8C (s/n 90-0175) belonging to the 93rd ACW, the second of this version of the J-STARS programme, in reality began its career in December 1967 as 707-338C-H with Qantas under the name of 'City of Toowoomba'. (WingMasters collection).

Norden AN/APY-3 lateral scanning radar antenna added under the fuselage behind the forward undercarriage. The antenna of this radar mechanically tilts from side to side for elevation scanning whilst azimuth scanning is carried out electronically. Made particularly resistant to electronic counter measure jamming, the plane can carry out eight-hour missions, prolonged if needed by in flight refuelling as a probe is installed above the cockpit. The E-8C radar, with its 120° sweep, covers an area 50,000 km² (19,305 sq miles) and can detect objectives situated between 50 and 250 km (31 and 155 miles) from the plane and functioning in several different ways.

Opposite.
Originally destined for Western Airlines, this 707-347C-H was finally bought by the Canadian air force in May 1971. Locally designated 'CC-137', it was used by No 437 Squadron before becoming one of the USAF E-8 J-STARS. (WingMasters collection)

Above.
Boeing A20 n°629 of RAAF No 33 Squadron refuelling a F/A-18 Hornet. After having used old civil 707s (four of which were Qantas 328C) as military transports, starting in 1971 under the name of A20, the RAAF had IAI transform four into two-point tankers. They were fitted with wing tip pods and put into service starting in 1990. These aircraft are due to be start being replaced in 2009 by the KC-30B, the military version of the Airbus A330. (RAAF)

- The WAS/MTI (Wide Area Surveillance and Moving Target Indicator) follows ground targets in a 512 km² (197 sq miles) zone and is even capable of differentiating between wheeled and tracked vehicles. Working in high resolution, this system allows for a precise identification of possible targets, which permits the elaboration of attack plans adapted to each situation. The WAS/MTI also has a maritime mode and has proved its capacities in detecting fast-moving helicopters.
- The SSM (Sector Search Mode), is a 'zoom' able to focus in detail on a small area (30 square kilometres/12 square miles) with a 60 second revisit time.
- The APM (Attack Planning Mode) is a high definition mode for the final determination of targets to attack; radar revisit time is every six seconds.
- The SAR/FTI (Synthetic Aperture Radar/Fixed Target Indicator) produces a map of photographic quality of the

geographical area under surveillance with precise indications on fixed objectives (bridges, airports, buildings and so on). In SAR mode, the radar has a range of 175 kilometres (108 miles) on each side of the E-8C in flight, meaning that during an eight-hour flight, no less than one million square kilometres (386,100 sq miles) can be mapped.

The data collected in real time by the systems of the E-8C can be stored and shown on the operator screens or printed as the aircraft carries a laser printer. They can also be retransmitted to ground stations using the SCDL system (Surveillance and Control Data Link nicknamed 'skittle'), or to attack or AWACS planes thanks to the JTDIS system (Joint Tactical Information Distribution System).

Curiously, the E-8C was not given an official name; it generally had a crew of twenty-one men (and women), three for flying and eighteen operators for the on board systems installed in

Opposite.
Delivered to the Bundesluftwaffe in October 1968, this 707-307C was named August Euler and attached to the Flugbereitschaftstaffel (VIP transport squadron). (WingMasters collection).

Opposite.
This Israel government aircraft (c/n 20110) was first used as a VIP transport then transformed into a tanker. It was a former South African Airlines 707-344C, who used it under the name of 'Durban'. It was still in service in 2007. (V. Gréciet collection)

Opposite.
This C/KC-137E of the 14ᵉ Stormo of the 8° Gruppo, Aviazione Militare Italiana (Italian air force), began its career as 707-382B-H (c/n 19740) named 'Cidade de Luanda' with the Portuguese airline TAP in February 1968. Repaired after a belly landing at Lisbon in March 1972, it was sold to Aeritalia in January 1989 and transformed into a 707 T/T by the Italian Aeronavali company.
(S. Guillemin collection)

Opposite.
Before being sold to Fuerza Aerea Del Chile in November 1982, this 707-351C (c/n 19443), originally bought by Northwest, had a long civil career with the Chilean national airline Lan Chile. Transformed as a passenger transport at the end of 1974, it was still used by the 10th Transport Group of the FAC in 2006.
(Coll. WingMasters).

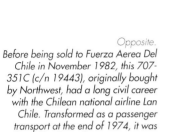

Above.
As part of the 'Peace Sentinel' program launched in 1981, Saudi Arabia ordered five E-3 and six tankers named KE-3A, a number that was finally increased to eight in 1984. Delivery was spread over 1986 to 1987, the maintenance of these aircraft being assured in the country by Boeing personnel or local sub contractors. On this photo, KE-3A s/n 82-0071 (c/n 23422), which was delivered to No. 18 Squadron of the Royal Saudi Air Force in June, is still in USAF livery. (WingMasters collection)

Below.
A South African Air Force Boeing 707 landing. Note the very discreet markings on the entirely medium grey camouflage.
(F. Lert).

the cabin [2]. The crew made up of USAF as well as US Army personnel could be increased to 34 men (six of which for flying the aircraft) for longer missions. Still in service today, the planes are constantly brought up to date and modernised, as much for the engines as the equipment, depending on information gathered from their operational use. The eleventh E-8C thus became the first of the 'Block 20' series equipped with new computers and consoles. The whole fleet had to be brought up to this standard. In 2005, it was decided to modernise the cockpit, that dated from the 1950s; the obsolete instruments and controls had to be replaced by a 'glass cockpit'. The first modified aircraft was put into service in 2007. A modernisation of the engines is also envisaged; the actual TF33 do not give enough power when the aircraft is at full gross weight, as is the case during a wartime mission with a full crew. Using the CFM 56 has been deemed too expensive; it is likely that a less efficient, but a lot less expensive solution will be chosen, perhaps using the JT8D turbofans instead, and in place of the actual

JT3D, the necessary modifications remaining within reasonable limits. A prototype, made in partnership with Pratt & Whitney and a Texan company named Seven Q Seven, and equipped with engines of this type, therefore took to the air in August 2001. An official contract was signed, according to which the whole E-8C fleet will be given new engines; the first trials should take place in 2008 and the first transformed plane put into service the following year. This upgrade will also affect the engine pylons and cowlings and a recent study has shown that this solution will nevertheless be less expensive than simply keeping in service the antique JT3Ds whilst making the re-engined E-8C safer, more available and, above all, capable of operating from a higher number of airports with shorter runways.

The other military 707s.

Apart from these specialist military versions used by the United States, many countries throughout the world use, or have used, the Boeing 707, mostly in its 'Intercontinental' version (-320) for three types of main mission, general transport, in particular VIPs, in flight refuelling and electronic warfare.

It would be too long to draw up a complete list of these militarised 707s, often by the sole fact that they were used by air forces which range, in alphabetical order, from Abu Dhabi in Zaire, these nations often using only one plane

2. The number of operator posts has constantly increased as the number of planes has decreased. Thus, the E-8A had only ten consoles whilst the E-8A should have had fifteen.

'Egyptian 01' seen in flight in December 1986. This 707-336C-H (c/n 20919/SU-AXJ) was delivered to the Egyptian government in August 1974 and used for the transportation of the President of the Republic. It has been replaced in this role by an Airbus A340.
(J. Guillem collection)

(Dubai, Colombia, Morocco, Paraguay, etc.), mostly for transporting their respective governments. Many of these aircraft, having most of the time a considerable potential, were later upgraded as flying tankers. Several companies such as Omega Air in the United States, or IAI in Israel, not forgetting Boeing itself, with its aircraft officially named KC-137, specialised in this upgrade that consisted of adding extra fuel tanks in the fuselage and refuelling pods under the wing tips (two point tankers) and or under the fuselage (three points). IAI also supplied five countries [3] of the Boeing 707s upgraded for electronic warfare and the reception of various data (SIGINT/ELINT).

In reality, only four countries, as well as the United States and France, have a fleet of military 707s, some bought new,

Top.
After a long civil career with TAP, this 707-328B-H was sold to the government of Zaire in November 1986. Named 'Mount Hoyo' and assigned to the Force Aérienne Zaïroise for VIP flights, it was withdrawn from service in May 1995 and scrapped at Lisbon in 2006.
(J. Guillem collection)

Above.
This 707-351B (c/n 18686), modified into a VIP transport, was seized at Stansted (Great Britain) in June 1990 before its delivery to the government of Liberia. Acquired a few weeks later by Executive Aviation, it was still for sale in 2006...
(J. Guillem collection)

Opposite.
This 707-3P1C-H (c/n 21334) originally used by AAA, was bought in July 1977 by the government of Qatar.
(Coll. J. Guillem).

Below.
Named 'Windsor Town' ' within RAAF No 33 Squadron, this 707-338C-H (c/n 19627) began its career with Australian airline Qantas before being sold to the country's air force in March 1979. This plane is now stored at the Richmond base.
(Wingmasters collection).

constantly upgraded and used for particular missions. West Germany was the first to buy, at the end of 1968, four 707-307C renamed C-137 that had the particularity of bearing both American and German serial numbers. All these aircraft were replaced in 1990 by Airbus A.310.

Canada received between 1970 and 1971, five 707-347C originally destined for Western Air Lines, and were given the designation CC-137 and name 'Husky' by the Canadian air force. These planes in fact replaced the KC-135 that Canada had planned to buy but which did not happen before the production lines of these planes closed. Attached to No. 437 Squadron, two of these planes were modified as tankers in 1972, with refuelling pods added to the wingtips. They began to be replaced in 1994 by the CC-150 Polaris (local designation of the Airbus A310), five CC-137 were re-purchased by the USAF to be upgraded to E-8C.

Iran, a loyal ally of the United States until the Shah was overthrown in 1979, ordered between 1974 and 1978; thirteen 707-3J9C in two distinct batches in the framework of a programme named 'Peace Station'. The first six aircraft were equipped with an in-flight refuelling probe identical to that of the KC-135. The following three were equipped as passenger transports and the last three as tankers, with wing mounted refuelling pods designed by Beech, something which was later installed on all the tankers.

The thirteenth and last plane, a specially equipped VIP transporter with a civil number, was reserved for the Shah himself. During the first Gulf war, in 1980-81, at least one of these Boeings, upgraded by E-Systems, was used as an ELINT listening platform with the Iranian air force of the time, recently renamed IRIAF (Islamic Republic of Iran Air Force). Another was no doubt upgraded by IAI to an electronic warfare aircraft.

Israel, another country with a large fleet of military 707s

3. Angola, Argentina and Spain (one aircraft each); India (two) and South Africa (four).

Bought in September 1975 by the Pelita AS airline, this B707-3M1C (c/n 21092) served until November 1982 with the Indonesian Air Force before becoming one of this country's governmental aircraft. (V. Gréciet collection).

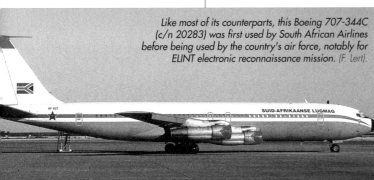

Like most of its counterparts, this Boeing 707-344C (c/n 20283) was first used by South African Airlines before being used by the country's air force, notably for ELINT electronic reconnaissance mission. (F. Lert).

Above, right.
After the definitive closure of the KC-135 production line, Boeing looked into transforming former civil 707s into tankers. Two demonstrators were made to this end, such as this '707 Tanker Transport', a three-points tanker, a former TWA 331C-H (c/n 18757) bought in 1982, militarised and equipped with pods under each wing and aft of the fuselage. This first demonstrator was then sold to the Spanish air force and was still in service in 2007. (D. Breffort collection)

Below.
With a rather discreet livery, like most of its counterparts, this Heyl Ha' Avir tanker is an old 707-3J6B (c/n 20716) bought by Israel in 1993, and equipped with a refuelling boom under the rear of the fuselage. This aircraft was still in use in 2007. (V. Gréciet collection).

destined for different missions, benefited from the experience of its national manufacturer in the upgrading of four engine jet aircraft as well as tankers into electronic warfare platforms. The difference with the countries we have just mentioned is that the Hebrew state never bought new aircraft, but rather used old civil aircraft, usually from the national airline, El Al.

Above.
First delivered to the CAAC, the 707-3J6C-H (c/n 20721) was sold in 1993 to Israel. Used as a transport aircraft by Heyl Ha' Avir, this aircraft had different code numbers, whilst its communication system was much improved as proved by the extra antenna on the fuselage.
Today it is used as a tanker.
(V. Gréciet collection).

Delivered to Saudia in 1975, this 707-368C-H (c/n 21104/ST-DRS) was sold to Sudan Airways in November 1983 and used by the Sudanese government until April 1985 with the code 'Sudan 001 '.
(J. Guillem collection)

This 707-321 (c/n 18084/ TY-BBW) was only used during a year (1987-88) by the government of Benin. At first stored in the United Kingdom, then at Ostend (Belgium) where it is here photographed in 1988, it was finally sold as a wreck in July 1997.
(J. Guillem collection)

Top.
Amongst the most surprising Boeing 707 conversions is the Israeli IAI Company Phalcon. Equipped with three radars placed in the nose bulge and fuselage sides, this aircraft has the dual role of airborne radar and flying command post (AEWC&C). It also has larger ELINT and COMINT capacities. As well as the Hebrew state, the Chilean Fuerza Aerea uses one of these aircraft, named locally 'Condor' since 1995. (J. Guillem collection)

Opposite.
After more than ten years of career with Northwest, this 707-351C-H (c/n 19635) was firstly acquired by PIA in July 1977 then by the Pakistan Air Force in April 1989. Flown by No 12 Squadron with the serial 68-19635, it was withdrawn from service and put up for sale.
(J. Guillem collection)

Below.
Landing at Orly of 'Togo 1', the Boeing 707-3L6B (c/n 21049/ 5V-TGE) of the Togolese government in which president Gnassingbe Eyadema died on 5 February 2005. This aircraft is now used by the government of Mali (TZ-TAC), its engines having been equipped of 'Stage 3' silencers.
(J. Guillem collection)

These were specially upgraded and integrated into the Heyl ha'Avir which gave them not only their own designation, but also a name. Although the information concerning the military is in Israel particularly difficult to obtain, it is, however, sure that the first aircraft was a 707-329 upgraded into a flying tanker in 1983 by IAI Bedek ('KC 707'). The fleet of Israeli tankers, locally named 'Saknayee' (pelican) and put into service by the 120 Tayeset based at Lod, comprised between seven and nine aircraft; some were equipped, as well as their refuelling probe installed under the fuselage, with two extra pods. Some aircraft also had limited electronic warfare equipment. Apart from these planes, Israel also upgraded several 707-320 into airborne command posts ('Tavas'/woodpecker), electronic warfare and counter measu-

Opposite.
This 707-3L6B-H (c/n 21049) delivered in November 1977 to the government of the United Arab Emirates, is the last Boeing 707-320B to be built. It was used for VIP transport until 1994.
(V. Gréciet collection)

Below.
Transformed by the Israeli IAI company in March 1985, this Boeing 707-328C-H (c/n 19575), delivered to American Airlines in May 1968, was sold to Fuerza Aerea del Peru in February 1988 where it is still in service, essentially for transport missions. Note the national flag painted on the rudder. *(V. Gréciet collection)*

Below.
Chili still has three military Boeing 707 such as this '351', a 351C (c/n 19443) used for transport. *(F. Lert).*

Below.
Used by Boeing as a crew training aircraft, this 707-320C-H (c/n 19870) was initially sold to Varig in 1969, then in 1986 to the Brazilian air force who transformed it into a KC-137E tanker. It is still used by the 2° Esquadrão, 2° Grupo de Transporte 'Corsário' at Galeão.
(Wingmasters collection).

Below.
Firstly used by Northwest between 1961 and 1971, this 720-051B was acquired by the Republic of China (Taiwan), modified into a VIP transport and used by president Tchang Kai-Chek and his successors. It is now preserved in the RoCAF Museum at Kangshan.
(J. Guillem collection)

res (EC-707 'Chasidah' - stork), reconnaissance (RC-707 'Barboor' - swan), electronic signal collection platforms (SIGINT) or quite simply transport planes ('Re'em' - unicorn-at least three planes).

Today, some of the older planes have been retired from service, but most of the fleet is still used by Heyl ha'Avir and have undergone frequent upgrades and modifications, their

serial numbers having been often changed for reasons of military security. Amongst the most spectacular modifications, and the most immediately visible on the exterior, are the planes equipped with the Phalcon system, developed by Israel Aircraft Industries and mainly calling upon a phased array radar.

These aircraft differed by their large nose bulb that replaced the rotodome of the E-3 Sentry, but also by their wide rectangular fairings on each side of the fuselage in the same way as the USAF RC-135. Destined to serve as both flying radars and airborne command posts (Airborne Early Warning, Command and Control or AEWC&C), these aircraft were also capable of gathering information over a wide area (COMINT and ELINT). As well as the Israeli air force, Chile has also used an aircraft of this version since 1995, locally named 'Condor' which is in fact an old Lan Chile 707-385C upgraded by IAI.

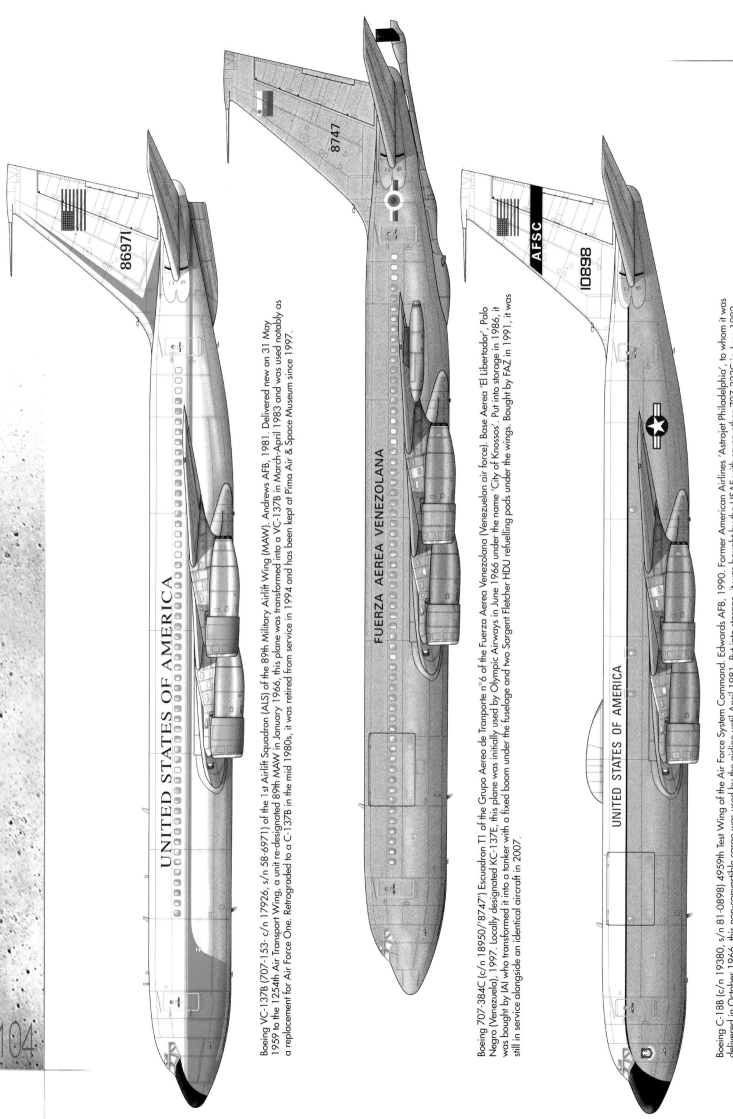

86971

8747

AFSC

10898

UNITED STATES OF AMERICA

FUERZA AEREA VENEZOLANA

UNITED STATES OF AMERICA

Boeing VC-137B (707-153 - c/n 17926, s/n 58-6971) of the 1st Airlift Squadron (ALS) of the 89th Military Airlift Wing (MAW). Andrews AFB, 1981. Delivered new on 31 May 1959 to the 1254th Air Transport Wing, a unit re-designated 89th MAW in January 1966, this plane was transformed into a VC-137B in March-April 1983 and was used notably as a replacement for Air Force One. Retrograded to a C-137B in the mid 1980s, it was retired from service in 1994 and has been kept at Pima Air & Space Museum since 1997.

Boeing 707-384C (c/n 18950/'8747') Escuadron T1 of the Grupo Aereo de Tranporte n°6 of the Fuerza Aerea Venezolana (Venezuelan air force). Base Aerea 'El Libertador', Palo Negro (Venezuela), 1997. Locally designated KC-137E, this plane was initially used by Olympic Airways in June 1966 under the name 'City of Knossos'. Put into storage in 1986, it was bought by IAI who transformed it into a tanker with a fixed boom under the fuselage and two Sargent Fletcher HDU refuelling pods under the wings. Bought by FAZ in 1991, it was still in service alongside an identical aircraft in 2007.

Boeing C-18B (c/n 19380, s/n 81-0898) 4959th Test Wing of the Air Force System Command. Edwards AFB, 1990. Former American Airlines 'Astrojet Philadelphia', to whom it was delivered in October 1966, this non-convertible cargo was used by the airline until April 1981. Put into storage, it was bought by the USAF with seven other 707-323C in June 1982. Designated C-18A, it was first used for EC-18B ARIA crew training and then became the only C-18B, leased by Grumman Aerospace, kept at Melbourne (Florida) and used for various tests. Its conversion to a E-8C was envisaged for a while but did not take place and it was first stored at the AMARC at Davis-Monthan (Arizona) where it can be found today.

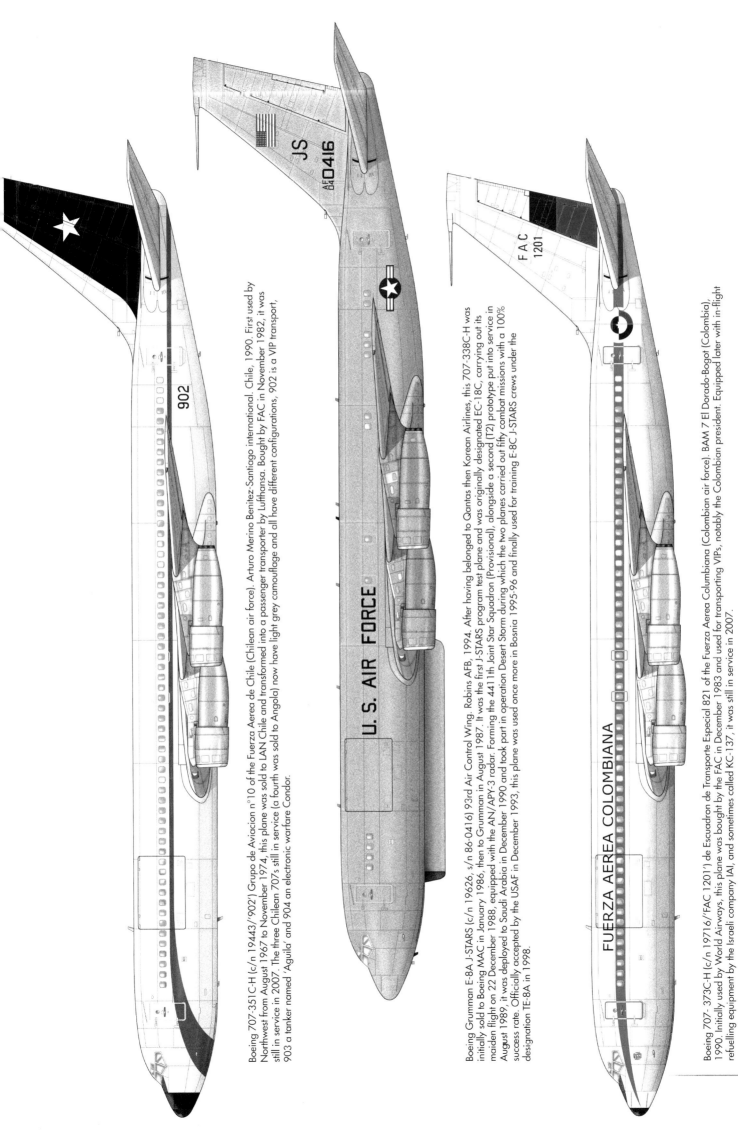

Boeing 707-351C-H (c/n 19443/'902') Grupo de Aviacion n°10 of the Fuerza Aerea de Chile (Chilean air force). Arturo Merino Benitez-Santiago international. Chile, 1990. First used by Northwest from August 1967 to November 1974, this plane was sold to LAN Chile and transformed into a passenger transporter by Lufthansa. Bought by FAC in November 1982, it was still in service in 2007. The three Chilean 707s still in service (a fourth was sold to Angola) now have light grey camouflage and all have different configurations, 902 is a VIP transport, 903 a tanker named 'Aguila' and 904 an electronic warfare Condor.

Boeing Grumman E-8A J-STARS (c/n 19626, s/n 86-0416) 93rd Air Control Wing. Robins AFB, 1994. After having belonged to Qantas then Korean Airlines, this 707-338C-H was initially sold to Boeing MAC in January 1986, then to Grumman in August 1987. It was the first J-STARS program test plane and was originally designated EC-18C, carrying out its maiden flight on 22 December 1988, equipped with the AN/APY-3 radar. Forming the 441 1th Joint Star Squadron (Provisional), alongside a second (T2) prototype put into service in August 1989, it was deployed to Saudi Arabia in December 1990 and took part in operation Desert Storm during which the two planes carried out fifty combat missions with a 100% success rate. Officially accepted by the USAF in December 1993, this plane was used once more in Bosnia 1995-96 and finally used for training E-8C J-STARS crews under the designation TE-8A in 1998.

Boeing 707- 373C-H (c/n 19716/'FAC 1201') de Escuadron de Transporte Especial 821 of the Fuerza Aerea Columbiana (Colombian air force). BAM 7 El Dorado-Bogot (Colombia), 1990. Initially used by World Airways, this plane was bought by the FAC in December 1983 and used for transporting VIPs, notably the Colombian president. Equipped later with in-flight refuelling equipment by the Israeli company IAI, and sometimes called KC-137, it was still in service in 2007.

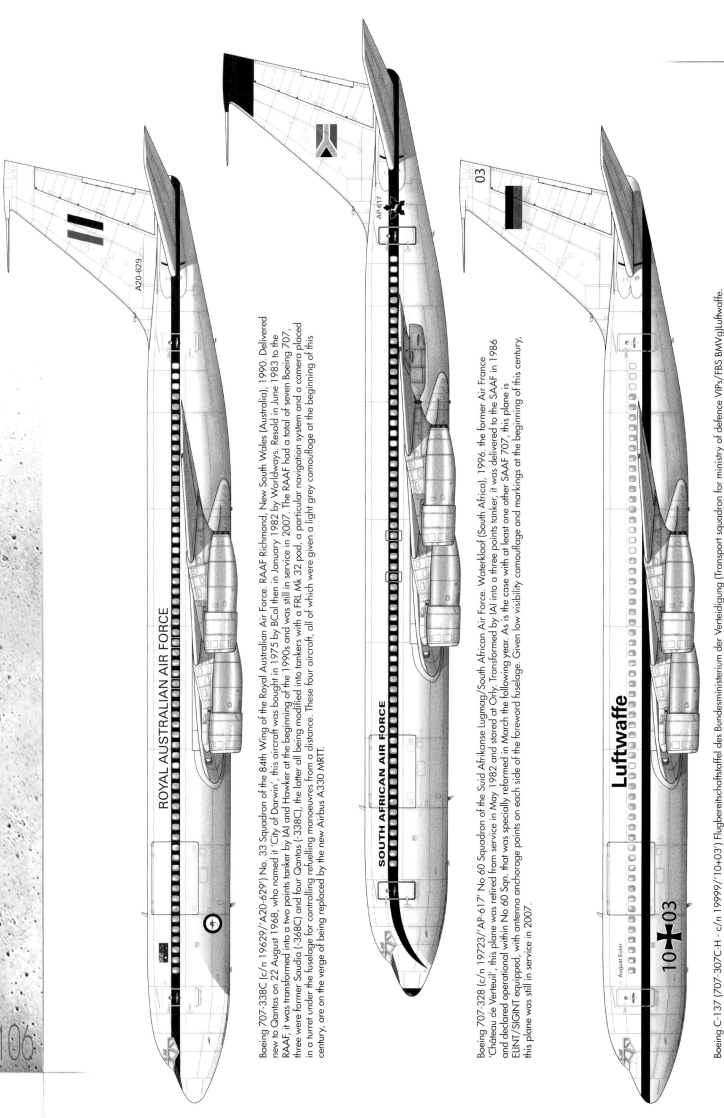

ROYAL AUSTRALIAN AIR FORCE

A20-629

Boeing 707-338C (c/n 19629/'A20-629') No. 33 Squadron of the 84th Wing of the Royal Australian Air Force. RAAF Richmond, New South Wales (Australia), 1990. Delivered new to Qantas on 22 August 1968, who named it 'City of Darwin', this aircraft was bought in 1975 by BCal then in January 1982 by Worldways. Resold in June 1983 to the RAAF, it was transformed into a two points tanker by IAI and Hawker at the beginning of the 1990s and was still in service in 2007. The RAAF had a total of seven Boeing 707, three were former Saudia (-368C) and four Qantas (-338C), the latter all being modified into tankers with a FRL Mk 32 pod, a particular navigation system and a camera placed in a turret under the fuselage for controlling refuelling manoeuvres from a distance. These four aircraft, all of which were given a light grey camouflage at the beginning of this century, are on the verge of being replaced by the new Airbus A330 MRTT.

SOUTH AFRICAN AIR FORCE

03

AP-617

Boeing 707-328 (c/n 19723/'AP-617' No 60 Squadron of the Suid Afrikanse Lugmag/South African Air Force. Waterkloof (South Africa), 1996. the former Air France 'Château de Verteuil', this plane was retired from service in May 1982 and stored at Orly. Transformed by IAI into a three points tanker, it was delivered to the SAAF in 1986 and declared operational within No 60 Sqn. that was specially reformed in March the following year. As is the case with at least one other SAAF 707, this plane is ELINT/SIGINT equipped, with antenna anchorage points on each side of the foreword fuselage. Given low visibility camouflage and markings at the beginning of this century, this plane was still in service in 2007.

Luftwaffe

August Euler

10+03

Boeing C-137 (707-307C-H - c/n 19999/'10+03') Flugbereitschaftstaffel des Bundesministerium der Verteidigung (Transport squadron for ministry of defence VIPs/FBS BMVg)Luftwaffe. Cologne-Wahn, 1998. Delivered new to the air force of the Federal Republic of Germany in October 1968, this plane was named 'August Euler'. Equipped with new silencers on its engines in 1987, it was retired from service in 1997, replaced by an Airbus A310 and put into storage at Hamburg. The four German C-137 (a designation used despite the presence of a cargo door) all bore a serial number of American origins (10+01 to 10+04/68-11071 to -11074).

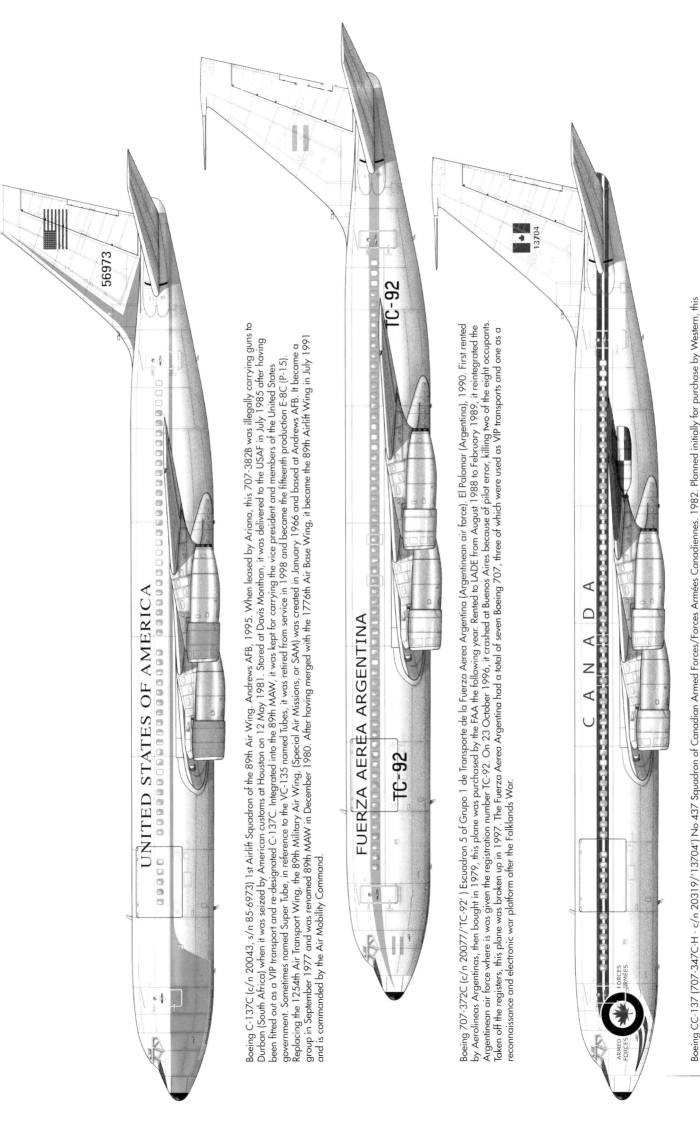

UNITED STATES OF AMERICA

56973

Boeing C-137C (c/n 20043, s/n 85-6973) 1st Airlift Squadron of the 89th Air Wing. Andrews AFB, 1995. When leased by Ariana, this 707-382B was illegally carrying guns to Durban (South Africa) when it was seized by American customs at Houston on 12 May 1981. Stored at Davis Monthan, it was delivered to the USAF in July 1985 after having been fitted out as a VIP transport and re-designated C-137C. Integrated into the 89th MAW, it was kept for carrying the vice president and members of the United States government. Sometimes named Super Tube, in reference to the VC-135 named Tubes, it was retired from service in 1998 and became the fifteenth production E-8C (P-15). Replacing the 1254th Air Transport Wing, the 89th Military Air Wing, (Special Air Missions, or SAM) was created in January 1966 and based at Andrews AFB. It became a group in September 1977 and was renamed 89th MAW in December 1980. After having merged with the 1776th Air Base Wing, it became the 89th Airlift Wing in July 1991 and is commanded by the Air Mobility Command.

FUERZA AEREA ARGENTINA

TC-92

TC-92

Boeing 707-372C (c/n 20077/'TC-92') Escuadron 5 of Grupo 1 de Transporte de la Fuerza Aerea Argentina (Argentinean air force). El Palomar (Argentina), 1990. First rented by Aerolineas Argentinas, then bought in 1979, this plane was purchased by the FAA the following year. Rented to LADE from August 1988 to February 1989, it reintegrated the Argentinean air force where is was given the registration number TC-92. On 23 October 1991, it crashed at Buenos Aires because of pilot error, killing two of the eight occupants. Taken off the registers, this plane was broken up in 1997. The Fuerza Aerea Argentina had a total of seven Boeing 707, three of which were used as VIP transports and one as a reconnaissance and electronic war platform after the Falklands War.

CANADA

13704

FORCES
ARMÉES

ARMED
FORCES

Boeing CC-137 (707-347C-H - c/n 20319/'13704') No 437 Squadron of Canadian Armed Forces/Forces Armées Canadiennes. 1982. Planned initially for purchase by Western, this plane was delivered to the RCAF in May 1971 and used until 1997 when it was bought by Boeing Grumman to become the ninth production E-8C (P9 - s/n 95-0124). The Canadian Armed Forces received a total of five CC-137 (the local designation of the military Boeing 707, including two aircraft (13703 and 13704) which were modified by Boeing as two point tankers in October 1972, after the installation of a Beech 1800 refuelling system.

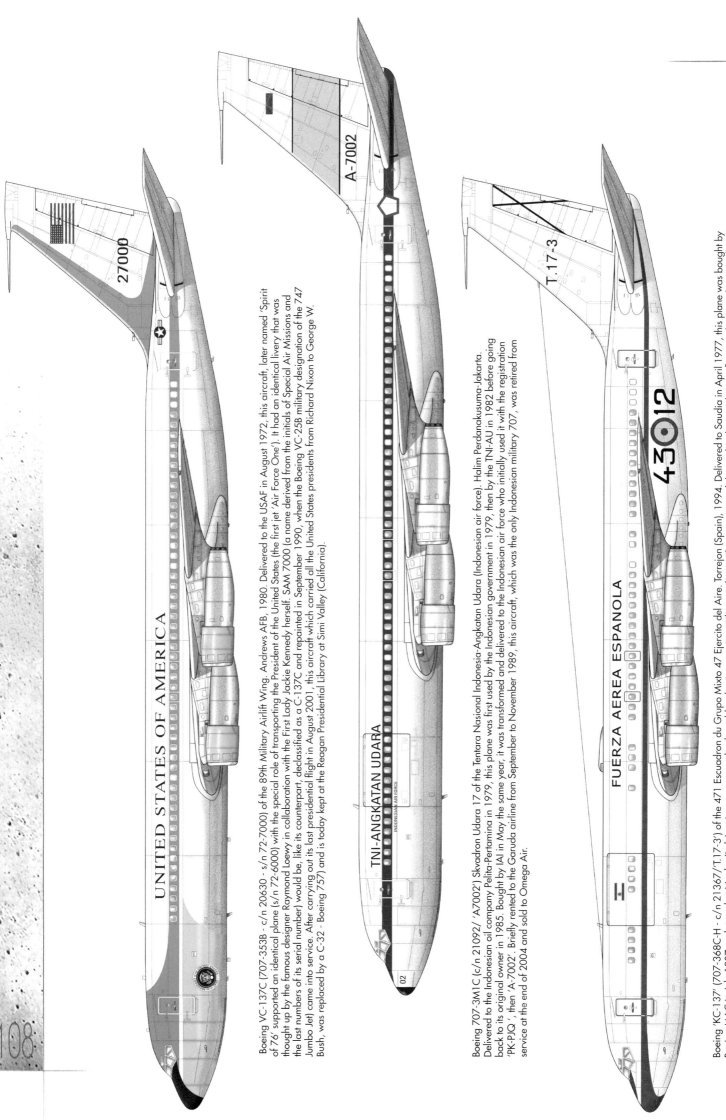

UNITED STATES OF AMERICA

27000

Boeing VC-137C (707-353B - c/n 20630 - s/n 72-7000) of the 89th Military Airlift Wing. Andrews AFB, 1980. Delivered to the USAF in August 1972, this aircraft, later named 'Spirit of 76' supported an identical plane (s/n 72-6000) with the special role of transporting the President of the United States (the first jet 'Air Force One'). It had an identical livery that was thought up by the famous designer Raymond Loewy in collaboration with the First Lady Jackie Kennedy herself. SAM 7000 (a name derived from the initials of Special Air Missions and the last numbers of its serial number) would be, like its counterpart, declassified as a C-137C and repainted in September 1990, when the Boeing VC-25B military designation of the 747 Jumbo Jet) came into service. After carrying out its last presidential flight in August 2001, this aircraft which carried all the United States presidents from Richard Nixon to George W. Bush, was replaced by a C-32 - Boeing 757) and is today kept at the Reagan Presidential Library at Simi Valley (California).

TNI-ANGKATAN UDARA

A-7002

Boeing 707-3M1C (c/n 21092/ 'A7002') Skvadron Udara 17 of the Tentara Nasional Indonesia-Angkatan Udara (Indonesian air force). Halim Perdanakusuma-Jakarta. Delivered to the Indonesian oil company Pelita-Pertamina in 1979, this plane was first used by the Indonesian government in 1979, then by the TNI-AU in 1982 before going back to its original owner in 1985. Bought by IAI in May the same year, it was transformed and delivered to the Indonesian air force who initially used it with the registration 'PK-PJQ ', then 'A-7002'. Briefly rented to the Garuda airline from September to November 1989, this aircraft, which was the only Indonesian military 707, was retired from service at the end of 2004 and sold to Omega Air.

FUERZA AEREA ESPANOLA

T.17-3

43012

Boeing 'KC-137' (707-368C-H - c/n 21367/'T.17-3') of the 471 Escuadron du Grupo Mixto 47 Ejercito del Aire. Torrejon (Spain), 1994. Delivered to Saudia in April 1977, this plane was bought by Boeing MAC in July 1987 and stored at Naples (Italy) as it was supposed to be sold to the Aeronautica Militare Italiana. The transaction did not take place and it was flown to the United States where it was transformed by Boeing into a two points tanker with two Sargent Fletcher 34-000 HDU pods under the wings. Sold to the Spanish air force in November 1989, it joined a second tanker (the three points Boeing demonstrator) bought the year before and serving with 451 Escuadron. This T.17 (local designation for a Boeing 707 with the EdA) was still in service in 2007.

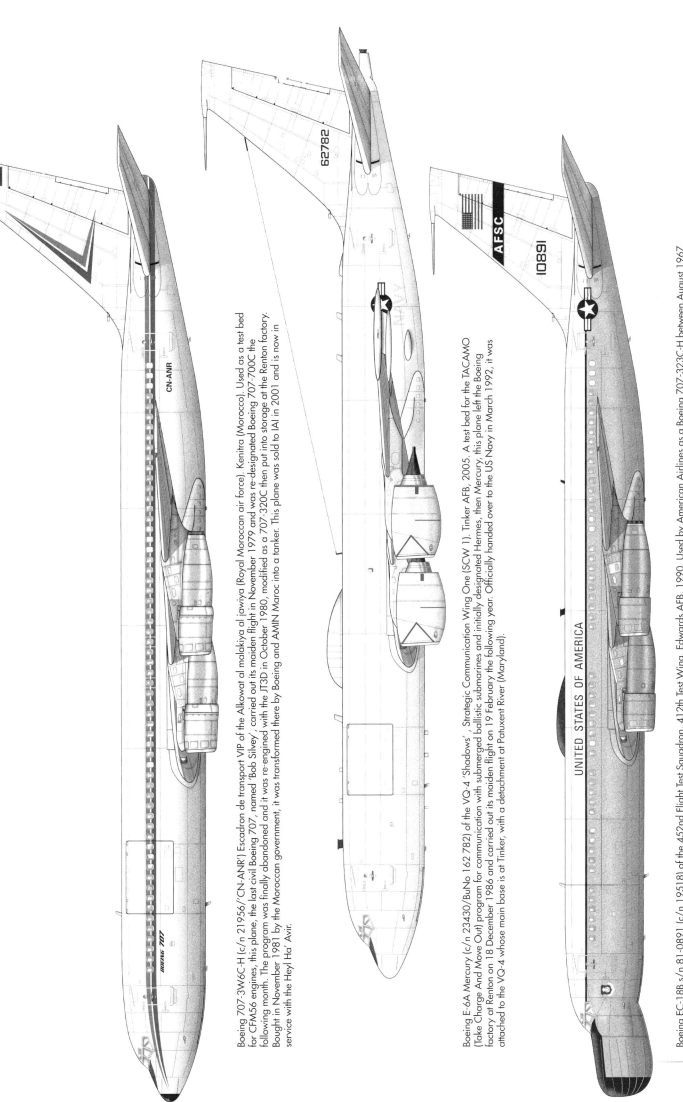

Boeing 707-3W6C-H (c/n 21956/'CN-ANR') Escadron de transport VIP of the Alkowat al malakiya al jawiya (Royal Moroccan air force). Kenitra (Morocco). Used as a test bed for CFM56 engines, this plane, the last civil Boeing 707, named 'Bob Silvey', carried out its maiden flight in November 1979 and was re-designated Boeing 707-700C the following month. The program was finally abandoned and it was re-engined with the JT3D in October 1980, modified as a 707-320C then put into storage at the Renton factory. Bought in November 1981 by the Moroccan government, it was transformed there by Boeing and AMIN Maroc into a tanker. This plane was sold to IAI in 2001 and is now in service with the Heyl Ha' Avir.

Boeing E-6A Mercury (c/n 23430/BuNo 162 782) of the VQ-4 'Shadows', Strategic Communication Wing One (SCW 1). Tinker AFB, 2005. A test bed for the TACAMO (Take Charge And Move Out) program for communication with submerged ballistic submarines and initially designated Hermes, then Mercury, this plane left the Boeing factory at Renton on 18 December 1986 and carried out its maiden flight on 19 February the following year. Officially handed over to the US Navy in March 1992, it was attached to the VQ-4 whose main base is at Tinker, with a detachment at Patuxent River (Maryland).

Boeing EC-18B s/n 81-0891 (c/n 19518) of the 452nd Flight Test Squadron, 412th Test Wing. Edwards AFB, 1990. Used by American Airlines as a Boeing 707-323C-H between August 1967 and August 1981, this plane was first stored at Waco (Texas) then sold to the USAF in February 1982. Initially transformed into a C-18A, it next became one of the EC-18B ARIA (Advanced Range Instrumentation Aircraft) whose role was to support the EC-135N fleet. Bigger than the latter, the EC-18B ARIA carried a higher payload and was of a higher performance, notably on take-off. This plane, which carried out its first mission in January 1986, has been stored at Edwards since 2001. The 452nd FLTS equipped with, in addition to the EC-18B, EC-135E and NKC-135B and E, depended originally on the Air Force System Command (AFSC) which was replaced by the Air Force Materiel Command (AFMC) in July 1992.

THE BOEING E-3 SENTRY

Popularly known under the generic term, AWACS (Airborne Warning And Control System), the Boeing E-3 Sentry is without doubt the best known of all the military 707s and the last of a long line that began with the 'Dash 80'. Having seen the light of day at the end of the 20th century, it is promised a long career and deserves its own chapter!

The concept of a plane able to foresee an enemy attack, thanks to its on board detection and surveillance equipment, is certainly as old as aviation itself. It came back in force after the Second World War, mainly by the United States who were deeply shocked by the surprise attack at Pearl Harbor in December 1941. They did not want, in the context born of the Cold War, to face such a situation, especially as the threat had moved to the Soviet Union that now had nuclear weapons.

To this end, various land and sea based systems were designed, in particular the famous DEW (Distant Early Warning [1]) Line, a warning radar network installed in the far north, including Canada, and destined to give sufficient early warning of the arrival of strategic bombers passing via the Pole. This land-based network soon showed its limitations, notably due to the existence of 'gaps' where no surveillance could be carried out. The decision was taken to deal with these gaps by using planes that had been modified as flying radars, operating in relays, twenty-four hours a day, every day of the year. The equipment necessary to this new role took up a lot of space and also required a lot of personnel. It was decided, at the beginning of the 1950s, to use in this new role the military version of the Lockheed Super Constellation, a plane known for its speed and carrying capacities [2].

Above.
A not yet modernised E-3C (s/n 82-00006) of the 965th AACS of the 552nd ACW seen in flight. The aircraft of the various squadrons of this unit are only outwardly distinguishable by the coloured strip at the top of the tail fin. Apart from their usual role in large-scale military operations, the USAF Sentry aircraft have also taken part in anti drug missions, notably over the Caribbean Sea. (USAF).

1. Literally remote alert line.
2. See *Lockheed Constellation, from Excalibur to Starliner. Legends of the sky n° 1. Histoire & Collections.*

An E-3C of the 970th Expeditionary Aerospace Air Control Squadron (EAACS), landing at the Turkish base at Incirlik in 2002. (USAF)

Opposite.
Registered in the Duchy of Luxemburg and served by crews from the fourteen member countries of the Alliance, the seventeen NATO Sentry aircraft, like this E-3A (90454), bear the NATO AEW Force emblem beneath their windscreen. (F. Lert)

Below, right.
The official presentation of the first EC-137D (s/n 71-1407) on 25 January 1972. Like its counterpart, this aircraft would later be modified to a E-3A. (USAF).

Above.
In order to define the AWACS concept, two prototypes were made from civil Boeing 707-320B airframes and designated EC-137D. Each one was equipped with a different radar, made respectively Hughes and Westinghouse. Boeing 707-320B, s/n 71-1408, the second prototype, undertook its maiden flight on 10 January 1972 and was transformed successively to a E-3A in 1977 and a E-3B. (WingMasters collection).

Below.
The civil origins of the EC-137D (here the second prototype, s/n 71-1408 equipped with the Westinghouse radar) are immediately visible by the cabin windows that have simply been plugged. Transformed to a E-3B, this plane is today in service with the 552nd ACW. (WingMasters collection).

Put into service as much by the USAF (EC-121) as by the US Navy (WV-2/EC-121K), the 'Warning Star' carried out this task until the beginning of the 1980s, a period when their replacement was more keenly felt, given that the threat had evolved at the same time as technique had progressed.

The AWACS program

The USAF, therefore, began looking for a new aircraft to replace its EC-121; an aircraft that had to be jet engined, in order to carry a heavier load, and above all, to fly at a higher altitude, increasing the range of the on-board radar. The latter was a Doppler type and had great capacities of ground detection. This radar was initially designed as part of the programme ORT (Overland Radar Technology) launched in 1965, the main objective of which was to pick up, over land as well as sea, small size jet aircraft flying at very low altitude. The trials undertaken within this program resulted in the design of a Pulse Doppler radar which, as its name suggests, combined a succession of energy pulses and the Doppler effect which consisted of measuring the slight variation in the echoes sent and those received. Several aviation companies, therefore, put their name forward, notably Douglas that

had now become McDonnell Douglas, who proposed an aircraft based on its DC-8-60, carrying on its back a rotating radome held by four pylons. As for Boeing, they suggested using the 707-320B airframe, known for its performance and autonomy, and studied various configurations for the position of the radar (top of the vertical stabilizer, or more classically above the fuselage held by pylons like on the Grumman E-2C Hawkeye or the prototype Lockheed WV-2E/EC-121L). It also had engines identical to those on the civil 707 Intercontinental (four TF33 turbofans, the military version of the JT3D) or those of the B-52 (four pairs of TF34).

It was finally Boeing Aerospace that was declared the winner of the competition; the USAF signed a contract on 23 July 1970 for two prototypes powered by eight engines and destined to evaluate the two competing radar systems, the first designed by Hughes, the second by Westinghouse.

In order to cut costs, and above all, to speed up the bringing into service of these prototypes, Boeing finally decided to give up on the concept of an eight engined plane, even though it

was chosen by the army, and use the production 707-320B as a platform. Outwardly similar, apart from their radome, with masked over windows, and renamed after transformation the EC-137D, the first of them undertook its maiden flight on 9 February 1972, and the second the following day.

The trials took place in the Seattle region between April and September 1972, in different conditions as much geographical as meteorological, and against varied targets, from the F-4 fighter to the B-52 heavy bomber. When these tests were complete,

The maiden flight of a pre-production E-3, named Sentry shortly after, took place on 21 July 1975, the aircraft at this time not yet being equipped with its radar. The latter was placed in a slightly oval shaped radome measuring 9.14 m (40 feet) in diameter and 1.83 m (6 feet) thick, held by two pylons 4.27 m (14 feet) above the fuselage and very slightly inclined towards the front so that the range of the radar towards the ground would be increased. The fairing contained, mounted back to back and separated by a beam able to resist torsion, the liquid-cooled detection

Above.
Made from the airframes of the civil Boeing 707, access to the Sentry was via a door situated high up, necessitating mobile steps. This differed from the military versions (C-135 and versions) that were equipped with a lower positioned hatch and, above all, equipped with a retractable ladder. (F. Lert).

the Westinghouse AN/APY-1 radar was chosen and installed in a rotating radome placed on the aircraft's back.

Pre-production Sentry

The AWACS development program was launched in January 1973 and Boeing was given the task of making four out of the six envisaged pre-production planes, two of them were in reality only transformations of the EC-137D prototypes.

radar antenna and the IFF antennae; it turned in a clockwise direction at a rate that went from three rotations a minute in standby mode, to six per minute when functioning. Made up of two fibre glass radomes sandwiched together at the front and rear, the rotodome only slightly affected the Sentry's manoeuvrability and a weak aerodynamic drag compared to a standard Boeing 707.

The surveillance radar, whose antenna is made up of fifty three wave guides placed one over the other, can operate up

Opposite.
A E-3C of the 961st AACS taking off from its base at Kadena, Okinawa, in 2004. The Sentry aircraft of this squadron are identified by their red stripe painted on the tail fin and by the 'ZZ' code which is specific to this Japanese base. (USAF)

Below.
In order to carry out Sentry crew training, NATO uses two 707-TCA (for Trainer Cargo Aircraft). In reality these are two former Sabena 707-329C like this one here, which bear their constructor number (20199) on the tail fin. These two aircraft are painted in the same way as the E-3A and bear identical markings. (F. Lert)

Above.
Sleeve insignia of the Armée de l'Air
36e EDCA. (F. Lert)

to the level of the stratosphere, over land and sea. Two generators that are both installed on the engines allow for the gain of the megawatt needed to make this equipment function. The electromagnetic pulses, controlled by a computer to prevent too high losses in energy, form a beam that can be aimed either towards the ground, or to the sky up to the maximum altitude of any normal aircraft. All of the signals sent by the radar, as well as the echoes received, pass via circuits placed in the two rotodome struts. Finally, the navigation itself calls upon two hybrid Delco inertial units with an Omega receiver, a navigation Doppler and a Northrop calculator.

Flying at a cruising speed of Mach 0.72 at an average altitude of 8,800 km (5,468 miles), a Sentry thus has a range of more than 375 km (233 miles) for targets flying at low altitude and beyond the horizon, that is roughly 650 km (403 miles) for those flying at medium or high altitude. The AN/APY-1 or -2 radar, depending on versions being coupled to the IFF system, the operators can detect, identify and follow a friendly or enemy target whilst eliminating parasite echoes which, in normal times, would hamper the other radars.

THE DIFFERENT RADAR MODES OF THE SENTRY

The E-3's radar, that begins working at full power as soon as the aircraft reaches its patrol zone, is able to work in six different modes that can be used simultaneously during a single rotation of its antenna (ten seconds).

- The most straightforward is the passive mode where the radar does not emit any signal. Only antennae record all of the signals received, wherever they come from, with the on-board equipment determining their source, position and exact nature. This mode is very efficient in a particularly dense electronic counter measure environment and means that the Sentry can avoid being spotted, then jammed or even attacked by possible adversary.

- The BTH (Beyond The Horizon) mode at repetitive low frequency, permits long distance detection of objectives beyond the earth's horizon, but does not allow for the gathering of data relating to the altitude of these objectives. This mode only calls upon the radar's pulses, but not the Doppler effect.

- The most commonly used mode is the PDES (Pulse Doppler Elevation Scan) which calls upon the high

frequency repetition pulses of the Doppler radar that can determine with precision the altitude of objectives, thanks to a vertical sweep of the air space. Its only downside is a decrease in the system's range.

- The bi-dimensional mode, PDNES (Pulse Doppler Non Elevation Scan), derives from the previous one and functions in a similar way. It is used when it is necessary to increase radar's range and when determining the exact altitude of the objective is not primordial.

- In maritime mode, the radar, which emits a beam of repetitive low frequency waves, is capable of detecting surface vessels whatever the sea conditions whilst a digital system allows the sorting of the echoes received and, therefore, the elimination of those caused by waves or areas of land.

- The 'Interleaved' mode is a combination of two modes (PDES and BTH or PDNES and Maritime) for determining the altitude of objectives flying at great distances, or the presence of both ships and aircraft.

Above.
An Armée de l'Air E-3F console. The French 'SDCA' usually carry nine operators known as 'contrôleurs'.
(F. Lert).

A partial view of the cabin interior of an Armée de l'Air E-3F. The technical crew is usually made up of thirteen specialists. The various posts are installed perpendicularly to the cabin; a corridor is placed on the left.
(F. Lert).

Opposite, left.
E-3F n° 203 was the third
SDCA delivered to the Armée de l'Air.
Taken into account in September 1991, it bears,
like its counterparts, the traditional insignia of the escadrilles
constituting the 36ᵉ Escadre de Détection
et de Commandement Aéroporté. (F. Lert).

Above.
The RAF's seven Sentry AEW Mk I
(here 'ZH-104' in flight) are all based
at Waddington and are attached, with
their NATO counterparts, to the
NAEWFC (NATO Airborne Early Warning Force). Replacing the ancient
Avro Shackleton, all the British aircraft
are painted entirely grey and have low
visibility markings; the insignia of the
two squadrons equipped with these
planes are on each side of the tail fin.
The red eagle, visible in this photo, is
the insignia of No. 23 Squadron.
(V. Gréciet collection)

Below.
Like their American counterparts,
the French E-3F are painted entirely in
light grey ('Boeing Grey'), apart from
their radome which is black and white.
The Armée de l'Air was the last Sentry
customer, its aircraft being constantly
upgraded and capable of performing
to an equivalent, or higher standard
than those of the USAF. (F. Lert)

Above.
A close up of the front of E-3B s/n 75-0556 of the 961st
AACS 'Eyes of the Pacific', based in Japan and showing the
extra radome that is characteristic of this modernised version,
as well as the access door that is for both the cockpit and the
cabin. The pilots' names are painted beneath the windscreen.
(USAF)

Below.
A close up of the rear of a French E-3F and its detector
placed in this area. This system has only appeared here with
the modernised versions of the Sentry.
(F. Lert).

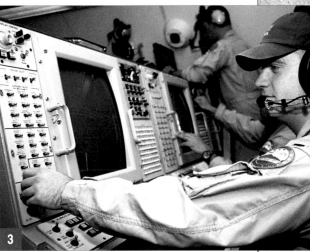

Above.
To celebrate the twenty-fifth anniversary of the AEWF in 2007, this NATO's E-3A (LX-N/90443) received this special and spectacular livery.
(J. Guillem collection)

Opposite, top to bottom .
1. Two radar operators at their post aboard a USAF Sentry. (USAF)
2. A E-3C systems operator of the 961st AACS inspects the systems before a flight at Kadena 2007. (USAF)
3. An operator in front of his console during operation 'Southern Watch'. (USAF)
4. Collected data can be presented in different forms on the Sentry's screens as it is visible on this operator's post of a 963rd AACS aircraft. (USAF)

On the various consoles in the cabin, data is supplied in the shape of graphs or tables, the on-board operators being tasked with surveillance, identification, weapons systems control and overseeing combat and communications. The radar, coupled to a computer, gathers and supplies global as well as detailed information, the data being received in real time. This information can be transmitted to the main command posts based on land or on board ships or, in the event of a crisis, sent to the NCA (National Command Authority). To avoid any interference due to the small space inside the cabin, filled with the systems operators' posts, the frequencies of the radio posts are controlled directly by the on-board computer.

The E-3 can be used for aerial support and then transmit their information so that interdiction, support for troops on the ground, reconnaissance, transport or in-flight refuelling missions can be put together. They can even be used for air defence, guiding interceptors towards their target situated far beyond borders whilst at the same time not infringing these themselves.

Capable of surviving in a electronic counter measure hostile environment, the Sentry is considered as being of a higher performance than any other analogue ground system as its mission can always be adapted to the risks, and can, therefore, be modified if need be. The E-3 is able to fly continuously for eight hours and its missions can be prolonged well beyond thanks to in-flight

The rotodome is in fact made up of two fibre glass radomes placed at the front and the rear which contain respectively, the detection radar antenna and that of the IFF (Identification Friend or Foe) placed back to back and separated by a beam. Differing from the rest of the plane, this radome is not painted so that the transmission of electro magnetic waves will not be perturbed. (USAF)

refuelling as all the aircraft are equipped with receptacles for this purpose. A second crew can take over in the cabin in the event of longer flights.

With the trials for the pre-production aircraft not yet complete, notably in the domain of 'survivability' in operations or in protection against scrambling, the American Congress authorised the production of 21 (22 [3]) production aircraft in November 1974.

E-3A 'Core' and 'Standard'

The first production Sentry aircraft began to enter service in the spring of 1977 with the 552nd ACW at Tinker, Oklahoma, under the generic name of 'Core E-3A'. This first block in fact comprised the two upgraded prototypes (in 1977 and 1978 but retaining their masked off windows), one of the pre-production aircraft, the twenty-one aircraft first ordered in 1974 and one from the next order; the eleven other 'Core' initially ordered were finally cancelled. All these aircraft are distinguished by their AN/APY-1 radar and their IBM CC-1 computer. The cabin has six SDC tactical information visualisation consoles, to which are added

two auxiliary visualisation units and thirteen communication channels.

Between 1980 and 1983, when the USAF decided to go back on its decision to cancel the initial order of eleven Core E-3A aircraft to replace it with another, this time for only eight. It made the most of the opportunity to also acquire a slightly improved version of the Sentry, designated 'Standard' or 'Common' E-3A.

Above.
An aerial view of the Sentry fleet based at Tinker in 1978.
(USAF)

Opposite.
A modernised E-3B (s/n 79-00002) of the 960th EACCS being prepared before a mission during operation 'Enduring Freedom', the United Nations intervention in Afghanistan following the terrorist attacks of 11 September 2001. One of the tasks of the Sentry consists of controlling and guiding the Allied aircraft escorting the C-17 aircraft carrying out humanitarian missions in the east of the country. (USAF)

3. This number depends in fact on the amount of E-3A of the 'Core' and 'Standard Common' type taken into account in the total number of 34 aircraft, including prototypes. The last 'Core E-3A' is sometimes included in the number of 'Standards' bringing the latter from 8 to 9 aircraft.

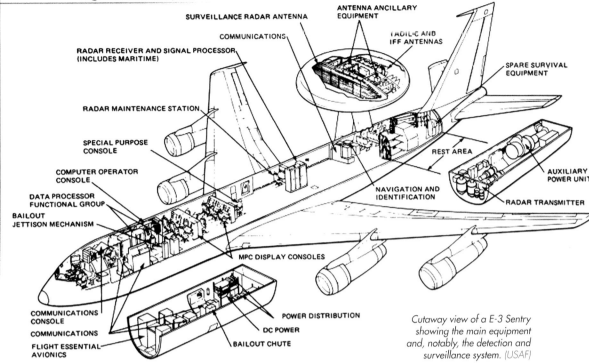

SURVEILLANCE RADAR ANTENNA

ANTENNA ANCILLARY
EQUIPMENT

COMMUNICATIONS

TADIL-C AND
IFF ANTENNAS

RADAR RECEIVER AND SIGNAL PROCESSOR
(INCLUDES MARITIME)

SPARE SURVIVAL
EQUIPMENT

RADAR MAINTENANCE STATION

SPECIAL PURPOSE
CONSOLE

REST AREA

COMPUTER OPERATOR
CONSOLE

AUXILIARY
POWER UNIT

DATA PROCESSOR
FUNCTIONAL GROUP

NAVIGATION AND
IDENTIFICATION

RADAR TRANSMITTER

BAILOUT
JETTISON MECHANISM

MPC DISPLAY CONSOLES

COMMUNICATIONS
CONSOLE

POWER DISTRIBUTION

COMMUNICATIONS

DC POWER

FLIGHT ESSENTIAL
AVIONICS

BAILOUT CHUTE

Cutaway view of a E-3 Sentry showing the main equipment and, notably, the detection and surveillance system. (USAF)

Top.
Like the Armée de l'Air Sentry, the British E-3D is equipped with a refuelling boom placed on the right above the cockpit. Here, a Sentry AEW.1 of No. 23 Squadron positions itself behind a USAF KC-135R to refuel in order to continue its long mission.
(No. 8 Sqn/RAF)

Below.
A RAF Sentry AEW.1 integrated into the USAF 963rd Expeditionary Wing during operation 'Iraqi Freedom' in 2003 and based in Saudi Arabia.
(USAF)

As technology had progressed since the launch of the AWACS program, new aircraft were equipped with the AN/APY-2 radar with new maritime search capacities, a new faster CC-2 computer, higher performance and more secure transmission and analyse equipment, and eleven radio posts instead of the seven previously installed.

Delivery of this second block went on until June 1984, a date on which the last Standard E-3A and, therefore, the last of the thirty-four first generation Sentry aircraft attached to the 552nd ACW, the only USAF unit equipped with this type. Afterwards, the whole Common E-3A fleet was upgraded and became the E-3C. Reactivated in July 1976, the 552nd AWACW (re-designated ACW shortly after) was given the task of training the crews, maintenance and logistical and software support of all the American Sentry aircraft. Dependent for administration on the 28th Air division, all these units based at Tinker can, at the shortest notice, deploy one or several aircraft anywhere in the United States or the world, depending on needs or threats. To this end, during periods of crisis, four E-3 are kept on alert in a zone away from the base. The support of the Sentry aircraft (air start trucks, air conditioning systems etc.) is carried out by the 443rd MAW at Altus, equipped with the C-5 Galaxy that can follow the planes wherever they go.

E-3B and E-3C

Within the framework of the upgrade program for part of the USAF Sentry fleet named 'Block 20', twenty-three Core E-3A,

including the two prototypes and a pre-production plane, were transformed into the E-3B starting in the middle of 1984. This upgrade tended to benefit these older aircraft with new equipment installed in the second block supplied to the USAF, this being a Westinghouse AN/APY-2 radar and a higher capacity IBM CC-2 computer (bubble memory with an increased capacity and higher powers of calculation), notably in maritime surveillance, class 2 JTDIS terminals, five extra data analysis posts, bringing the total amount of the latter to fourteen, a third high frequency radio or even five extra secure UHF radio posts. The first aircraft was modified at the Boeing factory, the others being transformed directly at the Tinker base with kits delivered by Boeing; they began to re-enter service in the second half of 1984.

One of these planes ('Yukla 27', s/n 77-0354, c/n 21554) was lost along with its crew (24 men including two from the RCAF) on 22 September 1995 whilst it was taking off from the Elmensdorf base, its two port engines (Alaska) having suddenly lost all power following a bird strike.

The following upgrade (Block 25) concerned the eight Standard E-3A and the last Core and put these planes, now designated E-3C, on a similar level to that of the new E-3B. These modifications mostly consisted of the addition of five extra analysis consoles and new exterior antennae. Another modernisation program for the entire American Sentry fleet (Block 30/35 Modification Program), developed from the US Army 'Quick Look' system, was launched in 1987 and was destined to increase reliability, ease general maintenance and increase the rate of availability of this type by notably providing it with

An indispensable component of any large-scale military operation, the Sentry is one of the first aircraft to be deployed by the USAF. (USAF)

characteristics identical to that of aircraft in service with NATO. The thirty-five aircraft still in service were, therefore, respectively brought up to the new E-3B Block 30 (twenty three planes) and E-3C Block 35 (nine planes) standard; this upgrade, which was completed in 2001, comprised several major improvements consisting of adding:

- An ESM (Electronic Support Measurer) AN/AYR-1, an electronic system already installed on the NATO E-3A permitting the passive detection and identification of the sources of aerial and land signals. This is immediately outwardly identifiable by two extra fairings, almost four metres in length, added along both sides of the fuselage in front of the wings, and also by two new bulges on the nose and tail.

- A JTDIS (Joint Tactical Information Distribution System) to make safe communications when data is transmitted, the latter is sent to a receiver, generally another plane, without any vocal contact.

- An increased memory for the IBM CC-2E with magnetic bubble memory on board computer in order for it to use not only the new ESM and JTDIS, but also any future equipment that may be installed.

- A GPS satellite positioning system for more precise navigation, rendering a navigator completely unnecessary.

- The addition of a secure anti-jam communication system 'Have Quick A-NETS'.

Finally, a last, for the time being at least, radar upgrade program (RSIP, for 'Radar System Improvement Program') was launched in 1999. It was destined for both USAF and NATO aircraft and aimed at improving the performance of electronic counter measures, but also increase the reliability and availability of planes

thanks to a modification to the on-board computers and software they use. The radar is now able to detect very small size objectives (drones) or furtive aircraft.

This RSIP program, established in collaboration with the USAF and NATO, coupled with the 'Extend Sentry Program', consisted of replacing the original cockpit with that of the Boeing 737-300 (digital and more analogical consoles). The program came to an end in 2004 when the last modernised Sentry re-entered into service.

Today, the USAF has a total fleet of thirty-two E-3 of different variants [4] (twenty three E-3B and nine E-3C). Twenty-eight are based at Tinker with the 552nd Airborne Control Wing made up of the 963rd 'Blue Knights', 964th 'Phoenix', 965th 'Falcons' and 966th 'Ravens' Airborne Air Control Squadrons, the last being more for crew and flight crew training, the systems operators with the TC-18E, as well as the flight or mission simulators), and the 513th Airborne Control Group of the reserve (AFRC), formed in March 1996. Two extra squadrons are based overseas; the 961st AACS with two planes at Kadena (Okinawa) and the 962nd AACS 'Eye of the Eagle', at Elmensdorf (Alaska), the 960th AWACS at Keflavik having been deactivated after the disintegration of the Soviet Bloc.

The USAF E-3 aircraft accompany, or precede, all of the United States military campaigns and they were, therefore, one of the key elements of the second Gulf War. They were amongst the first to arrive in Saudi Arabia at the end of the summer of 1990 in order to set up a veritable protective radar curtain for the

Top.
As part of operation 'Iraqi Freedom', the United States intervention in Iraq, a detachment of forty people and a E-3 Sentry of the 363rd Expeditionary Airborne Air Control Squadron were based in Saudi Arabia. It was from here that this squadron carried out its last mission after thirteen years of service. (USAF).

Above.
All of the USAF Sentry aircraft, like this E-3C (s/n 80-0137) are attached to the 552nd Air Control Wing at Tinker which has permanent overseas detachments, essentially on island of Okinawa (Kadena) and in Alaska (Elmendorf). The plane here is from the 963rd AACS and is recognisable by the black stripe painted at the top of the tail fin above the base code (OK). (USAF)

4. The third pre-production E-3 has been kept by Boeing in order to carry out different flight-testing campaigns. Sometimes named TS3 for Test System 3, and equipped identically to a pre-production E-3C, it is officially designated JE-3C.

An E-3C of 964th AWACS takes off from the Elmensdorf base, Alaska, in 2001 during operation 'Northern Edge'. (USAF)

Above.

The Armée de l'Air E-3F aircraft were bought in a joint operation with the RAF in order to decrease the purchase costs. Very similar to their British counterparts (engines, refuelling booms), the French Sentry has been modified in order to be used as a flying command post. (F. Lert)

Above.

An E-3C (s/n 83-00008) of the 363rd Expeditionary Airborne Air Control Squadron, 363rd Air Expeditionary Wing takes off from the Prince Sultan base in Saudi Arabia during a sand storm on 23 May of the same year. The whole wing was later disbanded and the United States left the Saudi kingdom to base itself in other Persian Gulf countries, notably Qatar. (USAF)

Above.

Insignia of the 552nd ACW from Tinker AFB.

Allies. During 'Desert Storm', they carried out over 400 missions, this representing no less than 5,000 hours on site, coordinating more than 120,000 sorties for coalition aircraft, and were at the origin of 38 of the 40 kills achieved during the operation.

Also used in antidrug operations in the Caribbean and Gulf of Mexico, the Sentry aircraft of the Air Combat Command have also been intensively used in the former Yugoslavia, Afghanistan (operation 'Enduring Freedom', and during the second Gulf War (operation Iraqi Freedom'), beginning in 2003. For the time being, their replacement is not on the cards; the fleet will have to fly until at least the end of the first quarter of this century. There is a good chance that the E-3's successor will be another Boeing product, the E-10 MC2A, based on the 767-400ER. In the meantime, a new modernisation program (Block 40/45 Modification Program) has been launched. It is destined to replace a large part of the on board equipment, notably the computers, the design of which goes back to the 1970s, with new, more powerful and faster examples [5]. The communications network, inside as well as outside, will be greatly improved, allowing for safer and more efficient digital transmission of data, improving at the same time the rate of availability and efficiency of the Sentry. At the moment, the exact contents of this program are not totally defined; however it is forecast that the first modified aircraft, designated E-3G, will begin to be delivered in 2009, the objective being to integrate the new Sentry into the SIAP program (Single Integrated Air Picture). This is a system still being studied and is destined to centralise, in real time, all of the data gathered via various means: land, maritime, space or aerial, concerning any type of objective in order to give it a unique 'treatment' number. This will, therefore, keep these planes in the front line until at least 2025-35.

For NATO, Great Britain, Saudi Arabia and France

The North Atlantic Treaty Organisation (NATO) first showed an interest in a radar surveillance aircraft in 1975. Having initially envisaged a fleet of 27 aircraft, it had to scale down this number after Great Britain pulled out of the project two years later. At the end of 1978, twelve of the NATO member countries [6] signed an agreement for the purchase of eighteen E-3A, which were delivered between 1982 and 1985. These are based in Germany at Geilenkirchen, where a three-kilometre runway was specially made, but registered in the Duchy of Luxemburg. These planes are operated by thirty crews that come from all of the Alliance's member countries implicated in the program, to which are added the British. The training of these crews, which began in the United States in 1982 with the 963rd AWAC Training Squadron at Tinker, is now carried out by two 707-TCA (for Trainer Cargo Aircraft), in reality two former Sabena 707-329 planes. Similar to the USAF E-3C, despite their designation, the NATO Sentry aircraft have avionics made by Dornier and were all equipped in Europe.

Operational since 1988 with the AEWF (Airborne Early Warning Force), one of these aircraft (c/n 22852/LX-N90457) was lost in Greece when taking off, one more because of a bird strike; however, no crew members were lost. Constantly upgraded, these planes are judged as being better than their United

---

5. The improvements of Blocks 40/45 comprise, amongst others, the Global Broadcast Service (GBS), a digital communication system that permits the gathering of weather and strategic data in the fastest way, the Data Link Infrastructure (DLI)which reduces the lapse time in transmissions, notably for the use of fighters in the event of particularly large/important targets, whilst new consoles and new computers, as well as more efficient software will be installed.
6. Belgium, Canada, Denmark, Greece, Italy, Luxemburg, Norway, Holland, Portugal, Turkey and the United States.

States counterparts. The RSIP program, carried out by DASA, ended in 2000 and a second modernisation (MTM or 'Mid Term Modernisation'), superior to the USAF Blocks 30-35 (GPS, MSI 'Multi Sensor Integration') and carried out by EADS, should be completed in 2008, the fleet being destined to remain operational until approximately 2025. Saudi Arabia, as part of the 'Peace Sentinel' program launched in 1981, also began taking delivery of five E-3A in September 1986. These planes, which did not have some of the most modern equipment installed on American or European aircraft, were, on the other hand, powered by CFM56 engines equipped with thrust reversers. Their radar system was modernised between 2001 and 2003. They are in service with No. 18 Squadron of the RSAF and operate along with the 707 (RE-3) electronic warfare versions owned by the kingdom.

Great Britain was the third country to buy this final version of the Boeing 707. In 1987, it initially ordered six, then finally seven, aircraft designated E-3D by Boeing and locally Sentry AEW Mk.1. This decision came after the cancellation of the Nimrod AEW.3 radar aircraft program designed by British Aerospace, necessitating the production of seven prototypes based on the evolution of the De Havilland Comet, curious turnabout thirty years later! These aircraft are fairly similar to the American E-3C, but like the Saudi planes, are powered by the CFM 56, much higher performance engines than the TF33/JT3D. They have a fixed in-flight refuelling boom, placed above the windscreen, along with the receptacle mounted on all Sentry aircraft, as well as LORAL 'Yellow Gate' counter measure wing tip pods. The first sortie by a British plane took place in May 1991 and the aircraft were declared operational on 1 July, the following year with No. 8 Squadron at Waddington. The unit was incorporated into NATO's AEWF in 1995.

The French Armée de l'Air was the last to purchase the Sentry, and, starting with the Boeing 707, including all versions as it received its fourth and final AWACS in 1991, thus brought to an end a lineage that had begun thirty-four years earlier. The French planes are globally identical to their British counterparts (CFM56 engines with thrust reversers, ELINT electronic data gathering system in wing tip pods etc.), but their refuelling boom was designed locally by SOGERMA. The decision to buy this type of plane,

THE USAF E-3 FLEET

C/N	S/N	Model	Note	C/N	S/N	Model	Note
20518	71-01407	E-3B		21752	78-00576	E-3B	
20519	71-01408	E-3B		21753	78-00577	E-3B	
21046	73-01674	E-3C	Retained by Boeing	21754	78-00578	E-3B	
				21755	79-00001	E-3B	
21047	75-00556	E-3B		21756	79-00002	E-3B	
21185	73-01675	E-3B		21757	79-00003	E-3B	
21207	75-00557	E-3B					
21208	75-00558	E-3B		22829	80-00137	E-3C	
21209	75-00559	E-3B		22830	80-00138	E-3C	
21250	75-00560	E-3B		22831	80-00139	E-3C	
21434	76-01604	E-3B		22832	81-00004	E-3C	
21435	76-01605	E-3B		22833	81-00005	E-3C	
21436	76-01606	E-3B		22834	82-00006	E-3C	
21437	76-01607	E-3B		22835	82-00007	E-3C	
21551	77-00351	E-3B		22836	83-00008	E-3C	
21552	77-00352	E-3B		22837	83-00009	E-3C	
21553	77-00353	E-3B					
21554	77-00354	E-3B	Lost in Alaska 22.09.1995				
21555	77-00355	E-3B					
21556	77-00356	E-3B		*NB. Except one aircraft retained by Boeing for trials, all USAF Sentries are used by 552nd ACW.*			

designated SDA (for *Système de Détection Aéroportée/* Airborne Detection System), by the Armée de l'Air, was taken in February 1987, but in fact had its origins in the 1970s. It aimed at completing the existing land-based radar network, notably by allowing the detection of planes flying at low, or very low altitude, whilst at the same time taking into account the particular French topography that is relatively hilly with areas of 'shadow'.

Various projects were studied (E-2C, Transall or a modified Airbus A300, or even, for a while, the British Nimrod). The

Above, left.
Based in Germany, at Geilenkirchen, the NATO E-3A aircraft are registered in Luxemburg and bear the arms of the Great Duchy on their tail fin. The Alliance's Sentry aircraft were, amongst other places, used in Bosnia during operation 'Deliberate Force'.
(WingMasters collection)

Above, right.
Saudi Arabia received five E-3A as part of the 'Peace Sentinel' program. All these planes are in service with No. 18 Squadron and, contrary to their official designation, differ from their United States counterparts by their CFM 56 engines and their simplified equipment compared to the western Sentry aircraft.
(Boeing).

Below.
The Sentry AEW Mk.I, the RAF designation of the E-3D, have CFM 56 engines like the French aircraft and were bought after the failure of the national Nimrod AEW.3 program. The aircraft here is 'ZH 103' photographed at the Ignatievo base in Bulgaria in 2003 during the 'Cooperative Key' program.
(USAF)

American AWACS system was considered to be the only viable option and the future aircraft were finally included in the military program law of 1984-1988. Great Britain had just cancelled its Nimrod programme and a program of Franco-British collaboration (JAFMO, 'Joint Anglo French Management Office') was brought into being to purchase a certain number of Sentry aircraft in the best possible economic conditions, by buying in quantity. The initial amount of three aircraft for the Armée de l'Air was finally increased to four in 1987.

The pilots of the future French SDA (almost all came from the FAS) were trained at Tinker with the 966th AEW & CTS of the 552nd ACW, the aircraft being received by the Armée de l'Air between October 1990 and June 1991. They were officially presented at Boeing Field on 22 August 1990 as the runway at Renton is not long enough for the Sentry; the first SDA was then sent to UTA Industries at Le Bourget. Like their counterparts, they are equipped with the bilingual JTDIS terminal and a transmission system for coded data. The French E-3F can now, as well as their surveillance and detection missions, be used as flying command posts. The French SDA are equipped both with the boom of their British E-3D counterparts (designed in collaboration with Sogerma and Zenith Aviation) and the USAF receptacle, and were amongst the first E-3 equipped with Have Quick A Net system. The cabin has fourteen UHF radio posts, three HF and two VHF/AM, whilst provisional cabling allows for the future addition of extra posts.

Constantly modernised since 1997, like most of the Sentry aircraft of other air forces, the E-3F were firstly equipped with an improved AN/AYR-1 IFF system (Identification Friend or Foe) then, in 2001, a contract was signed with Boeing for the installation of a GINS system (GPS Inertial Navigation System) which is a GPS system coupled with an altitude-calculating system allowing aircraft to integrate better in dense aerial traffic. Also installed were additional 'fourth generation' (PR4G) secure radio posts.

In 2002, it was decided to set up a modernisation program for the (RSIP) radar, the work being carried out in the Air France workshops

at Le Bourget with 'kits' supplied by Boeing and made by Northrop Grumman. The first plane re-entered service at the beginning of 2005.

In anticipation of the arrival of the Sentry within the Armée de l'Air, the Unité de Détection Aéroportée (UDA) 02.920 was formed at the BA 701 air base at Avord on 1 September 1989.

Transformed on 1 March the following year to the 36ᵉ Escadre de Détection Aéroportée and comprising the Escadrons 01.036 'Berry' and 02.036 'Nivernais', it carried on the traditions of the old 36ᵉ Escadre de Reconnaissance.

Declared operational on 19 June 1992, the 'escadre' (wing) became the 36ᵉ EDCA (Escadre de Détection et de Commandement Aéroporté) 'Berry' in September 2001. The French E-3F, equipped with extra capacities, became the SDCA (Système de Détection et de Commandement Aéroporté/airborne detection and command system). Each plane, in general, carries a crew of seventeen men [7], four of which are for the actual flying of the aircraft (pilot, co-pilot, navigator and flight mechanic) and thirteen specialists (communications technician and operator, radar technician, calculation and visualisation specialist and nine operators or controllers). The French Sentry aircraft take part not only in supporting aerial operations by controlling defensive (CAP), or offensive (OAS, COMAO) means, but also in-flight refuelling, logistical support, rescue on land and at sea (SAR/CSAR) and can also be used during defensive or offensive maritime operations (TASMO). Their secondary tasks comprise surveillance operations, notably alongside the French customs or when official events are held (international summits) as well as participating in inter army or inter allied exercises.

7. By comparison, the 'international' crews of the NATO Sentry aircraft is usually made up of fifteen men (and women), to which can be added instructors or observers. The flight crew comprises three people (pilot, co-pilot and navigator) and that of the technicians has twelve systems operators, one for communications, one for the on board computer, one for radar maintenance and nine for the radar, split up into three teams of three. These male and female operators are positioned in the forward and central area of the cabin; the rear is set out as a rest area with seats, bunks, kitchen and toilet.

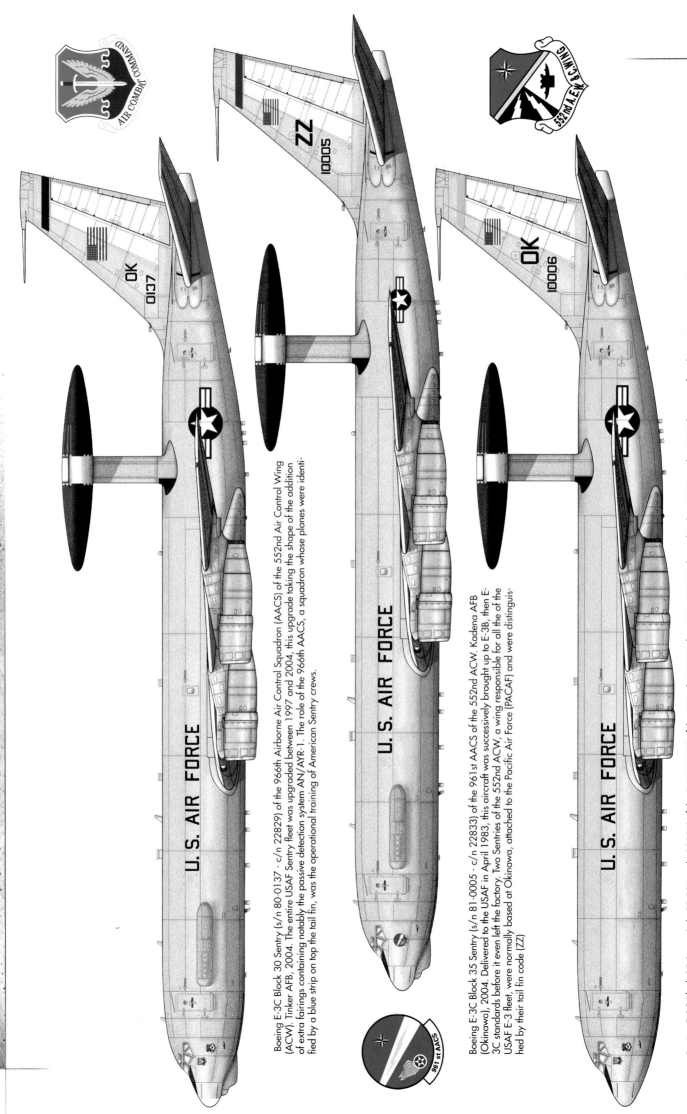

Boeing E-3C Block 30 Sentry (s/n 80-0137 - c/n 22829) of the 966th Airborne Air Control Squadron (AACS) of the 552nd Air Control Wing (ACW). Tinker AFB, 2004. The entire USAF Sentry fleet was upgraded between 1997 and 2004, this upgrade taking the shape of the addition of extra fairings containing notably the passive detection system AN/AYR-1. The role of the 966th AACS, a squadron whose planes were identified by a blue strip on top the tail fin, was the operational training of American Sentry crews.

Boeing E-3C Block 35 Sentry (s/n 81-0005 - c/n 22833) of the 961st AACS of the 552nd ACW. Kadena AFB (Okinawa), 2004. Delivered to the USAF in April 1983, this aircraft was successively brought up to E-3B, then E-3C standards before it even left the factory. Two Sentries of the 552nd ACW, a wing responsible for all the of the USAF E-3 fleet, were normally based at Okinawa, attached to the Pacific Air Force (PACAF) and were distinguished by their tail fin code (ZZ)

Boeing E-3C Block 25 Sentry (s/n 82-006 - c/n 22834) of the 965st AACS of the 552nd ACW. Tinker AFB, 1995. Delivered to the USAF in July 1983, this aircraft took part in operation Desert Storm in 1990-91. It is seen here before being upgraded. However, the presence of extra antenna on the fuselage allows us to distinguish previous versions, E-3A and B. It is one of the eight standard (or 'common') E-3A that were initially upgraded to E-3C Block 25, an identical variant to the E-3B Block 20.

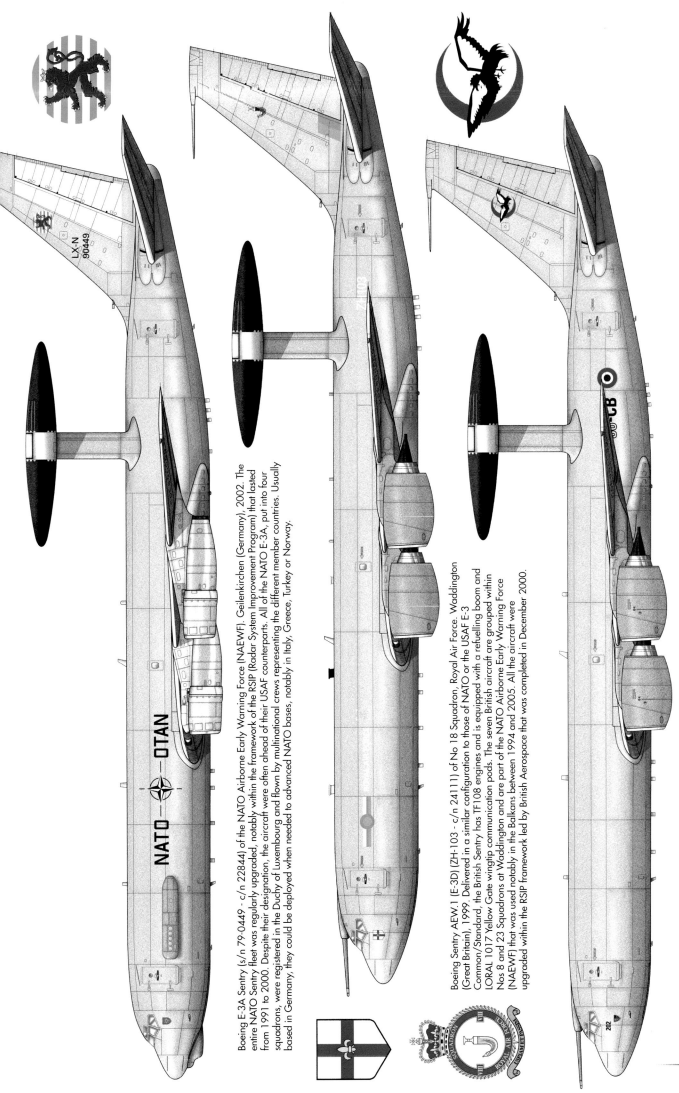

Boeing E-3A Sentry (s/n 79-0449 - c/n 22844) of the NATO Airborne Early Warning Force (NAEWF), Geilenkirchen (Germany), 2002. The entire NATO Sentry fleet was regularly upgraded, notably within the framework of the RSIP (Radar System Improvement Program) that lasted from 1991 to 2000. Despite their designation, the aircraft were often ahead of their USAF counterparts. All of the NATO E-3A, put into four squadrons, were registered in the Duchy of Luxembourg and flown by multinational crews representing the different member countries. Usually based in Germany, they could be deployed when needed to advanced NATO bases, notably in Italy, Greece, Turkey or Norway.

Boeing Sentry AEW.1 (E-3D) (ZH-103 - c/n 24111) of No 18 Squadron, Royal Air Force. Waddington (Great Britain), 1999. Delivered in a similar configuration to those of NATO or the USAF E-3 Common/Standard, the British Sentry has TF108 engines and is equipped with a refuelling boom and LORAL 1017 Yellow Gate wingtip communication pods. The seven British aircraft are grouped within Nos 8 and 23 Squadrons at Waddington and are part of the NATO Airborne Early Warning Force (NAEWF) that was used notably in the Balkans between 1994 and 2005. All the aircraft were upgraded within the RSIP framework led by British Aerospace that was completed in December 2000.

Boeing E-3F Sentry (36-CB - c/n 24116) of the 36ᵉ Escadron de Détection et de Contrôle Aéroporté (EDCA) 'Berry' of the l'Armée de l'Air. Base Aérienne 702 'Commandant Madon', Avord, 2001. Delivered in France in December 1990, this aircraft was accepted by the Armée de l'Air in July the following year. The French planes have the same engines as their British and Saudi counterparts and are equipped with a Sogerma designed refuelling boor. All of the E-3F were upgraded between 2004 and 2006 using Boeing supplied kits that were installed in France at the Air France workshops. Created 1 March 1990, the 36ᵉ Escadre de Détection Aéroportée (EDA) received its first Sentry in May 1991. Originally made up of two squadrons (001.036 'Berry' and 002.036 'Nivernais') which were given permission to paint their unit insignia on the tail fins ('Charlie-Bravo' with the vulture of the BR 43) in August 1992, they were renamed 36e Escadron de Détection et de Contrôle Aéroporté (EDCA) on 1 August 1993 and its squadrons became 'escadrilles' (flights).

123

The Boeing 707 in detail

The 707 was the first civil transport jet aircraft made by Boeing and had many technical characteristics that appeared on most of its successors.

Fuselage and cabin

The 707 fuselage was made entirely of metal, in accordance with the semi-single-hulled principle.

Measuring 3,74 m (12' 4") in diameter and 4,30 m (14') high, it contained, apart from the cockpit situated at the front, a cabin whose size varied depending on the version, but which measured, on average, 25 metres (82 ft) in length. Although the fuselage section appeared outwardly oval, it was in reality bilobal, that is to say made up of two circles, the junction of which was hidden by a spar that was itself covered on the exterior, giving an impression of structural homogeneity from the outside.

The fuselage was divided into four main sections going from the front to the rear: nose, passenger entry door, from the leading edge and trailing edge of the wings, from the latter to last pressurised bulkhead and the last section comprising the aft fuselage tip and the tail fin. The cabin floor was installed at the junction between the two fuselage lobes and its central part was an integral part of the wing structure.

The fuselage had four doors, two on the left and two on the right, respectively in front of the wing and just in front of the tail unit; the smaller right hand side doors were positioned slightly more forward than their counterparts. The design of these doors was revolutionary when the 707 entered into service, as they were equipped with a system that increased tightness and, therefore, avoided any possible decompression incidents when in flight. These 'plug type' doors were slightly larger than the opening they covered and tightness was achieved by a standard joint, but also through the internal pressure of the cabin. They opened from the outside, fitting against the fuselage after slightly pivoting on their vertical axis. The

aircraft also had emergency exits, at least two on each side, leading out onto the wing, notably on the short fuselage 707 (Qantas -138, for example) and the 720. It was also equipped with an emergency passenger oxygen system and escape slides. The latter were housed above the access doors and were completed by lifeboats, the number of which varied depending on the aircraft's configuration; these were stored in the cabin ceiling (two at the front, three or four in the centre and two at the rear). These lifeboats could hold 26 to 50 people

(Ph. Bruno collection)

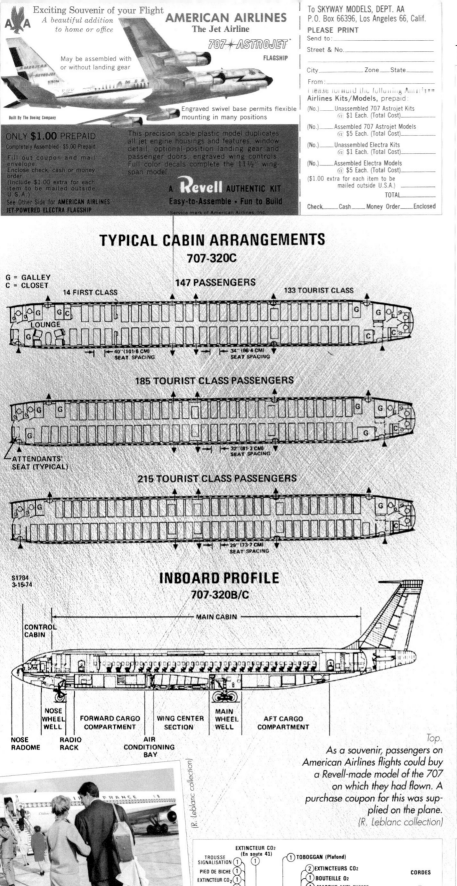

TYPICAL CABIN ARRANGEMENTS
707-320C

G = GALLEY
C = CLOSET

147 PASSENGERS

14 FIRST CLASS   133 TOURIST CLASS

LOUNGE

40" (101.6 CM) SEAT SPACING   34" (86.4 CM) SEAT SPACING

185 TOURIST CLASS PASSENGERS

ATTENDANTS' SEAT (TYPICAL)

32" (81.3 CM) SEAT SPACING

215 TOURIST CLASS PASSENGERS

29" (73.7 CM) SEAT SPACING

S1784
3-15-74

INBOARD PROFILE
707-320B/C

MAIN CABIN

CONTROL CABIN

NOSE WHEEL WELL | FORWARD CARGO COMPARTMENT | WING CENTER SECTION | MAIN WHEEL WELL | AFT CARGO COMPARTMENT

NOSE RADOME | RADIO RACK | AIR CONDITIONING BAY

Top.
As a souvenir, passengers on American Airlines flights could buy a Revell-made model of the 707 on which they had flown. A purchase coupon for this was supplied on the plane.
(R. Leblanc collection)

The Boeing 707 in detail

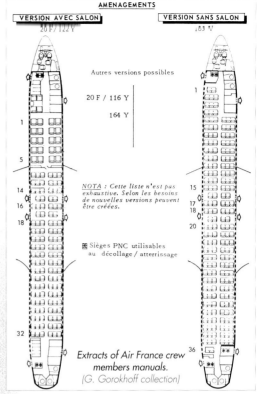

AMENAGEMENTS

VERSION AVEC SALON | VERSION SANS SALON

Autres versions possibles

20 F / 116 Y
164 Y

NOTA : Cette liste n'est pas exhaustive. Selon les besoins de nouvelles versions peuvent être créées.

⊠ Sièges PNC utilisables au décollage / atterrissage

Extracts of Air France crew members manuals.
(G. Gorokhoff collection)

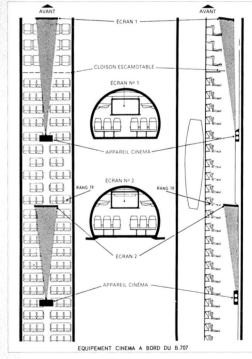

AVANT | AVANT

ÉCRAN 1
CLOISON ESCAMOTABLE
ÉCRAN Nº 1
APPAREIL CINÉMA
ÉCRAN Nº 2
RANG 19 | RANG 19
ÉCRAN 2
APPAREIL CINÉMA

EQUIPEMENT CINEMA A BORD DU B.707

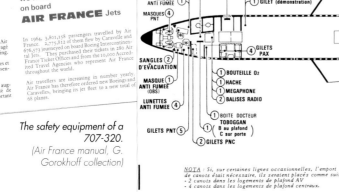

ètes le bienvenu
...d des Jets

AIR FRANCE

we welcome you on board
AIR FRANCE Jets

...58 passengers ont été transportés par Air ... en 1964. 2 775 812 d'entre eux ont voyagé ... des Caravelle et 676 573 à bord des Boeing.

...billets ont été délivrés par les 280 Agences et ...000 Agents de voyages agréés qui représentent Air France à travers le monde.

...me le nombre des voyageurs aériens augmente sans cesse, Air France a commandé de ...eaux Boeing et nouvelles Caravelle, portant à 68 unités le total de sa flotte « Jet ».

In 1964, 3,801,158 passengers travelled by Air France, 2,775,812 of them flew by Caravelle and 676,573 journeyed on board Boeing Intercontinental Jets. They purchased their tickets in 280 Air France Ticket Offices and from the 10,000 Accredited Travel Agencies who represent Air France throughout the world.

Air travellers are increasing in number yearly, Air France has therefore ordered new Boeings and Caravelles, bringing its jet fleet to a new total of 68 planes.

The safety equipment of a 707-320.
(Air France manual, G. Gorokhoff collection)

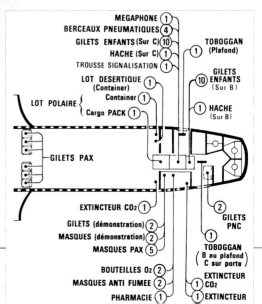

EXTINCTEUR CO2
(En soute 41)
TROUSSE SIGNALISATION (1)   (1)   (1) TOBOGGAN (Plafond)
PIED DE BICHE (1)   (2) EXTINCTEURS CO2
EXTINCTEUR CO2 (1)   (1) BOUTEILLE O2
HACHE (1)   (1) MASQUE ANTI FUMEE
GANTS AMIANTE (1)   (1) MASQUE (démonstration)
BOUTEILLE O2 (1)   (5) MASQUES PAX
MASQUE ANTI FUMEE (1)   (1) GILET (démonstration)
MASQUES PNT (4)
                             (4) MASQUES PNT
SANGLES D'EVACUATION (2)   (1) GILETS PAX
MASQUE ANTI FUMEE (OBS) (1) (1) BOUTEILLE O2
LUNETTES ANTI FUMEE (4)   (1) HACHE
                             (1) MEGAPHONE
                             (2) BALISES RADIO
GILETS PNT (5)   (1) BOITE DOCTEUR
                             (1) TOBOGGAN (B au plafond C sur porte)
                             (2) GILETS PNC

CORDES (2)
CORDES (2)

NOTA : Si, sur certaines lignes occasionnelles, l'emport de canots était nécessaire, ils seraient placés comme suit :
- 2 canots dans les logements de plafond AV
- 4 canots dans les logements de plafond centraux.

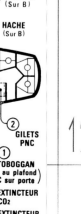

MEGAPHONE (1)
BERCEAUX PNEUMATIQUES (4)
GILETS ENFANTS (Sur C) (10)   TOBOGGAN (1) (Plafond)
HACHE (Sur C) (1)
TROUSSE SIGNALISATION (1)   GILETS ENFANTS (10) (Sur B)
LOT DESERTIQUE (1) (Container)
                                   HACHE (1) (Sur B)
LOT POLAIRE { Container (1)
             Cargo PACK (1)

GILETS PAX

EXTINCTEUR CO2 (1)
GILETS (démonstration) (2)   GILETS PNC (2)
MASQUES (démonstration) (2)
MASQUES PAX (5)   TOBOGGAN (1) (B au plafond C sur porte)
BOUTEILLES O2 (2)   EXTINCTEUR CO2 (1)
MASQUES ANTI FUMEE (2)   EXTINCTEUR (1)
PHARMACIE (1)

BOEING 707 320B/C GENERAL DESCRIPTION

and were equipped with a toggle, which set off a bottle of carbonic gas, inflating the lifeboat when launched.

The cabin was generally set out according to the customer's requirements and could be in a variety of layouts. Thus, the 707 aircraft put into service in the 1950s did not yet have different classes, with only one category of passenger carried and the cabin layout adapted accordingly.

As a general rule, the cabin could hold between 130 and 164 passengers; entry was usually by the front left door (when two classes of passengers were carried, the first class always entered by the front and the economy class by the rear door situated behind the wing),

the right hand side doors only being used exceptionally, often depending on how airports were set out. Inside were two toilets (with a sink and toilet) at the front and three at the rear, as well as two galleys equipped with oven, refrigerators, thermos flasks, percolators, kettles and even baby bottle warmers! Service on board was carried out with the help of trolleys that went up and down the aisles, although American Airlines had, at the beginning, used buffets (one at the front and the other at the rear) where passengers could help themselves. This airline's 707 planes were even equipped with a sitting room for six people at the rear of the cabin, just like luxury propeller airliners.

When the aircraft was specially set out to carry first class passengers (the latter could have various names such as Mercury etc.), up to 56, they were seated in pairs and separated by a small central table. If, on the other hand, the 707 was set out in 'tourist' configuration, the seats were placed three abreast, with the table being classically positioned at the rear of each seat. The space between each row was bigger than that on today's 'economy class' aircraft, and varied between 107 cm/42 inches (first class) and 87 cm/34 inches (tourist). When several classes were carried at the same time, they were separated by removable and adjustable panels, whereas the internal layout could be decorated according to the wishes of the airline, the cabin walls no longer being covered with fabric as was previously the case, but with a rigid covering.

One of the particularities of the Boeing 707 was the particular lay out of its rectangular windows; they were slightly smaller than average (usually measuring 23 cm x 32 cm - 9 in. x 12 in. -, but 25 cm x 36 cm - 10 in x 14 in - with American Airlines) and not placed opposite each row of seats, but between each fuselage frame, giving each passenger two window halves.

Another innovation that appeared with the 707 was the luggage compartments placed above the seats. These were usually held closed with hoods and they were generally missing on 'convertible' versions so that the compartments could be folded against the bulkheads when the cabin was transformed into a hold to transport freight. Passenger comfort was assured, notably, by an air conditioning system, initially working with Freon then with a closed circuit, using hot air taken from the engines and pressurised with the help of three turbo compressors whose air vents were positioned on the engine pod pylons, except for engine n°1 which did not have this.

Air France was one of the first airlines to install film viewing in its aircraft, starting in 1966 ('In-Flight Motion Pictures'). Films in French and English were shown thanks to two projectors and two screens each measuring 1,37 m by 0,85 m (4 ft 6 in. by 3 ft).

The convertible or 'Combi' 707 could carry 2.75 m (9 ft) wide containers, allowing a space to be left between the cockpit and the passenger cabin. In this case, the classic configuration was four standardized pallets and 119 passengers sat in rows of six abreast. A 707 cargo could carry a maximum load of fourteen of these pallets, representing a volume of freight that could reach 277 m³ (9,782 cu ft), whereas a 'Combi' could only carry a 210 m³ (7,416 cu ft) load in an 'all freight' configuration. The characteristic cargo door of this configuration was not a 'plug type' and opened from the top using hydraulic jacks placed on either side. The cargo aircraft floor was not only strengthened compared to the standard model, but also equipped with rollers to ease loading, as well as attachment points to tie down the freight. When a 'Combi' was transformed to just carry freight, the carpet was removed from the cabin, the seats taken out and rollers installed in the floor. Also, the interior covering was replaced by numbered panels essentially destined to protect the windows. It should be noted that the latter were much less numerous on planes originally designed to carry freight.

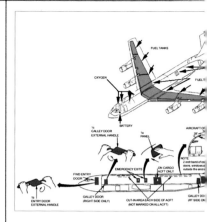

Above.
The cabin access doors (two per side) were of a new type, they were made airtight by both the seal placed around the edge of the door and the internal pressure. Each door was slightly larger than the opening it covered and opened towards the outside then positioned itself against the fuselage.
(E. Ratier)

Below.
Safety guidelines of a British Airways 707 showing the emergency exits and the position of the escape slides.
(R. Leblanc collection)

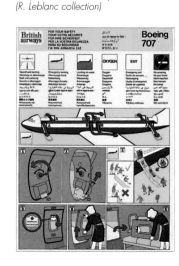

MOST UP-TO-DATE PLANES
e world's largest air network

26
OEING JET
ERCONTINENTAL

air travel : for you, Air France has selected the
planes.
pe's largest and one of the world's outstanding,
udes 26 Boeings and 42 Caravelles.

HE AIR FRANCE NETWORK

00 miles long, equivalent the 7 times the distance
d the earth. Air France's network serves 62 coun-
n all five continents. All major points throughout
orld can be reached by Air France to-day.

BOEING JET INTERCONTINENTAL

Il est utilisé pour les vols à grande distance (long-courriers).
Grâce à lui, New York, par exemple, n'est qu'à 7 h 30 de
vol de Paris.
Envergure . . . . 44,42 m
Longueur . . . . 46,61 m
Moteurs : 4 turbo-réacteurs Pratt et Whitney JT 3D3
Altitude de vol . . . . 13 000 m
Rayon d'action maximum . . . . 10 000 km
Vitesse maximum de croisière . . . . 950 km/h
Nombre de passagers 190

THE BOEING INTERCONTINENTAL JETLINER

Operates on intercontinental flights. Brings Paris within
7 ½ hours flying time of New York!
Wingspan . . . . 132'5"
Length . . . . 152'
Engines: 4 Pratt and Whitney JT 3D3 turbo-jets.
Cruising altitude . . . . 42,000 ft.
Maximum range . . . . 6,000 mi.
Maximum cruising speed . . . . 590 mph.
Number of passengers 190

(R. Leblanc collection)

*Opposite, from top to bottom.
On the panel over the pilots were
the switches for the interior and exterior
lighting systems, the windscreen wipers,
the de-icer and, above all, at the rear,
the engine ignition throttles.*

*Just in front of the engine throttle column,
in the centre of the instrument panel,
was the weather radar screen.*

*A view of the instruments on the Captai-
n's post with, in the centre, the artificial
horizon and on each side, the air speed
indicator (left) and the altimeter (right).
The constructor's name was in the centre
of the control wheel with this type of aircraft.*

*A close-up of the instrument panel placed
just over the engine throttles. On the left
is the weather radar and on the right the
radio adjustment buttons as well as the
(ILS, VOR) navigation aids. The exact
position of these instruments on this central console could vary, not only
depending on versions, but also the airlines' fleets. The row of dials is that of the
fuel flow to the engines.*
(D. Breffort collection)

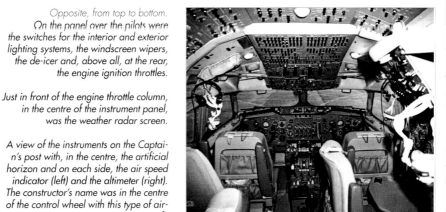

*Opposite.
The navigator's post, situated on the left,
behind that of the Captain.*
(E. Ratier)

MAIN INSTRUMENT AND CONTROL STAND PANELS

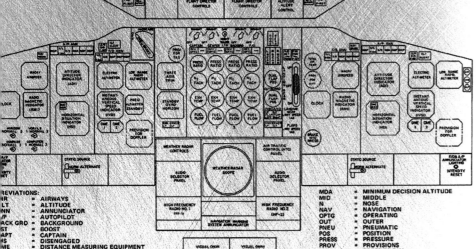

REVIATIONS:
R = AIRWAYS
LT = ALTITUDE
NN = ANNUNCIATOR
/P = AUTOPILOT
ACK GRD = BACKGROUND
ST = BOOST
PT = CAPTAIN
IS = DISENGAGED
ME = DISTANCE MEASURING EQUIPMENT
NG = DOWN
NE = ENGINE
SS = ESSENTIAL
XH = EXHAUST
VD = FLIGHT DIRECTOR
/O = FIRST OFFICER
/S = GLIDE SLOPE
YD = HYDRAULIC
= INDICATED AIRSPEED
= INOPERATIVE
= LEFT
= LEADING EDGE
= LOW PRESSURE

MDA = MINIMUM DECISION ALTITUDE
MID = MIDDLE
N = NOSE
NAV = NAVIGATION
OPTG = OPERATING
OUT = OUTER
PNEU = PNEUMATIC
POS = POSITION
PRESS = PRESSURE
PROV = PROVISIONS
P-DIM = PRESS TO DIM
P-RST = PRESS TO RESET
PWR = POWER
R = RIGHT
REV = REVERSER
RUD = RUDDER
SAT = STATIC AIR TEMPERATURE
TACH = TACHOMETER
TAS = TRUE AIRSPEED
TEMP = TEMPERATURE
VOR/ILS = VISUAL OMNI-RANGE/INSTRUMENT
LANDING SYSTEM
V/L = VOR/LOCALIZER
WARN = WARNING

1800
15-74

An official Boeing presentation brochure dating from 1955.

Most of the interior views were made in a studio using a mock up of the cabin and not in a real aircraft.

The cockpit

The configuration of the cockpit evolved very little as new versions of the Boeing 707 appeared; this characteristic allowed great versatility for crews trained to fly this type of aircraft, whereas the general tendency at this level will always to go towards a greater simplification.

The main instrument panel was modular and, therefore, easily dismantled piece by piece for easy maintenance. Behind this instrument panel, between the Captain's seat (left) and the co-pilot (right), was a central console with the power levers, trim, flaps and airbra-

kes, as well as the parking brake and ignition system for the engines. On the ceiling, the panels were more specially reserved for starting the de-icers, windscreen wipers or the internal and external lighting system.

The flight mechanic sat behind the co-pilot's seat on a swivel seat that could be set to a fixed position. At his disposal, installed in a panel placed on the right bulkhead, were various instruments and dials for controlling or starting the pressurisation system, air conditioning, fuel (gauges) and oil and hydraulic pressure; this panel also had an altimeter repeater or rate of climb indicator. The mechanic also had another set of power levers, which allowed him, for example, to

1. The aft galley of an Air France 707 in 1979. Note, on the left (above the head of the dashing flight attendant), the bar of the inflatable escape slide of the rear right-hand side door. In the centre, under the compartment for placing documents and money, is the percolator that was no longer in use at this time. At the bottom right is the top oven for reheating the 'tourist' meals. (G. Gorokhoff collection)

2. One of the innovations of the Boeing 707 was the presence of luggage compartments above the seats that closed with hoods. The internal layout depended on the airlines' requirements and used panels with a rigid cover. (E. Ratier)

3. An overhead light panel was placed over each row of seats and also had a call button for the cabin crew and the emergency oxygen masks. The windows were not positioned in the row of seats' axis but between them. (E. Ratier)

4. The interior decoration of the cabin varied from one airline to another. The different

classes of passengers were separated by adjustable panels. Seen here is the decor of an Air France 707-328. (E. Ratier)

5. Just before the entrance to the tourist class cabin are the fruit juice distributors on the left, below the compartments for the 'comodiprests' (trolleys holding the meal trays). (G. Gorokhoff collection)

6. The first class lounge (here on an Air France aircraft in 1979) was used in fact as an eating area for the flight attendants (it also transformed into a rest area and could be fitted with two bunks for the flight officers, notably during the Moscow-Tokyo-Moscow flight, although this configuration was, in fact, not used much.) (G. Gorokhoff collection)

7. The front of the first class cabin during sales. Note the rolled up screen, used for films, above the door. (G. Gorokhoff collection)

8. Summer 1969, the 'tourist' area of an Air France 707-328. The cabin luggage compartments are not closed. Note on the ceiling the compartment for the projector of the rear cinema, with the second further on towards the front. Above, in front of the latter, is the screen, which rolled down when films were shown. (G. Gorokhoff collection)

9. A Japanese hostess serving in first class with a fold down table on rollers, on an Air France 707-328 in 1980 (Moscow-Tokyo route). (G. Gorokhoff collection)

Serving First Class 'Senator' passengers on a Lufthansa 707 in the mid 1960s. Smoking laws were yet to come!
(Lufthansa)

(D. Breffort collection)

regulate the engines for greater efficiency at a given speed. In the event of an incident, he could use his swivel seat to gain access to the main controls situated between the two pilots. Just next to the mechanic's instrument panel was a cupboard for the crew's personal items. The navigator (when he was present) was sat to the left of the cockpit, behind the Captain, with his back to him. Under his position was a hatch leading to the lower deck and the hold (nicknamed 'hell hole'), containing the electronic equipment, of which some elements could be replaced when the plane was in flight. A fifth back-up seat was situated behind the pilot and could be folded up. It could be used for an instructor, observer, or even a visitor, but in very limited conditions of space and comfort. The difference with the military versions (KC, EC, RC-135, etc.) was that the flight crew did not have a separate entrance, but via the forward left door, the cockpit being separated from the cabin by a bulkhead equipped with a door.

The 707 was equipped with a LORAN hyperbolic navigation system (for LOng RAnge Navigation), two ADF and a RCA AVQ 10 weather radar, the antenna of which was placed in the front cone and which functioned on a 5.5 cm wavelength, capable of detecting storm zones according to the density of cloud mass and with a maximum range of 250 km (135 NM).

Production equipment (optional equipment could be added of the buyer wanted) also comprised of a DME (Distance Measuring Equipment) coupled with a VOR, which automatically established the distance of the aircraft from the ground, based VHF by giving its exact position. A Bendix designed FDS (Flight Direction System), grouped together all the information needed for flying within a single dial, whereas for planes destined to fly over polar regions, a specific gyrocompass allowed them to keep a precise heading when no magnetic reference was available.

Some aircraft were also equipped with a Litton LTN 51 inertial navigation system that gave coordinates of latitude and longitude as well as the possible margin of error compared to a predetermined

theoretical route, as well as the heading to take and the estimated time of arrival.

The arrival of the 707-300 version saw the appearance of a production system that allowed for automatic landing in bad weather (PALS, for Precision Approach Landing System) which was used for the first time on planes in regular service, with passengers, on 7 July 1967. Thanks to this system, the plane was guided automatically on its descent, with a very reduced drift compared to the centre of the runway (less than 15 m/50 ft) and a gap in slope less than 4 m (13 ft) with a 30 m (100 ft) ceiling, 350 m (1,150 ft) of visibility and a 40 km/h (21 kt) side wind.

Wings and rudders

For its 707 and unlike its large military jet aircraft designed before it (B-47, B-52), Boeing finally chose, as we have seen, to position the wings low on the fuselage. The wings were of the cantilever type, with a slightly positive dihedral (7°), each being made of two light alloy spars which formed a torsion box, whereas the central section of the wings was integrated into the fuselage. De-icing the wings, as well as the engine air intakes, was carried out using hot air from the engines.

Most of the wings contained fuel tanks (six in all); those situated at the wingtips were used as reserve tanks and, using gravity, filled those placed next to them. The main fuel tank, used first, was positioned in the centre, under the fuselage, and was originally divided by four bulkheads, then by seven.

The extra fuel tanks were situated, on the one hand, between the two engine pylons on each wing, and on the other hand, between the interior pylons and the fuselage.

The tanks were filled via pressurised fuel cocks placed under the lower surfaces; gravity fuel cocks placed on the upper surfaces meant that refuelling could take place when it was impossible to use the pressurised system. The engines were supplied with fuel via electric pumps positioned in each fuel tank, to which was added a central manifold.

In that way, the total fuel capacity varied between 65,888 litres (17,405 gal US) for 707-120 and 90,300 litres (23,855 gal US) for a 707-320B.

Each wing had hinged spoilers placed above the flaps, but independent of the latter, these two systems being destined to control the roll. These spoilers were moved hydraulically and deployed at a minimum angle of 30° and a maximum of 60° (during landing); if need be they could be used as airbrakes. The wings also had two pairs of ailerons, one at the tip and the other virtually in the centre;

Top left.
The 707 assembly line at Renton with the fuselages of the future cargo 707 on which the weather radars have not yet been installed.
(J. Delmas collection)

Above, from top to bottom.
The front undercarriage was equipped with twin wheels and retracted towards the front in the fuselage, the main doors only opening during the manoeuvre. A single landing light was positioned on the leg and complemented by four others, installed in pairs on the leading edge of the wings.
(E. Ratier and J. Delmas collection)

The main undercarriage was equipped with a bogie supporting four wheels. Note the size of the main shock absorber and the undercarriage torque link.
(E. Ratier)

To each its engine!

Model	Type
707-120	JT3C-6*
707-220	JT4A-3
720	JT3C-7
720B	JT3D-1 or -3
707-320	JT4A-11
707-420	Rolls Royce
707-120B	JT3D
707-320B/C	JT3D-3
707-320B-H**/C-H**	JT3D-7

* JT = Turbojet
**H is an unofficial suffix designating a plane equipped with JT3D-7 engines possessing a maximum take off weight of and 152,540 kg (336,290 lb)
NB. The JT3 is designated J57 in the USAF and equipped many aircraft (B-52/KC-135A and B/F-100/F-101 and F-102).
The JT3D is designated TF33 within the USAF (used on the C-141/B-52H and KC-135A)
The JT4A, also used on the DC-8-20 and 30 is the civil version of the J75 (F-105 and F-106).

Above.
Each wing was equipped with two double-slotted Fowler type flaps. These were hydraulically manoeuvred but had an electrical assistance in an emergency.
(D. Breffort collection)

Above.
The 707 had, in the standard configuration of four toilets, two at the front of the cabin on the right and two others on either side of the cabin at the rear. Each of them was equipped with a sink and toilet and a folding door.
(E. Ratier)

the first was only used at low speed, along with the flaps, whilst the others were used at all speeds. Each wing also had two pairs of Fowler type double slotted flaps, which were separated, by a small area of the fixed trailing edge. Locked between 20° and 30° on take off, they were used more for landing and their hydraulic system could be replaced, in the event of a problem, by back up electric motors. In order to increase lift, notably at the lowest speeds, the Boeing 707 had Krueger type flaps on the lower wing surfaces' leading edge which deployed forward thanks to jacks and retracted automatically as soon as the flaps were down at more than 6°. These flaps initially covered only part of the leading edge, but beginning with the 707-300, covered all of it, meaning that the approach speed was reduced by 12%.

Finally, a series of vortex generators was placed on the wing surfaces, including the tail assembly; these were made up of thin square shaped pieces of metal that were destined to diminish the wing and tail assembly's vibrations when the plane was flying at high speed.

The tail assembly

There were two different models of tail fin, one short and the other higher by 1.02 m (3 ft 4 in), and it was made around two alloy spars to which was added a false spar bearing the rudder hinges. The elevators were cast in one piece ('flying tail') and their incidence angle was set electronically, but could be controlled manually in the event

CONTROL SURFACES

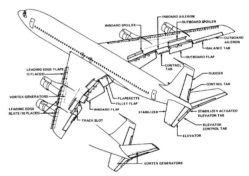

Opposite.
A flap placed at the wing root complements the two main double-slotted Fowler flaps.
(E. Ratier)

Above and below.
Each wing had moving spoilers positioned above the flaps. They were independent of the latter, controlled hydraulically and used to control the roll. Opening to a maximum angle of 60°, they could, if needed, be used as air brakes. Reflective strips on the upper wing surface show the pathway of the emergency exits.
(E. Ratier)

Opposite.
The tip of the left wing with the navigation light and part of the leading edge Krueger flap retracting towards the rear under the lower wing surface.
(E. Ratier)

Opposite.
The two Fowler flaps are separated by a small fixed area. As well as the vortex generators, the upper wing surface also has a retractable spoiler placed just over the second flap.
(E. Ratier)

of a problem. The tail fin's leading edge was equipped with an electric de-icer and there was a high frequency antenna placed at the top. This tail fin could be folded if the plane was stored in low-roofed hangers, but this was very rarely used in reality. The rudder was manoeuvred in three distinct ways, depending on its angle. Using a tab, only with aerodynamics for the first fifteen degrees and partially assisted from ten to fifteen degrees, then entirely hydraulically assisted by a servo actuator beyond this. To avoid the phenomenon of 'Dutch roll' (strong rocking combining rolling and yawing which is very dangerous as it is difficult to recover from[a]), the higher tail fin could be complemented, if need be, by a fin under the fuselage tail cone that could play the role of a shock absorber in the event of an excessive take off angle. Three models of these fins were installed on various versions of the 707 and differed essentially by their size and the shape of their leading edge, which was more or less inclined.

The aircraft bought new by the British airlines (BEA, BOAC etc.) were equipped with a fin that was specially shaped on the request of the British Air Registration Board; it was nicknamed the 'ARB fin' the ARB being Air Registration Board, the British equivalent of the American FAA or the French DGAC.

Undercarriage

The whole undercarriage was made up, for the front, of a single gear leg ending with twin wheels and, for the main undercarriage, two gear legs each supporting four wheels. The wheelbase of this undercarriage was 18 m (59 ft), that is five times that of a standard car. The wheels had tubeless tyres and the latter required as much materiel to make as that needed to equip twenty-five cars. The main undercarriage retracted towards the interior in a well situated behind the wing spar; its main doors closed immediately after the undercarriage was deployed in order to reduce drag; as for the retraction, this took ten seconds.

The front undercarriage retracted towards the front and its two

main doors also closed after the manoeuvre; only an extra door, placed behind the leg and acting as a deflector for any possible spray, remained down when the undercarriage was deployed. Braking was assured by a hydraulic system equipped with an anti-skid system and a pneumatic back up system could be used in the event of a break down, but only for a limited amount of seven emergency brakings.

Engines

Each engine was held by a pylon made mostly of magnesium, a metal whose drawback lay in that it could be affected by a possible

① INVERSEURS DE POUSSÉE

Pour faciliter le ralentissement au moment de l'atterrissage, ces dispositifs détournent le flux d'air rejeté par les réacteurs et le renvoient vers l'avant, créant une poussée inverse qui freine l'avion (ils n'existent pas sur Caravelle).

THRUST REVERSERS

To help brake the plane on landing, these devices throw the exhaust air from the jets forward, thereby creating a ''reverse thrust'' which slows up the aircraft.
(The Caravelle is not fitted with thrust reversers.)

② ANTENNES

Elles permettent à l'équipage de rester constamment en liaison avec les différentes stations de contrôle et lui transmettent de trèsnombreux renseignements sur les conditions de vol.

RADIO ANTENNAS

The radio antennas pick up and transmit messages to and from the various ground stations along the plane's route, and also ensure radio contact with the airport control tower at take-off and landing.

③ AÉROFREIN

Ces volets réduisent la vitesse de l'avion au moment de l'atterrissage. En outre, pour Boeing seulement, ils facilitent les virages pendant le vol.

AIR-BRAKES

When these flaps are raised, they reduce the aircraft's speed during landing. They are also used to facilitate banking during flight.

④ VOLETS

Les bords arrière de l'aile sont divisés en plusieurs parties qui peuvent être relevées ou baissées indépendamment. Elles permettent de modifier la portance des ailes au décollage et à l'atterrissage, et contribuent à freiner l'avion lorsqu'il s'est posé sur la piste.

CONTROL SURFACES

The trailing edge of the wing is divided on each side into several sections, which may be raised or lowered independently of one another to control the aerodynamic lift of the wing during take-off and landing, and also to help reduce the plane's speed when it touches down on the runway.

⑤ ATTÉNUATEURS DE BRUITS

Ces volets absorbent une grande partie du bruit produit par les réacteurs en assurant un meilleur mélange du flux d'air rejeté avec l'air extérieur.

NOISE SUPPRESSORS

These tubes absorb a large proportion of the noise produced by the jet engines. They ensure smoother contact between the exhaust air and atmospheric air.

⑥ GÉNÉRATEURS VORTEX

L'air glisse à 900 km les ailes. Dans certain les filets d'air risquen de la surface supérie faisant subir alors d' secousses à l'avion. Ce de métal, rangées en les ailes du Boing filets d'air à rester en le plan de l'aile et co douceur de vol. Pour rôle est joué par le arêtes métalliques pl diculairement au bo aile.

VORTEX GENER.

In flight, air flows over wing at 600 m.p.h. conditions, micro-strea from the upper wing sur the aircraft to sh small metal rods, arr rows along the wing c force the air-streams contact with the wing su contributing to smoot On the Caravelle, the vortex generators is pla deflectors placed perpe the tip of each end

BOEING JET

TOILETTES WC — 28 FAUTEUILS CLUBS — SORTIES DE SECOURS — 90 FAUTEUILS TOURISTES "Classe Economique" — TOILETTES WC

PORTE DE SECOURS — PORTE DE SECOURS

OFFICE — OFFICE

VESTIAIRE — POSTE REPOS ÉQUIPAGE — BAR — VESTIAIRE

ENTRÉE DES PASSAGERS — SORTIES DE SECOURS — ENTRÉE DES PASSAGERS — TOILETTES

Above.
When Air France brought into service its 'Intercontinental' Boeing 707-328 aircraft, it put forward the quality of its cabin layout and the on board service, in its publicity brochures.
(R. Leblanc collection)

Top, right.
The rear of a TEA 707 showing the secondary access door, the fin, the vortex generators under the stabilizer and the HF radio antenna on top of the tail fin. (J. Guillem collection)

engine fire, attached to a specially strengthened wing rib and placed parallel with the plane's flight line. Depending on the versions and some military aircraft - apart from the E-3D or F, E-6 with CFM56 engines - the Boeing 707-720 used four main models of jet engine, the essential difference residing in whether or not they had a turbofan.

Pratt & Whitney JT3C

Designed at the end of the 1940s, this 3.50 m (11 ft 6 in) long and 0.98 m (3 ft) diameter engine weighed 1,920 kg (4,230 lb) and was tested in flight in 1951. Its military version, the J57-P, was used on a considerable number of aircraft at this time (B-52, KC-135, F-100 Super Sabre, F-101 Voodoo, F-102 Delta Dagger as well as the Lockheed U-2 spy plane) and was installed respectively on the 707-120 (C-6 and C-6 Advanced) and the 707-020 (C-7, C-12).

Pratt & Whitney JT4A

Also used by the 707's great rival, the Douglas DC-8 with its 20 and 30 versions, this engine was longer than the previous one

(3.65 m/12 ft) and more powerful; its military designation was J75. Wider (1.09 m/3 ft 7 in) and heavier (2,290 kg/5,048 lb) it was mainly installed on the 707-220 and -320 in five main variants (A-3, -5, -9, -11 and -12). In order to reduce the noise levels, these engines could be equipped with silencer rings on their outlet. This modified the sound frequency of the waves emitted through dividing the exhaust fumes by putting them through twenty small diameter ducts. Thus, the exhaust fumes slowed down whilst mixing with the air when leaving the engines and the noise was, therefore, reduced.

Rolls Royce Conway Mark 508

Only used on the 707-420, it was the first large size production double flow turbofan. It was also the heaviest engine ever installed on a 707 (2,335 kg/5,147 lb) and measuring 3.45 m (11 ft 4 in) in length for a diameter of 1.06 m (3 ft 6 in). It too could be fitted with silencers.

Pratt & Whitney JT3D

This turbofan (double flow turbofan engine) was designed in 1959 and consisted of replacing, on a classic JT3 type turbofan engine, the first three stages of the low pressure compressor with a two-stage fan, whereas a third stage was added to the turbine at low pressure. In this way, two and half times as much air than before could be taken in, giving 50% extra thrust, whilst reducing both noise and fuel consumption. Designated TF33-P in its military version, the planes that were equipped with it, made new or re-engined, all received the B suffix to their basic designation (-120B, -320B) apart from the cargo versions (-C), the last to be made by Boeing and given from the outset this type of engine.

Six variants of this engine were used (D-1, D-3, D-3B and D-7, to which should be added the D-1-MC6 and D-1-MC7, in fact former JT3C-6 and C-7 engines that had been transformed), of which the differences were found in the power developed (from 6.6 t to 7.80 t/14,550 lb to 17,195 lb) and the unit weight (from 1,873 kg to 1,950 kg/4,130 lb to 4,300 lb).

Below.
This Aerocondor 720-023B (c/n 18023/HK-1973) was delivered new to American Airlines in April 1960. The right side secondary access doors, as the forward cargo compartment one, are open. (J. Guillem collection)

Opposite.
Side view of engine n°4 of one of Air Franc's 707-328 when being started. (R. Leblanc collection)

Below, left.
Maintenance on a JT4 engine of an Air France 707-328. Access is made easier by the large hinged hoods on each side, whilst the silencer ring is easily made out from this angle. (J. Delmas collection)

Above.
A JT4 engine of a USAF VC-137, the military version of the 707 that uses the same engines as its civil counterparts. (D. Breffort collection)

Opposite.
The JT4 engines differ from their JT3D turbofan counterparts by their narrower front opening, different profile and the oil radiator air intake underneath. The compressor air intake was present on all the pylons, except for that of engine n°1. (E. Ratier)

Below.
JT3D engines (by-pass turbofan) n° 3 and n° 4 of a Lufthansa 330B seen from the cabin windows. The mobile flaps of the extra air intake at the front, typical of this type of engine, are clearly seen, as is the compressor air intake at the tip of the pylon. (Lufthansa).

Some Boeing 707, those equipped with the JT3C-6 (707-120) engine, were equipped with a water injection system destined to increase thrust on take off and which was mainly used by the military KC-135, etc. This system used water stored in tanks placed between the main undercarriage wells, that was vaporised in the engine's compressor, greatly decreasing the ambient temperature (250° originally). The air having been made denser, its mass was, therefore, greater for an identical volume admitted, and on exit increased the thrust.

The main drawback, apart from the incredible volume of noise pollution and the black trails left by the engines, was an increase in the fuel consumption as more fuel was burnt without mixture. Also, the injection of water weakened the materials and equipment by pushing its resistance to the limit. Performance also varied depending on the ambient temperature and the altitude at take off. In general, the injection of 1,800 litres (475 gal US) of water meant a gain of around 900 kg (1,985 lb) of thrust, the water tanks being emptied in only two and a half minutes.

Each engine had extinguishers made up of two containers filled with an inert gas that when activated automatically shut off the hydraulic and fuel circuits. In the event of the extinguishers malfunctioning, those of the adjacent engine could be used as a back up.

The hydraulic system of the 707 was systematically doubled as a safety measure. Powered by pumps mounted on each engine, the system powered the flaps, undercarriage and its brakes, the spoilers, and the front wheel for steering the aircraft on the ground. In the event of one of these hydraulic system pumps breaking down, a second came into play, in priority to assure the working of the flaps, whilst an electric back up system could be used in an emergency, this being powered by alternators mounted on each engine.

*StarStream and DynaFan are service marks owned exclusively by Trans World Airlines, Inc.

Meet the team that saves you time

You fly to save time. Getting you there on time is a team operation at TWA. Skilled, seasoned flight and ground crews make on-timemanship a habit—to 70 U.S. cities *and* 15 overseas centers. Only TWA flies the StarStream,* newest of the transcontinental jets. Four mighty DynaFan* engines give the StarStream quicker take-off, swifter climb rate than any other coast-to-coast jet. The StarStream cruises at more than ten miles a minute, and has the tremendous power reserve so vital to maintaining precise flight schedules. On the ground, TWA saves you time with innovations like split-second electronic flight information, speeded-up check-in facilities, unique "carousel" baggage delivery. Compare what all airlines offer. Compare . . . and you'll fly TWA.

Nationwide
Worldwide
depend on

THE KC-135

As we have seen in the previous chapters, it was, in fact, the military version of the 367-80 that first entered into service. The USAF bought a specialised in-flight refuelling version in the summer of 1954, a few days after the maiden flight of the Dash 80.

Contrary to what the public generally believes, judging only from the exterior appearance, the civil Boeing 707 and the military KC-135, whilst sharing the same lineage, are in fact two different aircraft and only share a small percentage of common elements. Even their longevity is different, and even if the fleet of military aircraft, albeit upgraded and partially given new engines, has begun to show signs of ageing, that of the civil or military aircraft designed from the airframes of the latter (E-3, E-6, etc.), sometimes made later, will remain in service

until the middle of this century, almost one hundred years after the maiden flight of the ancestor, the 'Dash 80'.

Boom versus hose

Although when it began its first designs in 1952 that would lead to the 367-80 prototype Boeing was still little used to commercial multi-engined aircraft, on the other hand, it mastered much better not only jet bombers, but above all flying tankers that had become an essential element in the use of these bombers. Working in collaboration with Strategic Air Command, it knew the needs of the latter and notably the necessity for them to be rapidly equipped with a jet capable of refuelling its most up to date strategic bombers such as the B-47 and the B-52 that had just entered into service. The USAF asked Boeing, in 1947, to develop a way of in-flight refuelling, aimed mostly at the SAC bombers. On 28 March, 1948, two B-29s were transformed and equipped with the British 'hose and drogue' refuelling system consisting of a long hose with a basket at the end into which the receiving aircraft plugs a probe. Its efficiency was proven during a trial in which water was used. Other trials, with fuel this time, were carried out a few months later

and the USAF began to upgrade ninety-two Superfortresses into KB-29M, aircraft destined to make up the first Air Refuelling Squadrons or ARS.

At the same time, seventy-four B-29s were upgraded in order to receive fuel whilst in flight and initially re-designated as B-29L, then finally B-29M-R (R for Refuellable). As well as the Boeing lead trials, several B-29s were upgraded and tested in Great Britain by Flight Refuelling Ltd with an aircraft upgraded into a «three point» tanker equipped with two extra pods added to the wing tips. This configuration was later chosen for the B-50 (in fact a Superfortress with more powerful engines and a larger vertical stabilizer) of which more than one hundred were upgraded to KB-50J and K, first delivered to Tactical Air Command in 1957, the performance of which was improved by the addition of two jets placed in pods under the wings.

The hose system finally turned out to perform poorly, notably because it did not allow for a rapid transfer of a large quantity of fuel needed by the B-47, an aircraft that was a real kerosene guzzler. Boeing decided to design its own refuelling system that would no longer use a hose behind the tanker, but rather a telescopic, manoeuvrable boom capable of transferring an optimal volume of fuel (500 US gallons - 1 892 litres - against only 200 - 757 l for a classic hose).

The difference compared to the British system is that the receiving aircraft had to be equipped with a refuelling receptacle in which the boom, manoeuvred by an operator instal-

led in the tanker, plugged into [1]. Conclusive trials were carried out on two upgraded YKB-29J in October 1948. The USAF officially ordered, in May the following year, forty KB-29P[2] equipped with this system.

A total of one hundred and sixteen aircraft were upgraded and began to be delivered to the SAC in March 1950. The same year, the flying boom refuelling method was applied to the Boeing C-97, a transport aircraft derived from the B-29, taking its wings and engines. Three Stratofreighters were upgraded to KC-97A in December and were used as prototypes for the KC-97E. The first production version, of which sixty were made at Renton in 1951 and 1952, began to be delivered in July 1951. These planes were designed as tankers from the outset and were not the result of an upgrade; the same went for the following versions and they could, in theory be converted for a purely transport role, even if the dismantling of some of the tanks in the cabin of this configuration meant that this was hardly ever carried out. The upgrade into a flying tanker was made by installing the boom and its operator's post, where the latter would lay flat on a bunk, instead of and in the place of the two hold doors at the rear of the plane. The boom, equipped with ailerons/rudders (ruddelevators), was suspended by a cable hung under the tailplane and could be maintained almost vertically under the fuselage when it was not in use.

The second version of the refuelling Stratofreighter was the KC-97F, of which one hundred and fifty-nine were made, delivery to the SAC beginning in April 1952. They differed only by the slightly more powerful engines (300 extra hp units). It was followed by the KC-97G in July 1953, the main characteristic of which was the presence of two extra fuel tanks under the wings. This version was the most made with 592 delivered between May 1953 and July 1956. At the end of this same year, the SAC had a fleet of more than 1,300 B-47 Stratojets refuelled by 750 KC-97s of different versions.

From 1957, it was progressively replaced within first line USAF units by the new KC-135. However, the Stratofreighter saw a non negligible career with Reserve and National

---

1. The 'flying boom' system was first only used by the Strategic Air Command and the TAC (Tactical Air Command) initially, but above all the US Navy preferred the Probe and Drogue system. This absence of standardisation within the different United States air forces, still carries on, essentially between the 'landlubbers' and the 'sailors', even though the TAC has finally converted to the flying boom system.

2. The prefix K, for Kerosene, is attributed to all the transformed aircraft or originally designed as flying tankers.

IN-FLIGHT REFUELLING

An in-flight refuelling manoeuvre is almost always carried out in the same way, whatever the type of aircraft involved (fighter, bomber, transport, or even helicopters). After take off, a delicate operation for the older KC-135s, notably those equipped with water injection engines, which hardly allow any failures, making the use of short runways difficult (4,200 m/13,780 ft needed when fully loaded, a distance increased in hot weather), the tanker climbs initially to an altitude of 3,300 m/10,820 ft and accelerates until it reaches 520 km/h (323 mph). It next climbs to a higher altitude (7 500/8 800 m - 24,600/28,870 ft) in order to conserve its own fuel and reaches an area where air traffic is light. Arriving in the zone, the tanker flies a racetrack pattern, this being a closed circuit inside virtual quadrilaterals measuring 115 to 160 km (62 to 86 nm) for the long side and 65 to 90 km (35 to 48 nm) for the short sides.

The receiving planes, guided by ground control, approach the tanker and when thirty kilometres from the KC-135, the latter turns into the receiving aircraft's route then remains at a distance of five kilometres. The receiving planes then approach the tanker and pre-contact is made at roughly fifteen metres behind the boom, the operator having made sure everything is working beforehand. The boom operator guides the pilots with a system of coloured lights and radio. Pilots originally used a coloured stripe painted under the Stratotanker. Once the receiving aircraft is perfectly in line, the boomer, using his joystick, places the boom in the aircraft's receptacle and locks it into place using a hydraulic system. The fuel can then be transferred, carefully watched over by the co-pilot who makes sure that the KC-135's centre of gravity is not affected by the manoeuvre, or the turbulence caused by the receiving planes, especially the larger ones (B-52, C-5, etc.), the tanker's tail assembly having a tendency to rise in this case.

The flow of fuel depends on the receiving plane (2 950 kg - 6,500 lb - per minute for a cargo, but

only 905 kg - 1,995 lb/min for a fighter). During refuelling manoeuvres, which can even be carried out when the planes are turning, only two of the Stratotankers ten tanks are used, the rest being decanted from the other eight; the plane does not use different fuel for its own propulsion. When refuelling is complete, the boomer pulls the boom back and large aircraft allow themselves to 'fall' slowly. Fighters break off by accelerating to the left, the other flying alongside up to that point, moves to the right and positions itself for refuelling. Prior to the plane disengaging, just like at a petrol station, the boomer writes down the plane's serial number and type that he has just refuelled. This will be used by the SAC when it comes to sending bills to the different commands.

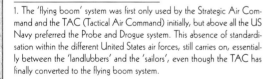

Opposite.
The KC-135 began its career without any camouflage or insignia; only the serial number, (here 57-1440) distinguished it. The delimitation on the fin (small size, characteristic of the first 582 planes made) is that of the walking area, the tail assembly being foldable on this plane, a configuration meant to ease storage in hangars, but rarely used.
(WingMasters collection).

Worse still, equipped with piston engines, the Stratotanker was forced to carry its own fuel and that it had to transfer, both different fuels, in specific tanks. We have seen in our first chapter how Boeing was pushed to study a better performing tanker, notably to answer the needs of the SAC (and above all its stormy boss, Curtis LeMay) that had just ordered its first B-52s. During the seventh flight of its Dash 80 prototype on 22 July 1954, a pretend refuelling with a B-52A was carried out, the real refuelling equipment (boom and boomer's post) was only installed the following year. As we said, apparently favourably impressed by this trial and without waiting for the results of the competition it had launched, the USAF announced a few days later on 5 August, that it would order twenty five interim tankers, followed shortly by eighty-eight aircraft and finally one hundred and sixty-nine more from February 1955 onwards, just as Lockheed was declared the winner of the KC-X competition of a new generation tanker.

Such a success led Renton to be accused of favouritism by the United States Congress and an inquiry was launched straight away. The annulling of the Lockheed choice and the orders for Boeing-produced tankers was even envisaged for a while, these planes being replaced by the B-36, or even B-52s transformed into flying tankers!

Guard units, of which it was the first tanker, beginning in 1957 and carrying on until the end of the 1970s. In order to improve its performance somewhat, during this second half of its career, eighty-one aircraft, renamed KC-97L, were equipped from 1964 onwards, with two General Electrics J47 engines, identical to those of the Stratojet, installed in pods under the wings.

The appearance of increasingly higher performance bombers (B-47 then the B-52), meant that the Stratofreighter was almost overtaken just as it reached its culminating point within the Strategic Air Command. Indeed, with its piston engines, it was not fast enough and, above all, performed poorly at high altitude, forcing the jet bomber pilots to leave their cruising altitude and cut back their speed to almost stalling point to refuel behind a tanker, sometimes flying at half their cruising speed.

Boeing wins by knockout!

Having beaten its rivals and in a position of official winner of the KX-F competition launched by the USAF due to the

big orders placed by the latter, Boeing had to quickly deliver its first tankers based on the Model 360-80 and designated Model 717. Compared to the Dash 80, the new plane, named by the military KC-135A, had a greater wingspan and wing surface, the wings were swept back to an angle of 35°. The fuselage diameter also differed, going from 3,35 m (132 inches) to 3,66 m (144 inches). Also, the undercarriage was reinforced in order to bear more weight, whilst a single cargo door was placed on the left hand side of the fuselage forward of the wing.

Finally - and most importantly! - a telescopic flying boom was added to the rear, under the fuselage and operated by a boomer laying flat on his stomach and viewing manoeuvres through a window nicknamed the balcony and protected by a fairing with a porthole.

Compared to the commercial Model 707, the appearance of which was programmed to coincide with the Stratotanker coming off the assembly lines, the KC-135 had a narrower fuselage but, above all, was made with a different aluminium, that lasted a little less long (aluminium 7178-T6) which explains why the whole tanker fleet, originally made to have a limited career [3], saw some of its aluminium replaced in the 70s and 80s to prolong the life of these planes still in service, from the 10,000 hours initially planned for, to 27,000 hours. This difference in construction was also visible from the exterior. The KC-135 had twenty-five areas of reinforcement at the rear section of the fuselage, destined to counter the effects of shock

*Above.
KC-135R s/n 58-0118 of the 92nd ARS of the 92nd ARW accompanied by Tornado F.3 of RAF No 617 Squadron during operation 'Iraqi Freedom' in 2003. The plane is equipped with Mk 32B wing pods allowing it to refuel planes equipped with an exterior boom thanks to the Hose and Drogue (HDU) system which today is installed on forty USAF KC-135. (USAF)*

waves felt here caused by the flow from the jets. Finally, as would also be the case with the 707, the first aircraft were equipped with a short tail fin and a non-assisted rudder, a bigger, assisted tail plane was introduced during construction, from the 583rd plane made and retrofited to planes previously built as it improved stability, notably in the case of the asymmetric functioning of the engines (break down or being voluntarily cut).

In all, 810 KC-135 A were made, of which 732 were delivered in twenty seven blocks, these appearing in the official designation of aircraft from the KC-135A-01-BN to the KC-135A-27-BN. Production spanned ten years with six to fifteen planes per month. The modifications made to the civil 707 during its elaboration phase always made it more different from the military refueller, to such an extent that two distinct assembly lines were made. The USAF, initially reticent, finally accepted that Boeing use the KC-135 tools to make its 707s, with the condition that this would not in anyway upset the delivery dates. In the end,

*Above.
The particularly colourful Nose Art of KC-135E s/n 57-1447, named 'Patriot' of the 18th ARW. This plane was retired from active service in May 2007. (USAF)*

3. The difference of the good old 707 of which some have nearly 100,000 flying hours!

*Opposite.
KC-135A s/n 63-8020 photographed at Frankfurt in July 1966. The upper section of the fuselage, as well as the fin and engines, have been painted in white, the rest of the plane being aluminium, a fairly unusual livery for a tanker.
(WingMasters collection).*

4. Eighteen months before the first production civil 707.
5. This name was chosen as a reminder of the lineage of Boeing made aircraft such as the Stratofreighter (C/KC-97), the Stratojet (B-47) or the Stratofortress (B-52).

an agreement was made, where Boeing could use for its civil jet, the tools and equipment financed by the government. They would have to reimburse a lump sum to the state based on the amount of planes made.

The first production KC-135A was rolled out on 20 July 1956, almost two years to the day since the maiden flight of the Dash 80, and at the same time that the last KC-97 left the factory. Named 'City of Renton' by this town's Mayor's wife, Mrs Baxter, s/n 55-3118, along with two other Stratotankers, remained with Boeing to be used during its campaign of tests. It carried out its maiden flight on 31 August 1956, eleven days before the date initially set [4], with Tex Johnston at the controls, assisted by R. L. 'Dix' Loesch. The second production aircraft only took off the following year on 14 February 1957. The series of tests that followed this maiden flight went by without any

notable incident, to such an extent that Tex Johnston declared that the KC-135 was a 'non story plane'. Some small faults were found however, such as an imperfect lateral stability (the phenomenon of 'Dutch Roll'), a certain stiffness in using the refuelling boom, or an excessive take-off weight when in war configuration which led to a climb rate that was not good enough.

The first planes were later delivered in June 1957 to the 93rd Air Refuelling Squadron of the 93rd Bomb Wing at Castle (California) and the number of Stratotankers [5] increased rapidly, the maximum number, 674 planes in service was reached in 1964 and the 732nd and last KC-135 was delivered on 12 January 1965. At the beginning, the aircraft were stationed at the same airfields as the B-52s in order to facilitate the planning of missions of these inseparable pairs. The first Stratotanker was also quickly used to beat various records. With General LeMay on board, one of its most ardent partisans, it flew from the base at Westover in Massachusetts, to Buenos Aires in Argentina in a thirteen hour non-stop flight between 11 and 12 November 1957, covering a distance of more than 10,100 kilometres and winning the Harmon International Trophy. A few months later, on 7 and 8 April 1958, another plane covered, non stop, the 16,450 kilometres between Tokyo and the Azores, the pilot this time being the boss of the 93rd Bomb Wing. Next to come were weight records (35 452 kg carried in 1958, more than the Tu-104) and those for altitude. On 27 July 1958, four aircraft of the 99th ARS attempted to break the speed record between their Westover base and London. This attempt was finally crowned with success (5h 27 outbound and 5h 51 inbound) but it resulted in the loss of one the first SAC KC-135s.

With the United States increasingly implicated in the conflict with each passing day, and the bombardment of North Vietnam inevitable, it was soon obvious that a fleet of tankers was needed. Indeed, at the beginning of June 1964, the Chief of Staff ordered the SAC to transfer six of its KC-135A based at Guam (Andersen AFB) to the Clark base in the Philippines in order to refuel the F-100Ds operating in Laos. In fact, the first Stratotanker operational missions in south east

On operations

Until the arrival of the KC-135A, the refuelling of the US Air Force's aircraft was carried out by different commands, such as those of the PACAF (Pacific Air Force), the Tactical Air Command or the USAFE (United States Air Force Europe). In November 1961, the General Staff of the USAF decided that, from now on, the Strategic Air Command alone would manage the entire Stratotanker fleet, shared out into thirty-two squadrons with twenty planes each, and that it would ensure the refuelling of units that did not have their own flying tankers. This situation lasted throughout the length of the war, SAC never abandoned its prerogatives to the 2nd Air Division, later the 7th Air Force, based at Saigon.

Asia had been carried out since 1961 for the reconnaissance F-101 Voodoo. The KC-135 saw service the following two years as support when the Tactical Air Command aircraft crossed the Pacific.

However, it was on 9 June 1964 that the first support mission for combat operations took place in Vietnam, the tankers refuelling the Super Sabres whose mission was to attack the anti-aircraft installations at Pathet-Lao in the Plain of Jars. This group, originally named 'Yankee Team Tanker Task Force', became, in September the same year, the 'Foreign Legion', made up of eight aircraft still destined to support American aircraft engaged in Laos, and that served until March 1965.

On 20 October 1964, ten Stratotankers were officially attached to south East Asia, replacing the KB-50s, normally

stationed at Kadena (Okinawa), but with an advanced base at the Don Muang aerodrome near Bangkok, where it served as an international airport, in Thailand. At the beginning, these aircraft, named 'Young Tiger Force' (4252nd Strategic Wing) would mainly refuel fighter bombers, before carrying out missions for the B-52s, mostly at operation 'Rolling Thunder' (an intensive bombardment of the supply lines of communist troops in South Vietnam) in June 1965, under the code-name of 'Arc Light'.

Rapidly, the number of jet engine tankers present in south east Asia was increased, going from fifteen ('King Cobra Task Force' based at Takhli, Thailand) in September 1965, to fifty five the following year with thirty aircraft used solely for operation 'Arc Light'. There were one hundred tankers in the Far East at the height of its use in this part of the world.

The living conditions of the crews and, above all, the ground crews, were initially very basic, the bases used not only void of all comfort, but often also lacking in necessary infrastructure for the maintenance of tankers, whilst the runways were more and more filled with increasing numbers of KC-135.

The situation improved a little in August 1966, with the completion of the much-delayed U-Tapao base in Thailand that immediately housed ten tankers as part of the 'Giant Cobra Force'.

The role of the KC-135 in south east Asia was of great importance, as without it a great many aircraft would have been lost, notably because the impressive quantity of fuel used by all combat missions would have rendered many planes incapable of regaining their bases. Without the intervention of the Stratotanker, there would have been no long distance fighter escort and no B-52 based at Guam would have been able to intervene, notably over North Vietnam. Flying almost twenty four hours a day, and as we have seen, in difficult conditions, the KC-135 would often save a fighter or a bomber returning from a mission, literally towing an aircraft hanging from its boom to a

friendly base, with the transferred fuel pouring from the bullet-riddled fuel tanks.

In 1965, the KC-135s carried out 9,282 sorties, refuelling 31,250 aircraft, numbers that constantly increased to such an extent that on the eve of the American withdrawal in 1972, the missions had seen a considerable increase and it was no less than 34,728 sorties and 67,655 aircraft that used the tankers. In 1968 alone, the Stratotankers transferred 450,000 metric tonnes (496,000 tons) of fuel and took part in a hundred 'rescues', refuelling at the last moment aircraft whose tanks were almost empty, sometimes in perilous conditions, notably in North Vietnam airspace. Indeed, it was not uncommon for anti aircraft missiles to be fired at them when they were flying particularly close to a combat zone. When refuelling operations officially came to an end in Vietnam, after the withdrawal of the United States, the KC-135s had carried out, between June 1964 and August 1973, 194,687 sorties during which 813,878 aircraft were refuelled with more than 5.5 billion litres transferred, numbers that do not require comment, especially if we add that no rendezvous was ever missed!

Although no Stratotanker was lost due to enemy action during the American intervention in Vietnam, the authorities admitted the loss of four aircraft during combat missions, all accidental, the first of which happened in September 1968 and the last in December 1969. Although the Strategic Air Command was the first, and for a while the only, to use the KC-135, the Tactical Air Command, which was previously equipped with the increasingly less practical KB-50 and KC-97 as they were not fast enough, would use the Stratotanker. Indeed, the SAC lent it its tankers which allowed its planes to intervene in a very short time (between eight and ten hours) almost anywhere in the world. For this, as the refuelling system was not the same in the two commands, the Stratotankers were equipped with a probe and drogue added to the original boom, allowing it to transfer fuel to aircraft not originally equipped with a refuelling receptacle (F-100, F-101, F-104, etc.). This adaptor, which would be used by the French on their C-135F and which today is installed on several USAF Stratotankers and ANG, is four metres (13 ft) in length and weights 55 kilos (121 lb) but no longer permits, once in place, the use of the boom in a classic way. The first colla-

boration between the SAC and TAC took place when the
KC-135A made it possible for the F-100D of the 354th FW
to go from Myrtle Beach, South Carolina, to Moron, in Spain,
in eight hours. The arrival of a new tanker even meant that the
SAC could put into place a technique named 'Wolf Pack',
made up of a KC-135 and four F-105 Thunderchiefs. The
tanker kept the accompanying aircraft flying, whilst carrying
spare pilots in its cabin. Despite its efficiency and the rapidi-
ty of deployment that it allowed, the original system was, all
the same, quickly abandoned at the beginning of the 1960s.

Versions, variants and by-products

On top of its primordial role as a flying tanker, the possibilities opened up by the Stratotanker were quickly exploited
and some aircraft were used as test beds for the elaboration
of production specialised versions.

- KC-135A (´Relay' or ´Combat Lightning')

Within the framework of a programme called ´Combat Lightning', two KC-135A were transformed in order to serve as
airborne radio relays supporting the command and control force
of south East Asia. Indeed, a AN/ARC 89 radio was installed in the cabin increasing the range of land stations, notably
for aircraft operating over North Vietnam. The KC-135A 'Relay'
(an unofficial nickname only), was identifiable from the exterior
by its nineteen small antenna placed on the fuselage and nine
below; it could not carry as much fuel as a standard Stratotanker. However, they were used several times as tankers, in
emergencies, when they were the only aircraft available in a
zone. Initially, that is too say, October 1966, these aircraft based
at Okinawa, then U-Tapao, orbited above the Gulf of Tonkin
and were used to relay messages to attack and rescue aircraft
on automatic missions.

In 1967, three other tankers were upgraded and equipped as well with a secure communication system. They were used to ensure a twenty-four hour coverage of combat zones, changing bases several times during their deployment. The 'Combat Lightning' program having ended in 1973, two planes were reconverted as standard KC-135A, whilst the five others conserved part of their specific equipment before being finally upgraded to KC-135E (three aircraft) and KC-135R (two aircraft).

- KC-135A 'Command Support Aircraft'

Several KC-135A were used by various USAF high commands as support aircraft. Some were specially equipped with improved communication and navigation systems. Apart from 'Speckled Trout', an aircraft was used by USSTRICOM (United States Strike Command) to accompany the tactical deployment of fighters, and another was used by the USAFE. Finally, the SAC had at least three aircraft of this type, named 'Casey' (for CS Command Support) 01, 08 and 015 and attached to the 8th and 15th Air Forces.

- KC-135B

This designation was given to seventeen Stratotankers with TF-33-P-9 engines that were finally, before their delivery to the USAF, re-designated EC-135C (first fourteen aircraft) and EC-135J (the last three).

- KC-135D

Four MAC RC-135A (see the following chapters) were transformed into flying tankers at the end of the 1970s and transferred to the SAC who renamed them KC-135D before attaching them to the 55th SRW base at Offutt. Re-engined with the TF 33 in 1990, they kept, however, their original designation.

- KC-135Q

Fifty six KC-135A were upgraded in order to refuel the Lockheed A-12 and SR-71 which used a specific fuel, JP-7 which was particularly corrosive and required specially designed tanks. Equipped with specific navigation equipment (a third radio UHF, TACAN and SATCOM) destined to ease rendezvous with the Blackbirds, as well as secure communication system that passed via the refuelling boom, all these aircraft were attached to the 9th Strategic Reconnaissance Wing (349th and 350th ARS) at Beale, in California, the 367th Strategic Reconnaissance Wing (909th ARS) of the 15th Air Force based at Kadena (Okinawa) and the 380th Bomb Wing (310th and 380th ARS) of the 8th AF at Plattsbugh (State of New York). It carried 37,788 kg (83,308 lb) of JP-7 and 49,896 kg (110,000 lb) of classic JP-4, the KC-135Q was equipped with a second filling point for its extra tanks, whilst extra ballast was added to the nose to help the plane maintain a certain stability once the JP-7 was transferred, the latter only being in the fuselage tanks. Finally, an extra light was installed at the top of the tail fin on the trailing edge to ease night-time refuelling manoeuvres as the Blackbirds were painted black and their refuelling receptacle was hard to see in these conditions.

This light was later installed on all of the USAF Stratotankers. Two KC-135Q were officially lost during their career, whilst fifteen were officially designated 'polyvalent', that is capable of refuelling classic aircraft as well as the SR-71.

Also, only twenty-one of them could be considered as being 'complete', the thirty-five others only being 'partial' as they were not equipped with the ARN-90 TACAN and LORAN-AL navigation systems; the third UHF radio was not installed either and sometimes replaced by an additional VHF. The KC-135Q, of which the official designation should have been KC-135C, began to be used in the utmost secrecy between April and July 1962, in support of the triple sonic A-12 fighters that were followed by the strategic reconnaissance version of the SR-71 and deployed in Vietnam in support of the Blackbirds, starting at the end of 1967 from the Okinawa base. These tankers were absolutely indispensable to the use of Blackbirds, as the latter, because of the nature of their fuel and tanks, that only became completely sealed at altitude after heating up, took off with a very limited amount of fuel and had to be, therefore, refuelled very quickly after having taken off.

- KC-135E

The Stratotanker fleet began to be modernised in 1975 when the aircraft was re-skinned [6]. A second series of upgrades began in 1981 and concerned this time the reserve aircraft, those in use were upgraded more completely, as we will see further on. Indeed, in August 1981, the USAF launched calls for tenders for the upgrading of the KC-135A, not surprisingly won by Boeing a few weeks later. Thus began the 'Airline Re-engine Program' that consisted of taking civil JT3D engines from 707s and completely upgrading them to obtain military TF-33-PW-102. As these engines were originally equipped with thrust reversers, a throttle identical to that of the 707 and 720 was installed in the cockpit. Also installed at the same time were several civil instruments and equipment (automatic pilot, a different air conditioning system).

The original power was now increased (8 164 kg/17,636 lb thrust against 6 236 kg/13,227 lb units) and a 9% bigger horizontal tail group was also added to compensate the natural tendency to nose up of the new plane, renamed KC-135E. The new engines, now rid of their water injection system, reduced fuel consummation by approximately 14% and reduced noise by 85%, and above all, 90% less polluting, two important criteria given that reserve tanker units in the United States are generally based at national and international airports.

Finally, despite an increased weight, the KC-135E, recognisable by its extra antenna placed on top of the tail fin, were now capable, thanks to their superior power, able to use shorter runways than before, and above all, transfer approximately 20% more fuel. The process of upgrading, which lasted around sixteen weeks per machine, began on 30 September 1981 and lasted nine years, the first KC-135E being delivered in July 1982. In fact, this program of upgrades was not only limited to tankers, but also concerned two NKC-135E, as well as a certain number of EC-135 and C-135E, a total of 161 aircraft were finally modified.

This re-engine program was, in reality, a stop gap measure, essentially because the TF-33 engines used, even completely upgraded, were not designed to last the planned forty years. Using these engines only extended the lifespan by around 6,000 hours. Also, because of their age, their maintenance and spare parts were more and more costly. At the beginning of 2003, the USAF thus announced the withdrawal of sixty-eight KC-135 (essentially within

6. The high resistance (except to time...) aluminium alloy used originally on the KC-135A (7178-T6), was designed to only last for 10,000 flying hours. In 1976, Boeing began to re-skin certain areas of the lower wing surfaces (approximately 140 m2) that were the most exposed, with aluminium 2024 with aluminium 7075 reinforcements. Carried out at approximately the 8,500 flying hours mark, this lengthened the aircraft's flying cycle to 27,000 hours. In total, the Reskinning Program/TCTO 989 concerned 746 aircraft (KC, EC and RC-135) at the rate of six a month and was completed in 1988.

squadrons due to receive the KC-135R), whilst the sixty-eight remaining aircraft would have to be used until 2006, the planned date for the replacement KC-767, based on the civil 767. A program that was finally abandoned at the beginning of 2006.

- KC-135R

At the same time as part of its fleet began to be upgraded within the framework of the program which led to the KC-135E,

first time on 27 November 1979 (see the chapter six 'The upgraded versions'). These new engines were heavier than those they replaced and had to be mounted on different pylons equipped with extra attachments. The wing areas near the pylons also had to be reinforced, as well as certain areas of the fuselage, notably at the exit of the auxiliary power unit (APU) now installed in the left rear of the fuselage. This system, characteristic of this version and made up of two Turbomach TT62, now allowed the KC-135R to be entirely autonomous and used without ground assistance.

The main undercarriage was also reinforced and improved, notably equipped with brakes that had an anti wheel spin system already installed on the KC-135E. The other upgrades concerned the improvement of the wings' leading edges in order to ease air flow, rudder controls and a modernised cockpit with a different automatic pilot and a dive control system for use when refuelling, notably with large planes such as the C-5 Galaxy.

the USAF looked at a more ambitious plan to bring their tankers up to date. Seven solutions were looked at, but the one finally chosen consisted mainly of replacing the original engines by the military version of the CFM56-2B-1, the F-108-CF-100, the result of a partnership between General Electrics and the French SNECMA. With each engine weighing the same as a J57, it was quieter, cleaner and, above all, more powerful (10,080 kg of thrust). They used less fuel, a factor that greatly reduced the amount of fuel used by the plane. In order to prove that this was the right choice, a demonstrator was made using the airframe of the last Boeing 707 to be made, and equipped with four CFM56. Named the 707-700, this one off aircraft flew for the

7. KC-135P-7 with four TF33P-7 engines, new stabilizers and new undercarriage. KC-135ME (for Mixed Engine) with two interior CFM 56 and two exterior J7. KC-135H, with four TF 33P-7 but 707-300 wings, bigger stabilizers and anew, strengthened undercarriage. Finally the KC-135Y with either CFM 56 or JT10D and a 'supercritical' wing.

Of course, the KC-135R was equipped with a larger horizontal stabilizer already mounted on the KC-135E. Finally, a TEMS system (Turbofan Engine Monitoring System) meant that a 'photo' could be taken of the engine parameters and as well as optimal maintenance whilst increasing general safety.

The first upgraded plane, (s/n 61-0293, named 'The Schocker') flew for the first time on 4 August 1982. It was equipped with an extra Pitot boom on the nose. The first unit to be equipped with this aircraft in July 1984, was the 384th ARW based at McConnel (Kansas), just next to the Boeing factory at Wichita. At the outset, the UASF wanted to upgrade all of its KC-135 still in service, that is 642 aircraft, before 1993.

However, due to the heavy costs of such an enterprise, and above all, because of drastic budget cuts, this number was reduced to 250 aircraft, then, because of savings made, to 467 in 2002. The last KC-135R was delivered in October 1993 and some other specialised versions were also concerned (KC-135E, RC-135). When used, it became apparent that the maintenance of aircraft equipped with F108 engines was less expensive than those with different engines, whilst the conversion of planes not yet upgraded would reduce maintenance costs by 95% and fuel consumption by 15%.

Thanks to these engines' superior performance, the KC-135R saw its load of kerosene increase by 65% at a range of 2,775 km (1,725 miles) and 150% at 4,630 km (2,875 miles), whilst noise emissions dropped from 126 dB to 99 dB. In that way, in 2002, it was estimated that the KC-135 fleet could fly another 35 years and that renting a Boeing 767 transformed into a tanker would cost approximately 15% more than upgrading a KC-135E to an R!

- KC-135T

Once the upgrading KC-135R program came to an end, it was transferred to the fifty-four original KC-135Q that became, between November 1993 and December 1995, the KC-135T. These planes were upgraded in an identical fashion whilst conserving their SR-71 refuelling capacities for the special JP-7 fuel.

The last upgrades?

In order to permit the KC-135 fleet still in service to fly until 2040, the date fixed as the extreme limit of the airframe's lifespan, essentially due to corrosion problems with the metals, a modernisation program was launched at he very end of the 20th century. Named PACER CRAG (Compass Radar & Global Positioning system), and elaborated by Rockwell Collins, it consists of getting rid of the post of navigator in most missions and upgrading the cockpit (a technique known as 'glass cockpit'). The most up to date navigation instruments are installed (LCD screens, Collins colour weather radar screen, GPS system, a ground proximity warning system EGPWS, modernised on board computer) as well as the new TACS (Traffic alert and Collision Avoidance System) destined to ease formation flying, notably in areas of dense aircraft traffic. Launched in May 1995, this upgrade program was carried out by BAE Systems at Mojave (California) in successive blocks between March 1999 and September 2002, those of Block 10 were only partially upgraded, whereas Block 20 underwent the whole Pacer CRAG program.

April 2002 saw the beginning of the KC-135 communication and navigation systems upgrades with the framework of the GATM (Global Air Traffic Management systems) program. Thus equipped, the aircraft were capable of flying in a busy aerial environment, whilst the distances between them were reduced significantly. This satellite-assisted navigation system

began to be installed in April 2002, the first planes thus equipped being delivered at the beginning of 2003.

During operation 'Desert Storm', during which Stratotankers of all versions were much called upon, it became obvious that the single boom refuelling system was not enough with receiving planes literally queueing up behind the tanker. It was, therefore, decided to install two extra refuelling pods at the wingtips in order to transform the K-135s into 'three point' tankers (a system named 'multi-point refuelling'). Each pod holds a soft hose that can be fed out with horizontal tension achieved thanks to a spring. The hose has a basket at the end which folds into the pod, into which the receiving aircraft place their boom.

The Mk 32b system, designed by the British Flight Refuelling Ltd had been tested successfully in 1999 and a first batch of twelve aircraft was upgraded in February 2000, the pods installed being identical to those mounted on the KC-10A Extender. Part of the fleet (45 aircraft) will be finally upgraded between now and the end of 2008 at Tinker, thanks to upgrade kits (a total of 150 ordered) supplied by Boeing. The installation of these extra pods imposed a certain number of modifications to the aircraft concerned, notably with the wing and fuselage tanks, whilst new gauges and circuit breakers had to be installed in the cockpit.

Finally, in 2002, the first trials began to transform the tankers into airborne relays. The KC-135 was specially chosen for this secondary mission as it was frequently engaged close to combat zones. Named ROBE (Roll On Beyond line of Sight Enhancement), this system rendered the Stratotanker capable of relaying information between the F-15s and E-8s and ground bases.

What replacement for the KC-135?

The maintenance costs for the KC-135 fleet increases all the time (it has, for example, doubled between 1993 and 2003) and forecasts are far from optimistic (a 6% annual increase from today until 2017) and the replacement of the Stratotanker has become imperative. However, with nearly 500 aircraft still in service, this can only take place progressively, concerning a first batch of one hundred. Originally, it was planned that the Stratotanker's replacement would be another Boeing, derived directly from the civil 767, not bought by the USAF, but rented from the aviation company. However, in January 2006, the Secretary of Defence of the time, Donald Rumsfeld, announced the cancellation of the rental contract, the decision being put forward as a budgetary cutback that was also part of a wider reorganisation of the USAF which included, apart from the retirement of the E-4B, the abandon E-10 MC2A program, the elimination of the fifty eight B-52s still in service, and the continuation of the upgrades for the KC-135 and KC-10. In January 2007, the US Air Force officially

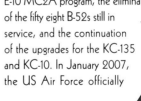

Above.
KC-135E (s/n 57-1505), 132nd ARS 'Maniacs' of the 101st ARW of the Maine ANG. The plane is equipped with the Hose and Drogue system installed in its refuelling boom and originally only used by French tankers. The pylons of the internal jet engines of this version are equipped with an additional air intake placed over the engine pod. (F. Lert)

Opposite.
During the period when the Armée de l'Air re-engined its C-135F fleet, it leased three USAF KC-135R including s/n 57-1439 seen here, used by ERV 93 from December 1992 to June 1994. (F. Lert)

launched the KC-X program, as well as an Request For Proposal, in the following terms.

The KC-X program is the first of three programs by the USAF destined to replace the whole of the ageing KC-135 fleet that has been in service for more than fifty years.' The USAF has planned to spend eight billion dollars by 2010 on the development and trials of a new aircraft which will be designated KC-45A, and estimates that the first squadron of sixteen aircraft could be operational in 2013.

Only two concepts are in the running in this program. Firstly the KC-767AT (Advanced Tanker), put forward by the Boeing led group of Smiths Aerospace, Rockwell Collins, Vought Aircraft Industries, Honeywell and Spirit AeroSystems. This aircraft, derived from the civil cargo Boeing 767-200, is equipped with a boom and fly by wire controls, new wingtip refuelling pods, a third generation boom control system, and finally a cockpit with digital instruments from the civil 777.

The other proposition, named KC-30, is the result of cooperation between Northrop-Grumman and the European consortium EADS. It is based on a military version of the EADS Airbus A330 MRTT (Multi Role Tanker Transport), itself

Below.
KC-135R (s/n 62-3551) of the 100th ARW on the runway at Mildenhall. The plane has nose art representing crossed American and British flags. (USAF)

derived from the civil A330 made by Airbus of which nearly nine hundred aircraft have been ordered in the passenger and cargo version. This aircraft, also twin engined, presents several advantages compared to the Boeing, notably with a higher fuel load capacity (27% more than a KC-135R today), due to its generally larger size. The cockpit is entirely digital with electronic controls, and the fuselage is wider and can take, not only more passengers (280 or 120 stretchers), but also a higher quantity of cargo (thirty two normal size pallets, almost twice as much as a C-17 Globemaster III).

These secondary possibilities have no doubt contributed to tipping the scales in its favour. The KC-30 can be used not only as a tanker, but also as a strategic transport aircraft, whilst being equipped with autoprotection systems that are totally absent on the KC-135. Indeed, to general surprise, as Boeing was considered as the 'official supplier' to the USAF, notably in the domain of tankers, it was finally the Northrop Grumman-EADS North America KC-30 that was officially chosen by the USAF on 1 March 2008. Four development planes are to be made initially, followed by 175 production aircraft that will be assembled at Mobile, Alabama. This order, estimated to be worth 40 billion US dollars, is added to those gained by the same aircraft in Australia, Saudi Arabia, the United Arab Emirates and Great Britain (optional). However, this spectacular decision only represents the first round in the process of repla-

8. With the withdrawal of a part of the USAF tankers fleet, an important quantity of Stratotankers became available and interested some clients as France (3 aircraft), Turkey (7) and Singapore (4).
9. Thanks to a single in-flight refuelling, the Mirage IV's range goes up from 2,870 km (1,783 miles) to 5,500 km (3,417 miles).
10. Firstly opposed to France's wish of independence regarding its homeland defence, United States finally comply with its request, mainly after its support during the Cuba's missiles crisis.
11. An aircraft (s/n 63-8473/F-UKCD) was lost by accident at Hao (French Polynesia) on 1 July 1972, when one of its engines shut off during a night take-off. All four crew members were lost despite the pilot's efforts to take his plane back to land safety.

cing the whole fleet of USAF tankers, as a second competition (KC-Y) will be organised in a non-defined period and will concern, according to the official terms, 'several hundred aircraft', during which Boeing counts on getting revenge by this time using its brand new 787 'Dreamliner', an aircraft that will have all the advantages in terms of modernity as the current A330.

The French tankers

Up to the mid 1990s 8, France was, along with the United States, the only one to use the Stratotanker, its tankers having been specially bought within the deterrence

force wanted by general de Gaulle, one of the components being the twin engined Mirage IV bomber. These aircraft did not, with their own tanks, have a sufficient 'reach' to get to their targets situated at the time, in Soviet territory. It quickly became obvious that in-flight refuelling was necessary [9].

The decision to equip the Forces Aériennes Stratégiques, that were undergoing formation at the time, with tankers, was taken in 1962. However, the United States were initially very reticent at the idea of selling this type of aircraft. It was only two years later that it was finally accepted. [10]

The first of the twelve tankers bought by France landed at Istres on 3 February 1964, and deliveries continued until July 1965, the crews having been trained at Beale, whilst a specific unit, the 90e ERV (Escadre de Ravitaillement en Vol - in-flight refuelling wing) was created on 1 August 1963. Compared to their American counterparts, the aircraft destined for the Armée de l'Air had larger cargo and passenger carrying capacities. The cabin floor was, therefore, reinforced in order take heavier loads, whilst the two lobes making up the fuselage were

pressurised instead of just the one on a production KC-135A. It is for this reason that a specific designation was attributed, C-135F, the C- prefix signifying the cargo role of this of aircraft, whilst the F suffix simply signified France. The Mirage IV was not equipped with a refuelling receptacle and the booms were modified to receive the probe and drogue system that the Americans later used on some of their aircraft.

Later, at the end of the 1990s, the original rigid boom regained some of its original use when the E-3F entered into service. These were the first Armée de l'Air aircraft equipped with an in-flight refuelling receptacle.

The first operational flight of the FAS took place on 1 October 1964 when a Mirage IVA carrying a AN 11 nuclear bomb was refuelled by a C-135F. With the progressive growth of the FAS, it became necessary to reorganise the units and the 90e ERV was

disbanded on 30 May 1965. Its aircraft ended up in three squadrons that each had three or four tankers. These were attached to a strategic bomber unit in order to form combat pairs ready twenty-four hours a day. Thus, the ERV (Escadrons de Ravitaillement en Vol) 004.091 'Landes', were created, based at Mont-de-Marsan with the Mirage IV of the 91e Escadre de Bombardement, ERV 004.093, 'Aunis', based at Istres (with the 93e EB), and ERV 004.094 'Sologne' at Avord (with the 94e EB), to which is added the independent logistical support unit, GERMAS (Groupement d'Entretien et de Réparation du Matériel Spécialisé) 015.090.

The French nuclear deterrent saw a change of direction with the installation of new intercontinental S-3 missiles at the Plateau d'Albion. It was decided to reorganise the refuelling units, which were regrouped on 1 July 1976, within the 93e Escadre de Ravitaillement which was formed at the beginning of the same year and carried on the traditions of the 31e EB.

The C-135F remained at their respective bases, but the squadrons were successively renamed 001.093 (Istres), 002.093 (Avord), 003.093 (Mont-de-Marsan) and GERMAS 015.093 (Istres).

Like their USAF counterparts, the eleven C-135F still in service, were sent to the Boeing Wichita factory between 1977 and 1979 to be partially re-skinned so that they could remain in service beyond 2000, their flying life being increased by 27,000 hours. A few years later, it was the engines that were changed, once again at Wichita BMAC (Boeing Military Aircraft Company). Between 1985 and 1988, the aircraft were fitted with the F108-CF-100, identical to those on the KC-135R. This time, they were renamed C-135FR, the second suffix signifying re-engined, and were given the same camouflage as the 'aerial defence' Mirage F1 of the day.

A series of flight instrument upgrades began in 1990, whilst in September the following year, the Landes group was given a new designation, EIRV 003.093 and was more in the role of training new tanker crews at its base at Istres.

This new mission was made necessary by the drop in the age of crew recruits. ERV 002.093 'Sologne' was disbanded in July 1993 and its personnel and planes transferred to Istres. The entire 93ᵉ Escadre de Ravitaillement was disbanded the following month and its mechanics attached to the specialist technical support squadron that had just been created.

Extra Flight Refuelling Mk 32b pods were installed in the Air France workshops on all the planes in 1994 to turn them

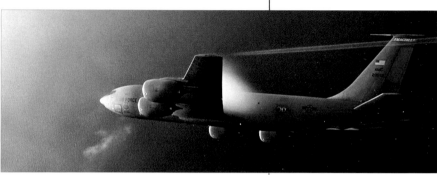

first combat mission as part of operation 'Lamentin'. They refuelled Jaguars during attacks against the rebels of the Polisario Front in Mauritania. The aircraft were then deployed in Africa 'Manta' in 1983 and 'Epervier' 1986 in Tchad, as well as the Gulf in 1990-91 as part of operation 'Daguet', the French tankers being based in Saudi Arabia. More recently, the C-135FR have been used in the former Yugoslavia, refuelling not only Armée de l'Air planes, but also those of the allied nations involved.

With the retirement of the Mirage IV, and the transfer of its original attack mission to the smaller Mirage 2000, France has greatly enlarged the use of its tankers that can now be called upon for overseas fighter deployments, as well as humanitarian

into 'three points' tankers. ERV 001.093 and 003.093, still in activity, were disbanded on 1 August 1996 and regrouped within ERV 093 'Bretagne' based at Istres and made up of three squadrons 'Rennes', 'Nantes' and 'Louve Romaine', the latter having more of a training role.

A final reorganisation (for the time being at least) took place on 1 September 2004 with the appearance of the in-flight refuelling GRV (Groupe de Ravitaillement en Vol) 093 'Bretagne' made up of four squadrons 'Nantes', 'Rennes', 'Fer à Cheval' and 'Louve Romaine' based at Istres-Le Tubé. In 1977, the Armée de l'Air C-135F aircraft took part in their

missions, the load capacity of the C-135FR being used with the latter. The replacement of these planes, although often talked about [12], has still not started. At the end of the 1990s, it was decided to buy old USAF aircraft which still had many flying hours left, in order to complete the fleet. Putting these planes, which also had to be re-engined, back into service, required several months. In the meantime, the decision was made to rent three USAF KC-135R [13] so that the Armée de l'Air could maintain its operational capacities. These were sent back to their original owner when the new aircraft began to be delivered in mid 1997.

New Customers

The USAF has progressively retired from service a large part of its KC-135 fleet. Some, stored at AMARC, Davis-Monthan, still have enough flying hours left in them to be of interest to some air forces who could make the most of the opportunity to equip themselves with a high performance jet tanker at an affordable price, especially as all these planes have been brought up to the KC-

---

12. By versions based upon the Airbus A300 or A310 whilst C-160 Transall or C-130 Hercules were also evoked.
13. Serial numbers 57-1439 (leased from December 1992 to June 1994), 62-3516 (August 1996 to July 1997) and 63-8033 (November 1996 to June 1997).
14. Originally it was planned to buy five aircraft, a figure finally reduced to three (s/n 62-3497—delivered in October 1997—, 62-3525-delivered in June 1997— and 62-3574 — delivered in July 1997). These planes kept their primary designation — KC-135R — within the Armée de l'Air, in order to differentiate them from the C-135FR acquired new.
15. Serial numbers: 57-2609, 58-0110, 60-0325, 60-0326, 62-3539, 62-3563 and 62-3567.
16. S/n: 59-1454, 61-0325, 63-8009 and 63-8016 (RSAF codes : 750 to 753).

- C-135FR 'Morphée'

France cruelly lacked a large long-range military aircraft for its overseas humanitarian missions. In 2006, a tanker (s/n 63-8471) was transformed by SOGEMA in Bordeaux, into a C-135FR 'Morphée' (Module de Réanimation pour Patient à Haute Elongation d'Evacuation) destined for strategic medical evacuations. It has two air conditioning systems to regulate the temperature to that of the ground when the engines are stopped, and is equipped with new electrical and oxygen circuits for specific medical systems. This variant can thus carry six seriously injured people and four other lighter cases, accompanied by a 12 strong medical team. When this equipment, which weighs seven tonnes, is not on board, the aircraft recovers its usual refuelling capacities. It is planned that three other planes will be thus modified, and be able to intervene, notably in the case of natural catastrophes, anywhere in the world.

135R standard. Apart from France, which completed its C-135FR fleet with three aircraft, beginning in 1997, Turkey bought seven aircraft 15, the first of which was officially delivered in October 1997. Two KC-13R had been rented beforehand to cover the interim period and crew training. The last aircraft was delivered in 1999, all the Türk Hava Kuvvetleri Stratotankers were now regrouped within the 101 Filo of the 10nci Ana Jet (based at Incirlik).

The last customer, for the time being at least, is the Republic of Singapore which received the first of the four planes purchased 16 in September 2000. All the aircraft, operational within No 112 Squadron since August 2002, are equipped with the multi-points refuelling system, and have been modernised within the Pacer CRAG program and can, when needed, be used for medical evacuations after a partial modification of their cabin.

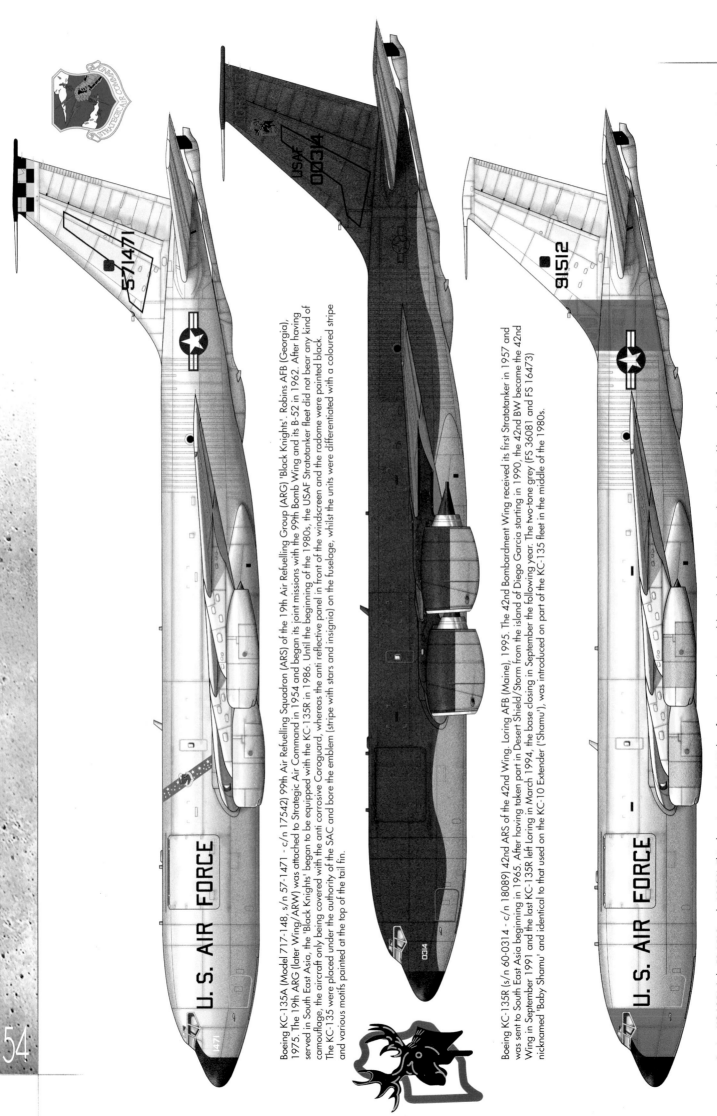

154

571471

147I

U.S. AIR FORCE

Boeing KC-135A (Model 717-148, s/n 57-1471 - c/n 17542) 99th Air Refuelling Squadron (ARS) of the 19th Air Refuelling Group (ARG) 'Black Knights'. Robins AFB (Georgia), 1975. The 19th ARG (later Wing/ARW) was attached to Strategic Air Command in 1954 and began its joint missions with the 99th Bomb Wing and its B-52 in 1962. After having served in South East Asia, the 'Black Knights' began to be equipped with the KC-135R in 1986. Until the beginning of the 1980s, the USAF Stratotanker fleet did not bear any kind of camouflage, the aircraft only being covered with the anti corrosive Coroguard, whereas the anti reflective panel in front of the windscreen and the radome were painted black. The KC-135 were placed under the authority of the SAC and bore the emblem (stripe with stars and insignia) on the fuselage, whilst the units were differentiated with a coloured stripe and various motifs painted at the top of the tail fin.

USAF 00314

ORING

0314

Boeing KC-135R (s/n 60-0314 - c/n 18089) 42nd ARS of the 42nd Wing. Loring AFB (Maine), 1995. The 42nd Bombardment Wing received its first Stratotanker in 1957 and was sent to South East Asia beginning in 1965. After having taken part in Desert Shield/Storm from the island of Diego Garcia starting in 1990, the 42nd BW became the 42nd Wing in September 1991 and the last KC-135R left Loring in March 1994, the base closing in September the following year. The two-tone grey (FS 36081 and FS 16473) nicknamed 'Baby Shamu' and identical to that used on the KC-10 Extender ('Shamu'), was introduced on part of the KC-135 fleet in the middle of the 1980s.

91512

U.S. AIR FORCE

Boeing KC-135A (s/n 59-1512 - c/n 18000). This plane is seen in its initial configuration when it was delivered to the USAF in October 1960 and bears at the front and rear the high visibility arctic stripes (orange 'day glo' FS 12197). The first 582 Stratotankers were equipped with a short tail fin which was replaced by a larger model on the following aircraft ; the old aircraft were equipped in the same way later. After having been used for a few months, this plane was modified to a KC-135Q, a particular version destined to refuel the Lockheed A-12 and SR-71 which used a special highly corrosive fuel and, therefore special equipment and tanks for the tanker.

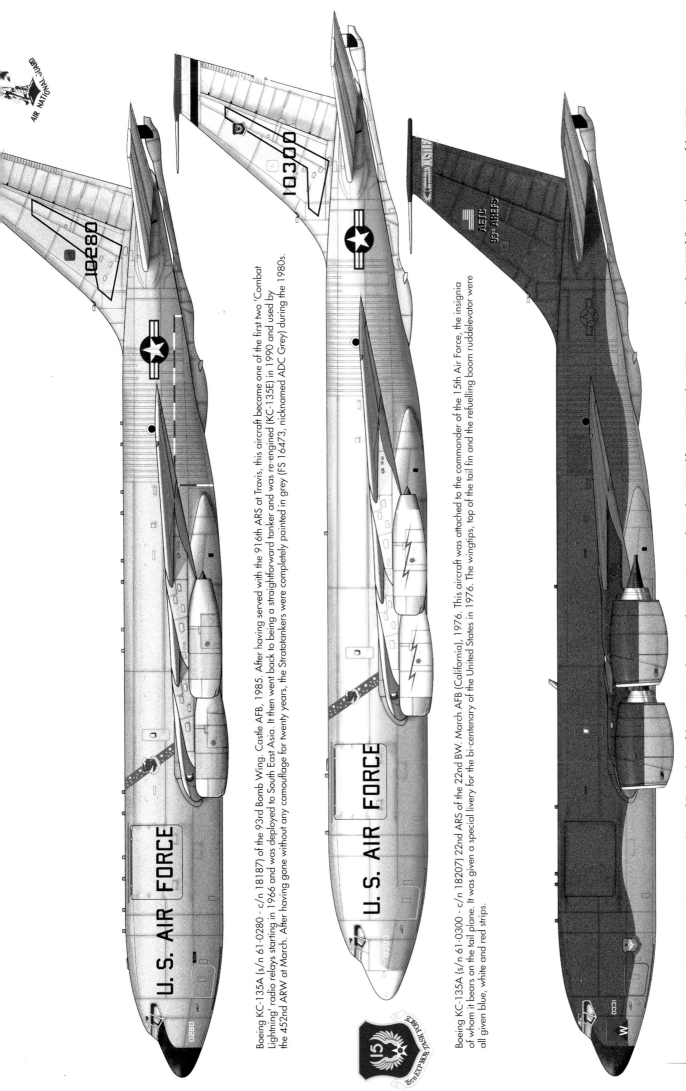

Boeing KC-135A (s/n 61-0280 - c/n 18187) of the 93rd Bomb Wing. Castle AFB, 1985. After having served with the 916th ARS at Travis, this aircraft became one of the first two 'Combat Lightning' radio relays starting in 1966 and was deployed to South East Asia. It then went back to being a straightforward tanker and was re-engined (KC-135E) in 1990 and used by the 452nd ARW at March. After having gone without any camouflage for twenty years, the Stratotankers were completely painted in grey (FS 16473, nicknamed ADC Grey) during the 1980s.

Boeing KC-135A (s/n 61-0300 - c/n 18207) 22nd ARS of the 22nd BW. March AFB (California), 1976. This aircraft was attached to the commander of the 15th Air Force, the insignia of whom it bears on the tail plane. It was given a special livery for the bi-centenary of the United States in 1976. The wingtips, top of the tail fin and the refuelling boom ruddelevator were all given blue, white and red strips.

Boeing KC-135R (s/n 60-0331 - c/n 18106) 93rd ARS of the 93rd BW of the AETC (Air Education and Training Command). Castle AFB (California), 1995. The AETC was created in July 1993 following the merger of the Air Training Command and the Air University and is responsible for training USAF personnel. The 93rd Bombardment Wing, based at Castle until 1995, then Fairchild (Washington State), was the main base for training Stratotanker crews. This aircraft , which was modified to a KC-135R in 1989, bears the two-tone grey camouflage scheme completed by black low visibility markings and a coloured stripe mentioning its home base.

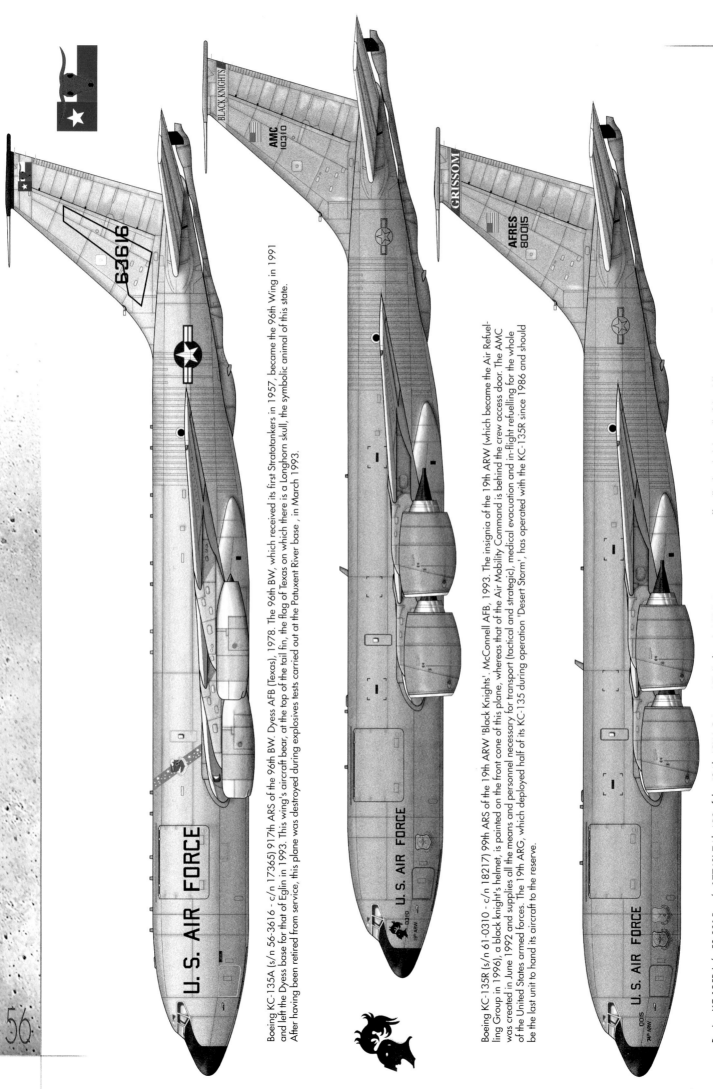

Boeing KC-135A (s/n 56-3616 - c/n 17365) 917th ARS of the 96th BW. Dyess AFB (Texas), 1978. The 96th BW, which received its first Stratotankers in 1957, became the 96th Wing in 1991 and left the Dyess base for that of Eglin in 1993. This wing's aircraft bear, at the top of the tail fin, the flag of Texas on which there is a Longhorn skull, the symbolic animal of this state. After having been retired from service, this plane was destroyed during explosives tests carried out at the Patuxent River base , in March 1993.

Boeing KC-135R (s/n 61-0310 - c/n 18217) 99th ARS of the 19th ARW 'Black Knights'. McConnell AFB, 1993. The insignia of the 19th ARW (which became the Air Refuelling Group in 1996), a black knight's helmet, is painted on the front cone of this plane, whereas that of the Air Mobility Command is behind the crew access door. The AMC was created in June 1992 and supplies all the means and personnel necessary for transport (tactical and strategic), medical evacuation and in-flight refuelling for the whole of the United States armed forces. The 19th ARG, which deployed half of its KC-135 during operation 'Desert Storm', has operated with the KC-135R since 1986 and should be the last unit to hand its aircraft to the reserve.

Boeing KC-135R (s/n 58-0015 - c/n 17760) 74th ARS of the 434th ARW. Grissom AFB (Indiana), 1995. From 1991, it was officially decided that all of the different versions of KC-135 still in service would be re-painted in dark grey (Dark Ghost - or Compass - Grey/FS 36320). The aircraft of the 434th ARW now bear the name of their base on the squadron colour stripe (blue for the 72nd ARS and red for the 74th) in the middle of their tail fin, whilst the United States flag has recently appeared here. The Air Force Reserve (AFRes), presently the Air Force Reserve Command (AFRC) gathers together Air Forces (4th, 10th and 12th) and supplies the personnel necessary for the USAF's main commands in the event of mobilisation, whereas its own fleet can be complemented by aircraft supplied by active units of the AMC.

156

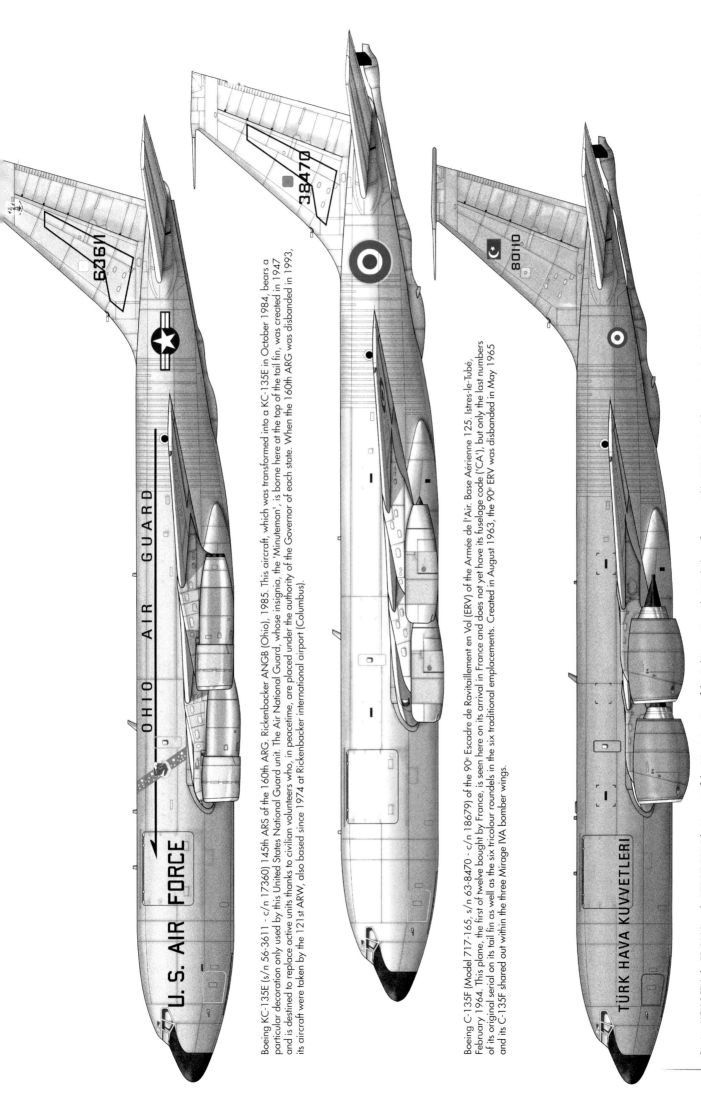

Boeing KC-135E (s/n 56-3611 - c/n 17360) 145th ARS of the 160th ARG, Rickenbacker ANGB (Ohio), 1985. This aircraft, which was transformed into a KC-135E in October 1984, bears a particular decoration only used by this United States National Guard unit. The Air National Guard, whose insignia, the 'Minuteman', is borne here at the top of the tail fin, was created in 1947 and is destined to replace active units thanks to civilian volunteers who, in peacetime, are placed under the authority of the Governor of each state. When the 160th ARG was disbanded in 1993, its aircraft were taken by the 121st ARW, also based since 1974 at Rickenbacker international airport (Columbus).

Boeing C-135F (Model 717-165, s/n 63-8470 - c/n 18679) of the 90e Escadre de Ravitaillement en Vol (ERV) of the Armée de l'Air. Base Aérienne 125. Istres-le-Tubé, February 1964. This plane, the first of twelve bought by France, is seen here on its arrival in France and does not yet have its fuselage code ('CA'), but only the last numbers of its original serial on its tail fin as well as the six tricolour roundels in the six traditional emplacements. Created in August 1963, the 90e ERV was disbanded in May 1965 and its C-135F shared out within the three Mirage IVA bomber wings.

Boeing KC-135R (s/n 58-0110 - c/n 17855) 101 Filo 'Asana' of the 10nci Ana Jets of the Turk Hava Kuvvetleri (Turkish air force). Incirlik, 2003. Retired from service by the USAF and declared surplus, this plane was put into storage at the AMARC depot at Davis Monthan in 1993. Transformed into a KC-135R at Wichita in June 1996, it was delivered to the THK via Mildenhall (Great Britain), on 13 December 1997. The seven Turkish KC-135R, which were preceded by two rented Stratotankers between 1995 and 1997, are equipped with a more modern boom than that of their USAF counterparts and Pacer CRAG for their flight instruments.

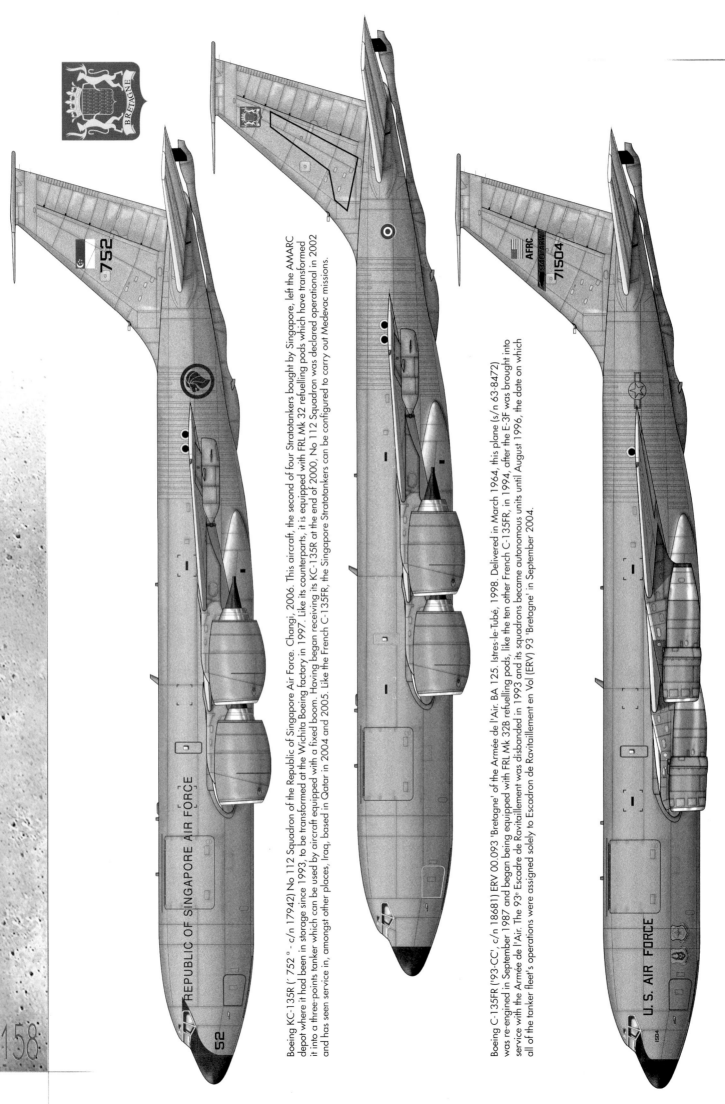

Boeing KC-135R ('752 ° - c/n 17942) No 112 Squadron of the Republic of Singapore Air Force. Changi, 2006. This aircraft, the second of four Stratotankers bought by Singapore, left the AMARC depot where it had been in storage since 1993, to be transformed at the Wichita Boeing factory in 1997. Like its counterparts, it is equipped with FRL Mk 32 refuelling pods which have transformed it into a three-points tanker which can be used by aircraft equipped with a fixed boom. Having began receiving its KC-135R at the end of 2000, No 112 Squadron was declared operational in 2002 and has seen service in, amongst other places, Iraq, based in Qatar in 2004 and 2005. Like the French C-135FR, the Singapore Stratotankers can be configured to carry out Medevac missions.

Boeing C-135FR ('93-CC', c/n 18681) ERV 00.093 'Bretagne' of the Armée de l'Air. BA 125. Istres-le-Tubé, 1998. Delivered in March 1964, this plane (s/n 63-8472) was re-engined in September 1987 and began being equipped with FRL Mk 32B refuelling pods, like the ten other French C-135FR, in 1994, after the E-3F was brought into service with the Armée de l'Air. The 93e Escadre de Ravitaillement was disbanded in 1993 and its squadrons became autonomous units until August 1996, the date on which all of the tanker fleet's operations were assigned solely to Escadron de Ravitaillement en Vol (ERV) 93 'Bretagne' in September 2004.

Boeing KC-135E (s/n 57-1504 - c/n 17575) 314th ARS of the 940th ARW. McClellan AFB (California), 1994. The Air Force Reserve Command only has two wings equipped with the KC-135E, the 927th ARW at Selfridge and the 940th ARW which began using it in 1977 from various bases in the region of Sacramento, including McClellan from 1993 to 1997.

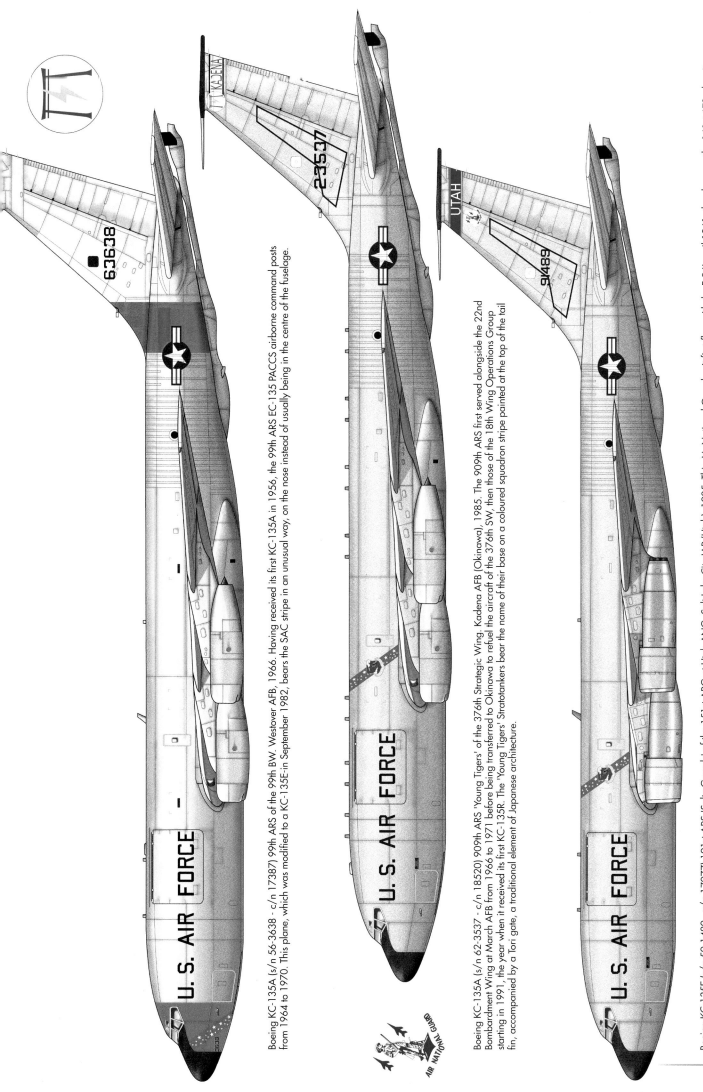

Boeing KC-135A (s/n 56-3638 - c/n 17387) 99th ARS of the 99th BW. Westover AFB, 1966. Having received its first KC-135A in 1956, the 99th ARS EC-135 PACCS airborne command posts from 1964 to 1970. This plane, which was modified to a KC-135E in September 1982, bears the SAC stripe in an unusual way, on the nose instead of usually being in the centre of the fuselage.

Boeing KC-135A (s/n 62-3537 - c/n 18520) 909th ARS 'Young Tigers' of the 376th Strategic Wing. Kadena AFB (Okinawa), 1985. The 909th ARS first served alongside the 22nd Bombardment Wing at March AFB from 1966 to 1971 before being transferred to Okinawa to refuel the aircraft of the 376th SW, then those of the 18th Wing Operations Group starting in 1991, the year when it received its first KC-135R. The 'Young Tigers' Stratotankers bear the name of their base on a coloured squadron stripe painted at the top of the tail fin, accompanied by a Tori gate, a traditional element of Japanese architecture.

Boeing KC-135E (s/n 59-1489 - c/n 17977) 191st ARS 'Salty Guards' of the 151st ARG at Utah ANG. Salt Lake City IAP (Utah), 1985. This Air National Guard unit first flew with the F-86L until 1961, then became the 161st ATS when it received the C-97. It was in October 1972, with the arrival of the KC-97L, that it took its present name, and was next equipped with the KC-135A (April 1978), the KC-135E (1982-1983) and the KC-135R at the end of the 20th century.

159

THE C-135

Believing that its 'Dash 80' demonstrator would inspire the US Air Force or the US Navy to order a large amount of a transport version of the future aircraft, Boeing equipped it with cargo doors to prove its efficiency.

However, at the time, the US Navy did not have sufficient funds to finance such a project, whilst the USAF, who had mostly invested in jet aircraft for its combat units (bombers and fighters), hesitated somewhat to do the same for its fleet of transport aircraft, MATS, created in 1948. The Berlin Air Lift in 1948, and above all, the Korean War, from 1950, made it blatantly obvious to the United States that it needed to renew its strategic transport aircraft. To fill this void, piston-

engined Douglas C-124 Globemaster II aircraft were quickly ordered in quantity, as was another Douglas, the C-133 Cargomaster, equipped with turboprops and for which only fifty were made. But, most importantly, a specific cargo plane program was launched, culminating a few years later in the Douglas C-141 Starlifter which became, for forty years, the USAF's main heavy transport aircraft.

Whilst waiting for the Starlifter to enter into service, the American Congress in May 1960, agreed to the purchase of fifty Boeings, designated C-135 and named Stratolifter [1]; this initial number was finally reduced to forty-five. To explain this decision, it should be remembered that at this time, the MATS only had three jet transport (C-137A), all the others being piston engined, and above all, that President Kennedy had announced in 1961 that the modernisation of the United States strategic transport was a priority. To achieve this, MATS would need modern planes, that is to say with a greater range, faster and capable of carrying heavier loads over greater distances. Several solutions were considered, notably a military cargo version of the Douglas DC-8 equipped with turbofans, or the

1. This name was a logical choice as it followed the lineage of those already used for other versions of the plane beginning with the Stratotanker (KC-135).

Above.
After a ten year career as a VC-135B, s/n 62-4125 was retrograded as a C-135B in March 1977 and used for VIP transport in Asia and Europe at the German base of Ramstein.
(WingMasters collection).

Boeing Model 735, derived from the KC-135 that was also equipped with JT3D turbofan engines and whose load (45,360 kg/100,000 lb maximum) could be put into the plane via the rear, the tail plane section being mobile, as on the military DC-8. A final solution, easily attainable, consisted of using as a base a Boeing Stratotanker and stripping it of its in-flight refuelling equipment. This proposition was the one finally chosen, as a stopgap solution whilst waiting for the arrival of the C-141 Starlifter that would begin to be delivered in 1965.

C-135A

The first fifteen aircraft, designated C-135A by the USAF and Model 717-157 by Boeing, were delivered between August 1961 and January 1962. Globally, they were KC-135A that had had their in-flight refuelling system removed (tanks, boom), apart from the boomer's compartment. The floor was strengthened and equipped with fixation points and the engines were Pratt and Whitney J57-59W.

These aircraft had a maximum take-off weight of 123,380 kg (272,000 lb) and could carry a little more than 41 tonnes (45 tons) over a distance of 4,350 km (2,700 miles). The hold, which was 24.20 m (79 ft 5 in) long and 3.27 m

Below.
VC-135 s/n 62-4126 of the 1st MAS
of the 89th MAW at the Edwards base
in 1982. The aircraft of this unit
specialised in VIP transport were pain-
ted in a particular way; the metal
areas were highly polished, notably
under the fuselage. (USAF).

(10 ft 9 in) wide, could take anything up to 2.12 m (7 ft) in height. Its total capacity was 170m³ (6,000 cu in) of cargo. The latter, placed on rollers, could be loaded using an internal F 71230 hoist installed in the door frame and which was complemented by a rail that ran along the cabin ceiling right to the end. Finally, when it was transformed into a cabin, the hold could take, depending on the internal lay out, 80 seated passengers in two rows or 160 passengers if the rows were

doubled. In a medivac configuration, the C-135A could also carry 44 stretchers or 54 seated wounded. In reality, the amount of passengers carried, as well as the crew (eleven men) was very often limited to 72, essentially due to the limited number of emergency exits. Whatever the load, this first version of the Stratolifter could fly at 850 km/h (530 mph) at an average altitude of 9,300 m (30,510 ft), this increasing to 13,000 m (42,650 ft) when the plane was empty. From 1962, a load transport system using normalised pallets was introduced with the MATS which was initially planned to be used on the future C-141, but which was also used by other cargo planes. The C-135A could thus carry eight 2.75 m x 2.23 m (9 ft x 7 ft 4 in) pallets and one 1.37 m x 2.23 m (4 ft 6 in x 7 ft 4 in) installed in the centre of the cabin, this allowed for a 0.50 m (1 ft 8 in) passage on each side. The Stratolifter did not really benefit from this standardisation, a plane rather disadvantaged by its cargo door that was placed

high up and which needed a lift for loading. In order to speed up the new MATS cargo planes, three KC-135A (s/n 60-0356, 60-0357 and 60-0362) were specially modified on the assembly lines and delivered in June-July 1961. Unofficially nicknamed 'falsies' they did not have the modifications introduced on the future production planes, notably the larger tail plane that improved lateral stability. These three were used to train future Stratolifter crews, but only had a short career with the MATS as they were modified in September the same year into KC-135A -II electronic reconnaissance planes as part of the Office Boy program. Put into service beginning in August 1961 with the 1611th Air Transport Wing, a wing was attached to the MATS, the two squadrons of which (18th and 41st ATS), were used by the EASTAF (Eastern Transport Air Force) and the WESTAF, the C-135 A quickly showed itself to be ill-suited for its mission as it did not perform well enough and, above all, was incapable of carrying heavy and,

moreover, bulky loads. Indeed, the cargo door, situated three metres above the ground, required the use of loading lifts, whilst its position at the front of the plane, as well as its narrowness, made it impossible to load anything too long round the corner (90°!) and into the hold. Also, the Stratolifter was not equipped with any access ramp; it could not carry either tanks or armoured vehicles, and even less an intercontinental missile; a huge handicap for an aircraft made for strategic transport. Worse, the C-135A, with its water injection engines, required long runways for take-offs and landings that had to be made of concrete to take its great weight, something which prevented it from being deployed anywhere other than international airports or specially equipped bases. To get to its final destination, cargo had to be shared out in other aircraft that were able to use smaller airfields or with shorter and less well-made runways. Another handicap present in this version was its much reduced range when carrying a heavy load. In this case, the quantity of internal fuel had to be limited, authorising only five to six hours of flight and in consequence ruling out any transpacific flights without a stopover.

Despite everything, the first C-135 A were used from their first year of being put into service in 1961, carrying National Guard soldiers in the United States to their different European bases during the crisis that began with the building of the Berlin Wall. At the end of their use as transport planes, that is to say in 1966, the MAC which took over from the MATS at this time relegated the Stratolifter to secondary missions and most of the C-135A still in service were used as a base for the new specialised versions such as the NC-135A, EC-135 N or EC-135E. A few aircraft had a less glorious end as they were used

as training airframes for mechanics and even for the study of a system of mechanised paint stripping (LARPS/Large Aircraft Robotic Paint System)!

C-135B

The last thirty aircraft of this transport version were delivered after the previous ones between February and August 196 and designated C-135B (Model 717-158), the maiden flight of the first aircraft taking place in February the same year. This time it was powered by TF-33- 5 engines fitted with thrust reversers-equipped turbofans that gave 40% extra thrust. In order to compensate for this increased power and to maintain the aircraft's trim, the horizontal tail plane was slightly enlarged, a model identical to that fitted to the civil Boeing 707 being used. Thanks to these new engines, the average altitude went from 9,800 m (32,150 ft) when at maximum weight and 13,100 m (42,980 ft) when empty, whilst the cruising speed of this cargo plane was now 865 km/h (538 mph). However, it was above all the distance that the plane needed to take off that benefited the most from this change as it went from 2,700 m (8,860 ft) for the C-135A to 2,100 m (6,890 ft) for the new version, with it being able to take off empty with 650 m (2130 ft) when it had previously needed 1,000 (3,300 ft).

The C-135B was able to carry a load of forty tonnes (44 tons) or 126 fully equipped soldiers and was, for a while, used as a medical transport (44 stretchers and 54 wounded with the accompanying medical personnel) before finally being replaced by the C-9A which was specifically designed

for this use. On the other hand, due to a lack of spare engines, the MATS voluntarily limited the number of passengers carried by these new Stratolifters to 90% of their capacity in order to put the engines under a little less strain, and especially as once more there were not enough emergency exits.

These higher performance and safer aircraft (their availability rate reached 93%) remained, however, just as ill-adapted to transporting bulky cargo, their main cargo door was still impractical and the loading and unloading operations could only take place on specially equipped bases of which there were not many. Logically it was the new 1611th ATW and its two transport squadrons that received the first C-135B, fifteen were also supplied to the 44th ATS at Travis, the only unit of the west coast of the United States to be equipped with the C-135. Overseas, a few squadrons put this transport version into service, such as the 7407th CSW at Rhein-Main, Germany, or the 6486th ABW at Hickam (Hawaii).

This new version of the Stratolifter took part in operation Big Lift in 1963, the aim of which was its reaction capacities to prove to the European allies and during which the entire 2nd Armored Division was transferred from Texas to the German base of Rhein-Main. This was a 9,000 km (5,590 miles) trip and required twenty five C-135, of both models. The year before, in October 1962, the Stratolifter collaborated with the first air bridge to use only jet aircraft, operation New Tape which kept Swedish troops supplied when on United Nations detachment in Congo.

Conscious of the limits of its Stratolifter, notably in the transportation of bulky loads, Boeing soon, that is in 1962, envisaged making a better adapted derivative. Using once again the 'double bubble' fuselage used on the C-97, the Advanced C-135 would thus be equipped with a cabin that was both longer and higher, accessible via a mobile ramp at the rear like that on the C-130. With this, very bulky loads (29,700 kg/65,500 lb maximum) could have been much more easily loaded into the

hold, notably gun carriers and even helicopters of the CH-47 Chinook category. Despite its undeniable qualities, this project was not followed up, mainly because the aircraft which was its direct rival, the C-141 Starlifter, had been production ordered a few months earlier. Replaced in their role as a strategic transport aircraft by the C-141 Starlifter, the C-135B still in service were used a great deal within the making of specialised versions. Ten of them became, therefore, the WC-135B (see following chapters) which were later modified themselves into the OC-135B and WC-135W.

Amongst the other versions which came from this aircraft and which we will look at more closely later, we should mention the RC-135E, RC-135W, RC-135S or the aircraft for training crews such as the TC-135W or the TC-135S.

VC-135B

In order to complete the VC-137 fleet for the transportation of VIPs, five C-135B received in 1967, a more luxurious internal layout and redesignated as VC-135B. They were attached to the 89th Military Airlift Wing at Andrews and served, notably, for the transportation of VIPs or high ranking staff officers. Compared to the military transport version of the Boeing 707, the C/VC-137, and C/VC-135 differed on the outside by the reduced amount of fuselage windows and, above all, by the remains of the boomer's position under the rear fuselage point which formed a characteristic bulge.

On the five VC-135B, for of them [2] were declassified in December 1977 as straightforward C-135B, losing the superb livery of Air Force One that they had had up to that point, whilst the fifth [3] was modified as a TC-135W training aircraft in February 1987.

C-135C

Three meteorological reconnaissance WC-135B [4] (following chapters) were converted into VIP transporters at the end of their operational career in 1975 (more luxurious internal layout than the standard Stratolifter, space communication systems) and therefore renamed C-135C. The main difference compared to the classic transporters was that these aircraft could be refuelled in the air as they were equipped with a refuelling receptacle that had not been removed when their mission role was changed. One of these planes (61-2669) became, with the 1st ACCS of the 1st CW at Andrews, the second 'Speckled Trout' [5], by replacing the KC-135A previously named this way (s/n 55-3126) and which had just been retired from service. After having been used to break several speed records in its category and attached to the USAF general headquarters, it was attached in 1994 to the 412th Test Squadron of the 412th Test Wing at Edwards (California) where it remained in service until 1996, as much for VIP transport, notably for the USAF general staff, as for trials for all sorts of on-board equipment or instruments such as the Glass Cockpit for example.

C-135E

Three old C-135A [6] became C-135E when they were re-engined with the Pratt & Whitney TF 33. The first two aircraft were attached to the 412th Test Squadron whilst the last was initially used by the 8th ACCS of the 552nd ACW at Tinker (Oklahoma) for personnel transport with the US Space Command before being transferred to the 89th Airlift Wing and finally the 15th Air Base Wing at Hickham at Hawaii.

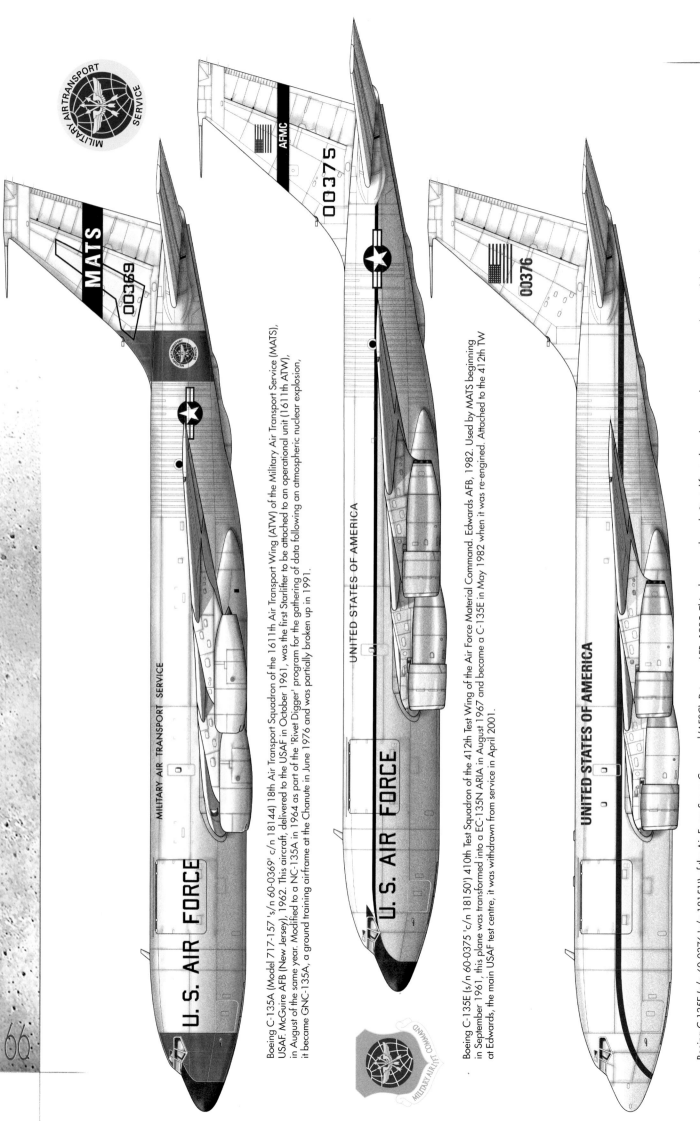

Boeing C-135A (Model 717-157 's/n 60-0369' c/n 18144) 18th Air Transport Squadron of the 1611th Air Transport Wing (ATW) of the Military Air Transport Service (MATS), USAF McGuire AFB (New Jersey), 1962. This aircraft, delivered to the USAF in October 1961, was the first Starlifter to be attached to an operational unit (1611th ATW), in August of the same year. Modified to a NC-135A in 1964 as part of the 'Rivet Digger' program for the gathering of data following an atmospheric nuclear explosion, it became GNC-135A, a ground training airframe at the Chanute in June 1976 and was partially broken up in 1991.

MILITARY AIR TRANSPORT SERVICE

Boeing C-135E (s/n 60-0375 'c/n 18150') 410th Test Squadron of the 412th Test Wing of the Air Force Material Command. Edwards AFB, 1982. Used by MATS beginning in September 1961, this plane was transformed into a EC-135N ARIA in August 1967 and became a C-135E in May 1982 when it was re-engined. Attached to the 412th TW at Edwards, the main USAF test centre, it was withdrawn from service in April 2001.

UNITED STATES OF AMERICA

Boeing C-135E (s/n 60-0376 'c/n 18151') of the Air Force Space Command (AFSC). Peterson AFB, 1985. This plane was the only Stratolifter to have been used as a transport plane until the end of its career. After having been attached to the Air Force Special Weapons Center, then to the AFSC in June 1965, it was modified to a VC-135A (general staff transport) in 1972-1973. It was re-engined in 1982 and re-designated at this time C-135E and used by the 89th MAW ; its interior was changed again in May 1984 and it became the personal aircraft of the Commander in Chief of the AFSC, a command responsible for all the United States' ballistic missiles. It was next attached successively to the 8th Tactical Deployment Control Squadron and the 8th ACCS. It ended its career with the 552nd Air Control Wing and went into storage in 2001.

UNITED STATES OF AMERICA

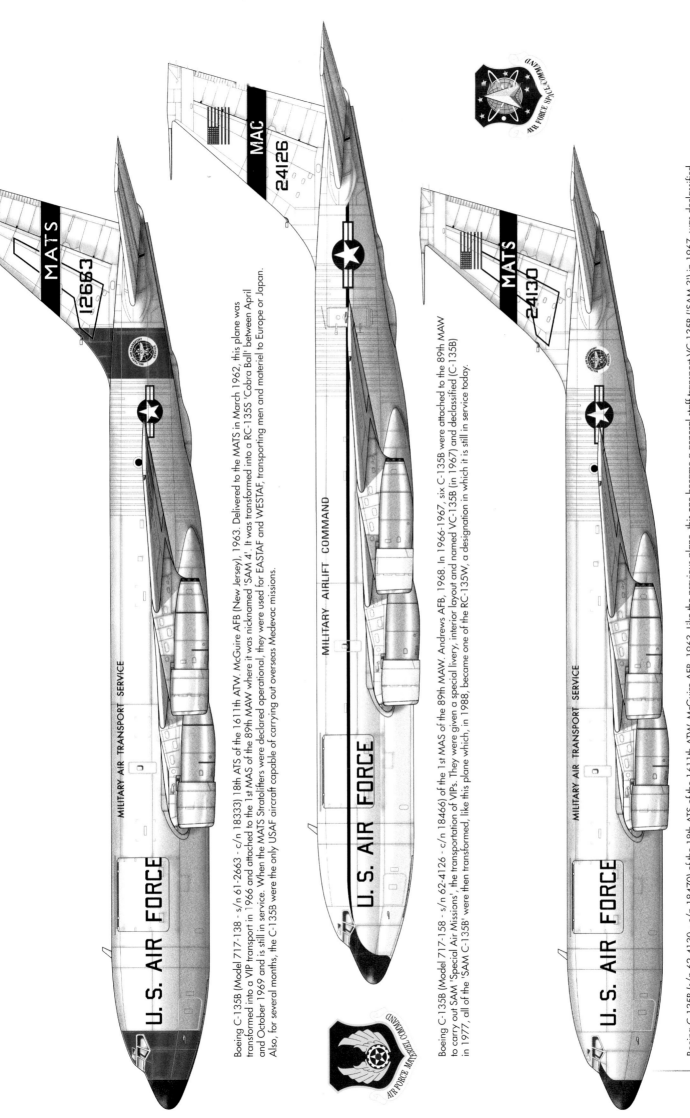

MATS

12663

MILITARY AIR TRANSPORT SERVICE

U. S. AIR FORCE

Boeing C-135B (Model 717-138 - s/n 61-2663 - c/n 18333) 18th ATS of the 1611th ATW. McGuire AFB (New Jersey), 1963. Delivered to the MATS in March 1962, this plane was transformed into a VIP transport in 1966 and attached to the 1st MAS of the 89th MAW where it was nicknamed 'SAM 4'. It was transformed into a RC-135S 'Cobra Ball' between April and October 1969 and is still in service. When the MATS Stratolifters were declared operational, they were used for EASTAF and WESTAF, transporting men and materiel to Europe or Japan. Also, for several months, the C-135B were the only USAF aircraft capable of carrying out overseas Medevac missions.

MAC

24126

MILITARY AIRLIFT COMMAND

U. S. AIR FORCE

Boeing C-135B (Model 717-158 - s/n 62-4126 - c/n 18466) of the 1st MAS of the 89th MAW. Andrews AFB, 1968. In 1966-1967, six C-135B were attached to the 89th MAW to carry out SAM 'Special Air Missions', the transportation of VIPs. They were given a special livery, interior layout and named VC-135B (C-135B) in 1977, all of the 'SAM C-135B' were then transformed, like this plane which, in 1988, became one of the RC-135W, a designation in which it is still in service today.

MATS

24130

MILITARY AIR TRANSPORT SERVICE

U. S. AIR FORCE

Boeing C-135B (s/n 62-4130 - c/n 18470) of the 18th ATS of the 1611th ATW. McGuire AFB, 1963. Like the previous plane, this one became a general staff transport VC-135B ('SAM 3') in 1967, was declassified (C-135B) in 1977 and is today one of the RC-135W. The thirty C-135B made were attached, at the beginning of their career, to the 1611th ATW (fifteen planes in the 18th and 415th ATS and the 1501st ATW (44th ATS, fifteen planes) at Travis AFB, the aircraft being frequently rotated from one base to the other. All the C-135B, after being used as transports, were modified, mainly for electronic reconnaissance versions (RC-135).

167

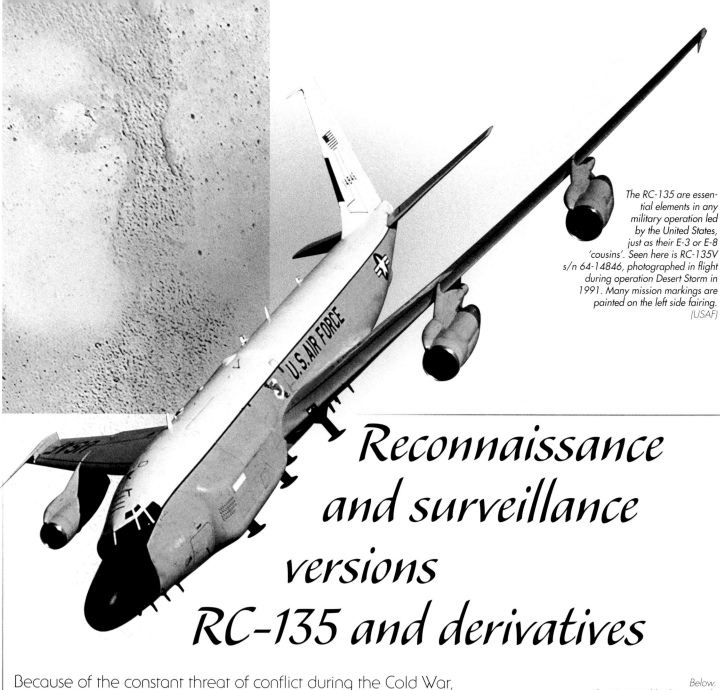

The RC-135 are essential elements in any military operation led by the United States, just as their E-3 or E-8 'cousins'. Seen here is RC-135V s/n 64-14846, photographed in flight during operation Desert Storm in 1991. Many mission markings are painted on the left side fairing.
(USAF)

Reconnaissance and surveillance versions RC-135 and derivatives

Because of the constant threat of conflict during the Cold War, reconnaissance and intelligence-gathering missions became increasingly important. Already equipped with specialised aircraft for these missions that were as thankless as they were perilous, the United States quickly saw in the new Boeing the ideal aircraft. It had a good range, could carry a large crew and a considerable amount of specialised equipment, but above all, as a civil jet transport, it looked much less aggressive than a military aircraft.

Below.
The RC-135A like this example replaced the RB-50 in cartography and geodesic surveillance missions carried out by the MATS, which became the MAC (Military Airlift Command) in 1966. These planes were completely covered in aluminium finish (Coroguard), with only an antireflection panel in front of the windscreen. S/n 63-8059 saw service beginning in 1971 as a support plane with the 55th Wing before being modified to a KC-135R.
(WingMasters archives)

Above.
With its numerous antenna on the
back of its fuselage, KC-135R
s/n 55-3121 was nicknamed
'Porcupine'. Initially a test bed
(JKC-135A), this plane successively
became a KC-135T in December 1969
after having received a new radome,
then a RC-135T in May 1971. It was
lost on 25 February 1985 in a crash
which killed three of its crew.
(WingMasters archives)

Opposite.
Ordered as a RC-135B,
s/n 64-14843 was delivered to the
USAF in November 1964 as
a RC-135C. This version is characterised by its short nose, a small tear drop
shaped radome under the front of the
aircraft and cameras installed in the
former boomer's compartment.
This aircraft is still used by the 55th
SRW after having been modified to a
RC-135V between 1973 and 1975.
(WingMasters archives)

Opposite.
Amongst the first planes to be specially
modified for reconnaissance is the
RB-50E, a version of the bomber
that was a direct descendent of the
famous Second World War
Superfortress bomber.
(USAF)

1. The U-2 became famous throughout the world
on 1 May 1960 when one was shot down by
the Soviet air defences and its pilot, Francis Gary
Powers, was sentenced to ten years in prison.
This incident was much publicised by the Russian authorities and the pilot was finally released
on exchange a few years later.

1950s, by versions derived from the B-47 Stratojet, and notably
by the RB-47B of which twenty-four were transformed between
1953 and 1954. On these aircraft, the original armament was
removed and the bomb bay modified to make room for the
eight cameras.

The RB-47E prototype took off on 3 July 1953 and was
a plane that was from the outset designed for reconnaissance and not the result of a transformation of a plane already in
existence. 240 of these were delivered to the SAC in the
months that followed. Apart from new, higher performance
jet engines, this version was characterised by a heavier weight
and a slightly longer nose. Shortly after, the US Air Force also
used fifteen RB-47K, modified RB-47E equipped with cameras
or weather reconnaissance systems for high or medium altitudes, as well as a variant specialised in electronic reconnaissance, the RB-47H equipped with radomes under the nose,
wings and the rear of the fuselage, as well as a compartment
added to the former bomb bay enclosing the receivers, recor-
ders and three operators! Carrying out its missions in often
perilous conditions, as these were strictly illegal, notably over
Soviet bloc territory, these planes were, as we can imagine,
extremely uncomfortable, the specialists being literally huddled
into a area that was as cluttered as it was impractical, for hours
at a time in an atmosphere of considerable tension.

As the spy planes, and principally the Lockheed U-2, whose
maiden flight was not until 1 August 1955 [1], were not opera-

Indeed, for strategic reconnaissance missions and all sorts
of intelligence-gathering until the end of the 1950s, the USAF
had used versions derived from multi-engined bombers such
as the RB-29A (ten modified aircraft used during the closing
months of the Second World War) and the RB-50B, of which
forty-four aircraft were made in 1947, equipped with four view-
taking positions with nine cameras, a weather reconnaissance
system and extra fuel tanks under the wings, whilst some of the
original armament (upper forward and caudal turret) were kept.

Four years later, in 1951, these RB-50B were once more
modified, this time to RB-50E, RB-50F and RB-50G, the fifteen
aircraft of this latest variant being given an improved radar,
increased armament and a crew made up of sixteen men. These
piston-engine aircraft were followed, at the beginning of the

Opposite.
The only RC-135E (s/n 62-4137) was distinguished by its side looking radar installed at the front of the fuselage. This area was made of glass fibre to ease the transmission of waves and was the cause of the accident of 5 June 1969 when the plane was lost along with all the crew. (USAF)

SIGINT, COMINT, ELINT… etc.

The general term SIGINT (Signal Intelligence) also covers other categories of intelligence such as: COMINT (COMmunication INTelligence), the listening, interception and treatment of communications across wavelengths (radio phonic, television, telephone) or emitted by any other source of electromagnetic origins (cable etc.)

ELINT (Electronic INTelligence): intelligence (frequency, power) obtained from electromagnetic emissions coming from electronic devices (radars, jamming systems, counter measures) not designed for communication, or caused by a nuclear explosion or a radioactive source.

TELINT (TELemetry INTelligence): The gathering of intelligence concerning electromagnetic emissions linked to trials or operational deployment of aerial or spatial systems of civil or military origin.

tional, and in any case not adapted for intelligence-gathering close to the ground, the Strategic Air Command initially looked into various solutions that would result in its having a fleet of modern reconnaissance and intelligence aircraft. These would have to be high performance with a long range, and above all, having the necessary space to carry out its missions in the best possible conditions, or at least in acceptable conditions.

With this in view, twenty-seven B-52 bombers were transformed into RB-52B (briefly designated XR-16), which carried in their bomb bays a pod containing either four cameras or electronic reconnaissance equipment and two specialist operators. These aircraft, attached to the 93rd Heavy Bombardment Wing at Castle AFB, in California, in June 1955, were rapidly deemed ill-adapted for the missions they were given, notably because of the narrowness of the bomb bay that meant that not all the required equipment could be installed. It therefore became quickly obvious that using a version derived from another Boeing would be the ideal solution.

Photos of the sole «River Amber» (RC-135E) are quite rare and often of a mediocre quality. It is seen here at the Shemva base in Alaska in 1962 when it was named 'Lisa Ann' (USAF)

Opposite.
'Rivet Brass 3', RC-135D s/n 60-0362, was the only one of the three aircraft of this version to be equipped with a large size radome.
(LTV)

Above.
Delivered in July 1962 to the USAF as a C-135B, s/n 62-4135 was initially the first RC-135M at the beginning of 1966, then the first RC-135W in 1980. (WingMasters archives)

With its four engines, the plane had a good autonomy (approximately eight hours), whilst its large capacity cabin could hold a lot of specialised equipment operated by numerous specialist operators. Another great advantage, as we have just seen, was its civil aircraft appearance, the future aircraft being a little less warlike than its predecessors, notably in the event of interceptions in delicate situations outside of authorised air routes when flying over sensitive regions.

As we will see, this led to several tragic mistakes when civil aircraft were thought to be, according to the protagonists, marauding military intelligence planes.

The beginnings

The first aircraft specially transformed for reconnaissance was the KC-135A. They were difficult to identify from the outside

Above.
Initially used in the AFSATCOM program (ultra high frequency tests), s/n 61-2662 was transformed into a RC-135S between June 1981 and November 1983. The exterior aspect of the 'Cobra Ball' varies slightly depending on the aircraft.
(WingMasters archives)

2. The 'J' prefix indicates a plane attached to temporary tests, whilst 'N' is used if transformed for permanent tests.

S/n 64-14849 was the last KC-135 to be made (but not, on the other hand, the last to be delivered). It was first modified to a RC-135C in the mid 1960s, then transformed into a RC-135U by General Dynamics in 1971, the configuration in which it has been photographed here. It began its new career in Vietnam and took part in operation 'Linebacker II' the following year.
(WingMasters archives)

due to the extreme secrecy surrounding their use. They were preceded, in 1961, by a plane, designated JKC-135A [2] and named 'Nancy Rae' used for data collection. Initially, a KC-135A was modified as part of the 'Big Safari' program (a code name attributed to the USAF services in charge of the development and transformation of specialised aircraft) for the recording of data notably that of electromagnetic radiation emitted after atmospheric nuclear tests by the Soviets. It was this aircraft which, in October 1961, recorded the explosion of a Russian atomic bomb during operation 'Speed Light'. The latter being a success, the decision was made to modify two more planes; the three aircraft were officially named 'Rivet Stand' in 1963

Opposite.
RC-135U s/n 63-9792 was modified to a RC-135V between 1975 and 1977. It is still in service with the 55th SRW as a 'Combat Sent 3'. At the beginning of the 1980s, all the RC-135 still in service were camouflaged in light grey (FS 16473) with the roof of the cabin painted white to deflect sun rays and decrease the internal temperature.
(WingMasters archives)

and were specialised in the gathering of intelligence concerning atomic explosions.

These aircraft remained very similar to a standard tanker and for this reason are still difficult to precisely identify today. Indeed, they kept their in-flight refuelling equipment, notably the aft boom, even though they were also equipped with a forward refuelling receptacle that allowed them to carry out long missions.

From the outside, the only clue to its new role was the presence of extra antenna, and notably five series of three antenna that were rapidly named 'Towel Bar' due to their particular shape on the fuselage, with another beneath. Because of these particular appendages, the planes were given all sorts of names such as porcupine or horned toad.

Finally, four small windows were added to each side at the front of the fuselage for various photographic equipment.

KC-135A-II (RC-135A)

The first officially identified reconnaissance version was the KC-135A-II, often mistakenly designated RC-135A, three of which were delivered beginning in December 1962. They were

Opposite.
Views of the underneath of the RC-135 are not common. This one, the first transformed RC-135U in flight, shows the shape of the 'cheek' fairings and the aft point, as well as the draining hose and the fairing replacing the refuelling boom and the boomer compartment on standard tankers.
(WingMasters archives)

Characteristics of the RC-135

Apart from a very few exceptions, all the derivatives of the C-135 specialised in reconnaissance and intelligence have similar characteristics. Thus, apart from the RC-135A, these planes can all be refuelled in the air as they have an ARR (Air Refuelling Receptacle), whilst the planes derived from the Stratotanker have some of their fuselage tanks removed in order to leave more space for equipment and on board technicians in the cabin.

All the 'true' RC-135, that is to say, the versions not obtained by modifying a KC-135, do not have a refuelling boom or a boomer's compartment but a dumping hose placed under the rear of the fuselage destined to dump some of the fuel to gain altitude rapidly in the event of an emergency.

Another almost general characteristic, the lengthened nose (except on the KC-135A and the RC-135A, C and U), that increased the aircraft's length to 40.70 m (135 ft) and in the interior of which the

retained AN/APN-59 navigation radar has been placed forward. This radar also has a recording device for flight data so that it can be analysed after the flight. The rectangular fairings placed on the side of the forward part of the fuselage (which is why they are nicknamed 'cheeks') are also typical to most of the RC-135.

Contrary to a still very widespread notion, they do not contain SLAR side-looking radar, but a large variety of antennae and small size receivers, such as notably the AEELS (Automatic Elint Emitter Locator System) - a system first tried out in 1962 on two NKC-135A modified by the ASD and LTV companies, taking up a total area of more than eighteen square metres. The average range of this equipment is approximately 250 kilometres (155 miles) and they obtain all sorts of information on potential objectives that can be transmitted to ground-based command posts in order to organise retaliation or preventive intervention. The exact

shape of these fairings varies according to their origin; thus, an expert eye can see slight differences between those designed by Martin (RC-135C, U and V) or E-Systems (RC-135U, V and W). These large bumps change the air flow around the front of the fuselage; a certain number of antenna and probes normally placed at this part had to be moved which explains why there are booms added over the wingtips for measuring pressure. These are in no way, as is sometimes indicated, and despite their similarity, high frequency antenna.

At the beginning, these data gathering aircraft were not, like their transport of refuelling counterparts, camouflaged, but simply covered in aluminium finish destined to protect their metallic structure from corrosion (Coroguard). Later, in order to decrease the temperature inside the cabin and cockpit, by deflecting sunrays, as is the case on civil transport aircraft, the RC-135 had the upper areas

of the fuselage and tall of the tail unit painted in gloss white. It was only in the beginning of the 1980s that they were entirely painted in gloss light grey (FS 16473); the cabin and tail unit, however, remained white, the colours being separated by a night blue stripe.

At the beginning of their career, and for nearly a quarter of a century, their markings were particularly discreet; only the national roundels were placed in the regulation areas, as well as the inscription US Air Force on each side of the fuselage. Their serial number, painted on the vertical stabiliser, was sometimes even voluntarily replaced by another to make them more difficult to identify for prying eyes. It was not until 1988 that an old tradition returned to SAC planes: that of nose art reappearing on the RC-135, whilst a few years later in 1994, the squadron was clearly indicated by a coloured stripe on top of the tail fin, like those on most of the KC-135.

used by the 4157th Strategic Wing at Shemya, in Alaska, a base chosen for its proximity with the eastern borders of the Soviet Union and China. These aircraft were immediately discernable exteriorly from the standard Stratotanker by its longer nose and it was rapidly named 'Hog Nose' or 'Thimble Nose', which characterised almost all reconnaissance versions of the (K)C-135 (see box). Apart from this appendage, booms appeared at the end of each wing tip, as well as several fairings enclosing antenna placed under the fuselage forward of the wings.

From 1963 onwards, at least one of these planes, capable of being refuelled in the air of course, was placed on 'Jig Time' alert, that is to say capable of taking off very quickly in order to collect data during an important but unpredictable event, such as, for example, the launch of a Russian ballistic missile from one of the bases situated in Kamchatka. In 1965, these

Below.
The first modified RC-135U (by General Dynamics between July 1970 and June 1971) taxiing, showing the particular shape of the antenna added on the lateral fairings, nicknamed 'Towel Rail' that were kept until 1991.
(WingMasters Archives)

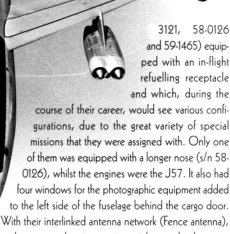

3. S/n 63-8058 to 63-8061, these aircraft
63-8062 to 63-8066 were cancelled.
4. Ten aircraft, serial numbers 63-9792
and 64-14841 to 64-14849.

planes were modified once more, this time to a RC-135D, as we shall see further on.

KC-135R

This designation, that should not be confused with the identical one which was later attributed to the Stratotanker powered by TF 33 engines, in fact applied to three aircraft (s/n 55- 3121, 58-0126 and 59-1465) equipped with an in-flight refuelling receptacle and which, during the course of their career, would see various configurations, due to the great variety of special missions that they were assigned with. Only one of them was equipped with a longer nose (s/n 58-0126), whilst the engines were the J57. It also had four windows for the photographic equipment added to the left side of the fuselage behind the cargo door. With their interlinked antenna network (Fence antenna), these planes were also given various nicknames by the crews or ground crews, such as 'Razorback' due to this wild pig's spiky hair.

One of these planes (s/n 591465), sometimes mistakenly identified as a RC-135R, was lost on 19 July 1967. The fleet was completed two years later, after the transformation of a former KC-135A (s/n 59-1514). It was in June 1963 that the first KC-135R (s/n 55-3121) was attached to the 55th Strategic Reconnaissance Wing at Offutt (Nebraska).

Three or four operators nicknamed 'Crows' were placed in the cabin and equipped with a listening system made up of a 3,600 m (11,811 ft) long cable that was deployed from the aircraf-

t's belly with a capsule containing several sensors at the end. The work initially carried out by this aircraft was considerable; another joined it shortly afterwards, then a third. The two surviving planes (s/n 58-0126 and 59-1514) went back to being tankers at the end of their careers as intelligence planes.

RC-135A Pacer Swann

In 1962, the USAF decided to replace sixteen of its old RB-50 aircraft with nine new specialised reconnaissance planes named the RC-135A. However, as the initial budget went over, this number was reduced initially to six planes and finally to four in 1964 [3].

The first flight of a plane of this version took place on 28 April 1965 and the planes were attached to the 1371st MCS (Mapping & Charting Squadron) of the 1370th Photo Mapping Wing at Turner (Georgia) in September of the same year. The unit was then sent to Forbes AFB in Kansas in August 1967.

The main equipment of the RC-135A was the AN/USQ 28, made up of an on board computer and two cameras installed under the fuselage where the first tank was usually placed under the belly. This Electronic Photo Mapping System automatically recorded, with each photo taken, the exact position of the plane and analysed the profile of the terrain, allowing it, amongst other things, to make corrections, notably in the plane's altitude. In order to avoid possible incidents caused by the overheating caused by the functioning of this new equipment, the internal cooling system was greatly improved.

Replaced by more modern reconnaissance versions, the RC-135A, whilst keeping its original designation, was used for classic transport missions before being modified to a KC-135D in 1979 and equipped with new fan TF33 engines in 1990.

RC-135B and RC-135C

Chronologically, the RC-135B was the first reconnaissance version specially designed by Boeing, but also the last model derived from the Stratotanker family made as such in the facto-

ry; all the following versions were in fact old modified aircraft.

Officially designated 'Model 739-445B', these aircraft [4] that were made between 1964 and 1965, were deemed ill adapted to their role as soon as they left the production line (end December 1964) and, therefore, stored at Glenn Martin at Baltimore until their specific equipment was installed as part of the 'Big Team' program. Once this was completed, the aircraft received a new designation, RC-135C, and were delivered beginning in January 1967 to the 55th Strategic Reconnaissance Wing at Offutt, replacing the RB-47H.

The 'Big Team' program consisted of equipping the planes with 'cheeks' that is to say large fairings placed on each side of the fuselage towards the front under the cockpit, containing a set of antenna. There was also a radome under the front of the nose that was initially rounded then later in a teardrop shape. A UHF antenna was also added above the tip of the right wing and was identical to that already on the top of the tail fin. This version was equipped with the characteristic long nose of reconnaissance aircraft.

In the plane itself was, apart from the usual flying crew (pilot, co-pilot, navigator and mechanic), a second navigator, three electronic warfare specialists nicknamed 'ravens', and two technicians for maintaining in-flight the on-board systems. In the case of lengthy missions, this crew could be completed by the addition of a fourth pilot and a third navigator. At the end of the 1960s, the number of on-board personnel was reduced to twelve men (two pilots, two navigators, three specialists, a maintenance technician and four system operators).

Compared to a classic KC-135, the RC-135C was equipped with an in-flight refuelling receptacle, whilst its boom was removed and replaced with a straightforward fuel tube. As for the boomer's compartment under the belly, this was now occupied by a container holding KA-59 optical equipment. Finally, one of the emergency exits at the front right of the fuselage was disused and various systems for the gathering and analysis of data were placed in the fuselage.

The RC-135C was given the first automatic reconnaissance system which allowed for the interception, localisation, identification and analysis of any signal of the slightest interest. If the latter was of particularly interest, an automatic alert was transmitted to the electronic warfare officer and was analysed whilst the plane was still in the air.

Named the 'vacuum cleaner' because of its ability to intercept all communications and signals over a vast range, and literally to catch everything in the electromagnetic spectrum, the RC-135C proved to be particularly efficient in Vietnam and south east Asia where it was deployed. There were not enough planes to carry out the mission they were given and they had to be supported by KC-135C reconnaissance only aircraft.

RC-135D 'Rivet Brass'

On 1 January 1965, three KC-135A-II [5] of the 4157th SW were officially re-designated RC-135D. These three 'Rivet Brass'[6],

the crew of which was relatively small compared to their counterparts (a crew normally made up of a pilot, co-pilot, two navigators, with two electronic warfare officers in the cabin) carried out missions named 'Burning Candy', beginning in 1969, from Kadena (Okinawa), over south east Asia.

came to an end, the three planes were declared surplus and went back to being standard KC-135A, the work being carried out by E-Systems in 1978-79, but nonetheless keeping their in-flight refuelling capacity (ARR).

RC-135E 'Rivet Amber'

This one-off aircraft, named 'Lisa Ann' until January 1967, was made by LTV at the beginning of the sixties using a former MATS C-135B (s/n 62-4137). Designed amidst great secrecy, its exact configuration is still the subject of controversy. Its main particularity consisted of a large size antenna covered by a fibreglass fairing joined to the front right of the cabin and which was linked to 7.5 megawatt radar.

The latter was based on the technique known as phased array where the different signal phases

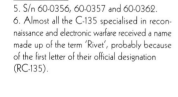

5. S/n 60-0356, 60-0357 and 60-0362.
6. Almost all the C-135 specialised in reconnaissance and electronic warfare received a name made up of the term 'Rivet', probably because of the first letter of their official designation (RC-135).

Despite their original designation, these planes, which could be refuelled in the air, were not equipped with a boom, but with a large size nose (the famous 'snout' characteristic of the reconnaissance versions), and two circular fairings on each side of the fuselage in front of the wings' leading edges that also contained antenna. Also, because of their specific engines (J57 jets), the 'Rivet Brass' had a slightly lower range than their counterparts.

The equipment installed on board the RC-135D evolved according to the missions; in time their external configuration was slightly modified: small tear drop fairings were, for example, added in front of the horizontal tail group, whilst one of them ('Rivet Brass 3') was given an extra circular radome under the fuselage, and another, near the wings' trailing edge. When the 'Burning Candy' missions

feeding a network of antenna are modulated in such a way that the radiation beams are reinforced in one direction and cut off in another. The whole cabin was, as we can imagine, set out completely differently and protected against radiation by lead walls. Getting from the front of the plane to the rear was impossible when the radar was working. As a consequence, the electric installations were reviewed, with an extra generator (the power of which was 350 kVA) being added under the left wing between the No.2 engine and the fuselage. A second pod, placed symmetrically to the right, contained a heat exchanger, the presence of which was made indispensable by the considerable heat generated by the functioning equipment.

These external pods were also the origin of numerous rumours about this aircraft and were often confused with auxiliary engines or air sample collectors.

Like most of its counterparts, the RC-135E also had probes in the shape of booms at the wingtips, a lengthened nose and was, of course, capable of being refuelled in the air.

With this special equipment, the RC-135E, based at Eielson AFB (Alaska) with the 4157th Strategic Wing, a wing replaced in March 1967 by the 6th SW and its 24th SRS, was destined to carry out the pursuit of objects entering the atmosphere, notably ballistic missiles whose trajectory could be recorded using optical equipment

RC-135M 'Rivet Cord'

Beginning in 1966, E-Systems transformed six former C-135B[7] in this new variant whose external characteristics were similar to those of the RC-135D, that is a lengthened nose, but with a slightly more square shape, large rectangular lateral fairings, in-flight refuelling receptacle, the original boom replaced by a rapid fuel draining hose, bilobal belly antenna and ovoid fairings in front of the horizontal stabilisers. Based at Kadena (Okinawa) where most of the tankers and SAC recon-

installed in the right side of the fuselage and protected by a window. These missions, carried out in a sensitive zone made up of the Bering Straits and the north Pacific, could be carried out thanks to its special radar, the SLAR (Side Looking Aerial Radar) never installed on a RC-135.

This radar could track a target 0.1m² (1.5 sq inch) from a distance of 550 km (340 miles) and one of 1 m² (10.75 sq. ft) from 1,850 km (1,150 miles)! It was during one of these missions, on 5 June 1969, that this aircraft, the only one of its kind, was lost in the Bering Straits, no doubt due to a structural fault in the forward part of its fuselage. The crew of nineteen perished in this accident.

naissance aircraft were based, that is to say a three hour flight from the Indochina peninsula, these aircraft, sometimes named 'Rivet Quick', were used intensively in Vietnam as part of the 'Combat Apple' program, sometimes in partnership with the RC-135R or the KC-135R.

Orbiting initially over the Gulf of Tonkin, then Laos or the Ho Chi Minh trail, depending on objectives, sometimes for twelve to thirteen hours, the Rivet Cord were used for gathering electronic intelligence (ELINT) or the interception of North Vietnamese communications (SIGINT).

They were combined with the EC-135L or the KC-135A 'Combat Lightning' used for relaying information to the land

7. S/n 62-4131 to 62-4135, 62-4138 and 62-4139.

THE RIVET JOINT FLEET

Serial n°	Name	Delivery date	Model	Origin	N° of order in the fleet
62-4125	—	1998	RC-135W	C-135B	
62-4127	—	1998	RC-135W	C-135B	
62-4129	Greyhound	1988	TC-135W	C-135B	
62-4130	—	1998	RC-135W	C-135B	
62-4131	Junk Yard Dog	March 1981	RC-135W	RC-135M	10
62-4132	Anticipation	November 1984	RC-135W	RC-135M	13
62-4134	The Flying W	August 1981	RC-135W	RC-135M	12
62-4135	Rapture	November 1980	RC-135W	RC-135M	9
62-4138	Jungle Assassin	July 1981	RC-135W	RC-135M	11
62-4139	Sniper	January 1985	RC-135W	RC-135M	14
63-9792	—	August 1977	RC-135W	RC-135U	8
64-14841	Red Eye	January 1978	RC-135V	RC-135C	7
64-14842	Fair Warning	January 1975	RC-135V	RC-135C	2
64-14843	Don't Bet on It	February 1975	RC-135V	RC-135C	3
64-14844	Problem Child	March 1975	RC-135V	RC-135C	4
64-14845	Luna Landa	November 1975	RC-135V	RC-135C	5
64-14846	—	December 1975	RC-135V	RC-135C	6
64-14848	—	August 1973	RC-135V	RC-135C	1
62-4128	—	October 1999	RC-135W	C-135B	15

based general staff or even planes in flight. The RC-135M, which usually carried a crew of fourteen specialists known as 'crows', carried out up to two missions a day in 1973, coordinating attacks against radar stations notably those of the northern capital, Hanoi, named 'Fan Song'. They also modified bombing operations underway against North Vietnam.

The 'Rivet Cord' was also used to support rescue operations or to organise the intervention of fighters or Combat Air Patrols (CAP), after having detected anti-aircraft missile sites or unusual North Vietnamese MiG activity. Often flying very close to the combat zones in order to be as efficient as possible, the RC-135 came under threat from enemy fighters trying to intercept

Opposite.
In 2000, 'Red Eye' RC-135V s/n 64-14841 took part in operation 'Southern Watch' observing aerial activity over Iraq with the 363rd Air Expeditionary Wing based at Prince Sultan AFB, in Saudi Arabia. (USAF)

them on several occasions. To counter this, it was quickly decided to use F-4 Phantom II fighters as escorts. They remained in the 'shadow' of these four engine aircraft to remain invisible to North Vietnamese radars. The MiG interceptors, after a few nasty surprises, soon decided to leave the RC-135M alone.

Replacing the B-47 aircraft and attached to the 82nd Strategic Reconnaissance Squadron, formed in August 1967, a detachment of the 4252nd SRW, normally based at Yokota (Japan), the Rivet Cord took part in almost all of the large scale operations lead by the United States in Vietnam during their 'Linebacker' I and II intervention, as well as 'Frequent Wind', the evacuation of Saigon in 1975. Despite the particularly difficult weather conditions (heavy rains) that put the men and aircraft under great strain, the RC-135M carried out nearly 3,250 sorties during their six-year spell in the Far East, spending 40,000 hours in the zone.

As we shall see further on, the 'Rivet Cord' were followed to Vietnam by two RC-135U (Combat Sent), operating on shifts for only three months from Kadena and which turned out to be much less efficient than their predecessors as they had to fly at higher altitudes because of their greater weight.

At the end of the conflict, the aircraft were put into service by the 55th SRW at Offutt, some of them operating overseas, notably at Mildenhall in Great Britain, and at the beginning of the 1980s, once again within the 'Big Safari' program, all the aircraft were upgraded and renamed RC-135W. (see further on).

RC-135S 'Cobra Ball' or 'Rivet Ball'

This designation applies to three specially modified aircraft for surveillance, still in the western Pacific, of Soviet (then Chinese) ballistic missile launches and the re-entering into the atmosphere of spacecraft, gathering at the same time all sorts of telemetric data (TELINT missions). For almost thirty years, that is until March 1995, these planes carried out their missions (named 'Burning Star') over international waters, but as close as possible to the Kamchatka Peninsula, a particularly sensitive area as it was close to Soviet missile launch sites. Put into service with a detachment of the 24th SRS based at Shemya (named 'The Rock') in the Aleutian Islands, these aircraft were on permanent alert as the launch dates, as we can imagine, were not announced beforehand. The crew (pilot, co-pilot, two navigators and a dozen systems operators) were therefore forced to live and sleep nearby until alerted by the Defence Special Missile And Astronautic Center (DEFSMAC).

The first 'Cobra Ball' was in fact a flying test bed, a JKC-135A (s/n 59-1491) modified in March 1963 and initially named 'Wanda Belle', then 'Rivet Ball' in January 1967. The plane

was lost on 13 January 1969 whilst landing at Shemva, a base that has always been known for its particularly difficult weather conditions. It was replaced by two former C-135B (s/n 61-2663 and 61-2664) that were modified within the 'Big Safari' program. The second of these aircraft ('Cobra Ball 2', s/n 61-2664) was also lost, again whilst misjudging a landing at Shemva on 15 March 1981. The fleet was completed by another transformed C-135B (s/n 61-2662, 'Cobra Ball 3').

Finally, in 1997, when the RC-135S had been, due to the end of the Cold War, attached two years previously to the 45th RS of the 55th Wing at Offutt (Nebraska), a last aircraft (the only RC-135X, s/n 62-4128) was modified to serve mainly as a rescue plane.

To train crews without having to mobilise an operational aircraft, and above all, taking the risk of losing it in an accident, a C-135B (s/n 62-4133) was modified to a TC-135S. From the outside it was identical to a standard RC-135 (fairings, external antenna etc.), but the specific equipment was not installed. All the 'Cobra Ball' have similar characteristics, a lengthened nose, large size rectangular fairings on each side near the front of the fuselage (cheeks), enclosing electronic receivers, another ovoid shaped fairing with a flattened surface placed on each side at the rear of the fuselage, probes placed above the wing tips, an in-flight refuelling receptacle, plus, on the right, several view-taking devices protected by round windows for filming long distance missile tests.

The specific equipment of the RC-135S comprises several infrared telescopes (RTOS, Real Time Optical System), for recording any object launched from a Soviet testing ground and re-entering the atmosphere. Thanks to the gathering and analysis of the launch parameters, the capacities of any missile, old or new, can be accurately determined.

Although the external appearance of the 'Cobra Ball' varied with time, often depending on missions, the equipment installed in the cabin (position of windows, a cover that could slide down to protect the optical equipment added to the right side), or the evolution of techniques, one of their main particularities, which greatly contributed to the myth of a 'mysterious plane' that it acquired, was the right wing upper surface and the internal part

Above.
This RC-135S, photographed in a turn, shows its right upper wing surfaces and black painted engine pods, as well as the red markings in this area. This particularity was destined to avoid any reverberations when recording the MIRV warheads of ballistic missiles. The 'Cobra ball' were re-engined with F108 engines at the beginning of this century. (USAF)

Opposite.
After having been transformed into the RC-135M in November 1966, s/n 62-4132 became the RC-135W at the end of 1984.
(V. Gréciet collection)

8. S/n 63-9792, 64-14847 & 64-14849.

Below.
S/n 64-14841 is one of the aircraft built from the beginning for reconnaissance, initially under the designation RC-135B, then finally RC-135C when they were delivered to the USAF. This four engine plane was upgraded to RC-135V in 1973-75 and is attached to the 343rd RS of the 55th Wing. The HF antenna cable linking the middle of the vertical stabiliser, above the antenna itself, (black fairing) to the fuselage is clearly visible seen from this angle. (F. Lert).

of the engine pods that were painted black at this area, something chosen to eliminate any reflections when recording, as the equipment was placed on this side.

A typical 'Burning Star' mission was carried out in the following way. Once the launch of a missile was detected (launched from land or a submerged submarine), the RC-135S took off and climbed to 35,000 feet (10,600 m), its working altitude, and was able to remain in in the air between ten and eighteen hours if refuelled in-flight. Thanks to its ATS system (Advanced Telemetry System), it looked for any signal sent on a determined wavelength and recorded it automatically.

Its cameras (MRC/Medium Resolution Camera and BFCS/Ballistic Framing Camera System) recorded all the data concerning the re-entry into the atmosphere of spacecraft (such as, for example, multiple warhead MIRV missiles), calculating their size and even the theoretical strength of the nuclear warhead. These missions were no longer needed when the Cold War came to an end, the RC-135S were given other tasks, notably that of keeping watch on tactical missiles (TBM or Theater Ballistic Missiles), in order to determine the point of impact of the latter. For a while it was thought of using them in the Middle East during the Gulf War for hunting down the Iraqi modified Scuds, the 'Hal Hussein', however the plan was not implemented… at least not officially.

In August 1995, the traditional adversary had changed and a 'Cobra Ball' was used to watch over Chinese missile tests off Taiwan.

In 2004, the 'Cobra Ball' equipment was once more upgraded, notably with the installation of the LATS (Large Aperture Tracking System), a 30.5 centimetre focal aperture that could give an extremely precise image of a distant object, and the MIRA (Medium wave Infra Red Array), a series of cameras mounted on each side of the fuselage that could analyse the electromagnetic spectrum of an object re-entering into the atmosphere. Also, the nose held a new weather radar that could calculate at any moment the exact position of the plane, notably in order to

avoid entering hostile airspace. The satellite communication system was also perfected, whilst the black painted starboard lower wing surface was conserved. Of no use now, this characteristic was nonetheless kept so that the myth would not be broken.

The 'Cobra Ball I and II' were also equipped with a new synthetic aperture Snake Eye, that gave a 360° image. This radar was installed in a turret placed under the fuselage. The upgrading of the RC-135S was recently completed by the installation of Pacer CRAG, GATM and JTIDS systems, the latter permitting communication with other planes equipped in the same way (E-3, E-8) as well as the transfer of data in real time with the whole of the 'Rivet Joint' fleet, whilst new F108 engines (the military version of the CFM 56) were installed in 2007. The RC-135S was the last version of this type to be re-engined. Today, with the change in the nature of threats, other specific missions have been allocated to the RC-135S, notably with secret nuclear tests, the detection of cruise missiles or furtive aircraft.

RC-135T 'Rivet Dandy'

After the crash of KC-135R s/n 59-1465 in July 1967, the USAF soon saw the need for an aircraft specialised in crew training for the reconnaissance RC-135. To achieve this, the only KC-135T (s/n 55-3121) was modified to a RC-135T in May 1971. This designation did not in any way indicate specific role (the letter T for trainer was normally used to designate training aircraft), but was a logical continuation of those attributed to this series of versions. Attached to the 55th SRW at Offutt,

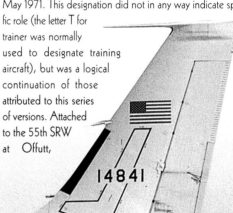

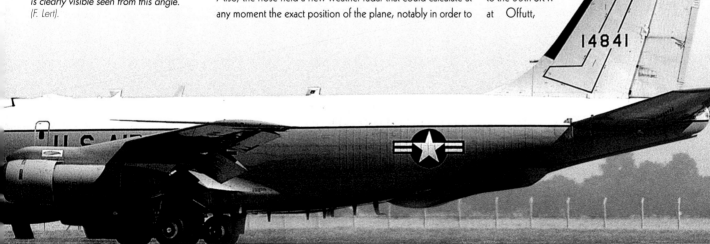

this plane was transformed into a training aircraft in 1973, some of its reconnaissance and observation was taken out, but the plane conserved its longer nose, in-flight refuelling receptacle, wingtip booms and, above all, its lateral fairings. which were now empty.

Re-engined with TF33 engines in 1982, this plane was also lost at Valdez in Alaska on 25 February 1985 when making an instruments landing.

Later, the fleet of 'school planes' was, as we will see in the following paragraphs, completed by two former C-135B which were specially modified to this end and re-designated respectively, TC-135S and TC-135W.

RC-135U 'Combat Sent'

In 1970, three of the ten RC-135C [8] were modified to RC-135U and delivered to the 55th SRW at Offutt the following year. These planes are certainly amongst the most easily identifiable of all the RC-135 as they are equipped with the usual rectangular lateral fairings (mounted with specially shaped antenna named towel rail until 1991). On the other hand, they did not have the usual 'snout'; it was replaced by the PPMS (Precision Power Measurement System) placed in the nose, under the rear of the fuselage, as well as in specific fairings added to the wing tips. This system permitted a 360° cover of all signals coming from all types of transmitters; millions of frequen-

cies were thus scanned and filtered in order to determine the most interesting. The particular signatures, coming from, for example, anti-aircraft radars (like those of Soviet origin, Odd Pair, Side Net or Top Steer) or missiles, were also memorised and stored in specific databases for later comparison.

The essential mission of the RC-135U was intelligence of a strategic nature concerning radar signals from all sources (based on land or on board ships or planes), the information gathered being carefully analysed and compared with pre-existing databases. The 'Combat Sent' could, therefore, be deployed all over the world for peace keeping missions, or as part of army interventions, the intelligence gathered being directly transmitted to military commands deployed on the ground. The original PPMS system was later completed by another, named EMM (Expert Mission Manager) for the authentication of the transmitting sources of signals and putting them into a priority list so that, on one hand retaliation could be set up against them, and on the other, set the detectors in a more optimal way to obtain better intelligence.

The RC-135U also have a fairing placed under the plane's 'chin', a radome under the belly, and strangely shaped antenna ('rabbit ears') just over the large lateral fairings at the front of the fuselage. Also, the former boomer's compartment under the tail plane was given a more angular fairing than on other versions and a HF antenna was added above the right wing near the wingtip. The aft point of the fuselage was also different, with a

9. 64-14841 to 64-14846 and 64-14848.
10. S/n 62-4125, 62-4128, 62-4130, 62-4131, 61-4132, 62-4134, 62-4135, 62-4138 and 62-4139.

rectangular fairing that is vaguely similar to a bomber turret (like that of the B-52), containing a high resolution camera, a television camera and radar detectors. One of the Combat Sent was even equipped with a system named 'Compass Era' made up of an infrared thermal imager, an interferometer-spectrometer and spectrum detectors.

The RC-135U began to be used at the end of the Vietnam War where it carried out missions named 'Combat Sent', and at least one of them was used after the accident at the Chernobyl nuclear power station in order to determine the exact nature of the explosion and to analyse the resulting radioactive cloud.

Beginning in 2002, the two RC-135U still in service were upgraded in the same way as the KC-135R and were given new F108 engines, as well as Pacer CRAG and GATM navigation systems.

RC-135V 'Rivet Joint'

Beginning in 1972, the LTV company undertook the transformation of seven non modified RC-135C[9] to 'Combat Sent', as well as one of the RC-135V (s/n 63-9792) to a new reconnaissance version logically named RC-135V and destined for observing an adversary's electronic activity. These too were equipped with a lengthened nose and rectangular fairings, could be refuelled in flight and had high performance communication systems which distinguished these planes from the previous examples with their four antenna named 'mushrooms', positioned in front of the main undercarriage well and linked to a MUCELS (Multiple position Comint Emitter Location System).

Like their counterparts, they were attached to the 55th Wing at Offutt, the RC-135V are part of the main aircraft dedicated

to reconnaissance and intelligence in service with the USAF. Some of them are often deployed overseas (Kadena, Mildenhall, Riyad etc.) to be closer to their mission zones. They are often intercepted, this notably being the case during the Cold War; the pilots sometimes chase off planes that get too close by releasing fuel or by suddenly slowing down. Choice prey for photographers, some of these meetings even led to a few amusing situations, such as when a 'Learner' sign or even the centrefold of Playboy magazine were stuck above the co-pilot's position for curious on-lookers...

Deployed today along with the other aircraft of the TAC (E-3, E-8, EC-135, etc.) with whom they are vocally linked or with automatic data transmission, the 'Rivet Joint' notably served in Grenada in 1982 (operation 'Urgent Fury'), Panama ('Just Cause'), or more recently in the former Yugoslavia (where, in 1993, a RC-135 allowed for a French Armée de l'Air pilot to be rescued after having traced his distress beacon), in Afghanistan ('Enduring Freedom') and in Iraq ('Iraqi Freedom').

At the outset of operation 'Desert Shield', the prelude to 'Desert Storm', the liberation of Kuwait, five RC-135V were rapidly deployed to Hellinikon in Greece, then to Riyadh in Saudi Arabia. These planes carried out four missions a day during the entire operation, orbiting over the border between Kuwait and Saudi Arabia, capturing all the signals emitted by the Iraqis, allowing, amongst other things, the making of an accurate map of enemy anti aircraft sites and their potential. During these missions they came under threat by MiG-23 or Mirage F-1, aircraft on several occasions, while one was damaged by a Scud missile when parked at a Saudi air base.

RC-135W 'Rivet Joint'

This other version of intelligence gathering (SIGINT), very similar to the RC-135U, stands out by its slightly longer lateral fairings, the addition of three large sabre antenna behind the main undercarriage wells and by the absence of additional air intakes on the engine struts. The latter are equipped with thrust reversers, whereas the engines of the RC-135V are not. To support the extra weight of these engines, the undercarriage has been strengthened, along with some structural elements, and the braking system has been upgraded.

At the beginning of 1978, the E-Systems company undertook the transformation of six RC-135M[10] in this new version, then the turn of three C-135B[10] brought up to this standard in 1996. In 1987, a training aircraft was attached to these planes, designated TC-135W (s/n 62-4129), also based at Offutt and with all the external characteristics of the other 'Rivet Joint', but not carrying any on board operational equipment.

Constantly upgraded, the 'RJ' could now transmit in time the data that had been collected by the AWACS thanks to the TADIL (Tactical Digital Information Link) or TIBS (Tactical Information Broadcast System), the on board specialists could localise record and analyse most of the signals emitted in the whole of the electromagnetic spectrum. The planes have been recently equipped with the JSAF (Joint Sigint Avionics Family), equipment that worked on a low frequency and able to detect and locate communications which before were clearly consi-

dered to be difficult to pick up. This system has a new circular antenna at the top of the tail fin on the RC-135W.

Having no doubt been used in antidrug operations, the 'Rivet Joint' can also be used as ABCP, Airborne Command Posts, or to carry out certain missions such as peace-keeping (operation 'Southern Watch' in Iraq in 1992), whilst their original strategic role became more and more tactical because of the evolution in threats.

Although they have greatly proved their efficiency, notably during and after the Gulf War, their existence has often been called into question, partly because of the geopolitical changes, but also because of the considerable costs of keeping them in service. After the collapse of the Soviet Block at the beginning of the 1990s, the USAF saw its budget reduced and for a time it was thought of replacing the four engined planes with drones.

However, although the nature of threats has changed, they have not entirely disappeared and the role of the RC-135 still appears to be essential within the organisation of United States military aircraft. In a world with many areas of instability, the gathering of intelligence still remains paramount, if only for peace-keeping by predicting threats. This no doubt explains why the 'Rivet Joint' are amongst the most used USAF aircraft. In 1995 alone, the fleet was deployed overseas for nearly half of the year, whilst in 1991, the 'Rivet Joint' broke the symbolic barrier of one thousand missions carried out by the RC-135 during 'Desert Storm'. An official report, dated 1992, even indicates that at this time, they carried out one hundred missions per month, representing a total of 18,000 flying hours annually.

The replacement of this fleet of specialised planes, even though it has not been officially launched, will become more and more urgent as the airframes grow older; despite the successive upgrades, they date from the 1960s. For many years, several replace-

Above.
One of the USAF « Rivet Joint » flying over the American coast. As well as the lateral fairings and the lengthened nose, these planes were distinguished by their numerous UHF/VHF antenna spaced out on the back of the fuselage. (USAF).

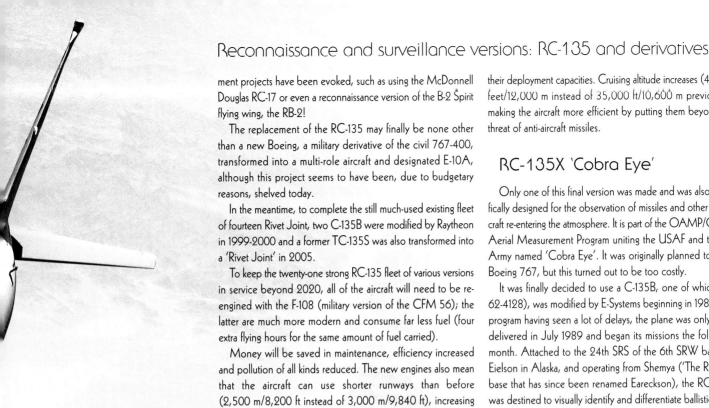

ment projects have been evoked, such as using the McDonnell Douglas RC-17 or even a reconnaissance version of the B-2 Spirit flying wing, the RB-2!

The replacement of the RC-135 may finally be none other than a new Boeing, a military derivative of the civil 767-400, transformed into a multi-role aircraft and designated E-10A, although this project seems to have been, due to budgetary reasons, shelved today.

In the meantime, to complete the still much-used existing fleet of fourteen Rivet Joint, two C-135B were modified by Raytheon in 1999-2000 and a former TC-135S was also transformed into a 'Rivet Joint' in 2005.

To keep the twenty-one strong RC-135 fleet of various versions in service beyond 2020, all of the aircraft will need to be re-engined with the F-108 (military version of the CFM 56); the latter are much more modern and consume far less fuel (four extra flying hours for the same amount of fuel carried).

Money will be saved in maintenance, efficiency increased and pollution of all kinds reduced. The new engines also mean that the aircraft can use shorter runways than before (2,500 m/8,200 ft instead of 3,000 m/9,840 ft), increasing

their deployment capacities. Cruising altitude increases (40,000 feet/12,000 m instead of 35,000 ft/10,600 m previously), making the aircraft more efficient by putting them beyond the threat of anti-aircraft missiles.

RC-135X 'Cobra Eye'

Only one of this final version was made and was also specifically designed for the observation of missiles and other space-craft re-entering the atmosphere. It is part of the OAMP/Optical Aerial Measurement Program uniting the USAF and the US Army named 'Cobra Eye'. It was originally planned to use a Boeing 767, but this turned out to be too costly.

It was finally decided to use a C-135B, one of which (s/n 62-4128), was modified by E-Systems beginning in 1983. The program having seen a lot of delays, the plane was only finally delivered in July 1989 and began its missions the following month. Attached to the 24th SRS of the 6th SRW based at Eielson in Alaska, and operating from Shemya ('The Rock', a base that has since been renamed Eareckson), the RC-135X was destined to visually identify and differentiate ballistic missiles penetrating into the atmosphere when these are halfway along their path. The gathered intelligence of various USSR missile tests came within the framework of the SDI (Strategic Defence Initiative), better known as Star Wars. Equipped with a longer nose, the 'Cobra Eye' (sometimes also designated Cobra Ball II) does not have the usual rectangular lateral fairings, but a sliding door in the right hand side of the fuselage in front of the wing, protecting the electronic detectors when these are not in use.

Capable of being refuelled in flight, its upper wing surface was painted black, officially to prevent reflections during observation operations, but also to give it the little mystery already surrounding the other planes that undertake secret missions, such as the RC-135S.

The program at the origin of the transformation of the plane turned out to be extraordinarily expensive; with the change in the nature of threats after the collapse of the Soviet Block, the RC-135X was retired from service in 1993.

Sent to the E-Systems factory at Greenville (Texas) and stripped of its specific equipment, it was finally transformed into a RC-135S 'Cobra Ball' a few years later, in order to complete the fleet of these specialised aircraft.

Below.
«Sniper », RC-135W s/n 62-4139 of the 343rd Reconnaissance Squadron making a run-up on a snow cleared runway at Offutt in 2004. This aircraft was the last RC-135M transformed into this final reconnaissance version of the four engine Boeing. This version had a Pitot tube wing tip, with the right one only mounted with a HF antenna.
(USAF)

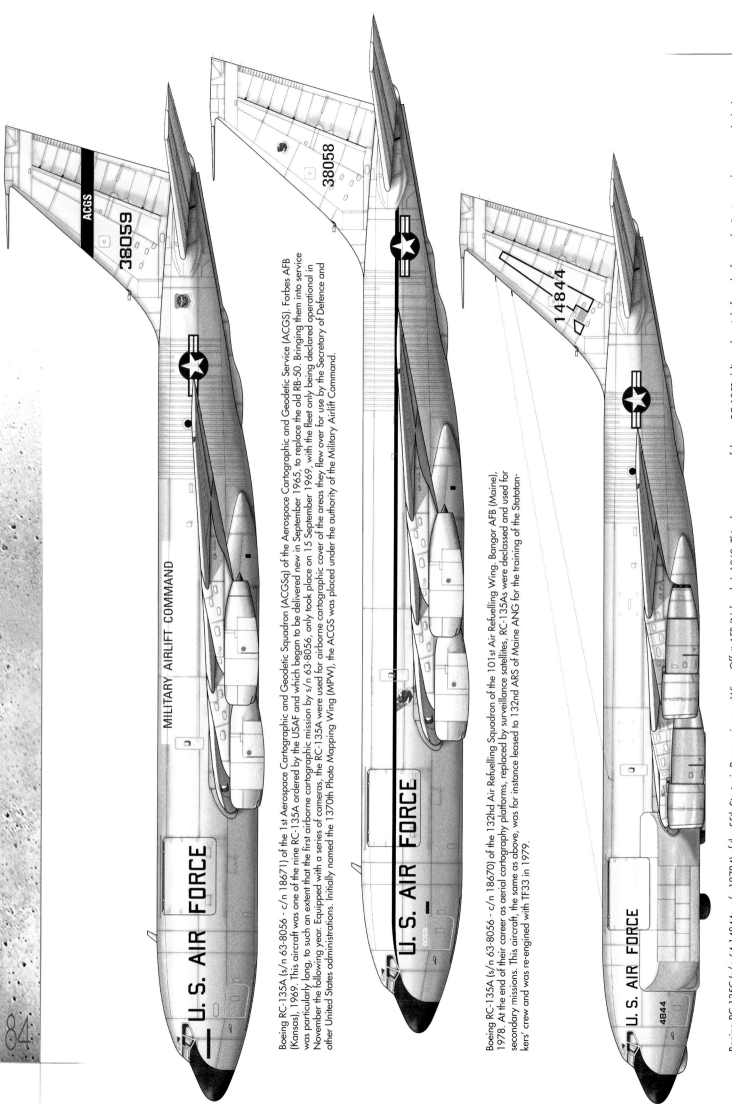

Boeing RC-135A (s/n 63-8056 - c/n 18671) of the 1st Aerospace Cartographic and Geodetic Service (ACGS). Forbes AFB (Kansas), 1969. This aircraft was one of the nine RC-135A ordered by the USAF and which began to be delivered new in September 1965, to replace the old RB-50. Bringing them into service was particularly long, to such an extent that the first airborne cartographic mission by s/n 63-8056, only took place on 15 September 1969, with the fleet only being declared operational in November the following year. Equipped with a series of cameras, the RC-135A were used for airborne cartographic cover of the areas they flew over for use by the Secretary of Defence and other United States administrations. Initially named the 1370th Photo Mapping Wing (MPW), the ACGS was placed under the authority of the Military Airlift Command.

MILITARY AIRLIFT COMMAND

Boeing RC-135A (s/n 63-8056 - c/n 18670) of the 132hd Air Refuelling Squadron of the 101st Air Refuelling Wing. Bangor AFB (Maine), 1978. At the end of their career as aerial cartography platforms, replaced by surveillance satellites, RC-135As were declassed and used for secondary missions. This aircraft, the same as above, was for instance leased to 132nd ARS of Maine ANG for the training of the Statotankers' crew and was re-engined with TF33 in 1979.

Boeing RC-135C (s/n 64-14844 - c/n 18784) of the 55th Strategic Reconnaissance Wing. Offutt AFB (Nebraska), 1968. This plane was one of the ten RC-135B delivered straight from the factory by Boeing and Martin and which were first put into storage before receiving their electronic reconnaissance equipment. Re-designated RC-135C, they began to be delivered to the 55h SRS at Offutt in November 1967, replacing the old RB-47H. This version was characterised, apart from its standard front and a bulge placed under the latter. In 1974-1975, this aircraft was transformed into a RC-135V.

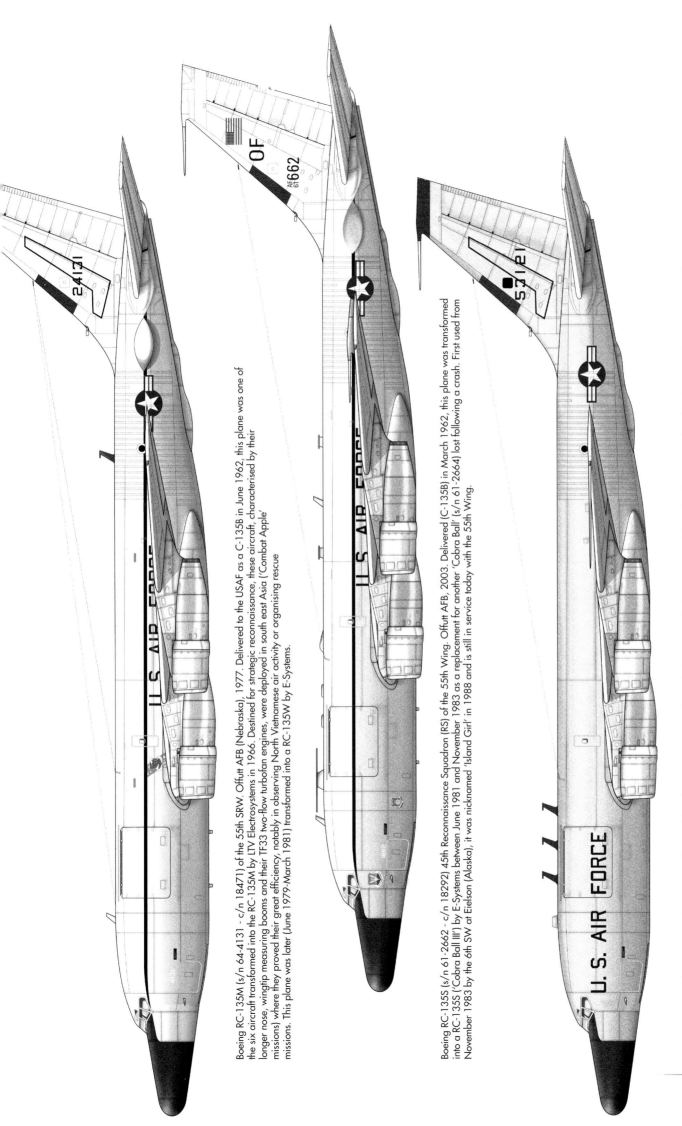

Boeing RC-135M (s/n 64-4131 - c/n 18471) of the 55th SRW. Offutt AFB (Nebraska), 1977. Delivered to the USAF as a C-135B in June 1962, this plane was one of the six aircraft transformed into the RC-135M by LTV Electrosystems in 1966. Destined for strategic reconnaissance, these aircraft, characterised by their longer nose, wingtip measuring booms and their TF33 two-flow turbofan engines, were deployed in south east Asia ('Combat Apple' missions) where they proved their great efficiency, notably in observing North Vietnamese air activity or organising rescue missions. This plane was later (June 1979-March 1981) transformed into a RC-135W by E-Systems.

Boeing RC-135S (s/n 61-2662 - c/n 18292) 45th Reconnaissance Squadron (RS) of the 55th Wing. Offutt AFB, 2003. Delivered (C-135B) in March 1962, this plane was transformed into a RC-135S ('Cobra Ball III') by E-Systems between June 1981 and November 1983 as a replacement for another 'Cobra Ball' (s/n 61-2664) lost following a crash. First used from November 1983 by the 6th SW at Eielson (Alaska), it was nicknamed 'Island Girl' in 1988 and is still in service today with the 55th Wing.

Boeing RC-135T (s/n 55-3121 - c/n 17237) 24th SRS of the 6th Strategic Wing. Eielson (Alaska), 1982. The first KC-135A delivered to the USAF and not kept by Boeing for tests, this one-off aircraft was transformed into a test bed (JKC-135A) in November 1966 then into a RC-135R reconnaissance plane in July 1967. Modified once more by LTV in 1969, it first became a KC-135T 'Rivet Stand', then the only RC-135T 'Rivet Dandy' in May 1971. Declassified two years later and stripped of its operational equipment, it was used a training aircraft for the crews of the 6th SW at Eielson. Re-engined 1982, it was lost in a crash near Valdez (Alaska), during an instruments approach; the three crew member's were killed in this accident.

185

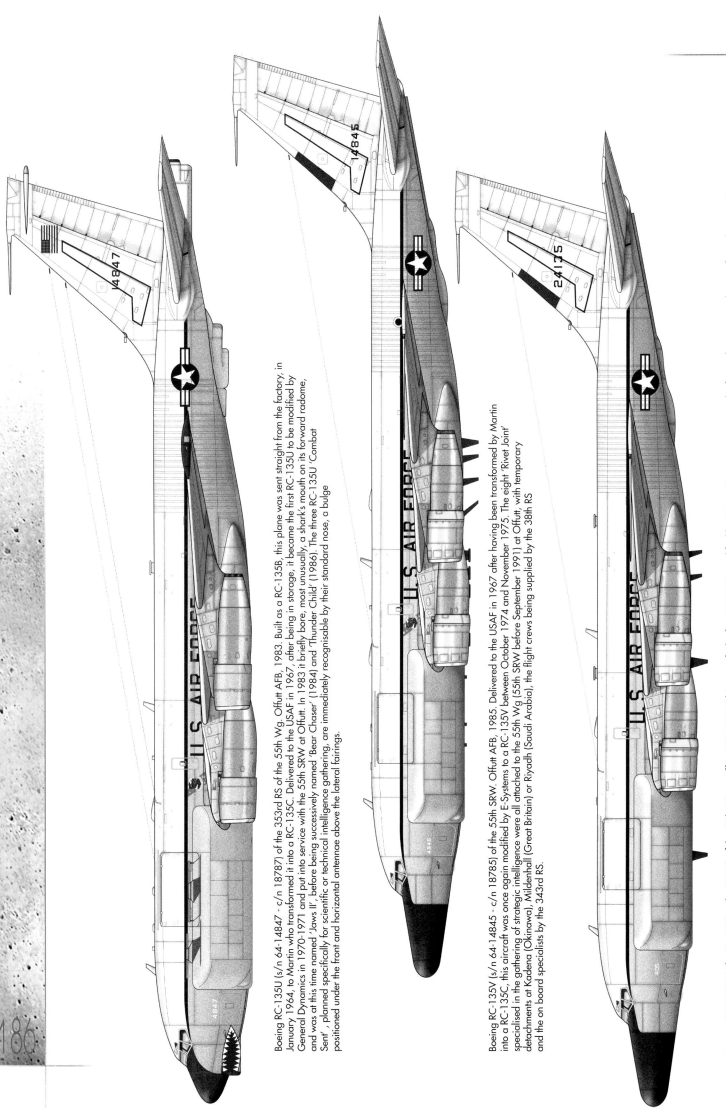

Boeing RC-135U (s/n 64-14847 - c/n 18787) of the 353rd RS of the 55th Wg, Offutt AFB, 1983. Built as a RC-135B, this plane was sent straight from the factory, in January 1964, to Martin who transformed it into a RC-135C. Delivered to the USAF in 1967, after being in storage, it became the first RC-135U to be modified by General Dynamics in 1970-1971 and put into service with the 55th SRW at Offutt. In 1983 it briefly bore, most unusually, a shark's mouth on its forward radome, and was at this time named 'Jaws II', before being successively named 'Bear Chaser' (1984) and 'Thunder Child' (1986). The three RC-135U 'Combat Sent', planned specifically for scientific or technical intelligence gathering, are immediately recognisable by their standard nose, a bulge positioned under the front and horizontal antennae above the lateral fairings.

Boeing RC-135V (s/n 64-14845 - c/n 18785) of the 55th SRW. Offutt AFB, 1985. Delivered to the USAF in 1967 after having been transformed by Martin into a RC-135C, this aircraft was once again modified by E-Systems to a RC-135V between October 1974 and November 1975. The eight 'Rivet Joint' specialised in the gathering of strategic intelligence were all attached to the 55th Wg (55th SRW before September 1991) at Offutt, with temporary detachments at Kadena (Okinawa), Mildenhall (Great Britain) or Riyadh (Saudi Arabia), the flight crews being supplied by the 38th RS and the on board specialists by the 343rd RS.

Boeing RC-135W (s/n 62-4135 - c/n 18475) of the 55th Wing. Offutt AFB, 1995. This aircraft, the first RC-135M modified by LTV in 1966 was once more the first in this version to be transformed into a RC-135W by E-Systems between 1978 and 1980 as part of the 'Big Safari' program. Like their RC-135V counterparts, to which they look very similar, apart from the position of the fuselage antennae, the seven Rivet Joint were all attached to the 55th Wing.

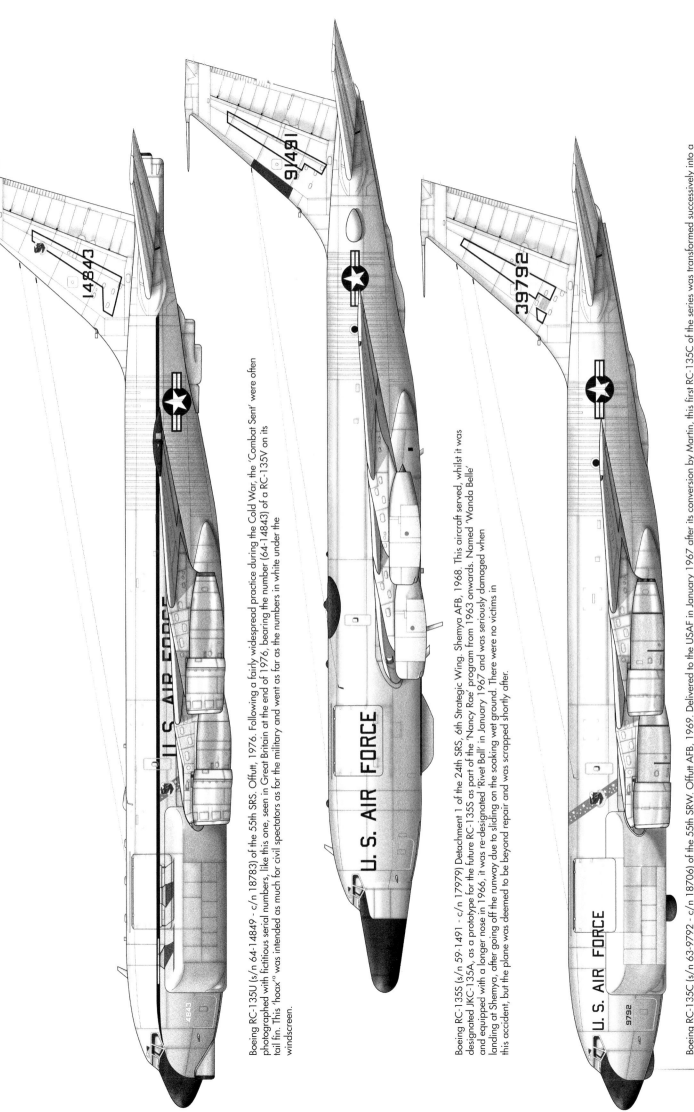

Boeing RC-135U (s/n 64-14849 - c/n 18783) of the 55th SRS. Offutt, 1976. Following a fairly widespread practice during the Cold War, the 'Combat Sent' were often photographed with fictitious serial numbers, like this one, seen in Great Britain at the end of 1976, bearing the number (64-14843) of a RC-135V on its tail fin. This 'hoax'ʳᵃ was intended as much for civil spectators as for the military and went as far as the numbers in white under the windscreen.

Boeing RC-135S (s/n 59-1491 - c/n 17979) Detachment 1 of the 24th SRS, 6th Strategic Wing. Shemya AFB, 1968. This aircraft served, whilst it was designated JKC-135A, as a prototype for the future RC-135S as part of the 'Nancy Rae' program from 1963 onwards. Named 'Wanda Belle' and equipped with a longer nose in 1966, it was re-designated 'Rivet Ball' in January 1967 and was seriously damaged when landing at Shemya, after going off the runway due to sliding on the soaking wet ground. There were no victims in this accident, but the plane was deemed to be beyond repair and was scrapped shortly after.

Boeing RC-135C (s/n 63-9792 - c/n 18706) of the 55th SRW. Offutt AFB, 1969. Delivered to the USAF in January 1967 after its conversion by Martin, this first RC-135C of the series was transformed successively into a RC-135U in 1970-1971 and became the first RC-135V modified by E-Systems between October 1975 and July 1977. Extremely efficient and able to gather, record and identify all signals emitted in their flight zone, the RC-135C, the first variant specifically designed for reconnaissance and not obtained through the transformation of an existing airframe, were successfully deployed in Vietnam.

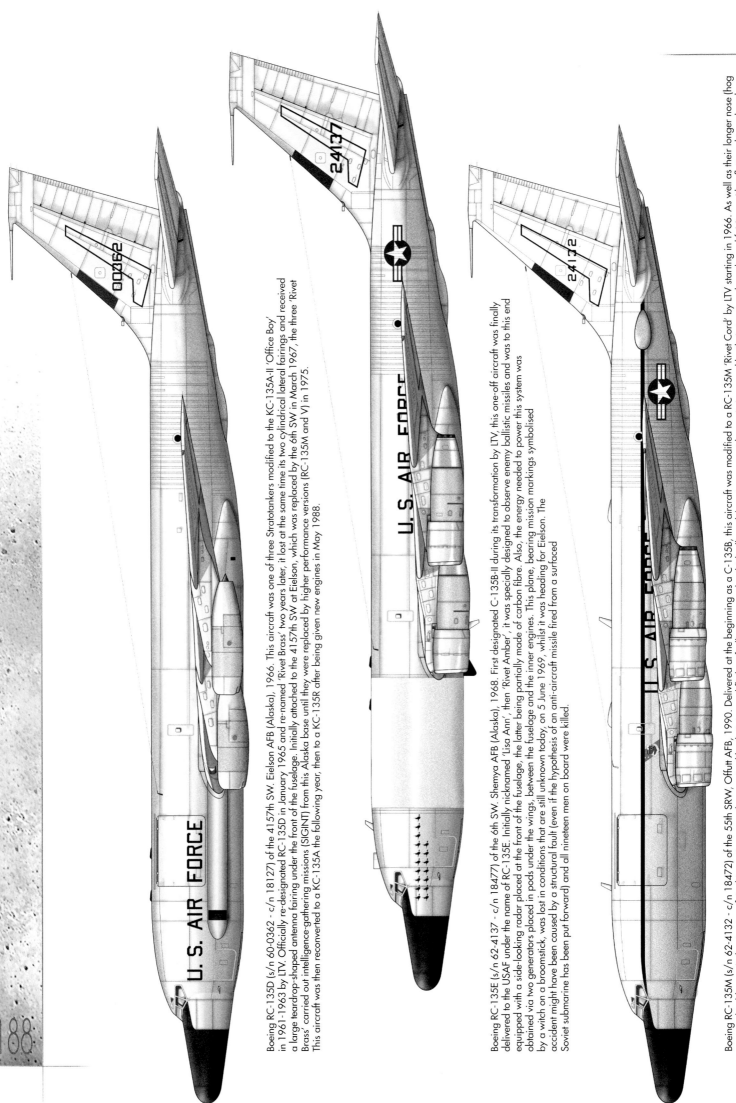

Boeing RC-135D (s/n 60-0362 - c/n 18127) of the 4157th SW. Eielson AFB (Alaska), 1966. This aircraft was one of three Stratotankers modified to the KC-135A-II 'Office Boy' in 1961-1963 by LTV. Officially re-designated RC-135D in January 1965 and re-named 'Rivet Brass' two years later, it lost at the same time its two cylindrical lateral fairings and received a large teardrop-shaped antenna fairing under the front of the fuselage. Initially attached to the 4157th SW at Eielson, which was replaced by the 6th SW in March 1967, the three 'Rivet Brass' carried out intelligence-gathering missions (SIGINT) from this Alaska base until they were replaced by higher performance versions (RC-135M and V) in 1975. This aircraft was then reconverted to a KC-135A the following year, then to a KC-135R after being given new engines in May 1988.

Boeing RC-135E (s/n 62-4137 - c/n 18477) of the 6th SW. Shemya AFB (Alaska), 1968. First designated C-135B-II during its transformation by LTV, this one-off aircraft was finally delivered to the USAF under the name of RC-135E. Initially nicknamed 'Lisa Ann', then 'Rivet Amber', it was specially designed to observe enemy ballistic missiles and was to this end equipped with a side-looking radar placed at the front of the fuselage, the latter being partially made of carbon fibre. Also, the energy needed to power this system was obtained via two generators placed in pods under the wings, between the fuselage and the inner engines. This plane, bearing mission markings symbolised by a witch on a broomstick, was lost in conditions that are still unknown today, on 5 June 1969, whilst it was heading for Eielson. The accident might have been caused by a structural fault (even if the hypothesis of an anti-aircraft missile fired from a surfaced Soviet submarine has been put forward) and all nineteen men on board were killed.

Boeing RC-135M (s/n 62-4132 - c/n 18472) of the 55th SRW. Offutt AFB, 1990. Delivered at the beginning as a C-135B, this aircraft was modified to a RC-135M 'Rivet Cord' by LTV starting in 1966. As well as their longer nose (hog nose or thimble nose), the six aircraft in this version were characterised by their internal flight refuelling receptacle which allowed them to carry out long missions, and by their two teardrop-shaped fairings with a flattened top placed on either side of the fuselage in front of the tail unit. This 'Rivet Cord' was modified to a RC-135W by E-Systems in November 1984 and is still in service with the 55th Wing at Offutt.

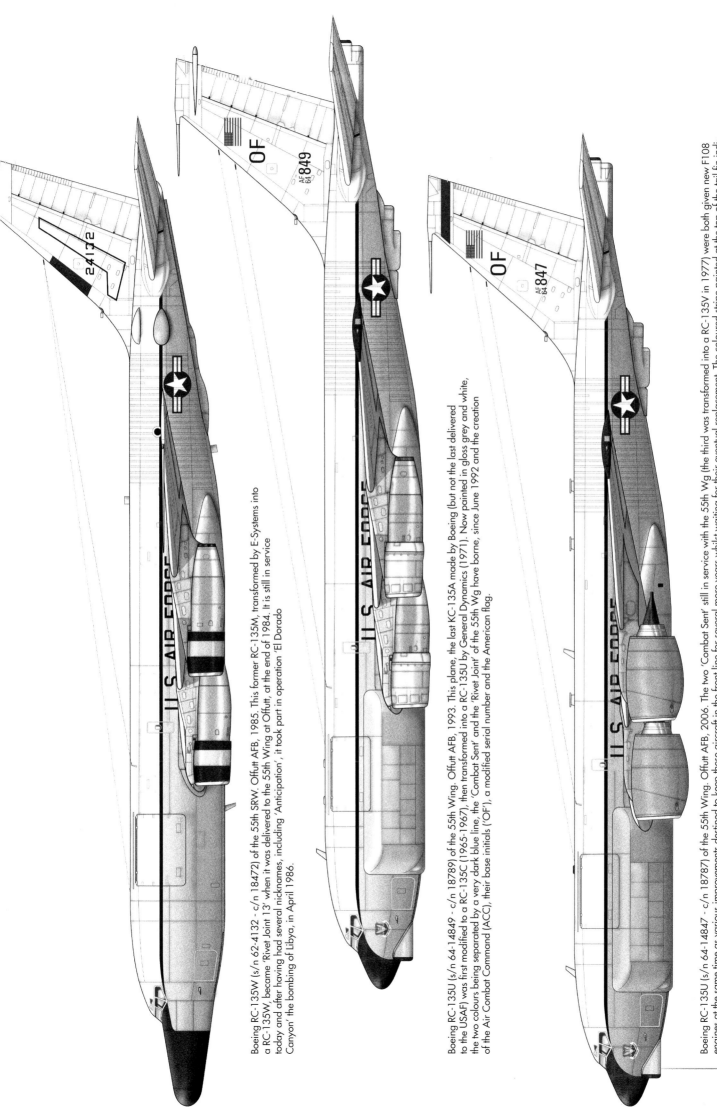

Boeing RC-135W (s/n 62-4132 - c/n 18472) of the 55th SRW. Offutt AFB, 1985. This former RC-135M, transformed by E-Systems into a RC-135W, became 'Rivet Joint 13' when it was delivered to the 55th Wing at Offutt, at the end of 1984. It is still in service today and after having had several nicknames, including 'Anticipation', it took part in operation 'El Dorado Canyon' the bombing of Libya, in April 1986.

Boeing RC-135U (s/n 64-14849 - c/n 18789) of the 55th Wing. Offutt AFB, 1993. This plane, the last KC-135A made by Boeing (but not the last delivered to the USAF) was first modified to a RC-135C (1965-1967), then transformed into a RC-135U by General Dynamics (1971). Now painted in gloss grey and white, the two colours being separated by a very dark blue line, the 'Combat Sent' and the 'Rivet Joint' of the 55th Wg have borne, since June 1992 and the creation of the Air Combat Command (ACC), their modified serial number and the American flag.

Boeing RC-135U (s/n 64-14847 - c/n 18787) of the 55th Wing. Offutt AFB, 2006. The two 'Combat Sent' still in service with the 55th Wg (the third was transformed into a RC-135V in 1977) were both given new F108 engines at the same time as various improvements destined to keep these aircraft in the front line for several more years whilst waiting for their eventual replacement. The coloured stripe painted at the top of the tail fin indicates that this aircraft belongs to the 45th RS 'Sylvesters'.

189

WC-135 and OC-135

Amongst the most surprising specialised versions designed from the C-
135 is the WC-135, whose role is
meteorological reconnaissance
and, above all, the OC-135, an observation aircraft born at the end of
the Cold War.

It is without doubt during the Second World War that
weather reconnaissance became of great importance; the
simple fact of being able to foresee weather conditions giving
a great advantage over an enemy. To this end, various equipment was designed, based at land stations or even at sea
(ships and buoys), which was quickly backed up by specially formed aerial units whose main mission was to collect
information and data that was as reliable as possible in as
short a time as possible. To this thankless, but essential task,
was added a second once the super powers had entered
into the atomic era; that of the surveillance of nuclear tests
conducted at altitude with air samples being taken. The
nuclear tests were generally kept secret, at least in their exact
nature, with information collected only by the
examination of collected particles, not only to
confirm that the nuclear explosion had really taken place,
but also the
type of
bomb used,
its strength, performance, as well as any eventual consequences, (dispersion of the cloud caused by the explosion),
localisation of fall out depending on air currents etc.
It was Dwight Eisenhower, the president of the United
States who, beginning in 1947, launched the 'Constant

Phoenix' program that saw the USAF given the task of detecting air burst nuclear explosions wherever they might take
place. To accomplish this, a small fleet of aircraft was specially modified, notably old four engine Superfortress bombers
transformed into the weather reconnaissance WB-29. It was
one of these planes, stripped of all weapons and equipped
with specific equipment, which detected a Soviet nuclear test
in 1949 whilst it was flying over the Pacific Ocean between
Japan and Alaska, a sensitive area if ever there was one.
These particular missions were, at
the beginning of the 1950s, given
to the WB-50, a plane that was
very close to the B-29, but more
powerful and with a higher tail fin, a
distant derivative of the British
Canberra bomber, made under licence in the United States.

WC-135B

As was the case with the tankers and
electronic reconnaissance aircraft, the
USAF quickly saw in the C-135 the

Opposite.

Opposite. The direct predecessor of the Boeing WC-135 was another plane made by the Seattle company, the WB-47B, a weather reconnaissance variant of the Stratojet, stripped of all weaponry. (USAF)

Above.
After having been used as a TC-135B for training the crews of the Boeing OC-135B, s/n 61-2667 became, from 1996 onwards, the last of the WC-135W weather reconnaissance fleet and is attached to the 44th RS of the 55th Wing at Offutt.
(F. Lert).

1. With the exception of s/n 61-2668 and 61-2671.

perfect platform to carry out these long duration missions; the four-engine plane being, as we have said, capable of flying for a long time at a steady speed whilst carrying a heavy payload of the special equipment and its operators. The new aircraft were destined more to supply weather information at low or average altitude; the Lockheed U-2, which at this time had just entered into service, was given high or very high altitude reconnaissance missions.

Ten C-135B (s/n 61-2665 to -2674), delivered to the MATS in 1962 were, therefore, transformed three years later into the WC-135B; the W prefix was for weather and clearly identified its new role. From the outside it was close to the traditional cargo aircraft and could be refuelled in flight [1]; it did not have an in-flight refuelling boom, but had a drain hose like on most of the RC-135, whilst the boomer's compartment was faired and equipped with various special equipment. They were veritable weather stations and generally carried a minimum crew of seven men (pilot, co-pilot, navigator, weather officer, mechanic and two weather technicians whose role, amongst others, was to release the on board probes), a number that could be increased to more than thirty. The WC-135B was equipped with the AN/AMQ-25, an on board weather and geophysical laboratory that called upon a computer that compared and analysed the data. It also had high performance research systems (such as the ARE, Atmospheric Research Equipment) that comprised of detectors and different types

of probes, fixed and releasable, or even propelled by rockets. Faired scoops (U-1) were installed for collecting air samples when the plane was in flight; these were placed on each side of the fuselage, where it was strengthened, behind the emergency exits above the wings. These had filters and were analysed and imprisoned in high-pressure spheres thanks to a special on board compressor. During their career, some of these aircraft received a special layout; one of them, for example, had its old boomers compartment equipped with tubes for the pneumatic release of probes whilst the WC-135B fleet was modified beginning in 1988 in order to carry the 'Star Cast' electro-optical system for taking photographs of fast moving objects, notably space shuttles. The presence of this equipment led to the removal of one of the two air sample scoops and the installation of two windows, one of which was on the cargo door, protecting the position-calculating optical system.

From 1965 onwards, the WC-135B based at McClellan and Yokota (Japan) with the 55th and 56th Weather Reconnaissance Squadrons carried out missions throughout the world, including polar regions or off the African and South American coasts. As well as the surveillance of nuclear tests in the atmosphere, their role also included establishing very precise databases that could be used to improve the use of any type of flying object. In the event of a nuclear conflict, the influence of the weather on a missile, a B-52 type jet bomber, or even a flying tanker could be determining, notably on the amount of fuel used and, therefore, the range and efficiency in general. Indeed, it should be known that a ballistic missile, despite its constantly improving precision due to technical progress, was extremely sensitive to strong winds at high altitude which could put it off its course and miss its target, or even lead to its destruction when it re-entered the atmosphere.

The WC-135B were, therefore, much used to define and trace the routes going via the North Pole that strategic bombers would have to take if launching a strike against the Soviet Union. On a regular basis, they collected (at least once a week) the different parameters (temperature, wind speed, hygrometric degrees, atmospheric pressure) in order to make databases and carry out simulations to define the ideal route and the weather conditions on them. These weather reconnaissance planes were also used in much more peaceful circumstances, taking part, for example, in international weather research, using their detectors to make sure that treaties banning open air nuclear testing were respected. Two WC-135B were even used in May 1986 after the nuclear power station explosion at Chernobyl, collecting the debris that allowed not only for the evaluation of the incident,

but also its consequences. These planes were also used in operation 'Desert Shield' in order to draw up a precise weather map of Kuwait and Iraq (wind direction etc.), notably for use in the possible use of bacteriological or chemical weapons.

WC-135W, WC-135C and NC-135W

With the end of the Cold War, the need for weather reconnaissance decreased, whilst their career was put into question by the ageing airframes that were exposed to corrosion. In 1995, the three surviving aircraft [2] were, for purely administrative reasons to simplify designations, renamed WC-135W. One of them (s/n 61-2665) was retired from service and stored in 1996 so well that a second aircraft (s/n 61-2667), previously re-designated TC-135B and briefly used for training the Boeing OC-135B 'Open Skies' crews, replaced it the same year and remains today the only surviving example of this specialised version. From the outside it is similar to the standard WC-135B with its lateral scoops for collecting air samples in the upper strata of the atmosphere as part of the Constant Phoenix program. It is attached to the 44th RS of the 55th Wing at Offutt. Also destined to be retired from service due to a lack of funds to carry out its modernisation, it was finally modernised starting in 1999 and later returned to its original unit. At the end of the Looking Glass program (following chapter) in 1993, one of the former flying command posts (ABNCP), EC-135C s/n 62-3582 was attached to the 55th Wing at Offutt and used for service and training missions under the designation WC-135C. Contrary to what its prefix might suggest, it has no specialised equipment and notably no system for collecting samples.

Finally, a former WC-135B (s/n 61-2666), the only surviving example today, has been used as a flying test bed for new equipment designed by E-Systems. Initially designated WC-135W, its side scoops began to be removed in 1995 and it was equipped side fuselage fairings, a longer nose and antenna on and under the fuselage, some of which are for the MUCELS system or the satellite communication system (on top of the tail fin) so that it differs very slightly, at least from the outside, from the standard RC-135W of which it does not have any of the specific equipment. Also, the rear of the fuselage has oval fairings with a flattened surface typical of those of the

Cobra Ball (RC-135C). In 2000, this plane was re-designated to NW-135W in order to show its particular status as a platform for in-flight tests; today it is attached to a unit that was specially created for it, Detachment 2 of the

645th Materiel Squadron based at Majors Field and placed under the authority of the AFMC (Air Force Materiel Command).

OC-135 'Open Skies'

In July 1955, during a conference being held at Geneva, President Eisenhower launched the idea of an international treaty named Open Skies. This would allow all of the nations who signed the treaty to fly over and photograph each other's territory in order to get a precise idea of each other's technical advances, notably in the military domain. The information gathered thanks to this policy of transparency was also aimed at decreasing the risk of a major conflict through better reciprocal knowledge. Far from being innocent, this treaty was in fact thought up by United States that were, at this time, convinced that they were trailing behind compared to the USSR, a country whose industrial, and even scientific capacities were largely over estimated, mainly because of the lack of precise information that filtered through the Iron Curtain.

Naturally, the USSR to whom this treaty was aimed, refused this project, leading the Americans to gain information by other means, this time a lot less official, notably turning to flying over the territory of the Soviet Union with U-2 type spy planes. By chance, these flights began a year to the day after the proposition put forward by the American president. In fact, it was one of his successors, George Bush, who

2. S/n 61-1673 in storage. 61-2668, 61-2669 - 'Speckled Trout', see previous chapters - and 61-2671 first modified to the C-135B then the C-135C VIP transport. 61-2670, -2672 and -2674 transformed into the OC-135B. The prefix 'O' signifies 'Observation', whereas the suffix 'B' is taken from the original designation of these aircraft, C-135B.
3. Signed on 24 March 1992, the treaty was not applied until a few years later, notably after its ratification by Belarus and Russia. With no limitation in time, clauses allow for its revision by signatory countries after the first three years of existence, then every five years. At present, this treaty has been signed by Belgium, Bulgaria, Belarus, Canada, Denmark, Spain, the United States, Finland, France, Georgia, Great Britain, Greece, Hungary, Iceland, Italy, Kyrgyzstan, Luxembourg, Holland, Rumania, Russia, Czech Republic, Slovakia, Sweden, Turkey and Ukraine.

Above.
S/n 61-2670 was the last of three WC-135B transformed into the OC-135B in 1996. The two Sky Cast system windows, on the cargo door, have been retained, but this equipment, however, has been removed. This plane, like its counterparts, was in service with the 45th RS 'Sylvester' of the 55th Wing at Offutt.
(USAF)

4. Canada and Belgium chose, for example, the C-130 Hercules and Russia the Antonov An-30

Below.
Transformed into a OC-135B in 1994, WC-135B s/n 61-2672 was modified, like the rest of the 'Open Skies' fleet into a OC-135W, the final variant of this plane equipped with new hushkits on its engines and in which the flight mechanic's post was deleted.
(J. Guillem collection)

re-launched the idea in 1989, this being finally accepted during the Helsinki Conference in 1992. In order to put this new treaty into practice, each country that signed it [3] had to, amongst other things, define its own surveillance plane, the United States very logically choosing a derivative of the indestructible C-135, named for the occasion OC-135B [4].

It is the Defence Threat Reduction Agency or DTRA that is responsible for the organisation and coordination of the missions that fall within the treaty, according to which 42 flights can be authorised every year. These observation flights stem more from good will and transparency on the part of the member nations, especially as information of a sensitive character can now be obtained thanks to increasingly higher performance satellites. The flights can be carried out without warning or limitation over countries that have signed the treaty, the missions not exceeding 96 hours. Representatives of the signatory countries can take part in these flights and control the surveillance operations and are even authorised to take photographs. Three former WC-135B (s/n 61-2670, 61-2672 and 61-2674) were, therefore, modified between 1993 and 1996 and their weather reconnaissance equipment replaced by that of its new missions and authorised by the treaty (infra red scanner, synthetic aperture radar, photographic equipment). The in-flight refuelling receptacle was retained, as were the two Star Cast system windows, although the system itself was

the exposure according to atmospheric conditions (light, cloud presence etc.). This equipment is placed in air-conditioned containers in order to optimise its performance; each camera has twelve kilometres of film. The cabin has been completely reorganised and laid out (conference tables, seats, four-channel interphone for private conversations between certain occupants of the plane, fluorescent tube lighting so that surveillance and control operations are not disturbed) and can carry thirty passengers, including a four man OSIA (On-Site Inspection Agency) team, the Federal agency whose role is the application of the treaty in the United States, attached to the American Department of Defence. This team is made up of four men (mission head and his deputy, plus two specialised technicians and linguists), as well as representatives from the countries flown over, the flying crew being provided by the USAF. According to the terms of the treaty, these planes can, in theory, be lent to other signatory nations, the flying crew, however, is still provided by the Air Force, whilst all of the gathered data from these flights is available to all of the signatory countries.

Put into service by the 45th Reconnaissance Squadron ('Sylvester') of the 55th Wing at Offutt, the unit not only carries out missions but also the training of crews as well as aircraft maintenance, the OC-135B are equipped according to the layout of the treaty in such a way that they can carry out their missions without having recourse to the ground based systems, using the INS/GPS (Integrated Inertial Navigation System/GPS), a high performance navigation system, the data of which is constantly updated during the flight.

removed. The OC-135B is equipped with four cameras installed at the rear of the fuselage, three are of the KS-87E type (one mounted vertically and two obliquely) for taking photographs at low altitude (900 m/2,950 ft), these are placed in the former boomer's compartment. Another, a KA-91C for panoramic sweeping, is mobile from one side of the fuselage to the other and takes photographs at high altitude (10,000 m/32,800 ft).

Thanks to the DARMS (Data Annotation And Recording System), linked to an radar altimeter precise from zero to 15,000 metres (49,210 ft), each photo is annotated and accompanied by a certain amount of precise data (date, time, position of the plane, etc.), whilst the operators can change

Recently, these planes have been equipped with the Pacer CRAG navigation system, like most of their counterparts.

The first OC-135B mission took place in August 1994 when the representatives of the Ukraine flew over part of the United States territory. Another mission was carried out in very different conditions in 2005 when it was tasked with taking aerial photographs to evaluate the damage caused by hurricane Katrina in the south east of the United States, notably in the New Orleans area.

Although a fourth plane (the only TC-135B, s/n 61-2667) was originally attached briefly to the OC-135B 'Open Skies' fleet between 1993 and 1995, today there are only two planes, the third (s/n 61-2674) being kept airworthy as a backup.

All the planes have been re-designated OC-135W after the flight engineer's post was cut and the engines were equipped with Hush Kits to bring them into line with the regulations in use in the countries flown over, notably in western Europe and North America.

Above.
WC-135W s/n 61-2665 was used to test the hushkits of the engines destined for the OC-135. After having served with the 24th Reconnaissance Squadron of Detachment 1 of the 55th Wing, it was retired from service and went into storage in September 1996. (J. Guillem collection)

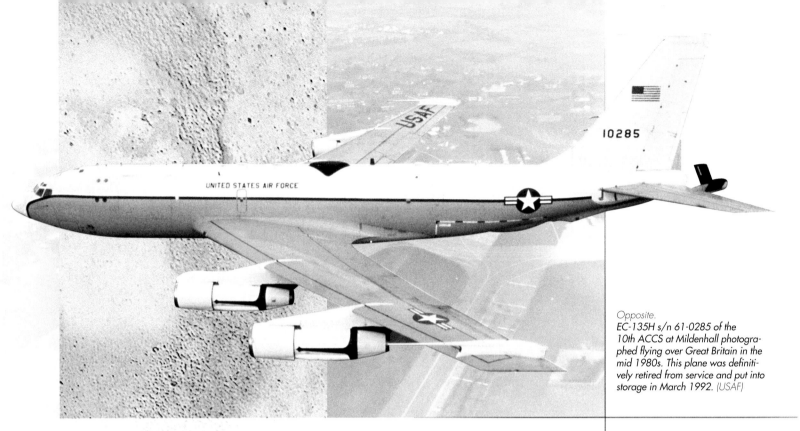

EC-135, the airborne command posts

The Cold War and, above all, the threat of a global nuclear conflict, was at the origin of another specialised version of the Boeing C-135, transformed this time into an airborne command post capable of directing reprisals in the event of the destruction of land based installations.

Deeply shocked after the surprise attack against Pearl Harbor on 7 December 1941, the United States constantly developed systems capable of not only anticipating this type of attack, but also assuring continuity in the chain of command whatever the circumstances.

With the Soviet Union achieving the status of a nuclear power, the situation became a little more complex as this time they had to take into account a new important parameter, that of a sudden strike on American territory using atomic weapons, leading to, by the scale of the destruction caused, the impossibility of undertaking any form of counter strike.

The beginning

In order to reduce this threat, at the end of the 1950s, the Strategic Air Command put a third of its fighter aircraft on fifteen-minute ground alert, whereas the long and medium detection network was improved ('Pinetree' radar stations from 1949 onwards, then the Distant Early Warning - the famous 'DEW line' - three years later) and the command centres, dispersed over various sites, were more concentrated in one site.

This attitude was reinforced by the politics of President John F. Kennedy, newly elected in 1960 that aimed at increasing the security of the United States, mainly by reducing their vulnerability in the face of a determined Soviet attack.

The precision of the enemy weapons, notably the ballistic missiles, constantly increased and it became rapidly apparent that in the event of large scale destruction caused by a surprise attack, the counter attack capacities of the country would be reduced and the 'balance of terror' would, therefore, be upset to the detriment of one side or the other. Also, although at the beginning it was thought possible to counter a conventional attack, even a massive one, with jet bombers, the appearance of almost indestructible intercontinental missiles, capable of hitting any area of the United States in less than thirty minutes after their launch, considerably modified the situation. This was even more the case with the launch of the first satellites, rapidly followed by the flight of the cosmonaut Yuri Gagarin; the head start of the Soviets in the

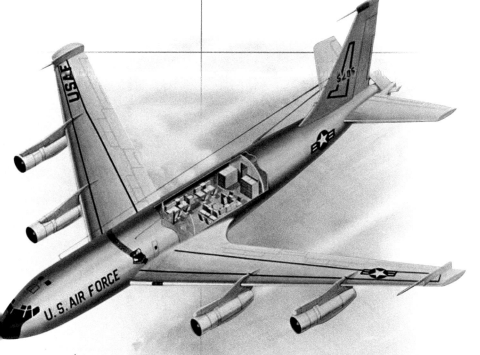

means of avoiding any threat was to install them in a plane, practically unreachable, especially if it remained over protected zones or, even better, escorted by fighter planes.

Thus was born the idea of the ABCP (Airborne Command Post) which was almost invulnerable as it was constantly in the air, and able to stand in for any decision-making centre if it was destroyed beyond repair or temporarily knocked out and unable to carry out its tasks.

From the end of 1958, the SAC envisaged using the capacities of the KC-135 (range, load capacity), even thinking of putting into service a specific variant in 1960. In May of this same year, a first aircraft (s/n 58-0022) was modified (specific cabin layout, installation of high performance communications equipment leading to the appearance of extra antennae on the fuselage) and began being tested out in July along with four other transformed aircraft at the Offutt base. The small crew was led by an AEAO (Airborne Emergency Actions Officer), initially a colonel, then a SAC general whose role consisted of taking command in the event of a loss in contact with the civil National Command Authorities (NCA) or the SAC general staff. The tests on the aircraft began in July 1960 with the 34th AREFS, the KC-135A aircraft being placed on fifteen-minute ground

military space domain was undeniable. The survival of the chain of command after a first strike and, therefore, the ability to strike back with an intensive bombardment using those forces that remained intact, became a priority.

A system named PACCS (Post Attack Command & Control System) was, therefore, developed; its first stage consisting of dispersing the SAC command centres in three different bases that were all very far from each other (Barksdale in Louisiana, March in California and Westover, in Massachusetts) rather than concentrating them on one much too vulnerable site at Offutt, Nebraska. This spreading out of the command centres was also combined with a new strategic doctrine that differed from that of the massive counter strike then in force. However, the land-based centres, although less immediately vulnerable, remained under open to attack and it very quickly became obvious that the only

alert notably in order to test the reaction time of the crews. These six months of tests were crowned with success, notably by showing that it was possible to maintain contact with the Joint Chief of Staff, but also with any land base or even any SAC aircraft in the air. The 'Looking Glass' program (thus named as these aircraft in flight had to take on the role of 'mirrors' for land based equipment and personnel) was officially launched in February 1961. Five replacement aircraft were, therefore, made initially, whereas six KC-135A ABCP were delivered to the 34th ARS between January and August 1962, the eleven aircraft rapidly forming the fleet of airborne command posts to which the code of 'Cover All' was attributed. From now on, every day, at least one aircraft should have been in the air to serve as an airborne command post, a

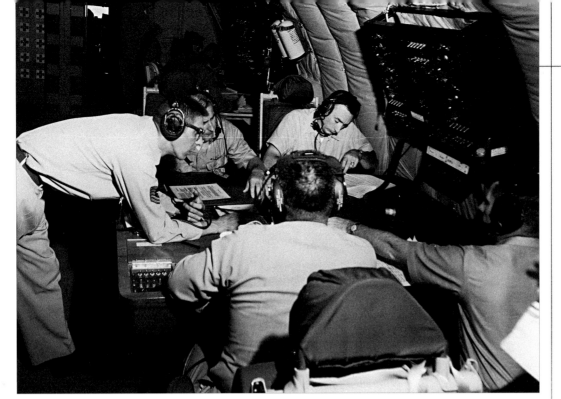

mission that lasted, on average, eight hours. Several other aircraft were kept on constant ground alert.

The ABCP fleet was at the origin of the formation of the 4363rd and 4364th Post Attack Command & Control Squadrons (PACCS) based respectively at Lockbourne (Ohio) and Mountain Home (Idaho). These planes were seconded, in 1962, by three AUXCP units (Auxiliary Airborne Command Posts), with identically transformed KC-135A attached to three SAC command centres and seconded themselves by four squadrons of Boeing EB-47L [1] acting as radio relays.

To complement this fleet, a certain number of other specially modified KC-135A were attached, also, starting in 1962, to the NCA to act as National Emergency Airborne Command Posts or NEACP, an abbreviation that was quickly transformed into 'kneecap'.

The KC-135A modified into airborne command posts which had notably served to define the concept and were considered as being transition models, began to be joined in February 1964 by seventeen 'second generation' aircraft. These were the KC-135B that could be refuelled in the air, equipped with complex communication systems and powered by the TF-33-P-5 turbofan. The designation of the airborne command posts was modified on 1 January 1965, principally in order to differentiate them from the standard tankers. The modified KC-135A were thus renamed EC-135A, and the KC-135B (at this time, three of them were not yet delivered) became the EC-135C. This modification was accompanied, in March of the same year, by a reorganisation of the ACP fleet, the EC6135A were thus attached to the refuelling squadrons at Lockbourne and Ellsworth (South Dakota), whereas the EB-47L was disbanded, and their missions taken over by the 'old' EC-135A.

A second reorganisation came in April 1970, all the EC-135 being this time attached to the 2nd, 3rd and 4th Airborne Command & Control Squadrons (ACCS) at Offutt (Nebraska), Grissom (Indiana) and Ellsworth, and in consequence attached to a particular geographical region of the United States (east, centre and west). However, their missions remained the same, that is to permanently maintain an aircraft in the air with, as support, a daily reserve on ground alert able to take off in less then fifteen minutes. The EC-135, in their various versions, accomplished their role for almost thirty years, without any major incident and hardly ever failing their mission as it was only on one or two occasions

1. In 1963, thirty-six downgraded B-47E were transformed into aerial relay aircraft under the designation of EB-47L. They carried two radio communications in their specially equipped bomb bay.

that a plane was forced to interrupt its mission and land because of serious medical problems.

Up to that point, the orders were clear, at least one airborne command post had to be in the air, in all weather and even, in the case of a breakdown, on one engine, twenty four hours a day and 365 days a year. It was only from 24 July 1990 that the in-flight alerts were suspended and replaced by others on the ground, or still in the air, but not exceeding twenty-four days per month.

The breaking up of the SAC, on 1 June 1992, accelerated the end of these 'Looking Glass' missions, especially as the geopolitical situation had much changed since the program was set up, principally in the collapse of the Soviet Bloc. Already

by this time, the EC-135 only flew once a day, and during a set lapse of time. Passed under the command of the United States Strategic Command (USSTRATCOM) but retaining similar missions, that is command continuity of the United States strategic forces in the event of an emergency, the 'Looking Glass' regrouped with the 7th Airborne Command and Control Squadron at Offutt (Nebraska), were finally retired from service on 1 October 1998 and their missions were taken over by other Boeings, the US Navy's E-6B Mercury.

The composition of crews on board the PACCS varied somewhat over time. At the beginning, as well as the flight crew (pilot, co-pilot, navigator, refuelling operator), the group of specialists in the cabin were made up of a communications officer, two radio operators, a data operator and a radio technician.

This specialised crew was placed under the orders of an Air Force general of the USSTRATCOM, of the United States Transportation Command (USTRANSCOM), of the Air

Combat Command (ACC), of the Air Force Space Command (AFSPC), or a US Navy admiral usually attached to the general staff of the ninth submarine fleet (Commander Submarine Group - COMSUBGRU - Nine) for the Pacific and that of the tenth fleet (COMSUBGRU Ten) for the Pacific. All of these specialists were divided into operational groups (seven at the system's heyday) and came from the different branches of the four main arms (USAF, US Navy, USMC and the US Army). Each group leader was responsible for training, cohesion and the work of the men (and women) under his authority.

At the height of the 'Looking Glass' program, the specialised crew was greatly increased (ten to eleven men in general, as well as the flight crew) and now comprised a SAC general, an operations controller, a specialist communications officer, an intelligence officer, weather experts, a logistics officer and various technicians. The officer in charge of remote missile launching and his time work in direct contact with the communications officer for remote missile launches.

A particular system allowed the 'Looking Glass' to transmit launch codes directly to missiles in their underground silos in the event of the usual command centres being rendered useless. The second officer was responsible, also with a team, for planning the mission and could show the 'Looking Glass' commander the various strategic options open to the president of the United States. As for the intelligence officer, he informed the entire crew of all the data in his possession and could thus make sure that the

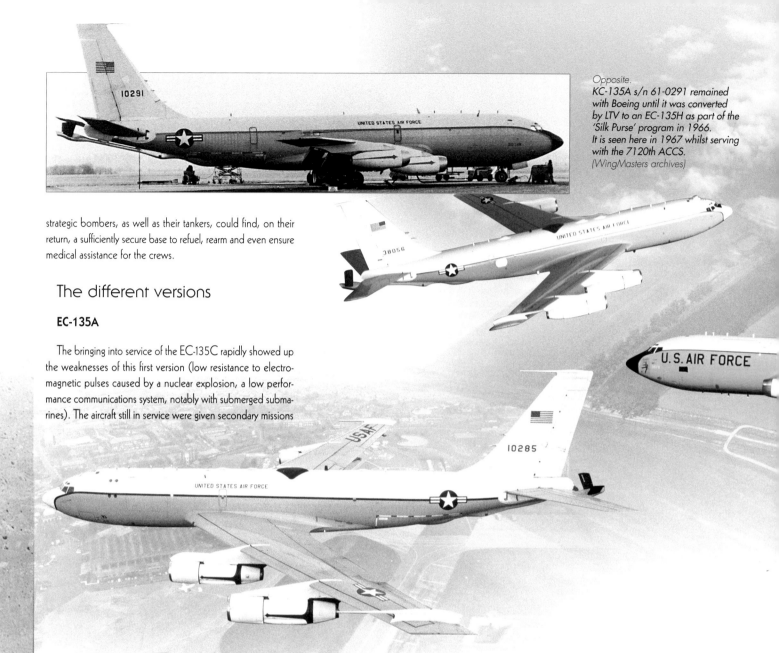

Opposite.
KC-135A s/n 61-0291 remained with Boeing until it was converted by LTV to an EC-135H as part of the 'Silk Purse' program in 1966. It is seen here in 1967 whilst serving with the 7120th ACCS. (WingMasters archives)

strategic bombers, as well as their tankers, could find, on their return, a sufficiently secure base to refuel, rearm and even ensure medical assistance for the crews.

The different versions

EC-135A

The bringing into service of the EC-135C rapidly showed up the weaknesses of this first version (low resistance to electromagnetic pulses caused by a nuclear explosion, a low performance communications system, notably with submerged submarines). The aircraft still in service were given secondary missions

and replaced, notably, by the old EB-47L in their role of radio relays. Powered by J 57 engines, they retained their boom and were, therefore, still capable of undertaking in-flight refuelling. They carried less fuel than a standard tanker due to the presence of equipment and the on board crew. They could be refuelled in the air and capable, in theory, of remaining airborne up to 72 hours, this limit being the point where the engine lubricant would start to run out.

In 1967, the six surviving aircraft [2] were modified as part of the ALCS (Air Launch Control System) program to be able to carry out remote launches of the ground based Minuteman II and Peacekeeper missiles. This procedure was carried out in April the same year and regularly tested later during operations named 'Glory Trip' during which a EC-135 launched a Minuteman generally based at Vandenberg in California, the

missile in these cases not equipped with its nuclear warhead. To this end, they were equipped with an in-flight refuelling receptacle as well as HF wingtip antennae and logically designated Airborne Launch Control Centers or ALCC. This system, which also functioned in a similar manner to that of the land-based command centres, allowed specialists on board the aircraft to completely replace the latter if needed to 'take command' to carry out the launches. This was undertaken in an unchanging ritual: following the authentication of the alert message received by the commander on board, the latter set off the ALCS system commanded by two keys that had to be turned simultaneously and kept by an on board senior officer and the communications officer, the two men being sat at different areas in order to avoid any mistake with catastrophic consequences. Before being retired from service in 1992 [3], the EC-135A had not been put into service since 1970, apart from by just the 4th ACCS at the bases of Ellsworth and Minot (North Dakota), and were able to lead five of the six Strategic Air Command Minuteman missile wings.

Below.
The first EC-135K (s/n 55-3118) was also the first KC-135A made and named 'City of Renton'. First used by Boeing as a test bed, it was delivered to the USAF in 1961 after having been modified to an airborne command post. Put into service with the 552nd ACW, it has been kept at the McConnell base since October 1996. This version was stripped of its in-flight refuelling boom unlike the other EC-135. (WingMasters archives)

2. S/n 61-062, 61-0278, 61-0287, 61-0289, 61-0293 and 61-0297. In 1967, five aircraft (58-0007, 58-0011, 58-0018, 58-0019 and 58-0022) were modified to EC-135P, two (s/n 61-0282 and 61-0285) to EC-135H and finally one (s/n 62-3579) to EC-135G.

3. One of these aircraft (s/n 61-0293) was first converted to a KC-135A tanker before becoming the first KC-135R.

4. S/n 62-3570, 62-3579, 63-7894 and 63-8001.

EC-135C

Seventeen KC-135B, designed at the outset as airborne command posts, began to be delivered to the SAC in February 1964 and were named EC-135C at the very beginning of the following year with three aircraft awaiting delivery. Destined to replace the EC-135A in the 'Looking Glass' program, this version, the most produced of all the ABCP, was characterised, apart from its higher tail fin (a particularity later retro-fitted on the previous versions), by its higher performance TF-33-P-9 turbofan engines, whilst several antennae appeared on and under the fuselage. The TWA (Trailing Wire Antenna) was placed, when not in use, in a fairing under the fuselage, offset to the right in front of the main undercarriage wells. These planes were equipped with a refuelling receptacle to increase their range and, like their predecessors, retained their boom and, therefore, their tanker capacities.

The EC-135C carried a crew made up of a flight crew comprising a pilot, co-pilot, navigator, refuelling operator, and an in-flight passenger specialist to which was added a SAC general, a planner and several intelligence specialists. At the beginning, these planes, considered as being the essential vectors of 'Looking Glass' missions, were based at the same place as the tankers or SAC reconnaissance aircraft, that is to say at Barksdale (913th AREFS of the 2nd AF), Westover (99th AREFS/8th AF) and March (22nd AREFS/15th AF). After, they were re-attached to the 2nd and 4th ACCS respectively at Offutt (nine aircraft) and Ellsworth (four). Like previously, and until the beginning of the 1990s, at least one EC-135C had to be constantly in the air whatever the conditions (weather or engine problems, etc.)

At the start of the 1990s, four EC-135C (s/n 62-3581, 61-3585, 63-8046 and 63-8054) had their equipment upgraded by the installation of an AFSATCOM satellite navigation system, better known by the abbreviation of MILSTAR. This was later used on the Boeing E-6 and was outwardly characterised by the presence of an ovoid-shaped fairing placed at the front of the fuselage. At the end of 1992, it was decided to leave in service only five EC-135C, placed under the orders of the US Strategic Command (USSTRATCOM) the headquarters of which were situated at Offutt and which had received authority over all of the American nuclear forces. In reality, there were eight aircraft that continued to be used, firstly by the 4th and 2nd ACCS then, starting in July 1994, only by the 7th ACCS. The missions of these aircraft (one of them,

s/n 63-8053, was lost at Pope AFB in September 1997) were finally taken over starting in September 1998 by the US Navy's Boeing E-6B Mercury aircraft on board which some of the EC-135C and notably the MILSTAR system was installed.

EC-135G

On 1 January 1965, three KC-135A modified into airborne command posts, as well as an EC-135A [4] were renamed EC-135G. This change in designation was justified by the fact that the on board systems were no longer manual as they were previously, but automatic. Three aircraft were attached to the 4th ACCS of the 28th BW at Ellsworth in order to serve as support to the EC-135A fleet of this unit, whereas the last was used within the 70th AREFS at Grissom as a radio relay, replacing the old EB-47L.

They could be refuelled in the air whilst at the same time keeping their boom and, therefore, at least in theory, retained their tanker capabilities. There were wingtip HF antennae as well as eight sabre antennae positioned on the fuselage and six others underneath, whilst an antenna cable ran from the top of the tail fin to the front of the fuselage. When they were used in their secondary role as radio relays, the interior layout was somewhat modified, the crew was now made up in this case of only two radio operators and a specialised technician.

In 1968, these four aircraft were equipped with an ALCS remote launch system, allowing them to launch intercontinental missiles when airborne. They were then all regrouped within the 4th ACCS before being retired from service in 1992.

EC-135H

Beginning in 1964, five KC-135A were transformed by LTV into the EC-135H, the airborne command post, in order to replace in these missions the old Douglas C-118A Liftmaster. One of these planes was kept on constant alert in the air until December 1969, the year on which they only remained on ground alert. To reduce the risks, an EC-135H was generally based in the Azores, in the event of aircraft based in Great Britain being destroyed on the ground following a surprise attack.

These planes were comparable to the other specialised versions (refuelling receptacle, HF wingtip antennae, six sabre antennae under the fuselage and two on top) and were characterised mainly by their trailing antenna housed under the belly, two ovoid fairings on the sides of the fuselage behind the wings' trailing edges and a flat

'saddleback' VLF antenna placed on top of the fuselage. In 1982, these aircraft were re-engined, their original J57 engines being replaced by the TF-33-PW-102.

One of them (s/n 61-0274) was attached to the 'Scope Light' program and was used as a support plane for the commander in chief of the Atlantic forces (CINCLANT) from the base at Langley, Virginia, before being modified to a EC-135P in 1988. The four other EC-135H (s/n 61-0282, 61-0285, 61-0286 and 61-0291) were part of the 'Silk Purse' program, the European branch of a worldwide network of airborne command posts. These were attached to the commander in chief of American forces in Europe (USCIN-CEUR) and those of NATO, initially from the Châteauroux base in France, then that of Mildenhall in Great Britain. The interior of their cabin housed a specialised crew generally comprising sixteen men (radio operators, teletypist, general staff personnel, etc.) supplied at the beginning by the only USCINCEUR then partly by the American high command in Europe, the SACEUR (Supreme Allied Command Europe). With their equipment being constantly modernised, the EC-135H were given new engines (TF33) beginning in 1982 and were definitively retired from service in 1991. Two of them (s/n 61-0282 and 61-0286) were then used as ground training airframes under the designation GEC-135H.

EC-135J

From 1965 to 1980, four EC-135C (s/n 62-3584, 63-8055, 63-8056 and 63-8057) were specially modified as part of the 'Night Watch' program destined to allow the NCA and more specially the president of the United States to have at his disposal a NEACP (National Emergency Airborne Command Post) in the event of a serious crisis and notably a nuclear war.

Launched in 1962, this program used four KC-135A at the beginning, one of which belonged to the SAC and was destined for training; they were kept on 24 hour alert starting in July the same year.

In 1965, these first planes were replaced by the EC-135J, which differed from the other airborne command posts, notably the EC-135H, by its profoundly modified cabin that was divided into two distinct compartments containing fifteen posts for the specialised technicians, to which was added next a suite for the president of the United States. Also, because of their particular functions, their communications equipment was greatly improved with notably the addition of a VLF antenna on top of the

fuselage. The 'Kneecaps' were all based at Andrews close to Washington DC, the home of most of the United States' administrations, and served with the 1000th ACCS which became the 1st ACCS in 1969. Deemed too small at the end of the 1960s, it was decided to replace these planes with the Boeing E-4B (the military designation of the 'Jumbo Jet'), but this project was put off for a long time before finally being carried out in 1974. The specific equipment of the EC-135H was then taken out and installed on the new E-4, the planes being sent to the 9th ACCS at Hickam (Hawaii) in order to replace the EC-135P 'Blue Eagle' of the commander in chief of the American Pacific forces (CINCPAC).

One of the EC-135J (s/n 62-3584) was lost on 29 May 1992 and the 9th ACCS had been disbanded a few weeks earlier. The three surviving aircraft were retired from service during this same year and one of them today is on display at the Tucson Pima Air Force Museum.

EC-135K

Three KC-135A [5], including the first (s/n 55-3118 'City of Renton'), were modified beginning at the start of 1961 as part of the 'Oxeye Daisy' program into airborne command posts, initially for the Tactical Air Command, then the Air Combat Command. Named 'Head Dancer', these planes were equipped with high performance radio systems and telewriters, whereas the soundproofed cabin was specially arranged and equipped with, amongst other things, carpet, tables, swivel seats and five bunks. The specialised crew comprised a commander assisted by his general staff and nine communications technicians.

Differing from most of the other EC-135, these aircraft were stripped of their in-flight refuelling system, the boom being replaced by a draining tube identical to that on the electronic reconnaissance RC-135, whereas HF antennae were added to the wingtips. On the other hand, these aircraft were not equipped with a receptacle and could not be refuelled in the air, also unlike most of their counterparts. Mainly destined to escort TAC fighter

5. S/n 55-3118, 59-1518 and 62-3536.

EC-135, the airborne command posts

planes during overseas deployment, the EC-135K served notably during transfer flights over the oceans, supplying weather information, carrying out navigation or organising in-flight refuelling in the event of an emergency for less well-equipped aircraft and notably single man fighter planes. They could, however, serve as back up command posts if needed, whilst they were also given special missions such as transporting VIPs, notably the government of the United States, their high performance communications equipment being used during these flights.

At the beginning, the TAC expressed a desire to have at least eight EC-135K to satisfy its needs within the framework of 'Head Dancer' missions; however this number was never achieved. A second aircraft (s/n 62-3536, a former Stratotanker ´ Zero-G' used by NASA) was only modified and delivered in 1970. Having been lost on 14 September 1977 after crashing into a

mountain near Kirtland (New Mexico), it was replaced by another KC-135A, 'Old Smoky'(s/n 59-1518) that had been used for tests with the Federal Aviation Administration (FAA) in only 1979; it was not put into operational service until the beginning of 1982.

After having served in various units at the beginning of its career, the first EC-135K was attached, in 1972, to the 8th Air Command & Control Squadron (ACCS) at the base of Seymour-Johnson in North Carolina, a squadron that became successively the 8th Tactical Deployment Control Squadron (TDCS) in 1974, and the 8th Air Deployment & Control Squadron (ADCS) in 1978 after having moved to Tinker (Oklahoma), and the new 8th ACCS in May 1996, the moment where it was finally transferred to the 89th Airlift Wing at the Andrews base.

Having begun their career during the Cuban missile crisis in 1962, the two EC-135K, re-engined with turbofans, saw service again during operations 'Desert Shield' and 'Desert Storm' in 1990-1991; the oldest (s/n 55-3118) was retired from service in 1996 and displayed the following year at the McConnell base. The surviving plane (s/n 59-1518) was transformed into a VIP transport for the 65th Airlift Squadron of the 15th Air Base Wing at Hickam (Hawaii) and renamed for this C-135K before being retired from service in the spring of 2003.

Opposite.
EC-135G s/n 63-7994 of the 70th AREFS of Grissom AFB. This version was originally designed to serve as an emergency airborne command post. Some aircraft were used temporarily as radio relays, carrying in this role a small three man specialised crew.
(V. Gréciet collection)

EC-135L

The replacement of the thirty-six EB-47L began in 1965, these planes having been used as radio relays for the general staff of the Strategic Air Command (CINCSAC) and the National Command Authorities (NCA) within the PACCS system. In the event of an emergency, two aircraft were used to establish a link between the National Military Command Center, the National Emergency Airborne Command Post, the SAC Airborne Command Post and the planes equipped with ALCC remote launch system.

Between 1965 and 1967, these old low-performance and above all uncomfortable bombers (some crew members had to squeeze themselves into the former bomb bay), were replaced by eight KC-135A [6], modified by Lockheed Aerospace and renamed EC-135L. These planes retained their refuelling boom, notably to be able refuel the aircraft taking over from them at the end of its mission, and were equipped with a series of extra antennae (nine on the fuselage and six underneath).

Five of them received a refuelling receptacle, whilst three (s/n 61-0281, 61-288 and 61-0302, these last two being transformed once more to a KC-135R after having new engines and the first re-designated KC-135E) became standard KC-135A tankers in 1970. The planes of this version were originally used by the 70th AREFS at Grissom and were kept on alert for the SAC on this base and that of Rickenbacker. An aircraft was then attached to Ellsworth with the 4th ACCS. In May 1967, two EC-135L were sent to the Far East and first based in Taiwan, then beginning in 1970, at U-Tapao in Thailand as radio relays within the Airborne Surveillance & Control System or AS&CS established in South East Asia in place of the KC-135A 'Combat Lightning' that had been sent to United States for modernisation. These planes carried out 24 hour a day radio cover missions from the Gulf of Tonkin and went back to their home base at the end of 1967 when the KC-135A 'Combat Lightning' became available once more.

Two other aircraft (s/n 61-0269 and 61-0283) carried out similar missions in 1991 in Iraq as part of operation 'Desert Storm'. These EC-135L notably served as over the horizon UHF radio relays for groups of attack aircraft, fighters, or even ground troops. Based at the Riyadh King Khalid international airport (Saudi Arabia), they belonged to the 305th ARW and were attached to the 1703rd ARW (Provisional). Used until March 1991, the two EC-135L notably served as communication relays between satellites and ground bases in the hunt for Iraqi Scud missile launch platforms.

This operation was, in a way, the swansong of this version as, until spring 1992, four surviving aircraft were retired from service and sent to the depot at Davis-Monthan, the fifth was put on permanent display at the Grissom base.

EC-135N

In 1967, eight C-135A were attached to the ARIA (Apollo Range Instrumented Aircraft, see following chapter) program, renamed EC-135N and equipped, amongst other things, with a large size bulbous nose housing a radar 2.15 metres (7 feet) in diameter. One of these planes (s/n 61-0237) was taken out of the program in 1985, had its special equipment removed and its nose replaced with a standard model. Retaining its original designation, it was initially attached to the 19th ARW at Robins (Georgia), along with the sole EC-135Y (see below) before being attached, in 1997, to the 91st ARS of the 6th ARW and served as an airborne command post for the chief of central command (CINCENT), responsible for missions taking place more particularly in the Middle or Far East, as well as North Africa.

Equipped with numerous antennae, notably for satellite links, this EC-135N, the last in this version, had, like most of its counterparts, wingtip HF antennae. Its replacement by a C-40, planned

6. S/n 61-0261, 61-0263, 61-0269, 61-0279, 61-0281, 61-0283, 61-0288 and 61-0302.

Below.
EC-135C s/n 62-3585 of the 2nd ACCS taxiing on one of the runways at the Offutt base during exercise 'Global Guardian' in 1999. The characteristic bulge of the MILSTAR system added to the 'Looking Glass' at the end of their career, is perfectly visible at the front of the fuselage. (USAF)

Above.
EC-135C s/n 62-3583 from the 2nd ACCS of the 55th SRW at the Offutt base at night. This plane was modified in 1965 and definitively retired from service in 1992.
(USAF)

Below.
The five EC-135H were destined to serve as airborne command posts for CINCEUR. After having been kept permanently in the air, the 'Silk Purse' were kept on ground alert at the bases of Mildenhall (Great Britain) and Lajes (Portugal). They were re-engined with the TF 33 in June 1982. S/n 61-0291 was retired from service in May 1991 after having been stripped of its equipment.
(S. Guillemin collection)

for 2002, did not finally happen, because of budget restrictions, until the following year.

EC-135P [7]

In March 1967, five old EC-135A were transformed and renamed EC-135P. They retained both their boom and refuelling receptacle and the cabin was given consoles, particular combat posts and equipment, as well as the usual series of sabre antennae positioned on (seven antennae) and under (five) the fuselage, as well as a trailing antenna (TWA) housed under the belly in front of the right hand side main undercarriage well and that of the MILSTAR satellite link system. These planes, in service with the SAC, were destined to be used as airborne command posts by the general staff of Pacific forces (CINCPAC) under the designation of 'Blue Eagle' [8] with the 9th ACCS at Hickam (Hawaii) and by that of the Atlantic (CINCLANT) under the name of 'Scope Light' [9] with the 6th ACCS at Langley (Virginia), along with the sole EC-135H already attached to this command. One of their main missions consisted of serving as communication relays with the fleet of missile launching submarines, either directly or via the Lockheed EC-130Q or Boeing E-6A Mercury.

One of these planes (s/n 58-0007) was destroyed by a fire on the ground on 31 January 1980 and briefly replaced (between April and June 1984) by an NKC-135E flying test bed (s/n 55-3129) previously used as a 'Zero G' plane. Two EC-135P (s/n 58-0011 and 58-0018) were downgraded to KC-135A in 1976, whilst the two surviving aircraft were re-engined with the TF 33. All these aircraft were finally retired from service at the beginning of 1992 and sent to the open-air depot (AMARC) at Davis-Monthan.

EC-135Y

In 1983, a KC-135A (s/n 55-3125) which had been previously used as a test bed by Air Force Systems Command (AFSC) before being renamed NKC-135A, was transformed into an airborne command post for the US Army Central Command (CENTCOM) that had just been created for the coordination of United States military operations in the Middle and Near East.

Re-designated EC-135Y, this sole example was used by the SAC and based at Robins (Georgia) with the 19th ARW. Its test equipment had been removed and installed once more, notably destined for communications; the original refuelling boom was, however, retained. An in-flight refuelling receptacle was added by the LTV Company, whilst it received new engines (TF 33) in May 1986. During the Gulf War in 1990-91, the EC-135Y based at Riyadh (Saudi Arabia) and attached to the 1700th ARS (P), served amongst other things as an airborne command post with the commander of the American forces, General Norman Schwarzkopf, and was used occasionally as a tanker.

Forced to return to the United States for maintenance in March 1991 and was replaced in its role by EC-135N s/n 61-0327 (see above) used as a CINCENT airborne command post. After having been attached to the 91st ARS of the 6th ARW during the summer of 1997, this aircraft, unique in its type, was definitively retired from service at the beginning of 1999.

---

7. See also following chapter ' Flying test beds '.
8. S/n 58-007, 58-0011 and 58-0018.
9. S/n 55-3129, 58-0019, 580022 and 61-0274.

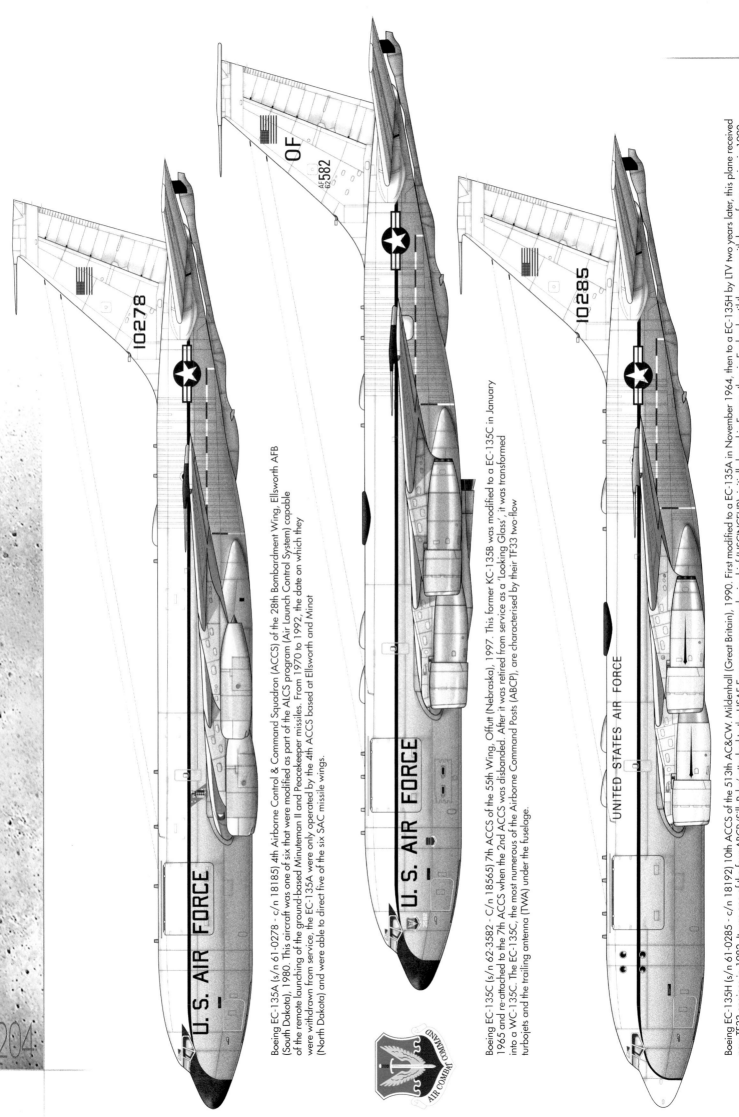

10278

AF
62 582

OF

10285

U.S. AIR FORCE

U.S. AIR FORCE

UNITED STATES AIR FORCE

AIR COMBAT COMMAND

Boeing EC-135A (s/n 61-0278 - c/n 18185) 4th Airborne Control & Command Squadron (ACCS) of the 28th Bombardment Wing, Ellsworth AFB (South Dakota), 1980. This aircraft was one of six that were modified as part of the ALCS program (Air Launch Control System) capable of the remote launching of the ground-based Minuteman II and Peacekeeper missiles. From 1970 to 1992, the date on which they were withdrawn from service, the EC-135A were only operated by the 4th ACCS based at Ellsworth and Minot (North Dakota) and were able to direct five of the six SAC missile wings.

Boeing EC-135C (s/n 62-3582 - C/n 18565) 7th ACCS of the 55th Wing, Offutt (Nebraska), 1997. This former KC-135B was modified to a EC-135C in January 1965 and re-attached to the 7th ACCS when the 2nd ACCS was disbanded. After it was retired from service as a 'Looking Glass', it was transformed into a WC-135C. The EC-135C, the most numerous of the Airborne Command Posts (ABCP), are characterised by their TF33 two-flow turbojets and the trailing antenna (TWA) under the fuselage.

Boeing EC-135H (s/n 61-0285 - c/n 18192) 10th ACCS of the 513th AC&CW. Mildenhall (Great Britain), 1990. First modified to a EC-135A in November 1964, then to a EC-135H by LTV two years later, this plane received new TF33 engines in 1982. It was one of the four ABCP 'Silk Pulse' attached to the USAF European commander in chief (USCINCEUR), initially based in France, then in England until they were withdrawn from service in 1992. The front tip of the fuselage, originally painted black, was repainted white after the engines were changed.

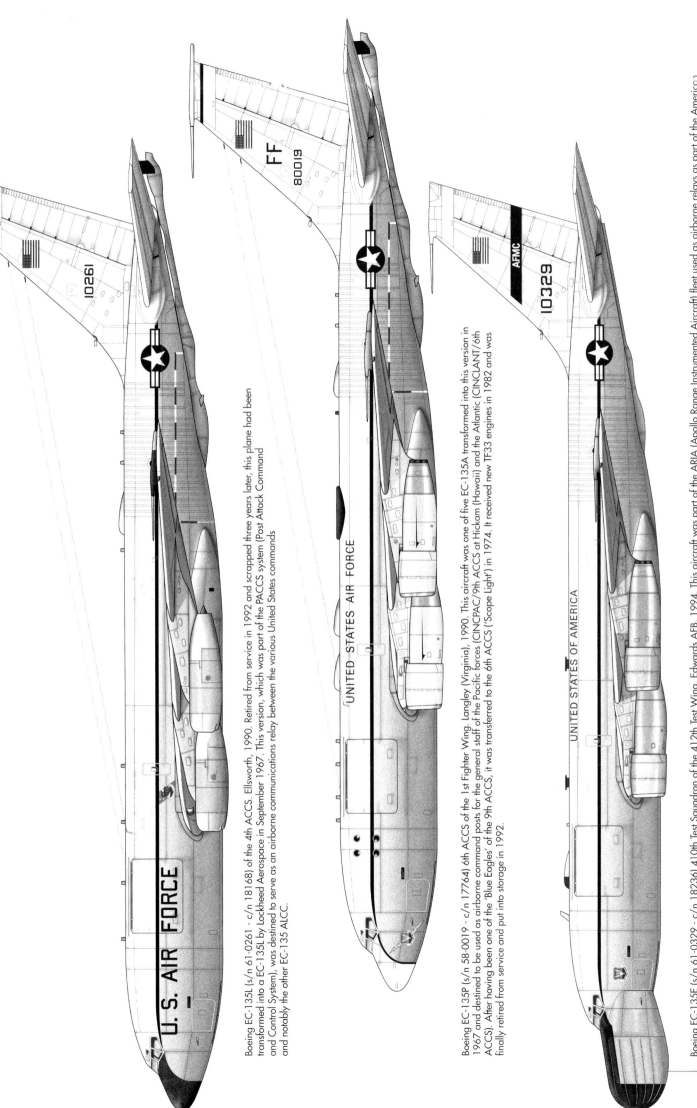

Boeing EC-135L (s/n 61-0261 - c/n 18168) of the 4th ACCS. Ellsworth, 1990. Retired from service in 1992 and scrapped three years later, this plane had been transformed into a EC-135L by Lockheed Aerospace in September 1967. This version, which was part of the PACCS system (Post Attack Command and Control System), was destined to serve as an airborne communications relay between the various United States commands and notably the other EC-135 ALCC.

Boeing EC-135P (s/n 58-0019 - c/n 17764) 6th ACCS of the 1st Fighter Wing. Langley (Virginia), 1990. This aircraft was one of five EC-135A transformed into this version in 1967 and destined to be used as airborne command posts for the general staff of the Pacific forces (CINCPAC/ 9th ACCS at Hickam (Hawaii) and the Atlantic (CINCLANT/6th ACCS). After having been one of the 'Blue Eagles' of the 9th ACCS, it was transferred to the 6th ACCS ('Scope Light') in 1974. It received new TF33 engines in 1982 and was finally retired from service and put into storage in 1992.

Boeing EC-135E (s/n 61-0329 - c/n 18236) 410th Test Squadron of the 412th Test Wing. Edwards AFB, 1994. This aircraft was part of the ARIA (Apollo Range Instrumented Aircraft) fleet used as airborne relays as part of the America space program. At the end of this program in 1972, the ARIA acronym was modified to Advanced Range Instrumented Aircraft and the plane was transferred to the 4950th TW at Wright-Patterson in December 1975. Modified once more, re-engined and re-named EC-135E, it served within numerous programs. In 1994 it was sent to the 412th TW at Edwards and was retired from service two years later in June 1996.

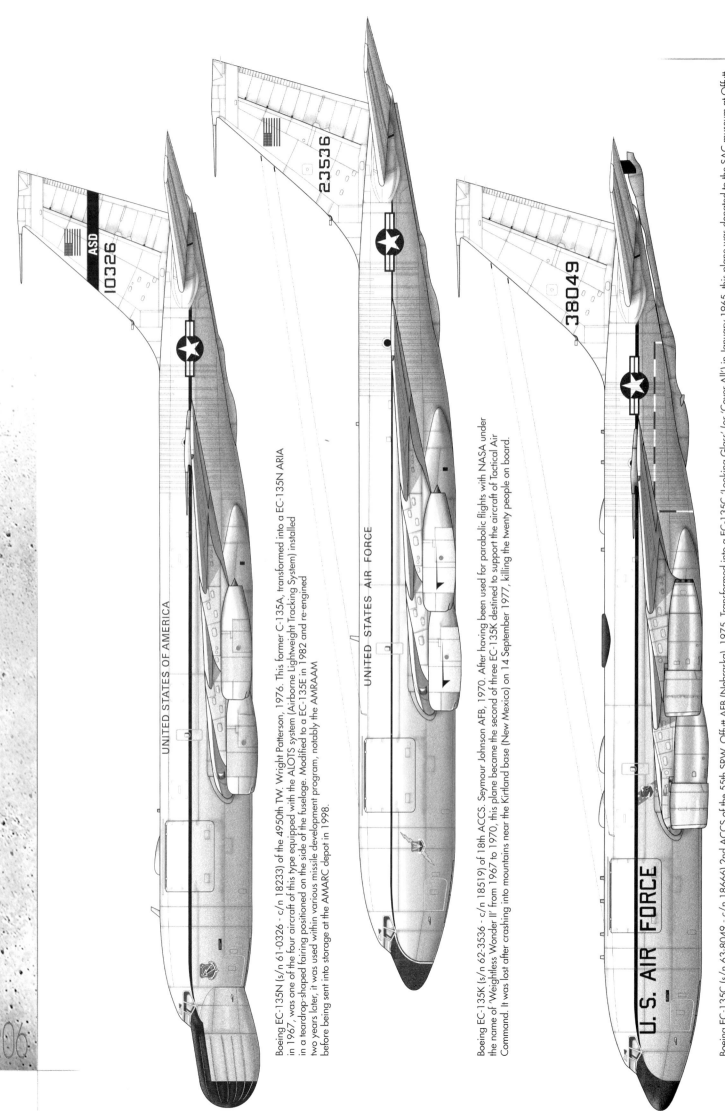

UNITED STATES OF AMERICA

10326 ASD

Boeing EC-135N (s/n 61-0326 - c/n 18233) of the 4950th TW. Wright Patterson, 1976. This former C-135A, transformed into a EC-135N ARIA in 1967, was one of the four aircraft of this type equipped with the ALOTS system (Airborne Lightweight Tracking System) installed in a teardrop-shaped fairing positioned on the side of the fuselage. Modified to a EC-135E in 1982 and re-engined two years later, it was used within various missile development program, notably the AMRAAM before being sent into storage at the AMARC depot in 1998.

UNITED STATES AIR FORCE

23536

Boeing EC-135K (s/n 62-3536 - c/n 18519) of 18th ACCS. Seymour Johnson AFB, 1970. After having been used for parabolic flights with NASA under the name of 'Weightless Wonder II' from 1967 to 1970, this plane became the second of three EC-135K destined to support the aircraft of Tactical Air Command. It was lost after crashing into mountains near the Kirtland base (New Mexico) on 14 September 1977, killing the twenty people on board.

38049

U.S. AIR FORCE

Boeing EC-135C (s/n 63-8049 - c/n 18666) 2nd ACCS of the 55th SRW. Offutt AFB (Nebraska), 1975. Transformed into a EC-135C 'Looking Glass' (or 'Cover All') in January 1965, this plane was donated to the SAC museum at Offutt at the end of its career where it is presently on display. After having initially been conserved with their lower surfaces covered with Coroguard, the EC-135 had their lower wing surfaces painted in gloss light grey (FS 16473). The upper areas of the fuselage were painted white, and like on commercial airliners, this was to reduce the internal temperature by deflecting sunrays.

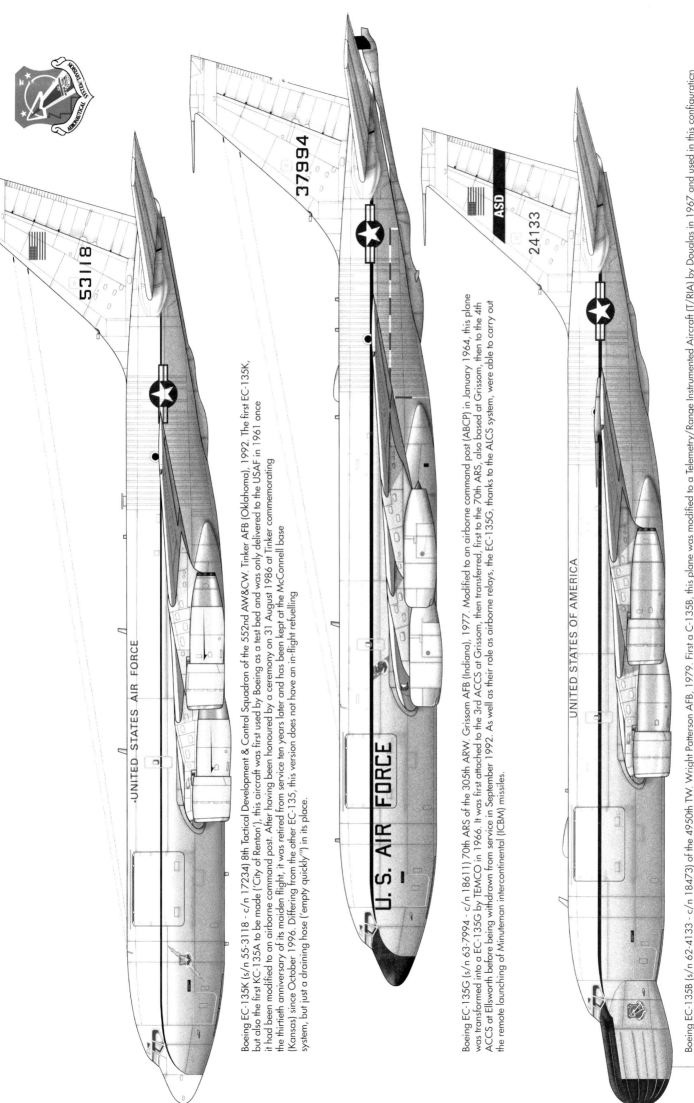

53118

UNITED STATES AIR FORCE

37994

U.S. AIR FORCE

ASD

24133

UNITED STATES OF AMERICA

Boeing EC-135K (s/n 55-3118 - c/n 17234) 8th Tactical Development & Control Squadron of the 552nd AW&CW. Tinker AFB (Oklahoma), 1992. The first EC-135K, but also the first KC-135A to be made ('City of Renton'), this aircraft was first used by Boeing as a test bed and was only delivered to the USAF in 1961 once it had been modified to an airborne command post. After having been honoured by a ceremony on 31 August 1986 at Tinker commemorating the thirtieth anniversary of its maiden flight, it was retired from service ten years later and has been kept at the McConnell base (Kansas) since October 1996. Differing from the other EC-135, this version does not have an in-flight refuelling system, but just a draining hose ('empty quickly'?) in its place.

Boeing EC-135G (s/n 63-7994 - c/n 18611) 70th ARS of the 305th ARW. Grissom AFB (Indiana), 1977. Modified to an airborne command post (ABCP) in January 1964, this plane was transformed into a EC-135G by TEMCO in 1966. It was first attached to the 3rd ACCS at Grissom, then transferred, first to the 70th ARS, also based at Grissom, then to the 4th ACCS at Ellsworth before being withdrawn from service in September 1992. As well as their role as airborne relays, the EC-135G, thanks to the ALCS system, were able to carry out the remote launching of Minuteman intercontinental (ICBM) missiles.

Boeing EC-135B (s/n 62-4133 - c/n 18473) of the 4950th TW. Wright Patterson AFB, 1979. First a C-135B, this plane was modified to a Telemetry/Range Instrumented Aircraft (T/RIA) by Douglas in 1967 and used in this configuration until 1971. Transformed next to a EC-135B ARIA after having been given the equipment of a EC-135N (s/n 60-0375), it had TF33 two-flow engines, whereas the EC-135N used the lower performance J57. Stripped of its front radar bulge and having become a destined for training the TC-135S 'Cobra Ball' fleet without any on board equipment, it is presently in service with the 55th Wing, as a RC-135W.

207

FLYING TEST BEDS

Out of the hundreds of KC-135 that were made, a small number were used almost from the beginning as flying test beds for the elaboration of all sorts of equipment, these often being later fitted to production aircraft.

At the beginning, this fleet was made up of sixteen KC-135A taken from the first examples to leave the factory and which were not delivered to operational units, but mainly used by the Air Research and Development Command (ARDC), the USAF command responsible for trials of new weapons and equipment in real conditions. These aircraft were rapidly given an extra prefix to distinguish them [1]; however, each one was attached to a type of trial or specific mission that it carried out for several decades and some are still in service today. For this reason, none of these JKC/NKC-135 had an identical and unchanging configuration, the airframes being adapted according to the needs of the moment.

The on-board equipment, the exact nature of which is still secret today, or at least not very well known, could vary and has been what led to the appearance on the fuselage of radomes, bossing up or all sorts of and various amounts of antenna. To these planes we must add a certain number of others that were modified with a particular objective in mind, notably in order to take part in a particular program such as the Apollo space missions amongst others.

The specialised test beds

As with the other types of specialised missions, the KC-135 was chosen to serve as a research platform due to its high performance (at the beginning of the sixties in any case), its spacious cabin that could take, notably thanks to its cargo door, a large amount of voluminous equipment, but also because of the amount of power produced by its electronic system which was indispensable for the electronic equipment that used up so much energy. Other advantages gained by using this four-engined Boeing were the airframe to which all sorts of additions of all shapes and sizes could be added (bosses, fairings, etc.), as well

Above.
In 1979, NKC-135A (s/n 55-3129) was attached to the NASA research centre at Dryden and was equipped with a measuring boom on the nose as well as a large size insignia on the tail fin. The previous year, it had been used for testing the wingtip winglets that were never mounted on production models despite having proved their efficiency.
(NASA).

1. JKC-135, the letter J indicates the temporary test character of the plane (Special Test Status, Temporary), a few years later this prefix was replaced by another NKC-135A (N for Special Test Status, Permanent) when these planes were considered as being purely test beds and that their reconversion to tankers was deemed too costly.

Below.
JKC-135A s/n 55-3124 photographed in 1958, whilst being used by the NACA, the ancestor of today's NASA, for various tests. This function is symbolised by the measuring boom added to the front.
(NASA).

Opposite.
NKC-135A s/n 55-3123 in its first configuration, carrying the ALOTS telescope system in its dorsal fairing. (WingMasters archives).

Below.
NKC-135E s/n 55-3132 'Big Crow' was used operationally for electronic warfare missions during operation 'Iraqi Freedom' in 2003. (USAF)

as the maintenance which was helped by the excellent availability of spare parts. After having been used by both Boeing and the USAF for tests, most of the planes in the flying test bed fleet were attached to the Flight and All Weather Test Division at the Wright Air Development Center (WADC), a section of the ARDC based at Wright-Patterson responsible for various projects.

In 1963, the ARDC became the Air Force System Command (AFSC) which was itself integrated into the AFLC (Air Force Logistics Command) in July 1992 in order to form today's Air Force Materiel Command (AFMC). As well as this main role, some aircraft were also used as test beds by other USAF services within the framework of specific programs.

In 1975, the whole fleet was reorganised within the framework of the 'Have Car' program of the 'Realign' project, and placed under the control of the 4950th Test Wing at Wright-Patterson, which was also given the ARIA and T/RIA aircraft (see following paragraph); some NKC-135 were eventually attached to other bases. With the unit having moved to Edwards in California in 1994, there were only six test beds still in service in 2007, with only one original NKC-135A which was renamed NKC-135E after having been re-engined.

s/n 55-3119

The second KC-135A to be made, this aircraft was sent to Wright-Patterson in July 1958 and re-designated shortly after to JKC-135A. Attached, the following year, to the RADC (Rome Air Development Center) at Griffis (New York State), it was mostly used for electronic counter measure research. Stripped of its refuelling boom in May 1962 when it was renamed NKC-135A, it lost its test bed status in September 1983 and was transformed into a support aircraft for the General Staff of the 55th SRW based at Offutt. This 'demotion' was made possible by the slight transformations that it had undergone beforehand.

s/n 55-3120

Specialised in the identification of infrared signatures, this JKC-135A was given a lot of fuselage windows which were at the origin

209

Opposite.
*After having begun its career as a 'Zero G' plane, NASA
began using NKC-135A s/n 55-3129 in December 1978.
Equipped with winglets, it carried out forty flights between
1978 and 1981 to test out this system that economised on
fuel, but which finally was not retained on this type of
aircraft. Photographed here at Edwards in October 1980,
it was later transformed into an EC-135P airborne
command post before definitively being put into storage in
January 1992.*
(WingMasters Archives).

*Reattached to the 'Recce Strike' program at the
end of 1963, NKC-135A s/n 55-3132 received
a fairing containing the special equipment at the
front right hand side of its fuselage.*
(V. Gréciet collection)

2. The FISTA program began in 1961 and was
originally intended to study the infra-red pro-
perties of nuclear explosions in the atmosphere.
After this type of test was forbidden, the program was modified and given the task of studying
the infrared characteristics of aircraft (detection,
identification from bases situated in the atmosphere, or space) and responsible for measuring
and studying the infrared characteristics of aircraft
(detection, identification from bases located in
the atmosphere, even in space) and, consequently, the influence of different types of paint
on the infrared signature of an aircraft.

of its different nicknames, the most frequently used being 'Flying
Piccolo' or 'Piccolo Tube'. In 1963, it took part in a research
program on the variations in the Earth's gravity and the exact shape
of the Earth that aimed at increasing the precision of intercontinental
ballistic missiles. In 1967, it became specialised in infrared signatures and was capable of differentiating between decoys or natural
phenomenon and real missiles re-entering the atmosphere.

This role became official in 1975
when it became part of the FISTA
system (Flying Infrared Signatures and

Technology Aircraft) [2]. Stripped of its refuelling boom in 1973, the
FISTA I was retired from service twenty years later in 1993 after thirty
years of loyal service. Its research equipment was then installed on
board FISTA II, the NKC-135E s/n 55-3135 that was declared
operational in 1995.

s/n 55-3121

Delivered in April 1957 to the WADC, this plane was first used
for the study of KC-135A all-weather flights, then for artificial icing
trials; a system was installed that could vaporise frozen water using

Below.
*Used from 1963 onwards in a
research program concerning the
transmission of radio waves and
equipped to this end with two radomes
containing cameras, NKC-135A s/n
55-3131 was used between
December 1979 and February 1981
for compatibility tests with the airborne
AWACS radar system later used on the
Boeing E-3 Sentry.*
(WingMasters archives).

JKC-135A s/n 55-3132 was modified by LTV in 1962 for testing the electronic reconnaissance equipment that preceded the future RC-135. It is seen here at the beginning of its career, still equipped with its short tail fin and with fairings mounted on the 'cheeks' and below the fuselage. (V. Gréciet collection)

Above.
Attached to Detachment 2 of the 418th FLTS, NKC-135E s/n 55-3132 was used as a target plane as part of the ABL airborne laser program installed on a Boeing E-4 (the military designation of the 747 Jumbo Jet). It bears the silhouette of a missile at the black painted front left hand side of the fuselage. The wing's leading edge and engine pods are also painted black. (USAF)

Below.
Having lost one of its engines during a flight on 5 February 1975, NKC-135A s/n 55-3132 was repaired and equipped with an in-flight refuelling receptacle and new engines. It is seen here at the beginning of the 1980s after having been given a camouflage scheme and new fairings at the front of the fuselage, in one of the many configurations used throughout its career as a test bed.
(WingMasters archives)

the rear boom. Modified in 1961-62 in order to take part in the 'Speed Light' program that researched Soviet atmospheric nuclear tests, it was given a series of extra antenna on its fuselage at the end of 1964 before being re-designated to JKC-135A in March the following year. It lost its flying test bed status in June 1967 and then became one of the reconnaissance KC-135R that preceded the RC-135, within the 55th Strategic Reconnaissance Wing at Offutt.

s/n 55-3122

Designated as JKC-135A from 1958 onwards, this aircraft was initially used for researching electronic counter measures (quick reaction capacity or QRC) and lost its refuelling boom and most of its fuselage fuel tanks. A radome made its appearance, containing counter measure detectors and the aft point was given a fairing that held the infrared alert detectors. In order to validate the on-board equipment, it was used as a 'target' during several authentic missile launches, that were, however, not given live warheads…

In 1969, it became a NKC-135A and was used for different electronic defence tests and was later used, in 1984, for the flight tests of the General Electrics F118-GE-100 engine that would be

used on the future B-2 Spirit, an engine equipped with a system that eliminated any atmospheric vapour trails. After being equipped with the MILSTAR satellite navigation system in 1990, this plane was definitively retired from service in 1993.

s/n 55-3123

This JKC-135A was mainly used within the framework of the ALOTS program (Airborne Lightweight Optical Tracking System) designed by Northrop. Its cargo door was equipped with a pylon-mounted pod containing an optical device. The fuselage had an observation dome that allowed for the optical pursuit of flying objects, notably missiles. For a while, the ALOTS was the largest airborne telescope with a diameter of 0.55 m and a focal length of more than 5 m. The telescope was served by a 70 mm rapid view camera and two television cameras. It then became one of the main test beds for the HEL airborne laser (High Energy Laser), renamed the ALL (Airborne Laser Laboratory) in 1977. This machine was used for defence as well as attack in the atmosphere and beyond, and was installed in a parallelepipedal fairing (often called 'canoe') placed at the front of the fuselage that also contained the optical devises of the tracking equipment. These systems used a lot of energy and the aircraft's jet engines were equipped with generators like those of on the B-52. The laser itself functioned with the help of cryogenic fuel and was installed in the centre of the fuselage; communication between the front and rear of the latter was not possible. The first trials of the 'flying laser' began at the beginning of May 1981 and a Sidewinder missile was destroyed during one of these tests. This aircraft was retired from service in May 1984.

s/n 55-3124

After having been used for tests with the NACA until 1958, this aircraft, redesignated JKC-135A, was modified by Bendix in 1962 as part of the 'Skyscraper' project aimed at tracking and recording objects re-entering the atmosphere. To this end, various equip-

ment was attached to its cargo door. In 1969, it became a NKC-135A and joined the fleet of test planes at Wright- Patterson in 1974. It took part in many programs, notably that which developed the AARB (Advanced Air Refuelling Boom) destined for the future KC-10 Extender. From 1991, it was used a ground training airframe at Sheppard (Texas) under the designation of GNKC-135. It was finally scrapped in 2000.

s/n 55-3125

Used for trials with NACA (the ancestor of NASA) as a JKC-135A, this plane was damaged on 12 November 1957 and replaced by its immediate predecessor, s/n 55-3124. Once repaired, it was used in different series of trials concerning electronic counter measures with the RADC. Re-designated as a NKC-135A in 1969, it was finally transformed into a flying command post in 1983, becoming the only EC-135Y attached to the US Army Central Command.

s/n 55-3127

Renamed JKC-135A in 1959, this plane was mainly used for research concerning the re-entry into the atmosphere of various objects, notably spatial, and more particularly for the radiation emitted by them in the final phase of flight. To this end, it was equipped with a fuselage fairing and two windows on the left side for the optical devices.

The upper wing surfaces and the internal side of the engines were painted black on this side to avoid any reflection. From 1980, it was used in different campaigns destined to improve the in-flight refuel-

ling performance of the KC-135. It notably received extra wing tip pods equipped with supple hoses as well as a light on top of the tail fin, a system that was already in use on the KC-135Q and which was later added to all the surviving Stratotankers.

Having been given an enlarged nose in 1986, similar to that on the production RC-135, the plane was retired from service in August 1992 after having been used one last time for the observation of an artificially created aurora borealis in the atmosphere.

it became an 'icing tanker', used for artificial icing tests on various types of aircraft.

A special 4,000 gallon (15 140 litres) was installed and its boom reinstalled for the vaporisation of frozen liquid.

s/n 55-3129

This plane began its career by carrying out parabolic 'zero-G' flights destined to achieve weightlessness during a short lapse of time [3]. To this end, all of the cabin was equipped with extra padding to avoid any accidents when returning to normal gravity. In 1968, it was re-designated to NKC-135A and became a laboratory for testing on board avionics, with notably a special fairing added to

s/n 55-3128

This aircraft, designated JKC-135A in 1958, also took part in the trials of electronic counter measure equipment after having been stripped of its refuelling boom and equipped with various fairings. Beginning in 1964, and until it was retired from service in May 1996,

its fuselage. It was also used as test bed for winglets in 1978. This system, despite its efficiency (an 8% reduction in fuel consumption), was finally never installed on the production KC-135. Attached to the NASA research centre at Dryden in 1979, it remained there until 1981 and was given, at this time, a fixed boom

3. As well as the JKC-135A 'Zero G' (s/n 55-3129), rapidly named 'Weightless Wonder' (and more trivially 'Vomit Comet'), three KC-135A were used by the USAF for parabolic flights before this mission was given to NASA's Reduced Gravity Office in August 1973. From August 1973 to October 2004, KC-135A s/n 62-3536 ('Weightless Wonder II'), 60-0378 ('Weightless Wonder III'), 59-1481 ('Weightless Wonder IV') and 63-7998 ('Weightless Wonder V', used between September 1995 and October 2004), were given the role of these weightlessness training missions for future astronauts. A normal mission lasted three hours, during which thirty to forty parabolic flights were carried out; the duration of the latter depending on the gravity reproduced, 'lunar' (1/6 of earth's gravity) or 'Martian' (1/3). In all, the Boeing 'Zero Gravity' carried out more than 80,000 parabolic flights from the beginning of the Mercury program until that of the ISS international space station.

As well as these missions, the NASA KC-135 aircraft were used for various experiments and notably used as support aircraft for the space shuttle (training crews in how to handle 'heavy' aircraft, taking the crews back if they landed at bases other than those originally planned for) and were, amongst other things, used as 'pathfinders' for the 747 that carried the space shuttle between Edwards (California) and Cape Canaveral (Florida). This was to avoid bad weather which could have damaged the ceramic tiles on the shuttle's lower wing surfaces.

Opposite.
Used for testing counter measure equipment, s/n 56-3596 was the first NKC-135A to be specially modified before being to transferred to the US Navy in 1975 where it was designated 'King Crow II' and attributed the BuNo 563596.
(WingMasters archives)

on its nose as well as strengthened wings. Re-engined in 1982 with TF33 turbofans, it was attached to the 6th SW at Eielson for the training of crews before finally being transformed in 1984 to a EC-135P for the commander in chief of the Atlantic forces (CINCLANT).

s/n 55-3131

When it became a JKC-135A, this aircraft was used for research into the effects of nuclear explosions in the ionosphere, and notably the radiation emitted. It was officially named the AIO (Airborne Ionospheric Observatory) in 1965 and equipped with domes on the fuselage, notably containing optical equipment such as 35 mm cameras. It took part in the trials for the E-3 Sentry until 1981 and was finally retired from service in October 1992.

s/n 55-3132

Designated JKC-135A in March 1960 and based at Wright-Patterson, this aircraft was very soon renamed NKC-135A and used as a flying laboratory in the programs for the elaboration of electronic reconnaissance programs such as the 'Recce Strike Program' in 1963 for which it was given a fairing on the right hand side of the fuselage as well as an extra cooling scoop.

In 1973 it was transferred to the Kirkland base and was involved in the 'Big Crow' program where it had to reproduce the electronic signature of a great number of aircraft, as well as the calibration of systems. To this end, it underwent a great many configurations (canoe fairing on the fuselage, different shaped nose and tail, carrying stations under the wings between the fuselage and the interior engines for the CME pods or decoy launchers, etc.).

In 1986, in order to give it sufficient autonomy, despite a reduced amount of fuel carried, it was equipped with an in-flight refuelling receptacle, most of its fuel tanks having been removed in order to gain space. At the beginning of 1991, it received new TF33 engines and was renamed NKC-135E and used for electronic warfare

missions during the Gulf War from its base at Dubai. As this book goes to press, it is still based at Kirtland and attached to Detachment 2 of the 418th FLTS.

s/n 55-3134

Attached to the Wright Patterson base in September 1958 just as it had been designated JKC-135A, this plane was part, two years later, of the TRAP program (Terminal Radiation Program) after having undergone the necessary modifications (dorsal fairing, eleven round windows added to the fuselage by Martin). In 1965, it was once again modified, this time by the E-Systems Company, with the addition of two lateral hatches to the left of the fuselage fairing. In 1967 it became a NKC-135A and was transferred to US Navy in May 1978, where it became the second aircraft of this type specialised in scrambling techniques in electronic warfare with the FEWSG (Fleet Electronic Warfare Support Group) at Norfolk, Virginia. Named 'Navy King Crow I', and its serial number having been changed to BuNo. 553 134.

As laid down by the regulations in use with the US Navy, it underwent various configurations in its new role depending on the

Above.
NC-135A s/n 60-0371 was used beginning in 1964 with the 'Rivet Digger' program for gathering data after a nuclear explosion. Much of the equipment was installed in a 'Canoe' fairing placed at the front of the fuselage. (WingMasters archives).

Below.
King Crow II, NKC-135 seen from another angle. We can make out the extra pylon placed between the two engines used for carrying loads or various equipment. (USAF)

4. s/n 63-0369 to 63-0372, 60-0376 and 60-0377. The fleet of these aircraft also comprised NC-135B (s/n 61-2662).

Opposite.
As with all the other military Boeings, the EC-135 ARIA like this 60-0372, were left in bare metal and were only camouflaged later in their career.
(USAF)

Above.
When taking part in the tests on the airborne laser ALL, several markings were painted on the front left hand side of NC-135A s/n 60-0371. The insignia painted under the cockpit is that of the ASD (Aeronautical Systems Division).
(USAF)

trials undertaken (different shaped noses and equipped with a search radar, covered fuselage windows, new sabre antenna on and under the fuselage, extra generators added to the engines and similar to those on the J/NKC-135A attached to the airborne laser program, as well as extra carrying stations added under the wings). Once these trials were over, this aircraft was deemed too expensive to keep airworthy and it was retired from service in February 1996, after having seen more than a quarter of a century of service!

s/n 55-3135

Characterised by its fifty open windows on the right hand side of the fuselage, this JKC-135A began its career as part of the trials concerning atomic alert procedures (ORSEP). In 1970, it was

135E. It was given the equipment removed from 'FISTA I' (NKC-135A s/n 55-3120) when the latter was retired from service in 1993. It was then used as a flying test bed for the elaboration of electronic counter measure systems that were part of the 'Big Crow' program. In 1995, it was declared operational in its new role, and 'FISTA II' thus took part in elaboration of future aircraft equipped with the smallest possible electronic signature, before finally being retired from service in 2004.

s/n 56-3596

This aircraft that became 'Navy King Crow II' in 1975 in fact began its career at Wright-Patterson as a KC-135A and was very quickly equipped with a AN/APS 73 side-looking radar placed

Stripped of its dorsal fairing in 1977, NC-135A s/n 60-0371 was used as a test bed for the airborne laser ALL until 1984.
(WingMasters archives).

Below.
Transformed into a C-135B T/RIA by Douglas in 1967, s/n 62-4128 retained its characteristic nose, even after the end of this program in 1971. It was then used as a test bed for various programs before becoming a RC-135X between July 1983 and July 1989.
(WingMasters archives)

renamed NKC-135A and had a radical change of role as it was specialised in the gathering of data concerning in-flight refuelling procedures, notably for all the new types of aircraft (fixed wing or rotary) put into service by the USAF, like, for example, the F-22 Raptor. For this, thirty of its cabin windows were removed, whilst measuring equipment was installed, taking the place of the fuselage fuel tanks that were removed.

In May 1982, it received new TF33 engines and became a NKC-

in a special profiled fairing as part of the 'Recce Strike' program. It was then, despite what its name might suggest, the first NKC-135A delivered to the US Navy who notably used it for electronic warfare missions and more particularly for the development of the Aegis anti aircraft missile system, being used here as protection and electronic scrambler. Its career with the US Navy was longer than that of its counterpart as 'King Crow II' was retired from service in June 1995. [4]

s/n 59-1491

Out of the whole fleet of flying test beds, this aircraft had the shortest career. It was first used as a support plane with the TRAP program for studying radiation whilst it was still only a KC-135A. In 1961 it was attached to the 'Nancy Rae' program for the development of an optical system to observe Soviet missile tests, and for this role it was based in the Aleutians. Renamed JKC-135A in February 1962, it was transferred to the Strategic Air Command at the beginning of the following year and became the first RC-135S 'Rivet Ball' to be lost in an accident on 13 January 1969.

This is, for example, the case of six C-135A which were transformed into NC-135A by General Dynamics starting in 1964. After the international treaty signed the following year which banned atmospheric nuclear testing, the first three of these aircraft (60-0369 to 60-0371), were kept on permanent alert and attached to the AFSC for analysing any real or supposed atomic explosion.

Equipped with sixteen round windows on the right hand side of the fuselage (on s/n 60-0370, they were, on the other hand, placed on the left near the cargo door so that the aircraft could fly in the opposite way to the others or in parallel) and a fairing containing electromagnetic detectors installed over the front of the fuselage, these planes had no markings (roundels, stencils) on the upper wing surfaces and the inside areas of the pods of the corresponding engines.

In order to collect the optical and spectrum data and analyse radiation, the 'Rivet Dagger', as they were named, orbited in a clockwise direction around the area of an explosion.

These surveillance missions ended in 1976 and two aircraft were retired from service; however, the third (s/n 60-0371) was not retired until 1994 after having been used in different military or scientific programs (studying eclipses, observing comets or cosmic rays).

For the 'Pacer Clerk' program, the Federal Aviation Administration (FAA) used two KC-135A for certifying air routes at high altitude. Registered as 'N96', the first (s/n 59-1518), named 'Old Smoky' because of its particularly polluting engines, was based at Hickam (Hawaii) and was used to aid navigation over the Pacific before

Other programs, other aircraft

As previously stated, apart from the sixteen aircraft that were used as flying test beds almost as soon as they left the production lines, other C/KC-135 also served within specific programs and for quite long periods of time, some still being in service today.

Below.
Delivered to the USAF in 1961 as C-135A, le s/n 60-0374, it became a EC-135N (ARIA) in 1966. Amongst other things, it took part in AG-129A cruise missile tests.
(WingMasters archives)

5. 61-0331, 62-4128, 62-4133 and 61-2664 (in 1968).
6. s/n 60-0372, 60-0374, 60-0375, 61-0326 to 61-0330.
7. 61-0328 was lost after a crash in May 1981. S/n 61-0372 and 61-0375 were modified to NC-135E. Finally, s/n 61-0327 was stripped of its special equipment and became an airborne command post (ABCP), but still kept its original designation for the Central Command (CINCCENT) along with EC-135Y s/n 55-3125.
8. s/n 61-0331, 61-2664, 62-4128 and 62-4133.

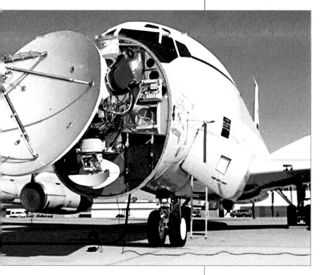

Above.
The radome has been removed from this EC-135N A/RIA 5 (Apollo/Range Instrumented Aircraft) baring the 2.10 m (7 ft) swivelling parabolic antenna installed on these aircraft.
(USAF)

Below.
This side view allows us to make out, apart from the special markings painted at the front, the characteristic shape of the nose of C-135B (T/RIA) s/n 62-4128, lengthened by more than three metres and installed in 1967. After having undergone various configurations and participated in several programs, this plane finally became the sole RC-135X; one of the its specific capacities being its ability to carry out observation on both sides, something the standard 'Cobra Ball' could not do.
(WingMasters archives)

being transformed into a EC-135K airborne command post.

The second aircraft used by the FAA (s/n 59-1481), was a former NASA 'Zero G' (Weightless Wonder IV) which was retired from service in 1996. NC-135W (s/n 61-2666) began its career as a C-135B before joining the WC-135B weather reconnaissance fleet. In May 1995, it was modified to a WC-135W as part of the 'Big Safari' program.

Outwardly resembling a rivet joint with its widened nose, its fuselage fairings (these 'cheeks' being, in fact, fake as they contained no equipment), it received this designation in 2000 and is still used today for the design and development of electronic equipment with the Raytheon E-Systems Company. NKC-135C (s/n 63-8050) was a former EC-135C airborne command post that in 1993, was initially attached to the HEL/ALL airborne laser program. Renamed NKC-135B in October 1996, it was used as a test bed for electronic countermeasure and scrambling systems for new radars in a real electronic warfare environment and earned its current designation. In theory never used in operations, this NKC-135C was, nevertheless, deployed from Ouran during operation 'Iraqi Freedom' in 2003, carrying out electronic warfare support missions.

Equipped with a bulbous nose, various antenna, extra carrying stations under the wings and rectangular canoe fairings, it has also kept its original refuelling boom. In 2006, it became one of the 'targets' for the new (ABL) YAL-1A airborne laser designed by Boeing. At this time, the black painted left hand side at the front of the fuselage was decorated with the white silhouette of a missile.

ARIA and TRIA

In the sixties and seventies, several C-135B and EC-18B (former civil Boeing 707-320) were modified in order to participate in various American space programs. Indeed, it was in the early sixties that NASA and the American Defence department expressed the desire to have a very mobile pursuit and telemetry platform as part of the Apollo program and other unusual flights.

The planes chosen had to serve as radio relays between the space capsule and the flight director based at Houston (Texas), whilst at the same time collecting different data and participating in recovering the craft after they had landed in the sea.

At the beginning, the fleet should have comprised of twelve aircraft of this type, a number that was finally reduced to eight. The four remaining aircraft [5] were transformed into the C-135B TRIA. Douglas and Bendix were, therefore, given the task of modifying eight C-135A to EC-135N A/RIA [6] (Apollo/Range Instrumented

Aircraft) equipped with a bulbous nose, a particular prominent and characteristic neck (3 m/10 ft long), that was rapidly named 'Droop Snoot' or 'Snoopy Nose'. Four of them were also equipped with the ALOTS pursuit system previously tried out on JKC-135A s/n 55-3123, this equipment being carried in a pod mounted on the left side of the fuselage.

The EC-135N were declared operational in January 1968 with the 6549th Test Squadron integrated into the Air Force Eastern Test Range at the Patrick base in Florida. The first ARIA mission took place during the Apollo VIII mission in 1968 and saw the involvement of eight aircraft; three based in Bermuda, two at Hickam (Hawaii), and three in Florida. The ARIA flew over the Atlantic when Saturn V was launched, then over the Pacific when the capsule returned. A single aircraft was able to cover an area of 13,000 km^2 (5,020 sq miles) of ocean which made possible a great reduction in the amount of specialised ships (ARIS for Apollo Range Instrumented Ships) in the surveillance of space missions.

A standard mission lasted for approximately ten hours and was only limited by the amount of fuel carried as the EC-135N could not be refuelled in flight, whilst the usual crew was made up of 23 men.

In 1972, at the end of the Apollo program, the ARIA acronym was modified to signify from now on, Advanced Range Instrumented Aircraft, the planes being transferred to the 4950th Test Wing of Wright-Patterson en December 1975 where they were underwent significant modifications (new engines etc.) and served, under the new designation of EC-135E, as test planes in many new programs (development of ballistic or cruise missiles, design of the future space shuttle for example). The surviving aircraft [7] were sent to Edwards in 1994 where they served with the 412th TW. However, they were considered too expensive to maintain and were transferred to other programs, notably that of Joint Stars.

On 3 November 2000, the last EC-135E (s/n 60-0374) remaining in service was retired and displayed at the museum of the Wright-Patterson base.

As we have already seen, four C-135B [8] were modified to the EC-135B T/RIA (Telemetry Range Instrumented Aircraft) by Douglas Aircraft Co's Modification Division at Tulsa (Oklahoma) in 1967 and used by the AFSC from Patrick base as support for the EC-135N ARIA, mainly in telecommunications. Outwardly, these planes looked like the EC-135N, notably with an identical nose; on the other hand, none of them received the ALOTS system. They remained for a very short time in this configuration as the first (s/n 61-0331) had its characteristic bulbous nose removed and disappeared following its crash into the Pacific on 13 June 1971 when it was part of the 4950th TW at Wright-Patterson.

The second EC-135B (61-2664) was modified en RC-135S and was also lost in an accident, whilst the third (s/n 61-4128) became the sole RC-135X. As for the last T/RIA (s/n 62-4133), it was transformed to a TC-135S training aircraft.

24128

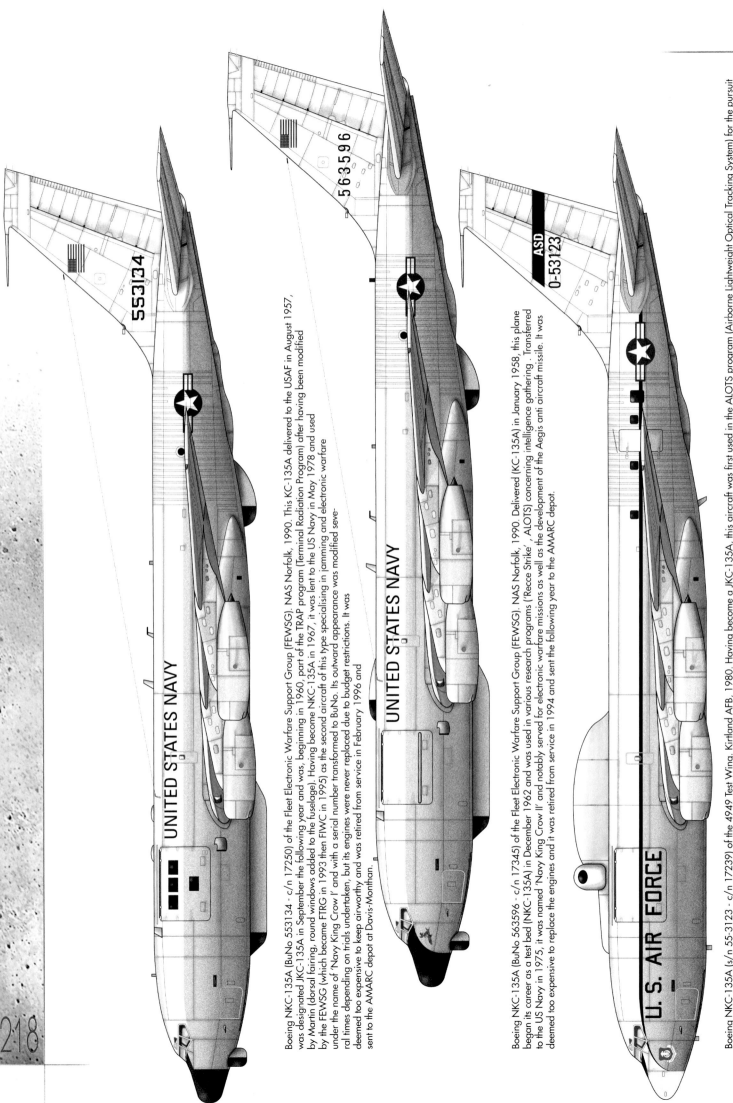

553134

Boeing NKC-135A (BuNo 553134 - c/n 17250) of the Fleet Electronic Warfare Support Group (FEWSG). NAS Norfolk, 1990. This KC-135A delivered to the USAF in August 1957, was designated JKC-135A in September the following year and was, beginning in 1960, part of the TRAP program (Terminal Radiation Program) after having been modified by Martin (dorsal fairing, round windows added to the fuselage). Having become NKC-135A in 1967, it was lent to the US Navy in May 1978 and used by the FEWSG (which became FTRG in 1993 then FIWC in 1995) as the second aircraft of this type specialising in jamming and electronic warfare under the name of 'Navy King Crow I' and with a serial number transformed to BuNo. Its outward appearance was modified several times depending on trials undertaken, but its engines were never replaced due to budget restrictions. It was deemed too expensive to keep airworthy and was retired from service in February 1996 and sent to the AMARC depot at Davis-Monthan.

563596

Boeing NKC-135A (BuNo 563596 - c/n 17345) of the Fleet Electronic Warfare Support Group (FEWSG). NAS Norfolk, 1990. Delivered (KC-135A) in January 1958, this plane began its career as a test bed (NKC-135A) in December 1962 and was used in various research programs ('Recce Strike', ALOTS) concerning intelligence gathering. Transferred to the US Navy in 1975, it was named 'Navy King Crow II' and notably served for electronic warfare missions as well as the development of the Aegis anti aircraft missile. It was deemed too expensive to replace the engines and it was retired from service in 1994 and sent the following year to the AMARC depot.

ASD
0-53123

Boeing NKC-135A (s/n 55-3123 - c/n 17239) of the 4949 Test Wing. Kirtland AFB, 1980. Having become a JKC-135A, this aircraft was first used in the ALOTS program (Airborne Lightweight Optical Tracking System) for the pursuit of rockets and missiles, before becoming one of the main test beds for the airborne laser HEL (High Energy Laser, then ALL - Airborne Laser Laboratory - in 1977) under the designation NKC-135A. Retired from service in May 1984, it was then transferred to the Wright Patterson base where it has been kept at the USAF museum since 1988.

218

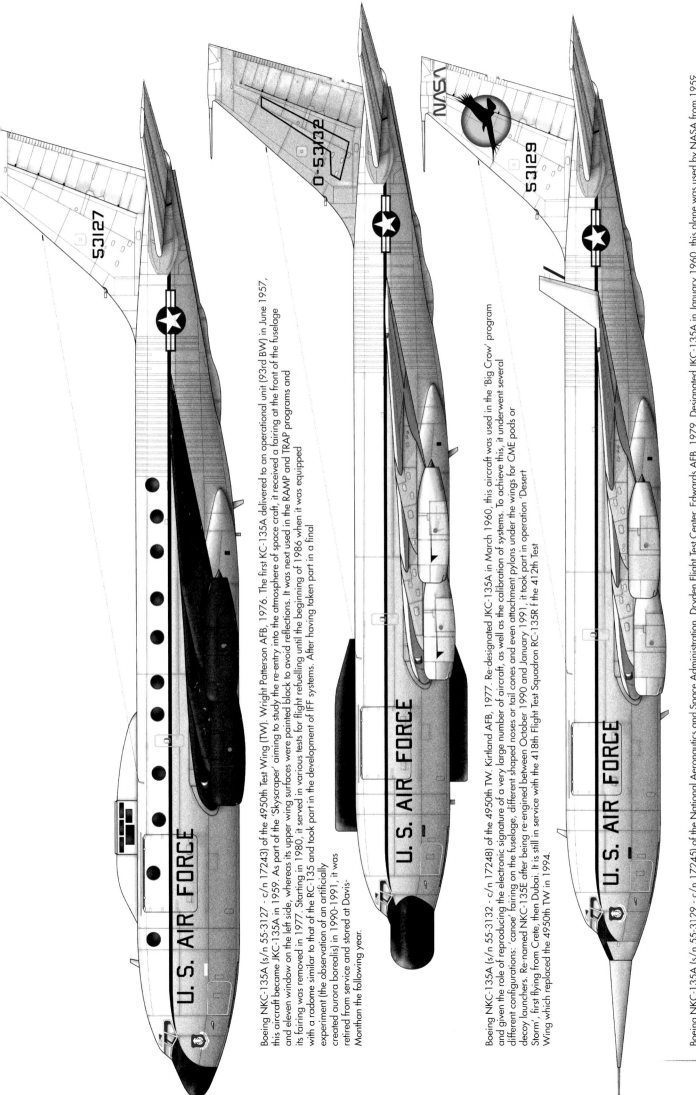

53127

Boeing NKC-135A (s/n 55-3127 - c/n 17243) of the 4950th Test Wing (TW). Wright Patterson AFB, 1976. The first KC-135A delivered to an operational unit (93rd BW) in June 1957, this aircraft became JKC-135A in 1959. As part of the 'Skyscraper' aiming to study the re-entry into the atmosphere of space craft, it received a fairing at the front of the fuselage and eleven window on the left side, whereas its upper wing surfaces were painted black to avoid reflections. It was next used in the RAMP and TRAP programs and its fairing was removed in 1977. Starting in 1980, it served in various tests for flight refuelling until the beginning of 1986 when it was equipped with a radome similar to that of the RC-135 and took part in the development of IFF systems. After having taken part in a final experiment (the observation of an artificially created aurora borealis) in 1990-1991, it was retired from service and stored at Davis-Monthan the following year.

O-53132

Boeing NKC-135A (s/n 55-3132 - c/n 17248) of the 4950th TW. Kirtland AFB, 1977. Re-designated JKC-135A in March 1960, this aircraft was used in the 'Big Crow' program and given the role of reproducing the electronic signature of a very large number of aircraft, as well as the calibration of systems. To achieve this, it underwent several different configurations: 'canoe' fairing on the fuselage, different shaped noses or tail cones and even attachment pylons under the wings for CME pods or decoy launchers. Re-named NKC-135E after being re-engined between October 1990 and January 1991, it took part in operation 'Desert Storm', first flying from Crete, then from Dubai. It is still in service with the 418th Flight Test Squadron RC-135R f the 412th Test Wing which replaced the 4950th TW in 1994.

NASA 53129

Boeing NKC-135A (s/n 55-3129 - c/n 17245) of the National Aeronautics and Space Administration. Dryden Flight Test Center. Edwards AFB, 1979. Designated JKC-135A in January 1960, this plane was used by NASA from 1959 to 1968 for training future astronauts in zero gravity under the name of 'Weightless Wonder' (more than 12,000 parabolic flights carried out). Modified to a NKC-135A and equipped with a radome, it was lent again to NASA from December 1978 to January 1981 and equipped with winglets at the wingtips which, despite their efficiency, were not finally mounted on production aircraft. Having become a NKC-135E after receiving new engines in June 1982, it was attached to the commander in chief of the Atlantic forces (CINCLANT) after being transformed into a EC-135P in 1984. Retired from service in January 1992, it was sent to the AMARC depot at Davis-Monthan.

The KC-135 in detail

With their common origins, the Dash 80, the KC-135 and the Boeing 707 seem identical and are often mixed up by an ill-informed public that thinks the first is a straightforward military version of the second. In reality they are two different aircraft and only share a small amount of common elements.

Indeed, as soon as we take a more thorough look at each of these aircraft, we soon notice that they only really share their exterior appearance. Both have four engines, swept wings with the engines mounted on separate struts, a circular fuselage (at least from the outside) and a single tail unit. Also, at the beginning it was relatively easy to distinguish a KC-135 from a civil 707, if only because the first was almost always equipped with a refuelling boom and boomer's post. As time has passed, it has become a lot more complicated, notably when the military planes took on a more 'civilian' aspect (appearance of fuselage windows, disappearance of the refuelling boom), and civil planes became more military (windows taken away and the appearance of a refuelling boom)!

However, to simplify things, and before looking at the different parts of a (K)C-135, we can say that the military versions are characterised by a narrower fuselage (10 cm/4 inches less in diameter than a civil 707), is shorter (a KC-135 is 39.27 m/134 ft 6 in, whereas a 707-100 is 42.32 m/145 ft), and of course, has fewer windows, or sometimes none at all. The engine struts, at least at the beginning, do not have additional air vents, whilst the rear of the fuselage has visible slightly raised reinforcing.

The fuselage

The fuselage is made up of two levels; the lower level is, at least on the standard KC-135, for refuelling and contains tanks and pumps for the transfer of fuel. Behind the cockpit, the upper level of the fuselage, separated horizontally by a floor, is entirely empty and makes up, depending on configurations, a cargo hold or a cabin for carrying passengers, clips attached to the floor permitting the installation of seats.

Seen from the outside, as with the 707, the fuselage appears perfectly circular, the junction between the two airframe lobes being covered.

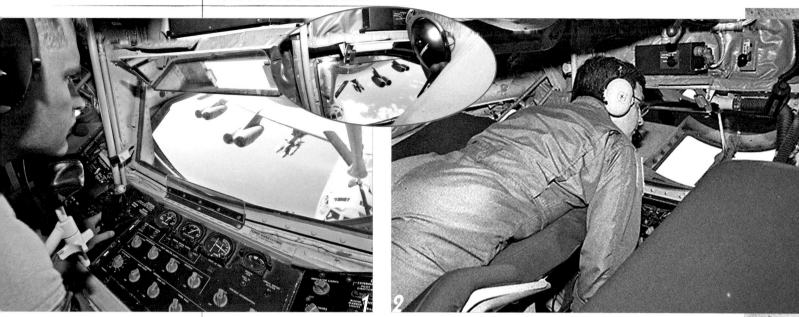

1 & 2. Lying on a bunk, the refueller - or boomer - controls the manoeuvre via a rectangular window, the main instruments and dials are just in front of him.
(USAF)

3. This spectacular view taken from a plane being refuelled perfectly shows the lifting system for the boom with its cable, the coloured zones painted on the extendable part, but also the alignment markings under the fuselage with the positioning lights and the yellow stripe indicating the axis of the Stratotanker.
(USAF)

4 & 5. Controlling the movements of the refuelling boom is carried out using a mini joystick placed on the boomer's instrument panel.
(USAF)

6 & 7. A profiled fairing equipped with a rectangular window protects the boomer's compartment and moves upwards during the refuelling manoeuvre, thus exposing the main window.
(USAF)

8. Two bunks are placed alongside that of the boomer for an instructor, observer or even a journalist. *(USAF)*

9. The boomer's bunk is equipped with a chin rest to make his position more comfortable during refuelling manoeuvres that often last for long periods of time. A system of inclined mirrors placed from one side of the rectangular window to the other increases the latter's field of vision via a periscopic effect.
(USAF)

1. In flight, the boom is manoeuvred using a rudder similar to that of a standard aircraft; it is a favourite place for putting unit insignia and numbers. Note, behind, the horizontal elevators. (F. Lert)

2. In order for it to be used with aircraft that are not equipped with refuelling receptacle, the boom can be equipped with a soft hose and drogue that is rolled out.
The extremity of the latter has an inflatable tube to ease the insertion of the fixed boom of the plane being refuelled. (F. Lert)

3. The extremity of the refuelling boom. A system indicates to the boomer that it is properly inserted before transferring the fuel. (USAF)

4. The extra pods placed at the wing tip (here that of a C-135FR) containing a soft hose and a drogue with an inflatable rim. The tension of the hose is maintained vertical thanks to a system of springs. The control of the refuelling manoeuvres is carried out from the flight mechanic's post, notably by using video cameras transmitting the pictures onto screens. (F. Lert)

5. Ground inspection of the inflatable refuelling basket of the 'hose and drogue' system. (USAF)

6. The interior of a KC-135 boom of the 100th ARW. The telescopic part and its extremity are perfectly visible from this angle. (USAF)

7. A female technician works on the boom of a KC-135, the mobile panels of which have been removed, allowing us to make out the complex internal mechanism. The entire interior is painted in yellow greenish zinchromate. (USAF)

As we have already seen, the life cycle of the KC-135 was designed to be of limited duration (10,000 flying hours) and to this end, its fuselage was made with a less robust aluminium alloy (7178-T6), notably over time. This explains why a program had to be carried out in the 1970s and 80s to change part of the lower surfaces (program ECP 405) in order to prolong the life cycle of these planes up to 27,000 flying hours, almost triple the number initially planned. This less robust fuselage skin also explains the presence of twenty five exterior reinforcement panels aft of the fuselage, to reduce the effect of shock waves caused by the jet flow at this part of the aircraft. Crew access is via a door at the front of the fuselage below the cockpit. It is equipped with a retractable ladder and its upper aperture is behind the pilot's seat on the left and can be used as an emergency exit.

A cargo door, measuring 2.90 m (9 ft 6 in) wide by 1.83 m (6 ft) high, is also placed on the same left-hand side in front of the wing and opens from the top using hydraulic cylinders. This cargo door characterises all the military versions (KC, EC, RC-135, etc.) and not only those originally destined only for cargo or passengers only (C-135). An emergency exit with door is present on both sides of the fuselage above the wings (there is a light fitted into the fuselage just behind the cargo door for lighting up the wing at this point). At the rear of the fuselage, also on both sides, is a pair of rescue hatches one above the other, the first by the wing's trailing edge, and above the boomer's position for the second.

The number of windows varies depending on the version; however, these remain in an extremely low number on tankers, the average being three on each side, including that on the emergency exit

The KC-135 and derivative engines

Turbojet
J57*-P29A (water injection/no thrust reverser)
J57-P43W (water injection/no thrust reverser)
J57-P59W (water injection/no thrust reverser)

Turbofan (with fan thrust reverser)
TF33**P-5 (with fan thrust reverser)
TF33P-9 (without fan thrust reverser)
TF33PW 102 (with 'core thrust reverser'/movable ejector)

The TF33 was developed from the J57 where the first three stages were removed and replaced by two new fan stages: the engine nacelle is then longer than on previous models and its section is nearly circular, seen from the outside.

* military designation of the JT3C.
** military designation of the JT3D

8. In order to ease maintenance, the whole boom can be removed. The boom of a C-135FR is seen here on a specially made maintenance trolley. (F. Lert)

9. Maintenance operations on the refuelling pod of a French C-135FR. The soft hose inside measures up to 27 metres (90 ft). The fuel flow is 1,360 kg (3,000 lb) per minute, the refuelling of fixed wing aircraft can be carried out with these pods between 320 and 580 kph. (F. Lert)

10. Initially, only the KC-135Q was equipped with a light on top of the tail fin, lighting up the receiving plane. This system, particularly efficient during nocturnal operations, was later spread to the entire KC-135 fleet still in service. (USAF)

11. The internal mechanism of a refuelling boom with notably, the extension of the telescopic tube contained in the main part. (USAF)

12. A KC-135 seen from the cockpit of the receiving plane. The alignment lights under the fuselage show all their usefulness in these conditions. (USAF)

13. One of the KC-135R of the 100th ARW undergoing maintenance in the hangars at Mildenhall, Great Britain. The flaps and the elevators are down, the spoilers deployed, whilst the reinforcing at the end of the fuselage can be made out thanks to differences in the paint here. (USAF)

over the wing. The cabin is pressurised and equipped with air conditioning and is sound-proofed. The floor is equipped for fitting passenger seats if they should be needed. The ceiling has rails equipped with a hoist to help the internal moving of bulky loads.

The tail unit

Originally, the first KC-135A that left the assembly lines were, as with the first 707, equipped with a short tail fin, as well as rudder that was not electronically controlled that tended to favour the 'Dutch roll' phenomenon (oscillation of the plane coupling yaw and roll) that was the cause of several serious incidents, notably when the plane was in automatic pilot.

In 1962, a new higher tail unit, coupled with a new automatic pilot, as well as a hydraulically assisted, more reactive rudder, were installed beginning with the 583rd aircraft made and retro-fitted on planes already in service. This improved the aircraft's stability, notably in the event of asymmetric engines (voluntarily stopping the engines, break downs etc.) A UHF antenna is placed on top, and at the front of the tail fin, to its rear, is a light that can be beamed downwards to light up the receiving aircraft during night-time refuelling. This system, originally designed to be fitted only on the KC-135Q designed to refuel the Lockheed A-12 and SR-71, was

then fitted on the whole tanker fleet. Finally, several radio navigation VOR antennae, as well as a AN/APN 69 radar beacon, were put into the tail fin. The variable position horizontal stabilisers are positioned by a worm, whilst the elevators are controlled manually.

The wings

The wings are swept back to 35° and both are equipped with a first aileron which functions whatever the aircraft's speed (all speed), placed between the interior and exterior double slotted flaps and a second that can only be used at low speeds, placed at the wingtips and only functioning at the same time as the flaps, thus improving stability at the lowest speeds.

A pair of spoilers is placed in front of each flap on the upper wing surfaces, permitting the control of roll when they are used separately and working as air brakes when they are synchronised. Finally, in order to improve lift at low speed (notably when landing), the lower wing surface leading edges are equipped with Krueger flaps that retract towards the rear.

The cockpit

The standard flying crew (pilot/captain, co-pilot - sat on his right - and navigator), access the plane via a door situated at the front, left-hand side, by the front wheel well. The two pilots, sat side by side, are separated by a central console which has, on its lower section, in front of the throttle levers, the instruments controlling the flow of transferred fuel, whilst the other instruments are placed on lateral consoles and a panel placed on the ceiling.

The navigator, who also acts as the flight mechanic, is installed behind the co-pilot on a swivel seat in front of the right side, and has both a table and instrument panel as he has to watch over the refuelling manoeuvre. Finally, an extra foldaway seat equipped with a console is also present in the cockpit behind the pilot, allowing for a fourth man (observer, instructor etc.) Behind the cockpit, separated by bulkheads leaving a central walkway, is a space containing, amongst other things, the electric and electronic equipment, as well as a sink and chemical toilets. The crews of the first KC-135 carried out celestial navigation and two small windows were installed in the cockpit roof to this end. This practise has since been advantageously replaced by an inertial unit and by a FSA (Fuel Saving Advisor) and CAS (Cockpit Avionics System) which coordinate and display information concerning navigation, the plane's performance and its fuel consumption. The windscreen is made up of six rectangular panels (two large ones at the front and four smaller ones at the sides) and was originally equipped with vents that both cleaned the windscreen and prevented them from fogging up. This system was replaced by a banal pair of windscreen

1 & 3. Different views of the cockpit of a USAF KC-135. The modernised aircraft (Pacer CRAG program) have been given cathode ray tube display replacing some of the analog instruments. (USAF and F. Lert)

2. View of the cockpit of a USAF KC-135 during landing at Istres during the Allied operations in Bosnia. The ceiling instrument panel is clearly visible, whilst the windows above the windscreen have been screened off with curtains. (F. Lert)

4. The interior of a C-135FR cockpit, with during landing at Istres and without the crew. Note that all the English instructions have been retained. A fold-up and pivoting seat, between the pilots, can take a crew member (in theory, an instructor, but also the boomer when he is not at work, observer etc.) (F. Lert)

5. The cockpit of a NKC-135 with the classic, non-modernised instrument dials. (V. Gréciet collection)

1 & 2. Two views of the navigators post. He also has the role of flight mechanic and is installed behind the co-pilot, facing the right side. As well as the weather radar, he has both a table and instrument panel, as he is responsible for supervising the fuel transfer operations. (USAF and F. Lert)

3. The Stratotanker retains its considerable cargo transporter or personnel-carrying capacities in its hold as we can see in this view of the interior of a KC-135R at Mildenhall during an assistance mission in Rwanda in 2004. (USAF)

4. A close-up of the front of a USAF KC-135Q decorated with superb 'nose art'. The two frontal windows of the windscreen are equipped with windscreen wipers whilst the upper windows assure a better visibility for the crew, notably when flying in formation. (F. Lert)

5. Filling the tanks of a KC-135 using the Pentagram system. The valves are inside the left main undercarriage well. (USAF)

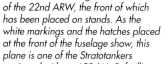

Below.
Maintenance operations on the forward undercarriage of a KC-135R of the 22nd ARW, the front of which has been placed on stands. As the white markings and the hatches placed at the front of the fuselage show, this plane is one of the Stratotankers equipped with an ARR (Air Refuelling Receptacle). (USAF)

Below, right.
The assembly line for the KC-135A at the Renton factory. In the foreground is the retracted tail fin (short first model) of s/n 58-0061. (Boeing)

wipers, a less modern but more efficient system. Above the windscreen, four small windows increase visibility and aid formation flying, notably when air traffic is dense or when the aircraft is turning, during landing phases for example.

The in-flight refuelling system

The main exterior characteristic of the KC-135, that we will also find on the its versions (EC-135, JKC-135 etc.), is the refuelling boom at the rear of the fuselage and the boomer's post with its three windows, one main one in the middle and two lateral. The boomer accesses his post via an opening in the cabin floor. During refuelling manoeuvres, the boomer lies flat on a bunk facing the rear that is equipped with a chin rest, with the boom joystick and different gauges and dials nearby. The post windows give a panoramic view of the planes coming to meet the tanker and two extra bunks are placed on each side of the main one for an instructor, pupil or even a photographer. As a matter of interest, it was originally planned for the boomer to be in a sitting position, a configuration used on the KC-10 Extender, but the prone position was finally chosen as it was deemed less tiring on long

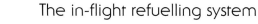

flights. As well as his main role, the boomer can also undertake the role of a loader if the KC-135 carries cargo, or that of steward if the plane is converted into a passenger carrier.

The boom itself, made by Boeing, is made up of two concentric tubular and telescopic sections (total dimension going from 8,50 m to 14,30 m/28 ft to 47 ft) with the fuel hose placed inside. Placed against the fuselage when not in use, the boom can be orientated thanks to its ruddelevators up to 30° on the sides and more than 12.5° to minus 50° in height. A system of coloured stripes (red, yellow and green) on the extending part is used to instantaneously judge its extension. In the case of break down, the manoeuvre can be carried out manually.

Two types of boom were made in succession, the second finally replacing the first. Firstly, the standard boom equipped with three cylinders placed on the external part of the ruddelevators is used up to 330 knots, and the now universally installed high speed boom that has no compensators and which can be used at any speed.

The fuel is supplied to the receiving aircraft after having been pressurised, and the boom receives the fuel via pipes set along the fuselage. The advantage of the rigid boom, notably compared to the soft hose equipped with a basket at its extremity, is the large quantity of fuel that can be transferred in a small

time, that is 1 000 gallons (4 545 litres) per minute. A refuelling probe is placed inside the telescopic boom whilst at its extremity, a flap opens as soon as it makes contact with the receiving aircraft's receptacle, allowing for safe fuel transfer, that is once the system has been locked. Originally, the aircraft coming to the Stratotanker for refuelling carried out their approach guided only by a painted fluorescent stripe on the KC-135 belly, a system that was then completed by two rows of lights placed on the forward lower fuselage area. These were much more efficient, principally during night time manoeuvres or in bad visibility.

The KC-135 has two tanks in each wing; the interior tank contains 8 611 litres (2 275 US gallons) and the second outside tank contains 7 805 l (2 062 US gal.). To these tanks are added two others still in the wings, placed at the exterior, both containing 1 642 litres (432 US gal.), and a main tank (27 656 l/7 306 US gal.), in the centre of the wing area in the aircraft's belly. In order to merit its name of 'Flying tanker', the Stratotanker has no less than nine tanks in its fuselage, under the floor of the hold ; the first four are placed forward and hold a total of 21 955 litres (5 800 US gal.). The five others, placed aft, contain 24 143 l (6 378 US gal.). Finally at the far end of the cabin, behind the bulkhead that is the limit of the pressurised area; a last, smaller sized tank holds 8 229 l (2 174 US gal.).

Although in theory all the fuel carried by the plane (118 104 l/31 200 US gal. or 90 700 kg/199,960 lb) can be transferred, generally only the fuselage tanks are used for refuelling manoeuvres, the fuel stored in the wing tanks being used by the KC-135 itself.

Initially, Boeing only used the fixed boom refuelling system. This limited the SAC Stratotankers' refuelling capacities to only aircraft equipped with an internal refuelling receptacle, thus excluding those of the Tactical Air Command (TAC), the US Navy, and some NATO countries. After having experimented with the Probe and Drogue system, that is a soft hose integrated into the boom itself, a system used by the French on their C-135F, a system that necessitated an adaptor four metres (13 feet) long and measuring a little more than fifty kilos, notably within the Wolf Pack framework that used SAC KC-135A with the TAC F-105D Thunderchief equipped with a fixed boom and not a refuelling receptacle, it gave more importance to this method, notably after having drawn on the lessons of the Gulf War during which many types of plane had to be refuelled.

In order to increase the efficiency of the tanker fleet, the USAF decided, in 1998, to launch MPRS program (Multi-Point Refuelling System). To achieve this, 45 KC-135 were modified to take wingtip refuelling pods that contained an extendable hose measuring a maximum of thirty metres with a basket equipped with an inflatable rim and lights for night time refuelling. Thanks to this system, aircraft equipped with a fixed boom could be refuelled,

whilst the traditional fixed boom could be kept, giving
the thus modified Stratotanker a much appreciated versatility.

To install these pods, very similar to those mounted on the
KC-10 Extender, the wings needed to be modified (strengthe-
ning, the addition of pipes and cables). The extra lights were
placed on the struts of the adjacent engines, the pods themselves and the boomer's fairing, notably for night time refuelling.
An extra panel was added in that of the boomer who could thus
control the manoeuvre in liaison with the co-pilot, notably thanks
to video cameras, whilst various instruments, as well as extra circuit breakers were also installed in the cockpit. These pods are
interchangeable and, therefore, still operational, even when an
aircraft is not. Launched in 1998, the MPRS program was tested operationally the following year, a first batch of twelve aircraft being equipped in February 2000 and the entire transformed Stratotanker fleet should be operational in September 2008.

Motorisation

The first KC-135A aircraft were equipped with four J57-P
(or F *)43W engines, the last suffix (W for Water) indicating
that a system of demineralised water is used. This system, which
necessitated the addition of a tank for the water inside the fuselage, meant that thrust was increased by increasing the density of
the air admitted when the water was injected in the air intake
duct and the diffuser. It was only used for take off, the tank only
holding enough to last for two minutes for each engine. Also, it
polluted, both by leaving long characteristic black trails behind
the aircraft, and the noise it made. It caused many problems
because of its extreme sensitivity to cold (risk of freezing). Above all, however, this system was difficult to use. Indeed, in the
event of a water pump breaking down when taking off, the plane found itself very unbalanced as two of its engines stopped
and, therefore, there was a risk of veering from its trajectory and
becoming difficult to control. The engine-produced compressed
air was used for pneumatic take off (engine n°4 started first, producing the energy needed to start the three others), the airframe
air conditioning, defrosting the astrodome, cockpit windows and
boomer's compartment, thanks to rain and fog removal vents.

Starting the 'first generation' engines was achieved with car-
tridges or with the help of an annex generator installed on a trai-

ler on the ground. Initially, these engines were made from tita-
nium to cut down their weight; however, this metal was extremely expensive and the decision was taken, when the Stratotanker fleet increased, to make them out of steel, less noble but
much cheaper. Thus, it was the J57-P-59W engines that were
used next, each one weighing 180 kg (400 lb) more, but, on
the other hand, costing 100,000 dollars (at the time! less. Afterwards, a first part of the fleet was re-engined with the TF33 turbofan that were less noisy and dirty and, above all higher performance whilst using less fuel and equipped with thrust reversers
(KC-135E). Finally, in the 1980s, a second batch of Stratotankers were given much more modern F-108 engines that performed better in all domains, from the military derivatives of the
CFM 56 (KC-135R/T).

---

*P when the engine is made by Pratt & Whitney, F when it is made by Ford
Aerospace.

BOEING 707 versions

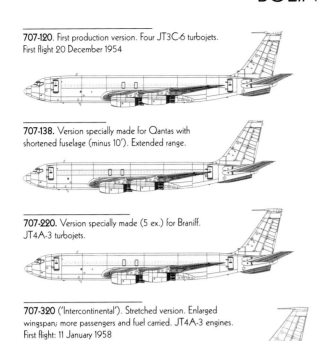

707-120. First production version. Four JT3C-6 turbojets. First flight 20 December 1954

707-138. Version specially made for Qantas with shortened fuselage (minus 10'). Extended range.

707-220. Version specially made (5 ex.) for Braniff. JT4A-3 turbojets.

707-320 ('Intercontinental'). Stretched version. Enlarged wingspan; more passengers and fuel carried. JT4A-3 engines. First flight: 11 January 1958

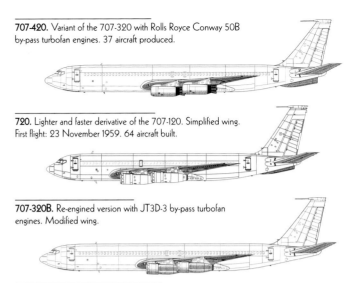

707-420. Variant of the 707-320 with Rolls Royce Conway 50B by-pass turbofan engines. 37 aircraft produced.

720. Lighter and faster derivative of the 707-120. Simplified wing. First flight: 23 November 1959. 64 aircraft built.

707-320B. Re-engined version with JT3D-3 by-pass turbofan engines. Modified wing.

707-320C. Convertible (passengers and/or cargo) version of the 707 similar to the 707-320B. Cargo door on the left side of the fuselage. The most produced version. Some aircraft buit as 'non modifiable cargos', unofficially designated 707-320CF

Characteristics of the BOEING 707 & 720

	707-120/220 (120B)	707-138	707-320 (320B and C)	720 (720B)
Power plant (x4)	P&W JT3C-6/JT4A-3 (JT3D)		JT4A-11 (JT3D-3 or D-7*)	JT3C-7 (JT3D-1 or -3)
Dimensions and weights				
Wingspan	130 ft 10 in	130 ft 10 in	142 ft 5 in (145 ft 8 in)	130 ft 10 in
Length (overall)	145 ft 1 in (144' 6")	134 ft 6 in	152 ft 11 in	136 ft 9 in
Height (w/modified tail)	42 ft	42 ft	41 ft 8 in (42' 5")	41 ft 7 in
Wing Area	2,433 sq ft (2510 sq ft)	2,433 sq ft	2,892 sq ft (2,942 sq ft)	2,510 sq ft
Max T/O weight	246,000 lb/257,000 lb (258,000 lb)	256,000 lb	301,000 lb** (327,000 lb)	213,000 lb (222,000 lb)
Performance				
Cruising speed (at 25,000 ft)	508 kt/526 kt (540 kt)	521 kt	522 kt (522 kt)	521 kt (540 kt)
Range (w. full payload)	2,465 NM/2,050 NM (2,640 NM)		4,155 NM*** (4,275 NM)	2,120 NM (2,085 NM)
Passengers (max.)	179/181/189	154	189 (189)	141 (149/156)

*707-320 B-H and C-H, **707-420 = 311,000 lb *** 707-420 = 4,225 NM

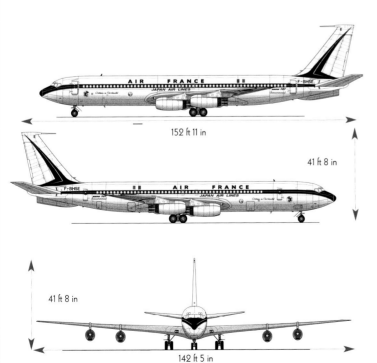

152 ft 11 in

41 ft 8 in

41 ft 8 in

142 ft 5 in

Boeing 707-328

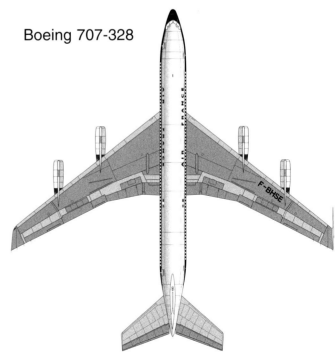

Boeing 707 production list

Constr. Number	Model	1st Operator	Delivery date	Note		Constr. Number	Model	1st Operator	Delivery date	Note
17158	B367-80	Boeing	5/07/1954			17663	B707-131	TWA	29/04/1959	
17586	B707-121	Pan Am	30/11/1958	A (17/09/65)		17664	B707-131	TWA	10/05/1959	
17587	B707-121	Pan Am	19/12/1958			17665	B707-131	TWA	13/05/1959	
17588	B707-121	Pan Am	15/08/1958	A (08/12/63)		17666	B707-131	TWA	28/05/1959	
17589	B707-121	Pan Am	29/09/1959			17667	B707-131	TWA	03/05/1959	
17590	B707-121	Pan Am	17/10/1958			17668	B707-131	TWA	16/05/1959	
17591	B707-121	Pan Am	30/10/1958			17669	B707-131	TWA	03/06/1959	A (06/11/67)
17592	B707-321	Pan Am	28/08/1958			17670	B707-131	TWA	25/06/1959	A (22/04/70)
17593	B707-321	Pan Am	19/07/1959			17671	B707-131	TWA	30/06/1959	A (13/10/76)
17594	B707-321	Pan Am	22/08/1959			17672	B707-131	TWA	01/08/1959	
17595	B707-321	Pan Am	01/09/1959			17673	B707-331	TWA	26/09/1959	A (08/03/72)
17596	B707-321	Pan Am	22/09/1959			17674	B707-331	Pan Am	09/10/1959	
17597	B707-321	Pan Am	03/10/1959			17675	B707-331	TWA	15/10/1959	
17598	B707-321	Pan Am	06/10/1959			17676	B707-331	TWA	05/11/1959	
17599	B707-321	Pan Am	19/10/1959			17677	B707-331	Pan Am	10/11/1959	
17600	B707-321	Pan Am	15/10/1959			17678	B707-331	TWA	03/12/1959	
17601	B707-321	Pan Am	27/10/1959			17679	B707-331	TWA	11/12/1959	
17602	B707-321	Pan Am	12/08/1959			17680	B707-331	Pan Am	11/12/1959	
17603	B707-321	Pan Am	12/12/1959			17681	B707-331	TWA	11/02/1960	
17604	B707-321	Pan Am	13/01/1960			17682	B707-331	TWA	11/02/1960	
17605	B707-321	Pan Am	28/01/1960	A (20/12/80)		17683	B707-331	Pan Am	15/03/1959	
17606	B707-321	Pan Am	06/03/1960			17684	B707-331	TWA	24/03/1960	
17607	B707-321	Pan Am	26/04/1960			17685	B707-331	TWA	21/04/1960	A (23/11/64)
17608	B707-321	Pan Am	28/04/1960	Test CFM-56		17686	B707-331	Pan Am	22/04/1960	
17609	B707-124	Continental	19/04/1959	A (01/07/65)		17687	B707-331	TWA	26/04/1960	
17610	B707-124	Continental	27/05/1959			17688	B707-331	TWA	06/06/1960	
17611	B707-124	Continental	16/07/1959	A (22/05/65)		17689	B707-331	Pan Am	01/06/196	
17612	B707-124	Continental	10/08/1959			17690	B707-331	TWA	13/06/1960	
17613	B707-328	Air France	21/10/1959	'Ch. de Versailles'/ A (27/07/61)		17691	B707-227	Braniff	11/06/1959	A (19/10/59)
						17692	B707-227	Braniff	13/11/1959	
17614	B707-328	Air France	12/12/1959	'Ch. de Chambord'		17693	B707-227	Braniff	08/01/1960	
17615	B707-328	Air France	12/12/1959	'Ch.de Fontainebleau'		17694	B707-227	Braniff	15/01/1960	
17616	B707-328	Air France	29/01/1960	'Ch. de Chenonceaux'		17695	B707-227	Braniff	01/02/1960	
17617	B707-328	Air France	20/03/1960	Ch. de Rambouillet'		17696	B707-138	Boeing	20/03/1959	
17618	B707-328	Air France	24/03/1960	'Château de Blois'		17697	B707-138	Qantas	20/05/1959	A (28/08/98)
17619	B707-328	Air France	13/05/1960	'Château de Pau'		17698	B707-138	Qantas	08/06/1959	A (07/02/68)
17620	B707-328	Air France	23/06/1960	'Ch. d'Amboise'/ Destroyed by bomb Ajaccio 07/09/1971		17699	B707-138	Qantas	15/07/1959	
						17700	B707-138	Qantas	13/08/1959	
						17701	B707-138	Qantas	21/08/1959	
17621	B707-328	Air France	07/11/1960	'Château de Josselin'		17702	B707-138	Qantas	18/09/1959	
17622	B707-328	Air France	24/03/1960	'Château de Chaumont'		17703	B707-436	Boeing/BOAC	09/05/1960	
17623	B707-329	Sabena	04/12/1959			17704	B707-436	Boeing/BOAC	16/05/1960	
17624	B707-329	Sabena	15/01/1960	A (15/02/61)		17705	B707-436	Boeing/BOAC	28/04/1960	
17625	B707-329	Sabena	13/02/1960			17706	B707-436	Boeing/BOAC	29/04/1960	A (05/03/66)
17626	B707-329	Amer. Airlines		10/04/1960		17707	B707-436	BOAC	13/05/1960	
						17708	B707-436	Boeing/BOAC	23/06/196	
17627	B707-329	Sabena	08/06/1960	A (15/02/78)		17709	B707-436	BOAC	15/07/1960	
17628	B707-123	American Al	23/10/1960	A (19/08/79)		17710	B707-436	BOAC	23/07/1960	
17629	B707-123	American Al	23/01/1959	A (28/01/61)		17711	B707-436	BOAC	22/09/1960	
17630	B707-123	American Al	31/12/1958			17712	B707-436	BOAC	29/09/1960	A (17/03/77
17631	B707-123	American Al	28/01/1959			17713	B707-436	BOAC	14/10/1960	
17632	B707-123	American Al	31/01/1959			17714	B707-436	BOAC	05/11/1960	
17633	B707-123	American Al	12/02/1959	A (01/03/62)		17715	B707-436	BOAC	16/11/1960	
17634	B707-123	American Al	27/02/1959			17716	B707-436	BOAC	09/12/1960	
17635	B707-123	American Al	27/03/1959			17717	B707-436	BOAC	22/12/1960	
17636	B707-123	American Al	03/04/1959			17718	B707-430	Boeing/ Lufthansa	10/03/1960	A (09/08/77)
17637	B707-123	American Al	23/04/1959							
17638	B707-123	American Al	12/05/1959			17719	B707-430	Lufthansa	03/02/1960	
17639	B707-123	American Al	21/05/1959			17720	B707-430	Lufthansa	01/10/1960	
17640	B707-123	American Al	28/05/1959			17721	B707-430	Lufthansa	24/04/1960	
17641	B707-123	American Al	05/06/1959	A (15/08/59)		17722	B707-437	Boeing/ Air India	07/03/1960	A (23/01/71)
17642	B707-123	American Al	24/061959							
17643	B707-123	American Al	29/06/1959			17723	B707-437	Air India	18/02/1960	A (22/06/82)
17644	B707-123	American Al	27/07/1959			17724	B707-437	Air India	19/02/1960	
17645	B707-123	American Al	31/07/1959			17725	B707-139B		13/05/1960	
17646	B707-123	American Al	24/08/1959			17820	B707-328	Air France	23/06/1960	
17647	B707-123	American Al	12/08/1959			17903	B707-139	Boeing/Western	07/06/1960	
17648	B707-123	American Al	14/09/1959			17904	B707-139	Boeing/Western	04/05/1960	A (07/04/64)
17649	B707-123	American Al	03/10/1959			17905	B720-441	Varig	10/01/1960	
17650	B707-123	American Al	14/10/1959			17906	B707-441	Varig	16/06/1960	A (27/11/62)
17651	B707-123	American Al	28/10/1959			17908	B720-022	United Airlines	29/07/1960	
17652	B707-123	American Al	21/11/1959	17653 to 17657 Cancelled		17909	B720-022	United Airlines	30/04/1960	
17658	B707-131	TWA	29/01/1959			17910	B720-022	United Airlines	21/05/1960	
17659	B707-131	TWA	17/03/1959			17911	B720-022	United Airlines	26/05/1960	
17660	B707-131	TWA	30/03/1959			17912	B720-022	United Airlines	09/06/1960	
17661	B707-131	TWA	03/04/1959			17913	B720-022	United Airlines	29/06/1960	
17662	B707-131	TWA	18/04/1959			17914	B720-022	United Airlines	26/06/1960	

A = Destroyed/damaged (withdrawal from service date)
Cvtd = Converted aircraft

Constr. Number	Model	1st Operator	Delivery date	Note
17915	B720-022	United Airlines	27/07/1960	
17916	B720-022	United Airlines	05/08/1960	
17917	B720-022	United Airlines	13/08/1960	
17918	B707-328	Boeing/ Air France	20/08/1960	'Ch. de Vizille'
17919	B707-328	Air France	20/08/1960	'Ch. de Maintenon'
17920	B707-328	Air France	21/09/1960	'Ch. de Sully'/ A (take-off Orly 03/06/62)
17921	B-707-328	Air France	18/09/1960	'Ch. de Valencay'
17922	B707-328	Air France	16/09/1960	'Château d'Anet'
17923	B707-328	Air France	07/111960	'Ch. de Villandry'
17924	B707-328	Air France	22/10/1960	'Ch. de Compiègne'
17925	B153B/VC137	USAF	04/05/1959	
17926	B153B/VC137	USAF	31/05/1959	
17927	B153B/VC137	USAF	30/06/1959	
17928	B707-344	SAA	01/07/1960	
17929	B707-344	SAA	22/08/1960	
17930	B707-344	SAA	22/08/1960	
18012	B707-124	Continental	17/03/1960	
18013	B720-023	American Al	30/07/1960	
18014	B720-023	American Al	24/07/1960	
18015	B720-023	American Al	13/08/1960	
18016	B720-023	American Al	22/09/1960	
18017	B720-023	American Al	01/09/1960	A (Shelling 12/06/82)
18018	B720-023	American Al	08/09/1960	A (Shelling 31/08/81)
18019	B720-023	American Al	19/09/1960	
18020	B720-023	American Al	10/10/1960	A (Bomb expl. 01/01/76)
18021	B720-023	American Al	14/09/1960	
18022	B720-023	American Al	03/12/1960	
18023	B720-023B	American Al	27/04/1960	
18024	B720-023B	American Al	03/02/1961	
18025	B720-023B	American Al	17/03/1961	
18026	B720-023B	American Al	17/02/1961	A (Shelling 16/06/82)
18027	B720-023B	American Al	27/02/1961	
18028	B720-023B	American Al	29/03/1961	
18029	B720-023B	American Al	28/03/1961	A (Shelling 16/06/82)
18030	B720-023B	American Al	10/04/1961	
18031	B720-023B	American Al	16/04/1961	
18032	B720-023B	American Al	19/04/1961	
18033	B720-023BF	American Al	23/05/1961	
18034	B720-023B	American Al	22/06/1961	A (Shelling 21/08/85)
18035	B720-023B	American Al	09/06/61	A (Shelling 02/06/83)
18036	B720-023B	American Al	02/07/61	
18037	B720-023B	American Al	21/07/61	
18038 to 18040	B707-153	Cancelled		
18041	B720-048	Aer Lingus	25/10/60	
18042	B720-048	Aer Lingus	24/01/61	
18043	B720-048	Aer Lingus	07/04/61	
18044	B720-022	United	22/12/60	A (22/04/76)
18045	B720-022	United	19/12/60	
18046	B720-022	United	14/01/61	
18047	B720-022	United	27/01/61	
18048	B720-022	United	02/02/61	
18049	B720-022	United	13/02/61	
18050	B720-022	United	06/03/61	18051 to 18053 cancelled
18054	B707-123B	American	25/05/61	
18055	B707-437	Air India	17/04/61	A (24/01/66)
18056	B707-430	Lufthansa	17/03/61	
18057	B720-030B	Lufthansa	08/03/61	
18058	B720-030B	Lufthansa	28/04/61	A (04/12/61)
18059	B720-030B	Lufthansa	02/05/61	
18060	B720-030B	Lufthansa	03/06/61	
18061	B720-047B	Western	07/04/61	A (16/08/76)
18062	B720-047B	Western	10/05/61	
18063	B720-047B	Western	07/06/61	
18064	B720-027	Braniff	11/02/61	
18065	B720-027	Braniff	22/03/61	
18066	B720	FAA	12/05/61	Crash test (01/12/84)
18067	B707-138B	Qantas	29/07/61	
18068	B707-138B	Qantas	16/08/61	
18069	B707-138B	Boeing	24/08/61	
18070	B707-458	El Al	22/04/61	
18071	B707-458	El Al	07/06/61	
18072	B720-022	United	01/12/61	
18073	B720-022	United	14/12/61	
18074	B720-022	United	21/12/61	
18075	B720-022	United	10/01/62	
18076	B720-022	United	17/01/62	
18077	B720-022	United	10/04/62	
18078	B720-022	United	24/04/62	
18079	B720-022	United	08/05/62	

Constr. Number	Model	1st Operator	Delivery date	Note
18080	B720-022	United	15/05/62	
18081	B720-022	United	01/06/62	
18082	B720-022	United	12/06/62	
18083	B707-321	Pan Am	16/05/61	
18084	B707-321	Pan Am	23/05/61	
18085	B707-321	Pan Am	13/06/61	
18086	B720-059B	Avianca	08/11/61	
18087	B720-059B	Avianca	16/11/61	A (27/01/80)
18154	B720-026	Braniff	09/08/61	
18155	B720-025	Eastern	14/08/61	
18156	B720-025	Eastern	25/08/61	
18157	B720-025	Eastern	02/02/61	
18158	B720-025	Eastern	20/09/61	
18159	B720-025	Eastern	27/09/61	
18160	B720-025	Eastern	17/10/61	
18161	B720-025	Eastern	17/10/61	
18162	B720-025	Eastern	08/11/61	
18163	B720-025	Eastern	23/10/61	
18164	B720-025	Eastern	23/10/61	
18165	B720-068B	Boeing/Saudia	20/12/61	
18166	B720-068B	Saudia	29/12/61	
18167	B720-047B	Western	11/07/61	
18240	B720-025	Eastern	09/01/62	
18241	B720-025	Eastern	13/11/61	
18242	B720-025	Eastern	22/11/61	
18243	B720-025	Eastern	08/12/61	A (13/09/74)
18244	B720-025	Eastern	16/12/61	
18245	B707-328	Air France	01/02/62	
18246	B707-328	Air France	16/02/62	
18247	B707-328	Air France	09/03/62	'Ch. de Chantilly'/A (22/06/62)
18248	B720-030B	Lufthansa	12/01/62	
18249	B720-030B	Lufthansa	23/03/62	A (15/07/64)
18250	B720-030B	Lufthansa	26/02/62	
18251	B720-030B	Lufthansa	29/02/62	
18334	B707-138B	Qantas	29/08/61	
18335	B707-321B	Pan Am	15/06/62	
18336	B707-321B	Pan Am	13/06/62	
18337	B707-321B	Pan Am	12/04/62	
18338	B707-321B	Pan Am	01/06/62	
18339	B707-321B	Pan Am	01/06/62	
18351	B720-051B	Northwest	22/06/61	
18352	B720-051B	Northwest	22/06/61	
18353	B720-051B	Northwest	11/07/61	
18354	B720-051B	Northwest	26/07/61	A (12/02/63)
18355	B720-051B	Northwest	31/08/61	
18356	B720-051B	Northwest	05/10/61	
18357	B707-458	El Al	13/02/62	
18372	B707-465	Cunard	27/02/62	
18373	B707-465	BOAC/Cunard	07/07/62	A (08/04/68)
18374	B707-329	Sabena	16/04/62	
18375	B707-328	Air France	11/05/62	'Ch. de Versailles'
18376	B720-062	Pacific Northern	23/03/62	
18377	B720-062	Pacific Northern	18/04/62	
18378	B720-040B	PIA	21/12/61	
18379	B720-040B	PIA	19/10/62	A (20/05/65)
18380	B720-040B	PIA	29/11/62	
18381	B720-051B	TWA	23/07/61	
18382	B720-051B	TWA	02/08/61	
18383	B720-051B	TWA	27/08/61	
18384	B720-051B	TWA	30/09/61	
18385	B707-131B	TWA	29/03/62	
18386	B707-131B	TWA	10/04/62	
18387	B707-131B	TWA	30/04/62	
18388	B707-131B	TWA	18/05/62	
18389	B707-131B	TWA	23/05/62	
18390	B707-131B	TWA	31/05/62	
18391	B707-131B	TWA	16/06/62	
18392	B707-131B	TWA	28/06/62	
18393	B707-131B	TWA	23/07/62	
18394	B707-131B	TWA	02/08/62	
18395	B707-131B	TWA	01/08/62	A (16/01/74)
18396	B707-131B	TWA	21/08/62	
18397	B707-131B	TWA	29/08/62	
18398 and 18399		Cancelled		
18400	B707-131B	TWA	31/08/62	
18401	B707-131B	TWA	21/09/62	
18402	B707-131B	TWA	26/09/62	
18403	B707-131B	TWA	28/09/62	
18404	B707-131B	TWA	12/10/62	
18405	B707-331B	TWA	11/03/63	

Constr. Number	Model	1st Operator	Delivery date	Note
18406	B707-331B	TWA	01/11/62	
18407	B707-331B	TWA	23/01/63	
18408	B707-331B	TWA	23/01/63	
18409	B707-331B	TWA	21/02/63	
18410	Cancelled			
18411	B707-436	BOAC	16/02/62	A (13/10/83)
18412	B707-436	BOAC	12/02/63	
18413	B707-436	BOAC	15/03/63	
18414	B707-437	Air India	07/03/63	
18415	B707-437	Air India	12/04/62	
18416	B720-024B	Continental	30/04/62	
18417	B720-024B	Continental	27/05/62	
18418	B720-024B	Continental	27/05/62	
18419	B720-024B	Continental	20/06/62	
18420	B720-051B	Northwest	09/07/62	
18421	B720-051B	Northwest	25/10/61	
18422	B720-051B	Northwest	15/11/61	
18423	B720-027	Braniff	13/12/61	
18424	B720-058B	El Al	10/05/62	
18425	B720-058B	El Al	23/06/62	
18451	B720-047B	Western	30/04/62	
18452	B720-047B	Western	27/07/62	
18453	B720-047B	Western	08/08/62	
18454	B720-060B	Ethiopian	28/08/62	A (09/01/68)
18455	B720-060B	Ethiopian	02/11/62	
18456	B707-328B	Air France	30/11/62	
18457	B707-328B	Air France	15/12/63	
18458	B707-328B	Air France	17/02/63	
18459	B707-328B	Air France	30/03/63	A (04/12/69)
18460	B707-329	Sabena	19/01/63	
18461	B353B/VC-137C	USAF	09/10/62	
18462	707-330B	Lufthansa	28/02/63	
18463	707-330B	Lufthansa	05/03/63	A (20/12/73)
18579	B707-321C	Pan Am	07/06/63	A (14/05/77)
18580	B707-321C	Pan Am	02/05/63	A (01/04/79)
18581	B720-027	Braniff	12/05/76	
18582	B707-373C	World Airways	12/05/76	
18583	B707-373C	World Airways	22/08/63	
18584	B707-351B	Northwest Orient	05/06/63	A (03/08/78)
18585	B707-351B	Northwest Orient	19/06/63	
18586	B707-351B	Northwest Orient	30/07/63	
18587	B720-024B	Continental	30/07/63	
18588	B720-047B	Western	03/04/63	
18589	B720-047B	Western	24/04/63	
18590	B720-047B	Western	02/05/63	A (08/01/81)
18591	B707-321C	Pan Am	07/06/63	
18592	Cancelled			
18685	B707-328B	Air France	13/01/64	
18686	B707-328B	Air France	30/01/64	
18687	B720-051B	Northwest	22/10/63	
18688	B720-051B	Northwest	23/01/64	
18689	B707-323C	American	19/11/63	
18690	B707-323C	American	13/12/63	
18691	B707-323C	American	20/12/63	
18692	B707-323C	American	31/12/63	A (31/08/91)
18693	B707-351B	Northwest Orient	09/09/63	
18694	B707-441	Varig	12/11/63	
18707	B707-373C	World	26/09/63	A (14/12/83)
18708	B707-337B	Air India	25/05/64	
18709	B707-373C	TWA	18/11/63	
18710	B707-351B	Northwest Orient	13/10/63	
18711	B707-331C	TWA	25/04/64	A (07/03/01)
18712	B707-331C	TWA	20/05/64	A (26/07/69)
18713	B707-331C	TWA	12/06/64	Cvtd TC-18E
18714	B707-321C	Pan Am	27/02/64	
18715	B707-321C	Pan Am	20/03/64	A (24/03/92)
18716	B707-321C	Pan Am	27/03/64	
18717	B707-321C	Pan Am	03/04/64	
18718	B707-321C	Pan Am	30/04/64	A (31/03/92)
18737	B707-348C	Aer Lingus	10/06/64	
18738	B707-373C	TWA	23/12/63	A (30/11/70)
18739	B707-138B	Qantas	19/08/64	
18740	B707-138B	Qantas	10/09/64	John Travolta
18745	B720-051B	Boeing	28/04/65	
18746	B707-351C	Northwest Orient	09/04/64	A (29/04/92)
18747	B707-351C	Northwest Orient	18/04/64	
18748	B707-351C	Northwest Orient	29/03/64	
18749	B720-047B	Western	21/05/64	
18756	B707-331C	TWA	06/08/64	
18757	B707-331C	TWA	29/08/64	
18758	B707-131B	TWA	29/10/64	
18759	B707-131B	TWA	13/11/64	
18760	B707-131B	TWA	10/11/64	
18761	B707-131B	TWA	31/12/64	
18762	B707-131B	TWA	23/12/64	
18763	B720-024B	Continental	23/07/64	
18764	B707-331B	TWA	15/01/65	
18765	B707-321C	Pan Am	30/04/64	
18766	B707-321C	Pan Am	09/05/64	
18767	B707-321C	Pan Am	21/05/64	A (03/08/75)
18790	B707-321C	Pan Am	03/12/64	A (12/06/68)
18792	B720-051B	Northwest Orient	26/06/64	
18793	B720-051B	Northwest Orient	27/06/64	
18808	B707-338C	Qantas	09/02/65	
18809	B707-338C	Qantas	05/03/65	
18810	B707-338C	Qantas	11/08/65	
18818	B707-047B	Western	25/09/64	
18819	B707-330B	Lufthansa	10/01/65	
18820	B720-047B	Western	21/01/65	
18824	B707-321C	Pan Am	31/12/64	A (26/12/68)
18825	B707-321C	Continental	21/08/64	A (25/11/92)
18826	B707-321C	Continental	17/09/64	A (02/01/73)
18827	B720-047B	Western	10/03/65	
18828	B720-047B	Western	19/05/65	A (01/08/82)
18829	B720-047B	Western	02/06/65	
18830	B720-047B	Western	17/06/65	
18831	B720-059B	Avianca	08/04/65	
18832	B707-321B	Pan Am	05/02/65	
18833	B707-321B	Pan Am	17/02/65	
18834	B707-321B	Pan Am	24/02/65	
18835	B707-321B	Pan Am	05/03/65	
18836	B707-321B	Pan Am	10/03/65	
18837	B707-321B	Pan Am	17/03/65	
18838	B707-321B	Pan Am	26/03/65	A (Bomb expl. 17/12/73)
18839	B707-321B	Pan Am	16/04/65	
18840	B707-321B	Pan Am	21/04/65	
18841	B707-321B	Pan Am	27/04/65	
18842	B707-321B	Pan Am	21/05/65	
18873	B707-337B	Air India	12/03/65	
18880	B707-348C	Aer Lingus	13/04/65	
18881	B707-328C	Air France	05/08/65	A (21/07/88)
18882	B707-123B	American	27/05/65	
18883	B707-123B	American	26/05/65	
18884	B707-123B	American	15/06/65	
18885	B707-123B	American	23/07/65	
18886	B707-324C	Continental	17/06/65	
18887	B707-324C	Continental	21/06/65	A (11/09/79)
18888	B707-351C	Northwest Orient	22/05/65	A (09/12/91)
18889	B707-351C	Northwest Orient	12/06/65	
18890	B707-329C	Sabena	17/04/65	A (11/05/80)
18891	B707-344B	SAA	27/08/65	
18913	B707-331B	TWA	29/01/65	
18914	B707-331B	TWA	09/04/65	
18915	B707-331B	TWA	25/05/65	
18916	B707-331B	TWA	10/12/65	
18917	B707-331B	TWA	21/12/65	A (Bomb expl. 13/09/70)
18918	B707-331B	TWA	12/01/66	
18921	B707-351C	Northwest Orient	13/08/65	
18922	B707-351C	Northwest Orient	15/09/65	
18923	B707-330B	Lufthansa	04/08/65	
18924	B707-336C	BOAC/Cunard	19/12/65	A (Bomb expl. 25/09/83)
18925	B707-336C	BOAC/Cunard	19/12/65	
18926	B707-330B	Lufthansa	05/10/65	
18927	B707-330B	Lufthansa	24/11/65	
18928	B707-330B	Lufthansa	28/12/65	
18929	B707-330B	Lufthansa	07/01/66	
18930	B707-330B	Lufthansa	19/01/66	
18931	B707-330B	Lufthansa	27/03/66	
18932	B707-330C	Lufthansa	11/03/66	A (11/04/87)
18937	B707-330C	Lufthansa	10/11/65	
18938	B707-323C	American	30/07/65	
18939	B707-323C	American	30/08/65	
18940	B707-323C	American	27/08/65	
18941	B707-328B	Air France	09/02/66	
18948	B707-384C	Olympic	11/05/66	
18949	B707-384C	Olympic	21/05/66	
18950	B707-384C	Olympic	18/06/66	
18954	B707-338C	Qantas	28/12/65	
18955	B707-338C	Qantas	03/02/66	A (14/03/83)
18956	B707-321B	Pan Am	29/01/66	
18957	B707-321B	Pan Am	15/02/66	
18958	B707-321B	Pan Am	25/02/66	A (22/09/80)

Constr. Number	Model	1st Operator	Delivery date	Note
18959	B707-321B	Pan Am	21/05/66	A (22/07/73)
18960	B707-321B	Pan Am	07/04/66	
18961	B707-382B	TAP	16/12/65	Cvtd TC-18F
18962	B707-382B	TAP	08/06/66	Cvtd TC-18F-E-6A
18963	B720-047B	Western	21/07/65	A (Bomb expl. 27/06/76)
18964	B707-351C	Northwest Orient	15/11/65	
18975	B707-349C	Flying Tiger	27/09/65	A (01/02/88)
18976	B707-349C	Flying Tiger	13/10/65	A (04/07/80)
18977	B720-060B	Ethiopian	20/09/65	
18978	B707-331B	TWA	25/01/66	A (22/12/75)
18979	B707-331B	TWA	03/02/66	
18980	B707-331B	TWA	05/02/66	
18981	B707-331B	TWA	05/03/66	
18982	B707-331B	TWA	04/04/66	
18983	B707-331B	TWA	04/04/66	
18984	B707-331B	TWA	20/04/66	
18985	B707-331B	TWA	21/05/66	
18986	B707-131B	TWA	25/03/66	
18987	B707-131B	TWA	16/04/66	
18988	B707-131B	TWA	28/04/66	
18989	B707-131B	TWA	06/05/66	
18991	B707-373C	World	22/10/65	
19000	B707-385C	Boeing	13/09/65	
19001	B707-348C	Aer Lingus	21/04/66	
19002	B720-024B	Continental	16/02/66	
19003	B720-024B	Continental	19/02/66	
19004	B707-358B	El Al	07/01/66	
19034	B707-351C	Northwest Orient	08/01/66	
19104	B707-327C	Braniff	21/05/66	
19105	B707-327C	Braniff	28/05/66	
19106	B707-327C	Braniff	18/06/66	A (09/06/73)
19107	B707-327C	Braniff	29/06/66	A (23/07/79)
19108	B707-327C	Braniff	27/07/66	A (26/07/93)
19133	B707-344B	SAA	09/01/67	
19160	B720-047B	Western	26/01/66	A (Shelling 21/08/85)
19161	B720-047B	Western	12/03/66	A (Shelling 16/06/82)
19162	B707-329C	Sabena	23/06/66	A (01/03/90)
19163	B707-351C	Northwest Orient	17/05/66	
19164	B707-351C	Northwest Orient	24/06/66	
19168	B707-351C	Northwest Orient	12/07/66	A (14/12/88)
19177	B707-324C	Continental	29/07/66	
19178	B707-324C	Varig	23/08/66	
19179	B707-373C	World	29/05/66	
19185	B707-123B	American	30/04/66	
19186	B707-123B	American	04/05/66	
19187	B707-123B	American	12/05/66	
19188	B707-123B	American	30/03/66	
19207	B720-047B	Western	29/07/66	
19208	B720-047B	Western	29/07/66	
19209	B707-351C	Northwest Orient	20/07/66	A (13/04/87)
19210	B707-351C	Northwest Orient	12/08/66	
19211	B707-329C	Sabena	30/08/66	A (13/07/68)
19212	B707-331C	TWA	18/06/67	
19213	B707-331C	TWA	29/08/67	A (23/10/81)
19214	B707-331C	TWA	29/09/67	
19215	B707-131B	TWA	12/11/66	
19216	B707-131B	TWA	08/03/67	
19217	B707-131B	TWA	02/04/67	
19218	B707-131B	TWA	29/03/67	
19219	B707-131B	TWA	14/04/67	
19220	B707-131B	TWA	22/04/67	
19221	B707-131B	TWA	13/05/67	
19222	B707-131B	TWA	27/05/67	
19223	B707-131B	TWA	13/07/67	
19224	B707-331B	TWA	15/03/67	
19225	B707-331B	TWA	04/04/67	
19226	B707-331B	TWA	31/05/67	
19227	B707-331B	TWA	06/08/67	
19235	B707-323C	American	31/08/66	A (30/01/79)
19236	B707-323C	American	28/09/66	Cvtd C-18A
19237	B707-323C	American	30/09/66	
19238	B707-387B	Aerol. Argent.	23/11/66	A (31/01/93)
19239	B707-387B	Aerol. Argent.	16/12/66	
19240	B707-387B	Aerol. Argent.	22/12/66	
19241	B707-387B	Aerol. Argent.	24/02/67	
19247	B707-337B	Air India	12/10/66	
19248	B707-337C	Air India	12/02/67	
19263	B707-351C	Northwest Orient	19/08/66	
19264	B707-321B	Pan Am	06/11/66	
19265	B707-321B	Pan Am	09/11/66	
19266	B707-321B	Pan Am	29/11/66	
19267	B707-321C	Pan Am	15/12/66	
19268	B707-321C	Pan Am	21/12/66	A (22/04/74)
19269	B707-321C	Pan Am	28/06/67	
19270	B707-321C	Pan Am	08/05/67	
19271	B707-321C	Pan Am	15/05/67	
19272	B707-321C	Pan Am	23/05/67	
19273	B707-321C	Pan Am	31/05/67	
19274	B707-321C	Pan Am	22/06/67	
19275	B707-321B	Pan Am	28/06/67	
19276	B707-321B	Pan Am	30/06/67	A (25/01/90)
19277	B707-321B	Pan Am	23/07/67	
19278	B707-321B	Pan Am	29/07/67	
19284	B707-340C	PIA	23/07/66	
19285	B707-340C	PIA	22/10/66	
19286	B707-340C	PIA	21/09/67	
19291	B707-328B	Air France	07/03/67	
19292	B707-328C	Air France	15/03/67	
19293	B707-338C	Qantas	28/01/67	Cvtd E-8C
19294	B707-338C	Qantas	08/03/67	Cvtd E-8C
19295	B707-338C	Qantas	06/09/67	Cvtd E-8C
19296	B707-338C	Qantas	10/10/67	Cvtd E-8C
19297	B707-338C	Qantas	23/10/67	
19315	B707-330B	Lufthansa	31/12/66	
19316	B707-330B	Lufthansa	30/01/67	A (17/05/89)
19317	B707-330C	Lufthansa	06/06/67	
19320	B707-341C	Varig	28/12/66	A (Fire 07/09/68)
19321	B707-341C	Varig	28/12/66	
19322	B707-341C	Varig	22/03/67	A (11/06/81)
19323	B707-123B	American	11/11/66	
19324	B707-123B	American	19/12/66	
19325	B707-123B	American	05/01/67	
19326	B707-123B	American	24/01/67	
19327	B707-123B	American	04/04/67	
19328	B707-123B	American	23/03/67	
19329	B707-123B	American	14/04/67	
19330	B707-123B	American	28/04/67	
19331	B707-123B	American	08/05/67	
19332	B707-123B	American	26/05/67	
19333	B707-123B	American	06/06/67	
19334	B 707-123	American	16/06/67	
19335	B707-123B	American	20/06/67	
19336	B707-123B	American	27/06/67	
19337	B707-123B	American	07/07/67	
19338	B707-123B	American	06/07/67	
19339	B707-123B	American	20/07/67	
19340	B707-123B	American	15/09/67	
19341	B707-123B	American	02/03/68	
19342	B707-123B	American	12/03/69	
19343	B707-123B	American	28/03/69	
19344	B707-123B	American	22/04/69	
19345 to 19349		Cancelled		
19350	B707-324C	Continental	02/12/66	
19351	B707-324C	Continental	01/02/67	
19352	B707-324C	Continental	21/04/67	
19353	B707-324C	Continental	27/05/67	
19354	B707-349C	Flying Tiger	21/06/66	
19355	B707-349C	Flying Tiger	06/02/67	
19361	B707-321B	Pan Am	09/09/67	
19362	B707-321B	Pan Am	14/09/67	
19363	B707-321B	Pan Am	21/09/67	A (Shot down 02/04/78)
19364	B707-321B	Pan Am	29/09/67	
19365	B707-321B	Pan Am	12/10/67	
19366	B707-321B	Pan Am	13/10/67	
19367	B707-321C	Pan Am	27/10/67	
19368	B707-321C	Pan Am	07/11/67	A (03/11/73)
19369	B707-321C	Pan Am	27/11/67	
19370	B707-321C	Pan Am	30/11/67	
19371	B707-321C	Pan Am	30/11/67	A (25/07/71)
19372	B707-321C	Pan Am	12/12/67	
19373	B707-321C	Pan Am	11/12/67	
19374	B707-321B	Pan Am	19/12/67	
19375	B707-321C	Pan Am	09/01/68	
19376	B707-321B	Pan Am	20/12/67	A (30/01/74)
19377	B707-321C	Pan Am	17/01/68	A (04/12/90)
19378	B707-321B	Pan Am	06/02/68	
19379	B707-321C	Pan Am	21/02/68	
19380	B 707-323C	American	21/02/68	Cvtd C-18A
19381	B707-323C	American	23/12/66	Cvtd C-18A-EC-18D
19382	B707-323C	American	02/10/67	
19383	B707-323C	American	02/11/67	
19384	B707-323C	American	21/11/67	Cvtd C-18A-EC-18D

Constr Number	Model	1st Operator	Delivery date	Note	Constr. Number	Model	1st Operator	Delivery date	Note
19410	B707-348C	Aer Lingus	01/07/67	A (10/09/82)	19716	B707-373C	World	02/04/68	
19411	B707-351C	Northwest Orient	30/09/67		19723	B707-328C	Air France	07/11/67	
19412	B707-351C	Northwest Orient	06/12/67	A (03/02/00)	19724	B707-328C	Air France	13/11/67	A (05/03/68)
19413	B720-047B	Western	13/05/67		19736	B707-360C	Ethiopian	17/01/68	A (19/11/77)
19414	B720-047B	Western	28/06/67		19737	B707-312B	Malaysian -Singap.	24/01/68	
19415	B707-399C	Caledonian	13/07/67						
19416	B707-365C	Airlift Int.	14/04/67	A (26/11/92)	19738	B707-312B	Malaysian -Singap.	08/04/68	
19417	B707-355C	Exec Jet/Airlift	19/05/67						
19433	B707-385C	Int Air Bahamas	06/12/66	A (25/03/91)	19739	B707-312B	Malaysian -Singap.	28/05/68	A (21/09/00)
19434	B707-351C	Caledonian	20/03/67						
19435	B707-331C	American	12/10/67	A (24/01/97)	19740	B707-382B	TAP	03/07/68	
19436	B707-131B	TWA	01/08/67		19741	B707-359B	Avianca	09/12/68	
19438	B720-047B	Western	18/08/67		19760	B707-384C	Olympic	19/02/68	
19439	B720-047B	Western	07/09/67	A (31/03/71)	19767	B707-399C	Caledonian	07/03/68	
19440	B707-327C	Western	17/02/67	A (07/07/81)	19773	B707-351C	Northwest Orient	05/06/68	
19441	B707-373C	Braniff	22/12/67	A (04/04/80)	19774	B707-351C	Northwest Orient	29/12/67	
19442	B707-373C	World	03/08/67		19775	B707-351C	Northwest Orient	03/05/68	
19443	B707-351C	Northwest Orient	15/04/71		19776	B707-351C	Northwest Orient	14/05/68	
19498	B707-336C	BOAC	12/08/67		19777	B707-351C	Northwest Orient	18/07/68	
19502	B707-358B	El Al	02/02/67		19789	B707-311C	Wardair	29/07/68	
19515	B707-323C	American	15/08/67		19809	B707-368C	Saudia	14/05/68	
19516	B707-323C	American	23/08/67		19810	B707-368C	Saudia	17/04/68	
19517	B707-323C	American	28/08/67		19820	B707-379C	Ethiopian	08/01/68	A (25/07/90)
19518	B707-323C	American	31/08/67	Cvtd C-18A	19821	B707-379C	Varig	19/01/68	
19519	B707-323C	American	11/09/67		19822	B707-379C	Varig	20/05/68	A (03/01/87)
19521	B707-328C	Air France	03/06/67	A (07/02/99)	19840	B707-345C	Seabord World	27/06/68	
19522	B707-328C	Air France	29/06/67		19841	B707-345C	Seabord World	04/11/68	A (11/07/93)
19523	B720-047B	Western	20/09/67		19842	B707-345C	Varig	26/02/68	
19529	B707-327C	Braniff	10/10/67		19843	B707-336C	BOAC	06/03/68	A (10/03/98)
19530	B707-327C	Braniff	18/10/67		19844	B707-366C	United Arab	06/08/68	
19531	B707-327C	Braniff	20/11/67	A (Bomb expl 14/04/00)	19845	B707-366C	United Arab	13/08/68	A (05/12/72)
19566	B707-331C	TWA	TC-18E		19866	B707-340C	PIA	26/02/68	
19567	B707-331C	TWA	26/06/68		19869	B707-324C	Continental	26/05/69	
19568	B707-131B	TWA	27/06/68		19870	B707-324C	Continental	26/08/68	
19569	B707-131B	TWA	11/03/68		19871	B707-324C	Continental	18/04/68	
19570	B707-331B	TWA	16/03/68		19872	B707-351B	Northwest Orient	24/04/68	A (11/07/89)
19571	B707-331B	TWA	27/03/68		19916	B707-328C	Air France	16/05/68	
19572	B707-331B	TWA	22/03/68	A (08/02/89)	19917	B707-328C	Air France	28/08/68	
19573	B707-331B	TWA	07/05/68		19961	B707-387C	Aerolinas Argentinas	04/12/68	A (27/01/86)
19574	B707-323C	American	21/05/68						
19575	B707-323C	American	04/06/68		19962	B707-387C	Aerolinas Argentinas	10/12/68	
19576	B707-323C	American	17/06/68						
19577	B707-323C	American	26/06/68		19963	B707-347C	Western	04/11/68	
19578 to 19580		Cancelled			19964	B707-347C	Western	04/11/68	
19581	B707-323C	American	31/10/67		19965	B707-347C	Western	22/06/68	A (10/10/88)
19582	B707-323C	American	27/10/67	A (22/10/96)	19966	B707-347C	Western	25/07/68	
19583	B707-323C	American	31/10/67	Cvtd C-18A - EC-18B	19967	B707-347C	Western	29/07/68	
19584	B707-323C	American	27/10/67	A (30/11/95)	19969	B707-382B	TAP	10/09/68	
19585	B707-323C	American	28/11/67		19986	B707-355C	Air France	19/09/68	Cvtd E-8C 97-0100
19586	B707-323C	American	11/01/68		19988	B707-337C	Air India	14/10/68	
19587	B707-323C	American	26/02/68		19996	B707-329C	Sabena	12/12/68	
19588	B707-323C	American	26/02/68	A (Shelling 08/01/87)	19997	B707-307C	Luftwaffe	19/08/68	
19589	B707-323C	American	15/03/68		19998	B707-307C	Luftwaffe	30/09/68	
19590	B707-365C	American	04/04/68		19999	B707-307C	Luftwaffe	30/09/68	
19621	B707-338C	Qantas	26/04/68	Cvtd E-8C	20000	B707-307C	Luftwaffe	15/10/68	
19622	B707-338C	Qantas	21/12/67	Cvtd E-8C	20008	B707-320C	Varig	31/10/68	
19623	B707-338C	Qantas	08/12/67		20016	B707-321C	Pan Am	18/11/68	Cvtd E-8C 95-0121
19624	B707-338C	Qantas	10/01/68		20017	B707-321C	Pan Am	03/10/90	
19625	B707-338C	Qantas	05/02/68		20018	B707-321C	Pan Am	12/12/68	
19626	B707-338C	Qantas	27/03/68	Cvtd E-8A-E-8C	20019	B707-321B	Pan Am	25/10/68	
19627	B707-338C	Qantas	04/04/68		20020	B707-321B	Pan Am	22/11/68	
19628	B707-338C	Qantas	04/05/68		20021	B707-321B	Pan Am	10/12/68	A (23/06/90)
19629	B707-338C	Qantas	16/05/68		20022	B707-321B	Pan Am	13/12/68	
19630	B707-338C	Qantas	12/06/68	A (17/10/88)	20023	B707-321B	Pan Am	17/12/68	
19631	B707-351C	Northwest Orient	22/08/68		20024	B707-321B	Pan Am	18/12/68	
19632	B707-351C	Northwest Orient	21/11/67		20025	B707-321B	Pan Am	08/01/69	
19633	B707-351B	Northwest Orient	14/10/67		20026	B707-321B	Pan Am	10/01/69	
19634	B707-351B	Northwest Orient	21/11/67		20027	B707-321B	Pan Am	24/01/69	
19635	B707-351B	Northwest Orient	26/03/68		20028	B707-321B	Pan Am	31/01/69	A (20/09/90)
19636	B707-351B	Northwest Orient	29/03/68		20029	B707-321B	Pan Am	06/02/69	
19664	B707-355C	Executive Jet	10/05/68	A (14/11/98)	20030	B707-321B	Pan Am	06/02/69	
19693	B707-321B	Pan Am	24/07/68		20031	B707-321B	Pan Am	04/03/69	
19694	B707-321B	Pan Am	09/11/67		20032	B707-321B	Pan Am	14/03/69	
19695	B707-321B	Pan Am	08/02/68		20033	B707-321B	Pan Am	23/06/69	
19696	B707-321B	Pan Am	22/02/68	A (12/12/68)	20034	B707-321B	Pan Am	14/03/69	
19697	B707-321B	Pan Am	14/03/68		20035	B707-384B	Olympic	23/06/69	
19698	B707-321B	Pan Am	28/03/68		20036	B707-384B	Olympic	31/03/69	
19699	B707-321B	Pan Am	09/04/68		20043	B707-396C	Wardair	19/12/68	
19705	B707-344C	SAA	17/04/68	A (20/04/68)	20056	B707-131B	TWA	23/01/69	
19706	B707-344C	SAA	24/04/68		20057	B707-131B	TWA	23/06/69	
19715	B707-373C	World	22/02/38	A (02/08/76)	20058	B707-331B	TWA	08/01/69	

Constr. Number	Model	1st Operator	Delivery date	Note
20059	B707-331B	TWA	23/01/69	
20060	B707-331B	TWA	12/12/68	
20061	B707-331B	TWA	15/01/69	
20062	B707-331B	TWA	03/03/69	
20063	B707-331B	TWA	07/03/69	A (Bomb expl. 08/09/74)
20064	B707-331B	TWA	02/04/69	
20065	B707-331B	TWA	07/04/69	
20066	B707-331B	TWA	01/05/69	
20067	B707-331B	TWA	07/05/69	
20068	B707-331C	TWA	12/06/69	A (14/09/72)
20069	B707-331C	TWA	17/06/69	
20076	B707-372C	Airlift	02/07/69	
20077	B707-372C	Airlift	16/07/69	A (23/10/96)
20084	B707-369C	Kuwait Airways	14/06/69	
20085	B707-369C	Kuwait Airways	11/07/69	
20086	B707-369C	Kuwait Airways	04/11/68	
20087	B707-323C	American	14/11/68	
20088	B707-323C	American	25/11/68	
20089	B707-323C	American	05/07/68	
20097	B707-358B	El Al	17/07/68	
20110	B707-344C	SAA	30/08/68	
20122	B707-358C	El Al	22/01/68	
20123	B707-330C	Lufthansa	17/04/69	
20124	B707-330C	Lufthansa	15/05/69	
20136	B707-382B	TAP	27/02/69	
20170	B707-323B	American	08/05/69	
20171	B707-323B	American	28/04/69	
20172	B707-323B	American	09/04/69	
20173	B707-323B	American	16/04/69	A (04/12/82)
20174	B707-323B	American	30/04/69	
20175	B707-323B	American	09/05/69	
20176	B707-323B	American	23/08/69	
20177	B707-323B	American	13/06/69	
20178	B707-323B	American	31/07/69	
20179	B707-323B	American	19/08/67	
20198	B707-329C	Sabena	09/09/69	
20199	B707-329C	Sabena	22/07/69	
20200	B707-329C	Sabena	17/06/69	
20224	B707-3B4C	MEA	22/07/69	A (Shelling 12/06/82)
20225	B707-3B4C	MEA	03/12/69	A (Shelling 28/12/68)
20230	B707-344C	SAA	18/11/68	
20259	B707-3B4C	MEA	18/11/68	
20260	B707-3B4C	MEA	28/08/68	A (23/03/01)
20261	B707-309C	China AL	01/10/69	
20262	B707-309C	China AL	28/10/69	A (27/02/80)
20275	B707-340C	PIA	07/11/69	A (26/11/79)
20283	B707-344C	SAA	18/12/69	
20287	B707-286C	Iran Air	31/12/69	
20288	B707-286C	Iran Air	17/03/70	
20297	B707-382B	TAP	13/02/70	
20298	B707-382B	TAP	25/03/70	
20301	B707-358C	El Al	26/01/70	
20315	CC-137	Canadian AF	25/02/70	
20316	CC-137	Canadian AF	28/02/70	Cvtd E-8C
20317	CC-137	Canadian AF	04/03/70	Cvtd E-8C
20318	CC-137	Canadian AF	10/03/70	Cvtd E-8C
20319	CC-137	Canadian AF	11/05/70	
20341	B707-366C	United Arab AL	24/04/70	
20342	B707-366C	United Arab AL	16/01/70	A (17/10/82)
20374	B-707-336C	BOAC	06/03/70	
20375	B-707-336C	BOAC	25/03/70	
20395	B707-330C	Lufthansa	16/10/70	A (26/07/79)
20428	B707-331C	TWA	23/07/70	
20429	B707-331C	TWA	25/08/70	
20439	Cancelled			
20456	B707-336B	BOAC	18/02/71	
20457	B707-336B	BOAC	17/04/71	A (13/06/85)
20474	B707-3F9C	Nigeria Airways	11/05/71	
20477 to 20479	Cancelled			
20487	B707-340	PIA	15/10/70	A (15/12/71)
20488	B707-340	PIA	23/12/70	
20494	B707-3D3C	Alia Jordanian	08/04/72	A (22/01/73)
20495	B707-3D3C	Alia Jordanian	31/10/73	Cvtd E-8C
20514	B707-3F5C	Portugal	23/09/71	
20515	B707-3F5C	Portugal	14/12/71	
20516	Cancelled			
20517	B707-336C	BOAC	28/05/71	
20518	EC-137D	Boeing	18/02/72	Test AWACS
20519	EC-137D	USAF	23/10/78	Test AWACS
20522	B707-3B5C	KAL	06/08/71	A (Bomb expl. 29/11/87)
20546	B707-369C	Kuwait Airways	15/01/72	A (30/06/96)
20547	B707-369C	Kuwait Airways	25/02/72	
20629	B707-3H7C	Cameroon A/L	20/11/72	
20630	B707-353B/VC-137	USAF	09/08/72	
20669	B707-3F9C	Nigeria Airways	16/01/73	A (19/12/94)
20714	B707-3J6B	CAAC	23/08/73	A (02/10/90)
20715	B707-3J6B	CAAC	17/09/73	
20716	B707-3J6B	CAAC	15/04/74	
20717	B707-3J6B	CAAC	10/05/74	
20718	B707-3J6C	CAAC	12/11/73	
20719	B707-3J6C	CAAC	22/11/73	
20720	B707-3J6C	CAAC	13/12/73	
20721	B707-3J6C	CAAC	14/01/74	
20722	B707-3J6C	CAAC	26/02/74	
20723	B707-3J6C	CAAC	19/03/74	
20741	B707-386C	Iran Air	01/05/73	
20760	B707-366C	Egyptair	30/03/73	A (22/08/96)
20761	B707-366C	Egyptair	29/05/73	
20762	B707-366C	Egyptair	29/06/73	
20763	B707-366C	Egyptair	20/09/73	A (25/12/76)
20803	B707-3K1C	Tarom	21/02/74	
20804	B707-3K1C	Tarom	03/06/74	
20805	B707-3K1C	Tarom	03/06/74	
20830	B707-3J9C	Iran AF	29/05/74	
20831	B707-3J9C	Iran AF	10/05/74	
20832	B707-3J9C	Iran AF	26/07/74	
20833	B707-3J9C	Iran AF	30/09/74	
20834	B707-3J9C	Iran AF	17/11/74	
20835	B707-3J9C	Iran AF	16/12/74	
20889	B707-370C	Iraqi Airways	27/08/74	
20890	B707-370C	Iraqi Airways	23/09/74	
20891	B707-370C	Iraqi Airways	07/10/74	
20897	B707-3J8C	Sudan Airways	17/06/74	
20898	B707-3J8C	Sudan Airways	10/07/74	
20919	B707-366C	Egyptair	21/08/74	
20920	B707-366C	Egyptair	15/11/74	
21046	E-3A	Boeing	28/04/74	Cvtd JE-3C — E-3C
21047	E-3A	USAF	E-3B	
21049	B707-3L6B	Boeing	08/01/75	
21070	B707-387B	Argentine AF	11/06/75	
21081	B707-368C	Govt Saudi Arabia	25/09/75	
21092	B707-3M1C	Pelita AS	25/09/75	
21096	B707-3L6C	Boeing	09/06/75	
21103	B707-368C	Saudia	14/10/75	A (29/10/91)
21104	B707-368C	Saudia	18/12/75	
21123	B707-3J9C	Iran AF	27/02/76	
21124	B707-3J9C	Iran AF	14/06/76	
21125	B707-3J9C	Iran AF	18/06/76	
21126	B707-3J9C	Iran AF	31/08/76	
21127	B707-3J9C	Iran AF	27/09/76	
21128	B707-3J9C	Iran AF	19/11/76	
21129	B707-3J9C	Iran AF	14/12/76	A (?)
21185	E-3A	USAF	18/08/78	Cvtd E-3B
21207	E-3A	USAF	23/03/77	Cvtd E-3B
21208	E-3A	USAF	29/05/77	Cvtd E-3B
21209	E-3A	USAF	21/10/77	Cvtd E-3B
21228	B707-3L5C	Libyan Arab	19/07/76	
21250	E-3A	USAF	21/11/77	Cvtd E-3B
21251	B707-368C	Saudia	23/12/77	
21334	B707-3P1C	Govt Qatar	28/07/77	
21367	B707-368C	Saudia	04/04/77	
21368	B707-368C	Saudia	27/06/77	
21396	B707-386C	Gov. Iran	03/05/78	
21428	B707-3F9C	Nigeria Airways	30/01/78	
21434	E-3A	USAF	19/01/78	Cvtd E-3B
21435	E-3A	USAF	25/05/78	Cvtd E-3B
21436	E-3A	USAF	22/06/78	Cvtd E-3B
21437	E-3A	USAF	29/09/78	Cvtd E-3B
21475	B707-3J9C	Iran AF	20/12/78	
21551	E-3A	USAF	29/09/78	Cvtd E-3B
21552	E-3A	USAF	20/11/78	Cvtd E-3B
21553	E-3A	USAF	19/12/78	Cvtd E-3B

Constr. Number	Model	1st Operator	Delivery date	Note
21554	E-3A	USAF	19/01/79	Cvtd E-3B A (22/09/95)
21555	E-3A	USAF	16/03/79	Cvtd E-3B
21556	E-3A	USAF	22/05/79	Cvtd E-3B
21651	B707-3K1C	Gov. Roumania	30/03/79	A (10/01/91)
21752	E-3A	USAF	14/09/79	
21753	E-3A	USAF	20/12/79	
21754	E-3A	USAF	03/06/80	
21755	E-3A	USAF	18/09/80	Cvtd E-3B
21756	E-3A	USAF	19/12/80	Cvtd E-3B
21757	E-3B	USAF	19/03/81	Cvtd E-3B
21956	B707-700	Boeing	18/11/81	Test CFM56
22829	E-3C	USAF	10/03/82	
22830	E-3C	USAF	04/12/81	
22831	E-3C	USAF	06/04/82	
22832	E-3C	USAF	23/07/82	
22833	E-3C	USAF	19/10/82	
22834	E-3C	USAF	20/04/83	
22835	E-3C	USAF	29/07/83	
22836	E-3C	USAF	01/11/83	
22837	E-3C	USAF	18/04/84	
22838	E-3A	NATO	19/06/84	
22839	E-3A	NATO	19/05/82	
22840	E-3A	NATO	19/08/82	
22841	E-3A	NATO	12/11/82	
22842	E-3A	NATO	10/03/83	
22843	E-3A	NATO	05/06/83	
22844	E-3A	NATO	27/06/83	
22845	E-3A	NATO	19/08/83	
22846	E-3A	NATO	12/10/83	
22847	E-3A	NATO	20/10/84	
22848	E-3A	NATO	27/04/84	
22849	E-3A	NATO	18/05/84	
22850	E-3A	NATO	02/11/84	
22851	E-3A	NATO	11/02/85	
22852	E-3A	NATO	07/11/84	A (17/07/96)
22853	E-3A	NATO	19/12/84	
22854	E-3A	NATO	18/03/85	
22855	E-3A	NATO	30/04/85	
23417	RE-3A	RSAF	22/01/82	
23418	RE-3A	RSAF	31/10/86	
23419	RE-3A	RSAF	29/08/86	
23420	RE-3A	RSAF	29/06/86	
23421	RE-3A	RSAF	23/12/86	
23422	KE-3A	RSAF	02/05/87	
23423	KE-3A	RSAF	24/06/87	
23424	KE-3A	RSAF	02/03/87	
23425	KE-3A	RSAF	16/06/87	
23426	KE-3A	RSAF	12/02/87	
23427	KE-3A	RSAF	08/07/87	
23428	KE-3A	RSAF	11/06/87	
23429	KE-3A	RSAF	16/09/87	
23430	E-6A	US Navy	13/08/87	
23889	E-6A	US Navy	18/03/92	
23890	E-6A	US Navy	07/09/89	
23891	E-6A	US Navy	02/08/89	
23892	E-6A	US Navy	02/08/89	
23893	E-6A	US Navy	06/10/89	
23894	E-6A	US Navy	18/12/89	
24109	E-3D	RAF	13/07/90	
24110	E-3D	RAF	22/05/91	
24111	E-3D	RAF	25/03/91	
24112	E-3D	RAF	08/07/91	
24113	E-3D	RAF	19/09/91	
24114	E-3D	RAF	21/11/91	
24115	E-3A	Armée de l'Air	09/03/92	
24116	E-3A	Armée de l'Air	22/05/91	
24117	E-3A	Armée de l'Air	23/07/91	
24499	E-3D	RAF	11/09/91	
24500	E-6A	US Navy	12/05/92	
24501	E-6A	US Navy	12/04/90	
24502	E-6A	US Navy	29/08/90	
24503	E-6A	US Navy	28/05/92	Cvtd YE-8B
24504	E-6A	US Navy	03/10/91	
24505	E-6A	US Navy	20/12/90	Cvtd E-6B
24506	E-6A	US Navy	25/04/91	
24507	E-6A	US Navy	02/08/91	
24508	E-6A	US Navy	01/08/91	
24509	E-6A	US Navy	21/12/91	
24510	E-3A	Armée de l'Air	15/02/92	

ABBREVIATIONS & ACRONYMS

AACS: Airborne Air Control Squadron
AB: Air Base
ABL: Airborne Laser
ABNCP: Airborne National Command Post
AC&CS: Airborne Command and Control Squadron
ACC: Air Combat Command
ACGS (Sq): Aerospace Cartographic and Geodetic Service (Squadron)
ACP: Airborne Command Post
ACW: Air Control Wing
ADC: Air Defense Command
ADCOM: Air (later Aerospace) Defense Command
AETC: Air Education and Training Command
AEW: Airborne Early Warning
AEWF: Airborne Early Warning Force (NATO)
AF: Air Force
AFB: Air Force Base
AFMC: Air Force Materiel Command
AFRC: Air Force Reserve Command
AFRES: Air Force Reserve
ALCM: Air Launched Cruise Missile
ALCS: Airborne Launch Control System
ALL: Airborne Laser Laboratory
A-LOTS: Airborne Lightweight Optical Tracking System
AMARC: Aircraft Maintenance And Regeneration Center
AMC: Air Mobility Command
AMW: Air Mobility Wing
ANG: Air National Guard
ARG: Air Refueling Group
ARIA: Apollo (Advanced) Range Instrumentation Aircraft
ARW: Air Refueling Wing
ATG/ATS: Air Transport Group (Squadron)
AW: Airlift Wing
AWACS: Airborne Warning And Control System
AW&CW (S): Airborne Warning And Control Wing (Squadron)
BuNo: Bureau of Aeronautics Number
BW: Bombardment/Bomb Wing
CENTAF: Central Air Force
CENTCOM: Central Command
c/n: construction number
CINCLANT: Commander in Chief, Atlantic
CINCPAC: Commander in Chief, Pacific Command
CINCPACAF: Commander in Chief, Pacific Air Forces
CINCSAC: Commander in Chief, Strategic Air Command
CINCUSAFE: Commander in Chief, United States Air Forces in Europe
COMINT: Communication Intelligence
DEW: Distant Early Warning
DOD: Department of Defense
ECM: Electronic Countermeasures
ELINT: Electronic Intelligence
ETTF: European Tanker Task Force
FAC: Forward Air Control
FEAF: Far East Air Forces
(later renamed PACAF)
FS: Fighter Squadron
FW: Fighter Wing
ICBM: intercontinental ballistic missile
ICM: intercontinental missile
J-STARS: Joint Surveillance Target Attack Radar System
LANTIRN: Low Altitude Navigation and Targeting Infrared System for Night
LORAN: Long Range Aid to Navigation
MAC: Military Airlift Command (replace MATS)
MATS: Military Air Transport Service (later renamed MAC)
MAW: Military Airlift Wing
MILSTAR: Military Strategic and Tactical Relay System
NAS: Naval Air Station
NASA: National Aeronautics and Space Administration
NEACP: National Emergency Airborne Command Post
NORAD: North American Air Defense Command
PACAF: Pacific Air Forces (first designated FEAF)
PACCS: Post attack Command and Control System
Prov: Provisional
RAAF: Royal Australian Air Force
RAF: Royal Air Force (United Kingdom)
RCM: Electronic countermeasure reconnaissance
RS: Reconnaissance Squadron
RW: Reconnaissance Wing
SAC: Strategic Air Command
SAGE: Semi-Automatic Ground Environment
SEA: Southeast Asia
SIGINT: Signal Intelligence
s/n: serial number
Sqn: Squadron
SRS: Strategic Reconnaissance Squadron
SRW: Strategic Reconnaissance Wing
SW: Strategic Wing (before1994)/ Space Wing (since 1994)
TAC: Tactical Air Command
TACAMO: Take Charge And Move Out
TAW: Tactical Airlift Wing
TELINT: Telemetry Intelligence
TRIA: Telemetry Range Instrumented Aircraft
TRS: Tactical Reconnaissance Squadron
TRW: Tactical Reconnaissance Wing before 1992; Training Wing since 1993
TS: Test Squadron
TW: Test Wing
UHF: Ultra High Frequency
USAF: United States Air Force
USAFE: United States Air Forces in Europe
USN: United States Navy
VIP: Very Important Person (s)
Wg: Wing
WRS: Weather Reconnaissance Squadron

C-137B
VC-137B declassified to a transport plane 3 aircraft (1998)

C-18A
Training version based on the Boeing 707-320C. 9 aircraft (1981)

EC-18B
C-18A equipped with a special radome for telemetric missions. 4 aircraft (1985)

EC-18D
C-18A modified for remote missile control. 2 aircraft

EC-137D
Prototype of the E-3A made from a Boeing 707-320B. 2 aircraft (1972).

EC-137E
Civil 707-300C transformed for the Commander of US SOUTHCOM. 1 aircraft

E-3A Sentry
Airborne early warning and control (AWACS) based on the Boeing 707-320B. 22 aircraft produced (1980) for the USAF and 23 for NATO and Saudi Arabia.

E-3B Sentry
E-3A fitted with improved electronic equipment. Most of the aircraft were later modernised to the E-3C with new CFM 56 engines. 10 aircraft made

E-6A Mercury
Communication relays for the US Navy based on the 707-320C. 16 aircraft made. (1987-90)

E-8A
707-320C modified as part of the joint USAF/US Navy Joint STARS attack and surveillance program. Original designation: EC-18C. 2 aircraft

E-8C
Airframe J-STARS transformed by Northrop-Grumman. 18 aircraft (1994).

JE-3C
E-3A modified, test bed. 1 aircraft.

KE-3A Sentry
E-3A equipped for flight refuelling and destined for Saudi Arabia. 8 aircraft made (1986-87).

E-3D Sentry (AEW.Mk. 1)
Identical version to the E-3A destined for Great Britain. 7 aircraft made.

E-3F Sentry
Identical version ti the E-3A destined for France. 4 aircraft made (1990-91)

TC-18E
Training version based on the 707-320C. 2 aircraft

TC-18F
Training variant for US Navy E-6A crews. 3 aircraft

VC-137A
VIP transport based on the Boeing 707-153 made whilst waiting for the arrival of the VC-137C. 3 aircraft (1959)

VC-137B
VC-137A re-engined. 3 aircraft (1963).

VC-137C
VIP transport based on Boeing

707-353B. 2 aircraft (1962).

YE-8B
Prototype made as part of the Joint-STARS program and based on the 707-320C. 1 aircraft made.

Model 707-3F3B
Argentina, 1 aircraft.

Model 707-3L6B
Malaysia, 2 aircraft.

Model 707-307C
Germany (designated C-137), 4 aircraft

Model 707-347C
Canada (designated CC-137C), 5 aircraft.

Model 707-366C
Egypt, 1 aircraft

Model 707-368C
Saudi Arabia, 1 aircraft

Model 707-3F5C
Portugal, 2 aircraft

Model 707-3M1C
Indonesia, 1 aircraft

Model 707-3J9C
Iran ('Peace Station'), 14 aircraft

Model 707-3P1C
Qatar, aircraft

E-8C
Battlefield surveillance aircraft derived from the joint USAF/US Army J-STARS program and built by Northrop-Grumman. 18 aircraft.

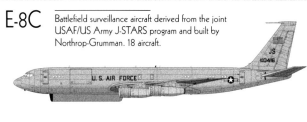

VC-137C
VIP transport version based on the 707-353B. 2 aircraft

E-6B MERCURY
Communication relay aircraft built for the US Navy and based on the 707-320C. 16 aircraft.

EC-135N
Version derived from the C/TC-18 for the pursuit of spacecraft and based on the 707-320C.

E-3 SENTRY
Airborne warning and control systems (AWACS).

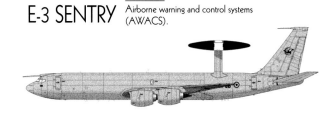

CUSTOMERS CODES

Code	Airline	Code	Airline	Code	Airline
20	Boeing		Air Force		Airways (BWIA)
21	Pan American World Airways	54	Mohawk Airlines	79	Saturn Airways, later Trans International A/L
22	United Airlines	55	Executive Jet Management		
23	American Airlines	56	Iberia Airlines	80	Bankers Trust
24	Continental Airlines	57	Swissair	81	All Nippon Airways
25	Eastern Air Lines	58	El Al	82	TAP Portugal
26	USAF/ MATS	59	Avianca	83	SAS
27	Braniff	60	Ethiopian Airlines	84	Olympic Airways
28	Air France	61	Federal Aviation Administration	85	American Flyers
29	Sabena			86	Iran Air
30	Lufthansa	62	Pacific Northern Airlines , later Western Airlines, later Delta Air Lines	87	Aerolíneas Argentinas
31	TWA, later American Airlines			89	Japan Air System later Japan Airlines Domestic
32	Delta Air Lines				
33	Air Canada	63	Faucett	90	Alaska Airlines
34	Transair Sweden	64	Mexicana	91	Frontier Airlines, later People Express
35	National Airlines	65	Cunard Eagle and British Eagle		
36	BOAC, later British Airways	66	United Arab Airlines later Egyptair		Continental Airlines
37	Air India	67	Cathay Pacific Airways	92	Southern Air Transport
38	Qantas				
39	Cubana	68	Saudi Arabian Airlines	93	Pacific Airlines, later Air California later American Airlines
40	Pakistan International Airlines	69	Kuwait Airways		
41	Varig Brazilian Airlines	70	Iraqi Airways	94	Syrian Arab Airlines
42	Nordair	71	Trans International Airlines, later TransAmerica	95	Northeast Airlines later Delta Air Lines
43	Alitalia				
44	South African Airways	72	Airlift International	96	Quebecair later Nordair
45	Seaboard World Airlines	73	World Airways		
46	Japan Airlines (JAL)	74	Iraqi Airways later Libyan Arab	97	Aloha Airlines
47	Western Airlines later Delta Air Lines	75	Pacific Western later Canadian Airlines	98	Air Zaire
48	Aer Lingus			99	Caledonian Airways
49	Flying Tiger Line	76	Trans Australia Airlines , later Australian Airlines, later Qantas		
50	Trek Airways				
51	Northwest Airlines				
52	Aeromexico	77	Ansett Australia		
53	United States	78	British West Indian		

Examples: a Boeing 707-138 is an aircraft from the -100 series, specially built for Qantas and a 707-430, a -400 series aircraft delivered new to Lufthansa.

This designation is kept during all the aircraft's life, whatever the successive owners may be.

Characteristics of the military versions of the BOEING 707

	E-3 Sentry	E-8C J-STARS
Type	Airborne Warning and Control System (AWACS)	Airborne command post/battle management aircraft
Crew	Flight crew: 4. From 13 to 19 in-board systems specialists	Flight crew: 4. At least 15 specialists from the USAF and 3 from the US Army
Power plant	USA/NATO: four Pratt & Whitney TF33-PW-100A 21,000 lb (93 kN) unitary thrust GB/France/Saudi Arabia: four CFM-56-2A-2/3 turbofan 24,000 lb (107 kN) unitary thrust	Four Pratt & Whitney TF33-102C 19,200 lb (85 kN) unitary thrust

Dimensions and weights

	E-3 Sentry	E-8C J-STARS
Length	152 ft 11 in	152 ft 11 in
Wingspan	145 ft 9 in	145 ft 9 in
Height	41 ft 4 in	42 ft 6 in
Wing area	3,050 sq ft	3,050 sq ft^2
Empty weight	162,000 lb (E-3D/F: 185,000 lb)	
Max. take-off weight	347,000 lb (E-3D/F: 334,000 lb)	336,000 lb

Performance

	E-3 Sentry	E-8C J-STARS
Max. speed	473 kt (E-3D/F: 515 kt)	390 to 510 kt (Mach 0.52 to 0.65)
		9 hours (without refuelling)
Range	4,000 NM (E-3D/F: 5,000 NM)	42,000 ft
Service ceiling	29,000 ft (E-3D/F: 43,000 ft)	

KC-135 and C-135: VERSIONS & VARIANTS

● **C-135A** 'Stratolifter' : transport version. No refuelling boom. Constructor designation: Model 717-157. 15 aircraft.

● C-135A 'Falsies' : 3 KC-135A (60-0356, 60-0357, 60-0362) transformed in the factory with a short tailfin and with an added refuelling boom.

● C-135B: version identical to the C-135A but equipped with turbofans and larger elevators. Constructor designation: Model 717-158. 30 aircraft (1961-62).

◆ C-135B T/RIA: C-135B modified with a bulbous nose. 4 aircraft

◆ C-135C: WC-135A converted to a transport plane with improved engines. 3 aircraft.

◆ C-135E: C-135A re-engined with Pratt & Whitney TF33 turbofans. 3 aircraft.

◆ C-135F: (F for 'France') refuelling version retaining its cargo capacity destined for France. Constructor designation: Model 717-164. 12 aircraft (1963-64).

◆ C-135FR: C-135F re-engined with CFM56 turbofans (1984).

◆ C-135N: EC-135N declassified to supply unit. Large nose retained. 4 aircraft.

◆ EC-135A: KC-135A modified to an airborne radio relay. 11 aircraft modified (1965).

◆ EC-135B: C-135B T/RIA modified with a nose radar and extra antennae. 2 aircraft transformed (1978).

◆ EC-135B ARIA (Apollo, then Advanced Range Instrumentation Aircraft): Modified C-135B, equipped with a bulbous nose and destined for the pursuit of missiles and spacecraft. 4 aircraft transformed.

◆ EC-135C: new designation of the KC-135B (airborne command post). 14 aircraft modified.

◆ **EC-135E**: Re-engined EC-135N used for various tests. 2 aircraft modified (1981).

◆ **EC-135G**: KC-135A transformed to an airborne command post and equipped for the remote launching of missiles. 4 aircraft transformed (1965).

◆ **EC-135H**: Airborne command post made from a KC-135A airframe. 5 aircraft transformed (1968).

◆ EC-135J: Airborne command post made from the KC-135B. 3 aircraft transformed (1965).

◆ **EC-135K**: KC-135A with improved communication equipment destined for logistical support for fighters during deployment. 3 aircraft transformed.

◆ **EC-135L**: Airborne command post (and crisis) made from a KC-135A. 8 aircraft transformed (1965).

◆ **EC-135N**: C-135A equipped with a larger nose destined for the pursuit of spacecraft as part of the Apollo (ARIA) program. 8 aircraft transformed (1967).

◆ **EC-135P**: Airborne command post made from the airframes of de KC-135A, NKC-135A and EC-135H. 5 aircraft transformed.

◆ EC-135Y: NKC-135A converted to an airborne command post. 1 aircraft (1984).

◆ GKC-135A: KC-135A modified into a ground training airframe. 1 aircraft.

◆ GNC-135A: NC-135A modified into a ground training airframe. 1 aircraft.

◆ JKC-135A: flying test bed (J = temporary conversion) made from a KC-135A airframe. 5 aircraft.

● **KC-135A 'Stratotanker'** : First in flight refuelling version. Constructor designation: Model 717-100A (29 aircraft.), 717-146 (68 aircraft.), 717-148 (635 aircraft.). Total = 732 aircraft.

KC-135A

C-135A
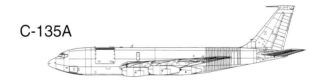

KC-135E

KC-135R
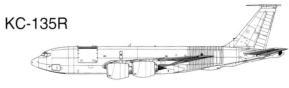

The nation's first jet transport-tanker is in the air

First production model of the Boeing KC-135 jet transport-tanker is shown above on one of its routine test flights. The Air Force has announced that production will be stepped up to a rate of 20 per month earlier than originally planned.

The KC-135 is a sleek, swept-wing craft capable of speeds in the 500-mile-an-hour range. It will refuel jet bombers and fighters while flying eight miles or more above the earth—at speeds best suited to jet flight. It is a versatile aircraft.

convertible in a matter of hours from tanker into a military transport. As a transport it offers the full potential of jet-age operation for carrying personnel and critical cargo.

Design of the KC-135 is based on that of a prototype model which already has behind it more than two years of intensive flight testing. The KC-135 incorporates many design advances that could come only from such a flight test program. This experience background enabled Boeing to cut production time on the first KC-135

by 20 per cent under normal estimates for a first production model.

The new Boeing transport-tanker also benefits from the knowledge Boeing has gained through developing and producing more than 1400 B-47 and B-52 multi-jet bombers, the backbone of the Strategic Air Command's nuclear weapons carrier forces. In the not too distant future, this team of revolutionary Boeing bombers will be joined by the newest Boeing jet, the KC-135 transport-tanker.

C/KC-135 VERSIONS

Year	Model	Designation	Quantity
1956	Model 717-100A	KC-135A	29
1957	Model 717-146	KC-135A	68
1958	Model 717-148	KC-135A	635
			Sub-total: 732
1961	Model 717-157	C-135A	15
1962	Model 717-158	C-135B	30
1963	Model 717-164	C-135F	12
1964	Model 717-166	KC-135B	17
			Sub-total: 74
1965	Model 739-700	RC-135A	4
1964	Model 739-445B	RC-135B	10
			Sub-total: 14
			Grand Total : 820

C/KC-135 PRODUCTION LIST

KC-135A
Produced from 1955 to 1964 at the Renton plant (Washington). 582 first aircraft with short tail, later enlarged.
Serial numbers:
55-3118 to 55-3146; 56-3591 to 56-3658; 57-1418 to 57-1514; 57-2589 to 57-2609; 58-0001 to 58-0130; 59-1443 to 59-1523; 60-0313 to 60-0368; 61-0261 to 61-0325; 62-3497 to 62-3580; 63-7976 to 63-8045; 63-8871 to 63-8888; 64-14828 to 64-14840 **Total: 732**
57 aircraft cancelled

C-135A
Cargo and passenger transport version, without refuelling boom. 3 KC-135A (s/n 60-0356, 60-0357 and 60-0362) factory modified into C-135A « Falsies » with short tail and refuelling boom. Production: 1961.
Serial numbers: 60-0369 to 60-0378; 61-0326 to 61-0330. **Total: 15**

C-135B
As C-135B but new engines and enlarged tail. Production: 1961-62.
Serial numbers:
61-0331, 61-0332, 61-2662, 61-2663; 61-2664 to 61-2674; 62-4125 to 62-4139. **Total: 30**

C-135F
Idem KC-135A. Aircraft acquired by France ('F'). Production: 1963-64.
Serial numbers: 63-8470 to 63-8475; 63-12735 to 63-12740 **Total: 12**

KC-135B
Identical to KC-135A but with different engines (turbofan). Production: 1963-65.
Serial numbers: 62-3581 to 62-3585; 63-8046 to 63-8052; 63-8053 to 63-8057. **Total: 17**

RC-135A
Production: 1965. **Serial numbers:** 63-8058 to 63-8061 **Total: 4**

RC-135B
Similar to C-135B, ELINT version. No refuelling boom. Production: 1964-65.
Serial numbers: 63-9792; 64-14841 to 64-14849 **Total: 10**

KC-135D
Four RC-135A redesignated KC-135D after being transformed into tankers (refuelling boom, etc.). Designation kept after re-engining with TF33 turbofans.
Serial numbers: 63-8058 to 63-8061

KC-135E
Designation of more than 150 KC-135A re-engined with TF33 turbofans.
Serial numbers:
55-3141; 55-3143; 55-3145; 55-3146; 56-3593; 56-3604; 56-3606; 56-3607; 56-3609; 56-3611; 56-3612; 56-3622; 56-3623; 56-3626; 56-3630; 56-3631; 56-3638; 56-3640; 56-3641; 56-3643; 56-3645; 56-3648; 56-3650; 56-3654; 56-3658; 57-1421; 57-1422; 57-1423; 57-1425; 57-1426; 57-1428; 57-1429; 57-1431; 57-1433; 27-1434; 57-1436; 57-1438; 57-1441; 57-1443; 57-1445; 57-1447; 57-1448; 57-1450; 57-1451; 57-1452; 57-1455; 57-1458; 57-1460; 57-1463; 57-1464; 57-1465; 57-1468; 57-1471; 57-1475; 57-1478; 57-1479; 57-1480; 57-1482; 57-1484; 57-1485; 57-1491; 57-1492; 57-1494; 57-1495; 57-1496; 57-1497; 57-1501; 57-1503; 57-1504; 57-1505; 57-1507; 57-1509; 57-1510; 57-1511; 57-1512; 57-2589; 57-2594; 57-2595; 57-2598; 57-2600; 57-2603; 57-2604; 57-2606; 57-2607; 57-2608; 58-0003; 58-0005; 58-0006; 58-0008; 58-0012; 58-0013; 58-0014; 58-0017; 58-0020; 58-0024; 58-0032; 58-0037; 58-0040; 58-0041; 58-0043; 58-0044; 58-0052; 58-0053; 58-0057; 58-0058; 58-0064; 58-0068; 58-0078; 58-0080; 58-0082; 58-0085; 58-0087; 58-0090; 58-0096; 58-0107; 58-0108; 58-0111; 58-0115; 58-0116; 59-1445; 59-1447; 59-1448; 59-1450; 59-1451; 59-1452; 59-1456; 59-1457; 59-1473; 59-1477; 59-1479; 59-1484; 59-1485; 59-1487; 59-1489; 59-1493; 59-1496; 59-1497; 59-1499; 59-1503; 59-1505; 59-1506; 59-1509; 59-1514; 59-1516; 59-1519; 60-0316; 60-0327; 61-0268; 61-0270; 61-0271; 61-0280; 61-0281; 61-0303; 62-3566.

KC-135Q
Version specially made for the refuelling of SR-71A, redesignated KC-135T after being re-engined with F108.
Serial numbers:
58-0042; 58-0045; 58-0046; 58-0047; 58-0049; 58-0050; 58-0054; 58-0055; 58-0060; 58-0061; 58-0062; 58-0065; 58-0069; 58-0071; 58-0072; 58-0074; 58-0077; 58-0084; 58-0086; 58-0088; 58-0089; 58-0094; 58-0095; 58-0099; 58-0103; 58-0112; 58-0117; 58-0125; 58-0129; 59-1460; 59-1462; 59-1464; 59-1467; 59-1468; 59-1470; 59-1471; 59-1474; 59-1480; 59-1490; 59-1504; 59-1510; 59-1512; 59-1513; 59-1520; 59-1523; 60-0335; 60-0336; 60-0337; 60-0339; 60-0342; 60-0343; 60-0344; 60-0345; 60-0346. **Total = 56**

KC-135R
Designation of the AMC KC-135A re-engined with General Electric/SNECMA F108-CF-100 and upgraded. More than 250 aircraft modified.
Serial numbers:
57-1418; 57-1419; 57-1427; 57-1430; 57-1437; 57-1439; 57-1440; 57-1454; 57-1456; 57-1461; 57-1462; 57-1469; 57-1470; 57-1454; 57-1456; 57-1461; 57-1462; 57-1469; 57-1470; 57-1472; 57-1473; 57-1483; 57-1486; 57-1487; 57-1488; 57-1493; 57-1499; 57-1502; 57-1506; 57-1508; 57-1514; 57-2597; 57-2599; 57-2605; 58-0001; 58-0004; 58-0009; 58-0010; 58-0011; 58-0015; 58-0016; 58-0018; 58-0021; 58-0023; 58-0027; 58-0030; 58-0035; 58-0038; 58-0051; 58-0056; 58-0059; 58-0073; 58-0076; 58-0079; 58-0083; 58-0093; 58-0098; 58-0100; 58-0104; 58-0109; 58-0120; 58-0122; 58-0123; 58-0124; 58-0126; 58-0130; 59-1444; 59-1446; 59-1453; 59-1455; 59-1458; 59-1459; 59-1461; 59-1463; 59-1466; 59-1469; 59-1472; 59-1475; 59-1476; 59-1478; 59-1482; 59-1483; 59-1492; 59-1495; 59-1498; 59-1511; 59-1515; 59-1517; 59-1521; 60-0313; 60-0314; 60-0315; 60-0321; 60-0322; 60-0323; 60-0324; 60-0329; 60-0331; 60-0333; 60-0334; 60-0341; 60-0347; 60-0353; 60-0356; 60-0357; 60-0359; 60-0360; 60-0362; 60-0364; 60-0365; 60-0366; 60-0367; 61-0264; 61-0272; 61-0275; 61-0276; 61-0277; 61-0290; 61-0292; 61-0293; 61-0294; 61-0295; 61-0298; 61-0299; 61-0300; 61-0302; 61-0304; 61-0305; 61-0306; 61-0307; 61-0308; 61-0309; 61-0310; 61-0311; 61-0312; 61-0313; 61-0314; 61-0315; 61-0317; 61-0318; 61-0321; 61-0323; 61-0324; 62-3499; 62-3500; 62-3504; 62-3506; 62-3507; 62-3508; 62-3510; 62-3511; 62-3513; 62-3514; 62-3515; 62-3516; 62-3518; 62-3519; 62-3521; 62-3523; 62-3524; 62-3530; 62-3531; 62-3533; 62-3534; 62-3537; 62-3540; 62-3541; 62-3542; 62-3543; 62-3544; 62-3545; 62-3546; 62-3547; 62-3548; 62-3549; 62-3550; 62-3551; 62-3552; 62-3553; 62-3554; 62-3555; 62-3556; 62-3557; 62-3558; 62-3561; 62-3564; 62-3565; 62-3568; 62-3569; 62-3571; 62-3572; 62-3573; 62-3574; 62-3575; 62-3577; 62-3580; 63-7976; 63-7977; 63-7978; 63-7979; 63-7980; 63-7981; 63-7984; 63-7985; 63-7988; 63-7991; 63-7992; 63-7993; 63-7995; 63-7996; 63-7997; 63-7999; 63-8002; 63-8003; 63-8004; 63-8006; 63-8007; 63-8008; 63-8011; 63-8013; 63-8015; 63-8020; 63-8021; 63-8023; 63-8024; 63-8025; 63-8028; 63-8029; 63-8030; 63-8032; 63-8033; 63-8036; 63-8037; 63-8038; 63-8039; 63-8040; 63-8041; 63-8871; 63-8872; 63-8876; 63-8880; 63-8883; 63-8884; 63-8885; 64-14828; 64-14829; 64-14830; 64-14831; 64-14832; 64-14834; 64-14835; 64-14840.

Characteristics of the KC 135 and DERIVATIVES

	KC-135	RC-135V/ (RC-135U)
Crew	Four-engined tanker 4 (pilot, copilot, navigator, air-refuelling operator)	Four-engined electronic reconnaissance aircraft Three pilots, two navigators and 21 to 27 embarked specialists. (Two pilots, two navigators, two embarked systems specialists; at least 10 electronic warfare specialists and at least 6 tactical specialists)
Power plant	KC-135A: 4 x Pratt & Whitney J57-P-59W with 13,000 lb unitary thrust KC-135E: 4 x Pratt & Whitney JT3D-3B with 16,000 lb unitary thrust KC-135R: 4 x CFM International F108-CF-100 with 22,000 lb unitary thrust	4 x Pratt & Whitney TF33-P-5 turbofans 21,600 lb unitary thrust (TF-33-P-9 with 16,050 lb unitary thrust)
Dimensions and weights		
Length	134 ft 6 in	135 ft
Wingspan	130 ft 10 in	131 ft
Height	41 ft 8 in (modified tail)	42 ft
Wing Area	2,433 sq ft	2,433 sq ft
Weight (unloaded)	98,465 lb	
Max take-off weight	301,600 lb (KC-135R=322,000 lb)	294,610 lb (299,000 lb)
Max. load (cargo configuration)	82,895 lb or 37 passengers	
Performance		
Max. speed	530 kt	
Cruising speed	462 kt at 36,000 ft	435 kt (350 kt)
Combat range	2,995 NM (max.). 1,000 NM (with 120,000 lb of fuel to transfer); 2,995 NM with 24,000 lb. (KC-135R =2,500 NM with 203,295 lb of fuel).	
Ceiling	45,000 ft	35,000 ft
Fuel transfer speed	About 6,615 lb/min with rigid boom— about 1,543 lb/min with hose	
Range		3,510 NM (w/o refuel.). (3,995 NM w/o refuel.)

◆ KC-135A 'Relay' : KC-135A modified to an aerial radio relay as part of the 'Combat Lighting' program. 7 aircraft transformed (1966-73).

● KC-135B: KC-135A modified into an airborne command post (ABCP) for the SAC and then renamed EC-135C. Constructor designation: Model 717-166. 17 aircraft (1963-65).

◆ KC-135D: RC-135A transformed into a tanker. 4 aircraft transformed (1972).

◆ **KC-135E**: KC-135A re-engined with turbofans taken from former civil Boeing 707 and with modernised avionics. 161 aircraft transformed.

◆ KC-135ER: Designation never officially used for the KC-135R (re-engined)

◆ KC-135Q: KC-135A specially modified to refuel the Lockheed A-12 and SR-71 Blackbird with JP-7 fuel. It has different navigation equipment and refuelling lights on top of the tail fin. 56 aircraft transformed (1966).

◆ KC-135T: KC-135Q equipped with identical engines to those on the KC-135R. Modernised avionics. 56 aircraft modified (1995).

◆ **KC-135R:** 1. KC-135A modified to an electronic reconnaissance aircraft. Later designated RC-135R. 5 aircraft transformed. 2. KC-135A and KC-135E modernised, re-engined with the CFM F108, improved avionics and an APU auxiliary generator. 432 aircraft transformed.

◆ NC-135A: C-135A transformed for the observation of atmospheric atomic tests. 3 aircraft (1964).

◆ NC-135W: WC-135W modified to a permanent test bed. 1 aircraft transformed (2001).

◆ **NKC-135A**: Flying test bed (N = permanent modification) derived from the JKC-135A. 21 aircraft.

◆ NKC-135E: NKC-135A re-engined with TF33 turbofans. 21 aircraft.

◆ OC-135B 'Open Skies' : WC-135B modified and equipped with cameras used as part of the 'Open Skies' international treaty. 3 aircraft transformed.

● RC-135A: KC-135A taken on the production lines and transformed for aerial reconnaissance. No refuelling boom. Constructor designation: Model 739-700. 4 aircraft (1965) Extra order for five aircraft cancelled. l RC-135B: Electronic reconnaissance version never used operationally and transformed into a RC-135C.
Constructor designation: Model 739-445B. 10 aircraft.

◆ **RC-135C**: Reconnaissance version obtained from a specially modified RC-135B. 10 aircraft transformed (1963).

◆ **RC-135D** 'Rivet Brass' : KC-135A (1 aircraft) and C-135A (3 aircraft) transformed for surveillance and photography of spacecraft and missiles re-entering into the atmosphere. 4 aircraft transformed (1962).

◆ **RC-135E** 'Rivet Amber' : C-135B equipped with a side sweeping radar positioned at the front of the specially transformed fuselage. 1 aircraft transformed.

◆ **RC-135M** 'Rivet Card' / 'Rivet Quick' : Electronic reconnaissance version made from C-135B and VC-135B airframes equipped with side fairings and large nose. 6 aircraft transformed (1967).

◆ RC-135R: New designation of the KC-135R.

◆ **RC-135S** 'Rivet Ball' / 'Cobra Ball' : Electronic reconnaissance version obtained by converting a KC-135A (1 plane) and the C-135B and destined for observing missile launches. 4 aircraft transformed.

◆ RC-135T: KC-135R modified to an electronic reconnaissance aircraft with large nose. 1 aircraft transformed (1971-85).

◆ **RC-135U** 'Combat Sent' / 'Combat Pink' : RC-135C modified and improved. 3 aircraft transformed (1971).

◆ RC-135V 'Rivet Joint' : Modernised electronic reconnaissance version obtained from a RC-135C and RC-135U. 8 aircraft transformed (1973).

◆ RC-135W 'Rivet Joint' : Former RC-135M equipped with identical equipment to that of the RC-135V. 8 aircraft transformed.

◆ RC-135X 'Cobra Eye' : Identical aircraft to that of the RC-135S destined for the pursuit of objects re-entering the atmosphere. 1 aircraft transformed.

◆ TC-135B: WC-135B modified into a crew training aircraft for the OC-135B. 1 aircraft.

◆ TC-135S: EC-135B modified into a crew training aircraft for the RC-135S with less equipment. 1 aircraft transformed (1984).

◆ TC-135W: C-135B modified into a crew training aircraft for the RC-135W with less on board equipment. 3 aircraft transformed (1987).

◆ VC-135A: Variant of the VIP transport made from a C-135A and 4 KC-135A. 5 aircraft.

◆ VC-135B: VIP transport version made from the C-135B. 5 aircraft.

◆ WC-135B: Weather reconnaissance variant made from the C-135B. 11 aircraft transformed.

◆ WC-135C: Temporary conversion of a EC-135C before the WC-135W entered into service. 1 aircraft.

◆ WC-135W 'Constant Phoenix' : C-135B modified to collect air samples. 2 aircraft transformed.

● Production version ◆ Conversion of existing aircraft

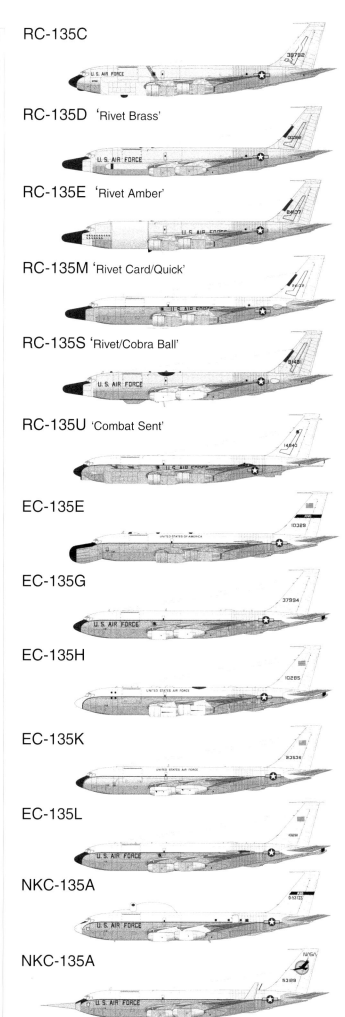

RC-135C

RC-135D 'Rivet Brass'

RC-135E 'Rivet Amber'

RC-135M 'Rivet Card/Quick'

RC-135S 'Rivet/Cobra Ball'

RC-135U 'Combat Sent'

EC-135E

EC-135G

EC-135H

EC-135K

EC-135L

NKC-135A

NKC-135A

Selected bibliography

- *Boeing 707, Pioneer jetliner.* R. J. Francillon. MBI.
- *Boeing 707/720.* J. Winchester. Airlife Classic Airliners.
- *The Boeing 707.* Profile Publications n° 192.
- *The Boeing C-135 Series.* D. Logan. Schiffer.
- *Boeing KC-135, more than just a tanker.* R. S. Hopkins III. Aerofax.
- *KC-135 in Action.* C. M. Reed. Squadron Signal n° 118.
- *Boeing aircraft cutaways.* M. Badrocke & B. Gunston. Osprey.
- *Boeing KC-135 Stratotanker.* R. F. Dorr. Ian Allan.
- *The Boeing 707, 720 & C-135.* T. Pither. Air Britain Publications.
Magazines :
- International Air Power Review.
- World Air Power.
- Air Enthusiast.

Acknowledgements

The authors would like to thank the following persons for their help in the making of this book:

Jean-Claude Bertrand, Philippe Bruno, Gérard Gorokhoff, Jean Delmas, Vincent Gréciet, Sébastien Guillemin, Renaud Leblanc, Frédéric Lert and Emmanuel Ratier.

A special acknowledgement goes to Jacques Guillem without whom this book would certainly not have been so rich and colourful.

Design and lay-out by Magali MASSELIN. Front cover drawing by BRUNO PAUTIGNY @ HISTOIRE & COLLECTIONS 2008.

A book from Histoire et Collections
SA au capital de 182 938,82 €
5, avenue de la République. F-75541 Paris CEDEX 11.
FRANCE
Téléphone: 01 40 21 18 20 Fax: 01 47 00 51 11
www.histoireetcollections.fr

Color separation by the Studio A&C
ISBN: 978-2-35250-075-9
Printed by Zure, Spain, European Union, October 2008.
@ Histoire & Collections 2008